REENTRY SOURCEBOOK

4TH EDITION

COLLECTION

WWW.FRESHSTARTLIBRARY.COM

Brought to you by the New Jersey State Library.

REENTRY
ESSENTIALS, INC.

Reentry Essentials, Inc.
2609 East 14th Street, Suite 1018
Brooklyn, New York 11235
I: http://www.ReentryEssentials.org
E: info@ReentryEssentials.org (TRULINCS Friendly)

TABLE OF CONTENTS

ABOUT THE SOURCEBOOK

The purpose of the Reentry Sourcebook is to help currently and previously incarcerated men and women locate and engage local community-based resource providers in the hopes of enhancing the likelihood of reentry success.

Every listing in the Reentry Sourcebook has been verified to ensure the most current and relevant information is presented. When a listing could not be verified, websites were utilized to obtain program descriptions and contact information.

The Reentry Sourcebook contains only a limited selection of resources available in the United States. By reviewing the Reentry Sourcebook, we hope individuals will become encouraged to explore further and to become aware of potential opportunities they might otherwise have overlooked. We have included resources that were relatively easy to contact, hoping that our readers would not be discouraged by wrong numbers or returned letters. If you feel we have missed a particularly valuable resource, let us know and we'll include it in our next edition. If you represent an agency that would like to be included in the Reentry Sourcebook, please contact us for inclusion.

ACKNOWLEDGMENTS

Thanks to the many currently and previously incarcerated men and women who have contributed their invaluable time and experiences to this project. Without their desire for accurate information and unwavering belief in this book, we would not have been challenged to dig so deeply, to probe so many resources, to look beyond the readily available answers for true solutions. Nor would we have had the motivation or the opportunity to test these findings and document the results so thoroughly.

We also wish to express special gratitude to the countless law enforcement professionals, whose suggestions and insight showed remarkable sensitivity and depth of knowledge. You are a group of competent people.

Finally, we wish to acknowledge the countless individuals, organizations, and companies who so generously offered ideas, information, and resources. This book has grown out of people's experiences – our own and many others. Sincerest thanks to all those who have gone before, from the pioneers who cleared the trails to the engineers who paved the road, so that the journey of so many might be easier.

INTRODUCTION

The United States has the highest documented incarceration rate in the world; in 2009, for every 100,000 residents, 754 were in jails or prisons. (1)

Everything about incarceration is directly related to reentry success. Reentry strategies vary widely across the United States signifying that reentry's much more than an option, it's a necessary process. How successful the overall reentry process is depends on the strategies and resources used including pre- and post-release planning, offender programming, and family and community integration.

Reconnecting with family and friends, establishing stable housing, finding and retaining quality employment, developing educational goals, and coping with addiction and substance abuse issues are just some of the obstacles that offenders must confront and overcome as part of the reentry process.

With less than 5% of the world's population (2) and 23% of the world's prison population (3) the challenges of incarceration in the United States are staggering.

The United States now spends more than $68 billion on federal, state and local corrections. (4)

The costs of reentry – both societal and economic – are high. Statistics indicate that more than two-thirds of state prisoners are rearrested within 3 years of their release and half are re incarcerated. (5)

A disproportionate number of offenders return to communities with no job, nowhere to live, and limited financial resources. The implementation and use of successful reentry strategies play a role in the overall success of those most in need while helping to reduce the cycle of recidivism.

In helping individuals to locate much needed resources, it is our sincere hope that the Reentry Sourcebook will aid in the overall success of all reentry stakeholders.

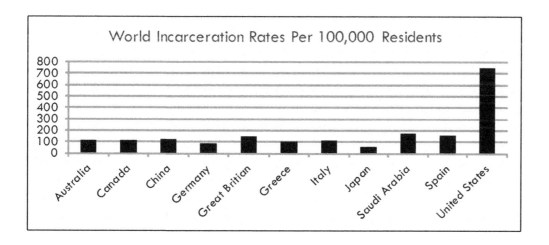

World Incarceration Rates Per 100,000 Residents

---

1. International Centre for Prison Studies (March 18, 2010). "Prison Brief – Highest to Lowest Rates". World Prison Brief. School of Law, King's College London.

2. "U.S. & World Population Clock". U.S. Census Bureau.

3. "World Prison Population List". 8th Edition. By Roy Walmsley. Published in 2009. International Centre for Prison Studies. School of Law, King's College London.

4. Pew Center of the States. "One in 31: The Long Reach of American Corrections". Washington, DC: The Pew Charitable Trusts, March 2010.

5. Langan, P.A. & D.J. Levin. "Recidivism of Prisoners Released in 2010". Washington, DC: U.S. Department of Justice, Bureau of Justice Statistics, 2012.

CHAPTER 1 | REENTRY RESOURCES & INITIATIVES

"Our greatest freedom is the freedom to choose our attitude." ~ Victor Frankl

There are many government and nonprofit agencies that offer programs and services designed to enhance the post-release success of individuals returning to society after a term of incarceration. The agencies and organizations listed in this section were compiled as a starting point to assist individuals, families and communities with locating and utilizing reentry resources in an effort to enhance post-release success.

REENTRY SERVICE DIRECTORIES

In many communities, government and nonprofit agencies have developed reentry-specific resource directories to help individuals and their families locate community-based service providers. The following links provide access to directories available on a national and state level.

NATIONAL DIRECTORIES

There are many national resource directories designed to assist individuals, families and communities in the reintegration process. As resources change frequently, the following is only a brief sampling of what may be available on a national level.

American Civil Liberties Union, *Prisoners' Assistance Directory*
https://www.aclu.org/files/assets/2012_prisoners_assistance_directory.pdf

Fair Shake Reentry Resource Center, *Reentry Packet*
http://www.fairshake.net/pdf/reentry_document_packet.pdf

Federal Bureau of Prisons, *Employment Information Handbook*
http://www.bop.gov/resources/pdfs/emp_info_handbk.pdf

Federal Bureau of Prisons, *National Directory of American Job Centers*
http://www.nicic.gov/files/folders/4338/download.aspx

Gay and Lesbian Advocates and Defenders, *Resources for Prisoners and Ex-Offenders in New England*
http://www.glad.org/uploads/docs/publications/resources-for-prisoners-and-ex-offenders-in-ne.pdf

Inside Book Project, *National Resource Guide*
http://insidebooksproject.org/s/IBP-ResourceGuide_February2015.pdf

Naljor Prison Dharma Service, *Resource Directory for Prisoners*
http://naljorprisondharmaservice.org/pdf/Resource%20Directory%20for%20Prisoners.pdf

Prison Book Program, *National Prisoner Resource List*
http://www.prisonbookprogram.org/wp-content/uploads/2013/08/NPRL.pdf

STATE DIRECTORIES

If available, links to state specific reentry service directories can be found by searching the Fair Shake "Resource Directory" page online at https://www.fairshake.net/reentry-resources/search-for-a-resource/.

LOCAL REENTRY SERVICE PROVIDERS

More than 600,000 men and women are released from state and federal prisons each year. To meet the growing demand for reentry related resources many organizations have expanded their existing programs or developed new ones to incorporate direct services for formerly incarcerated individuals and their families. Many of these organizations provide assistance with addressing issues related to mental health, substance abuse, housing and homelessness, health, education and employment, and families. A comprehensive listing of community-based reentry service providers is located within Appendix 1-A. Additionally, you may visit the Fair Shake "Search for a Resource" page online at https://www.fairshake.net/reentry-resources/search-for-a-resource/ to search through over 15,000 local, state and national resources.

NATIONAL REENTRY STAKEHOLDERS, ORGANIZATIONS & INITIATIVES

There are many stakeholders, organizations and initiatives that provide resources and technical assistance to offenders, families, communities and practitioners on a national level. The following organizations provide services and assistance nationally and should be utilized in conjunction with local community-based resources. Many of the following agencies will provide referrals to local reentry service providers upon request.

AMERICAN PROBATION & PAROLE ASSOCIATION
http://www.appa-net.org

The American Probation & Parole Association comprises individuals from the United States and Canada actively involved with probation, parole and community-based corrections, in both adult and juvenile sectors. Its constituents come from all levels of government including local, state/provincial, legislative, executive, judicial, and federal agencies. The American Probation & Parole Association has grown to become the voice for thousands of probation and parole practitioners including line staff, supervisors, administrators, educators, volunteers, and concerned citizens with an interest in criminal and juvenile justice. The American Probation & Parole Association's mission is to serve, challenge and empower its members and constituents by educating, communicating and training; advocating and influencing; acting as a resource and conduit for information, ideas and support; developing standards and models; and collaborating with other disciplines.

National Contact:

American Probation & Parole Association
P.O. Box 11910
Lexington, KY 40578
P: 859.244.8203

ASSOCIATION OF STATE CORRECTIONAL ADMINISTRATORS
http://www.asca.net

The Association of State Correctional Administrators is a membership organization comprised of the directors of state correctional agencies and the administrators of the largest jail systems in the United States. The association is dedicated to the improvement of correctional services and practices through promoting and facilitating the advancement of correctional techniques, research in correctional practices, and the development and application of correctional standards and accreditation. Formed in 1970, The Association of State Correctional Administrators was formally incorporated as a New York State not-for-profit corporation in 1985.

National Contact:

Association of State Correctional Administrators
213 Court Street
Middletown, CT 06547
P: 860.704.6403

CORPORATION FOR SUPPORTIVE HOUSING
http://www.csh.org

The Corporation for Supportive Housing helps communities create permanent housing with services to prevent and end homelessness by bringing together people, skills, and resources; providing high-quality advice and development expertise; making loans and grants to supportive housing sponsors; strengthening the supportive housing industry; and reforming public policy to make it easier to create and operate supportive housing.

National Contact:

Corporation for Supportive Housing
50 Broadway, 17th Floor
New York, NY 10004
P: 212.986.2966

COUNCIL OF STATE GOVERNMENTS
http://www.csg.org

Founded in 1933, the Council of State Governments is our nation's only organization serving all three branches of state government. The Council of State Governments is a region-based forum that fosters the exchange of insights and ideas to help state officials shape public policy. This offers unparalleled regional, national and international opportunities to network, develop leaders, collaborate and create problem-solving partnerships. The Council of State Governments coordinates and facilitates many programs and projects such as the Council of State Governments' Justice Center, Criminal Justice/Mental Health Consensus Project, Justice Reinvestment, National Reentry Resource Center and the Reentry Policy Council.

National Contact:

Council of State Governments
2760 Research Park Drive
Lexington, KY 40511
P: 859.244.8000

COUNCIL OF STATE GOVERNMENTS' JUSTICE CENTER

http://www.justicecenter.csg.org

The Council of State Governments' Justice Center is a national nonprofit organization that serves policymakers at the local, state, and federal levels from all branches of government. Staff provides practical, nonpartisan advice and evidence-based, consensus-driven strategies to increase public safety and strengthen communities.

The Justice Center evolved from the Council of State Governments' Eastern Regional Conference justice program to a national center in 2006, and serves all states to promote effective data-driven practices particularly in areas in which the criminal justice system intersects with other disciplines, such as public health to provide practical solutions to public safety and cross-systems problems.

The Justice Center's Board of Directors includes state legislative leaders, judges, corrections administrators, juvenile justice agency directors, and law enforcement professionals, who together represent a cross-section of the senior-level officials who shape criminal justice policy across the country.

National Contact:

Council of State Governments' Justice Center
22 Cortlandt Street, 22nd Floor
New York, NY 10007
P: 212.482.2344

NATIONAL REENTRY RESOURCE CENTER

http://csgjusticecenter.org/nrrc

The National Reentry Resource Center provides education, training, and technical assistance to states, tribes, territories, local governments, service providers, nonprofit organizations, correctional institutions working on prisoner reentry and individuals directly impacted by community reintegration. The National Reentry Resource Centers mission is to advance the reentry field through knowledge transfer and dissemination and to promote evidence-based best practices. Specifically, the National Reentry Resource Center provides a one-stop, interactive source of current, evidence-based, and user-friendly reentry information, individualized, targeted technical assistance for Second Chance Act grantees; and training, distance learning, and knowledge development to support grantees and advance the reentry field.

Established in 2008 by the Second Chance Act, the National Reentry Resource Center is administered by the Bureau of Justice Assistance, U.S. Department of Justice, and is a project of the Council of State Governments' Justice Center, along with key project partners including the Urban Institute, the Association of State Correctional Administrators, and the American Probation and Parole Association.

National Contact:

National Reentry Resource Center
22 Cortlandt Street, 22nd Floor
New York, NY 10007
P: 212.482.2344

Additional Resources:

National Reentry Resource Center, *About the National Reentry Resource Center*
http://csgjusticecenter.org/wp-content/uploads/2014/10/About-the-NRRC.pdf

FEDERAL INTERAGENCY REENTRY COUNCIL

http://csgjusticecenter.org/nrrc/projects/firc/

A project of the Council of State Governments' Justice Center under the National Reentry Resource Center, the mission of the Federal Interagency Reentry Council is to support the Administrations' efforts to advance public safety and wellbeing through enhanced communication, coordination, and collaboration across Federal agency initiatives that 1) make communities safer by reducing recidivism and victimization, 2) assist those returning from prison and jail in becoming productive citizens, and 3) save taxpayer dollars by lowering the direct and collateral costs of incarceration.

In furtherance of their mission, the Federal Interagency Reentry Council has created numerous Reentry Myth-Busters. Reentry MythBusters are fact sheets designed to clarify existing federal policies that affect formerly incarcerated individuals and their families in areas such as public housing, access to benefits, parental rights, employer incentives, Medicaid suspension/termination, and more.

National Contact:

Federal Interagency Reentry Council
22 Cortlandt Street, 22nd Floor
New York, NY 10007
P: 212.482.2344

Additional Resources:

Federal Interagency Reentry Council, *Reentry MythBusters*
http://csgjusticecenter.org/nrrc/projects/mythbusters/

Federal Interagency Reentry Council, *Reentry Snapshots*
http://csgjusticecenter.org/nrrc/projects/firc/snapshots/

Federal Interagency Reentry Council, *FIRC Reentry Week Fact Sheet*
https://csgjusticecenter.org/wp-content/uploads/2016/04/FIRC-Fact-Sheet_4.25.16_CSG.pdf

NATIONAL ASSOCIATION OF HOUSING AND REDEVELOPMENT OFFICIALS

http://www.nahro.org

The National Association of Housing and Redevelopment Officials is a professional membership organization comprised of 21,227 housing and community development agencies and officials throughout the US who administer a variety of affordable housing and community development programs at the local level. The National Association of Housing and Redevelopment Official's mission is to create affordable housing and safe, viable communities that enhance the quality of life for all Americans, especially those of low- and moderate-income, advocating for appropriate laws and policies which are sensitive to the needs of the people served, are financially and programmatically viable for the industry, are flexible, promote deregulation and local decision making; and fostering the highest standards of ethical behavior, service and accountability.

National Contact:

National Association of Housing and Redevelopment Officials
630 Eye Street, NW
Washington DC 20001
P: 202.289.3500

NATIONAL ASSOCIATION OF STATE ALCOHOL/DRUG PROGRAM DIRECTORS

http://www.nasadad.org

The National Association of State Alcohol/Drug Program Directors is a private, not-for-profit educational, scientific, and informational organization whose basic purpose is to foster and support the development of effective alcohol and other drug abuse prevention and treatment programs throughout every State. The National Association of State Alcohol/Drug Program Directors serves as a focal point for the examination of alcohol and other drug related issues of common interest to both other national organizations and federal agencies by conducting research, fostering collaboration, providing training and cross-training, providing technical assistance, promoting national standards, shaping policy, and ensuring stable funding.

National Contact:

National Association of State Alcohol/Drug Abuse Directors
808 17th Street NW, Suite 410
Washington, DC 20006
P: 202.293.0090

NATIONAL ASSOCIATION OF STATE MENTAL HEALTH PROGRAM DIRECTORS

http://www.nasmhpd.org

The National Association of State Mental Health Program Directors is an organization that advocates for the collective interests of state mental health authorities and their directors at the national level. The National Association of State Mental Health Program Directors analyzes trends in the delivery and financing of mental health services and identifies public mental health policy issues and best practices in the delivery of mental health services. The association apprises its members of research findings and best practices in the delivery of mental health services, fosters collaboration, provides consultation and technical assistance, and promotes effective management practices and financing mechanisms adequate to sustain the mission.

National Contact:

National Association of State Mental Health Program Directors
66 Canal Center Plaza, Suite 302
Alexandria, VA 22314
P: 703.739.9333

NATIONAL ASSOCIATION OF WORKFORCE BOARDS

http://www.nawb.org

The National Association of Workforce Boards believes that through the influence of committed private and public sector leadership, a high performance, quality workforce development system can be developed to meet the human resource needs of the competitive global economy that increasingly demands highly skilled workers. The National Association of Workforce Boards supports and promotes the work of its members through a comprehensive program of advocacy, technical assistance, and communications activities. Services are designed to help Board volunteers advance the public-private model among key policymakers, secure the role of the business sector in workforce development, enhance members' capacity and effectiveness, and learn from networking opportunities with the nationwide job training community. The National Association of Workforce Boards is the only group that advocates solely for Workforce Boards.

National Contact:

National Association of Workforce Boards
1701 K Street, NW, Suite 1000
Washington, DC 20006
P: 202.775.0960

NATIONAL CENTER FOR STATE COURTS

http://www.ncsconline.org

The National Center for State Courts provides up-to-date information and hands-on assistance to court leaders that helps them better serve the public. Through original research, consulting services, publications, and national educational programs, National Center for State Courts offers solutions that enhance court operations with the latest technology; collects and interprets the latest data on court operations nationwide; and provides information on proven best practices for improving court operations in many areas, such as civil case management. The National Center for State Courts is an independent, nonprofit, tax-exempt organization.

National Contact:

National Center for State Courts
300 Newport Avenue
Williamsburg, VA 23185
P: 800.616.6164

POLICE EXECUTIVE RESEARCH FORUM

http://www.policeforum.org

The Police Executive Research Forum is a national membership organization of progressive police executives from the largest city, county, and state law enforcement agencies. The Police Executive Research Forum is dedicated to improving policing and advancing professionalism through research and involvement in public policy debate. Incorporated in 1977, the Police Executive Research Forum's primary sources of operating revenues are government grants and contracts and partnerships with private foundations and other organizations.

National Contact:

The Police Executive Research Forum
1120 Connecticut Avenue NW, Suite 930
Washington, DC 20036
P: 202.466.7820

URBAN INSTITUTE

http://www.urban.org

The Urban Institute is a nonprofit, nonpartisan policy research and educational organization established to examine the social, economic, and governance problems facing the nation. It provides information and analysis to public and private decision makers to help them address these challenges, and strives to raise citizen understanding of the issues and tradeoffs in policymaking.

National Contact:

Urban Institute
2100 M Street, NW
Washington, DC 20037
P: 202.833.7200

FAIR SHAKE REENTRY RESOURCE CENTER

https://www.fairshake.net

Fair Shake is a national nonprofit organization dedicated to reducing the recidivism rate through personal and community focused ownership and engagement opportunities for inmates and former felons. Through an interactive blend of electronic tools, reentry awareness and community building, Fair Shake encourages released prisoners, and all related stakeholders, to participate in the successful reintegration of formerly incarcerated people back into society. Fair Shake offers non-traditional support that focuses on responsibility, tenacity, positive and realistic thinking and self-empowerment.

To learn more about Fair Shake and the resources available, individuals are encouraged to contact them directly for complimentary copies of their exclusive Reentry Packet and other valuable resources.

National Contact:

Fair Shake Reentry Resource Center
P.O. Box 63
Westby, WI 54667
P: 608.634.6363

Additional Resources:

Fair Shake Reentry Resource Center, *Fair Shake Ready-To-Print Reentry Packet*
https://www.fairshake.net/pdf/reentry_document_packet.pdf

Fair Shake Reentry Resource Center, *Fair Shake Ownership Manual*
https://www.fairshake.net/pdf/8.5X11_ownership_manual.pdf

Fair Shake Reentry Resource Center, *Fair Shake Transition Tips*
https://www.fairshake.net/pdf/transition_tips.pdf

Fair Shake Reentry Resource Center, *Fair Shake Full Color Brochure*
https://www.fairshake.net/pdf/fairshake_brochure_web.pdf

Fair Shake Reentry Resource Center, *Fair Shake Full Color Brochure Insert*
https://www.fairshake.net/pdf/fair_shake_brochure_insert.pdf

Fair Shake Reentry Resource Center, *Fair Shake Member Agreement*
https://www.fairshake.net/pdf/Fair_Shake_Member_Agreement.pdf

NATIONAL H.I.R.E. NETWORK

http://www.hirenetwork.org

Established by the Legal Action Center, the National Helping Individuals with Criminal Records Re-enter through Employment Network is both a national clearinghouse for information and an advocate for policy change. The goal of the National H.I.R.E. Network is to increase the number and quality of job opportunities available to people with criminal records by changing public policies, employment practices and public opinion. The National H.I.R.E. Network also provides training and technical assistance to agencies working to improve employment prospects for people with criminal histories.

National Contact:

National H.I.R.E. Network
Legal Action Center
225 Varick Street
New York, NY 10014
P: 212.243.1313

Additional Resources:

National H.I.R.E. Network, *Resources, Information & Assistance Clearinghouse*
http://www.hirenetwork.org/clearinghouse

National H.I.R.E. Network, *Publications Catalog*
http://www.hirenetwork.org/content/publications

PRISONER VISITATION AND SUPPORT

http://www.prisonervisitation.org

In 1972, Prisoner Visitation and Support was granted permission by the Federal Bureau of Prisons to visit all federal prisons and prisoners in the United States. In 1975, the U.S. Department of Defense granted Prisoner Visitation and Support access to all military prisons and prisoners in the United State. Today, Prisoner Visitation and Support volunteers see any prisoners desiring a visit, including those in Special Housing Units (solitary confinement), those on death row, and those transferred from prison to prison. Prisoner Visitation and Support is dedicated to human contact with those who seek visitors, they have no religious agenda, and offer no legal services.

National Contact:

Prisoner Visitation and Support
1501 Cherry Street
Philadelphia, PA 19102
P: 215.241.7117

U.S. DEPARTMENT OF JUSTICE | REENTRY PROGRAMS & INITIATIVES

As the primary law enforcement agency of the United States, the U.S. Department of Justice is responsible for overseeing and administering the nation's legal system and ensuring the fair and equal treatment of all citizens in accordance with the U.S. Constitution. There are many agencies within the U.S. Department of Justice; the following agencies provide direct oversight, resources and assistance to individuals, communities and professionals affected by rising recidivism and incarceration rates.

FEDERAL BUREAU OF PRISONS

http://www.bop.gov

As the primary correctional agency for the federal government, the Federal Bureau of Prisons oversees a national network of over 140 correctional institutions, community corrections centers, and comprehensive sanction centers that house and rehabilitate an inmate population of approximately 200,000 annually – the largest correctional system in the world. The reentry related programs and services offered by the Federal Bureau of Prisons are designed to help offenders be as productive as possible while incarcerated and ensure that individuals are prepared to return to society as productive, law abiding citizens.

REENTRY SERVICES

As part of its commitment to the successful community reintegration of federal offenders, the Federal Bureau of Prisons' recently activated a Reentry Services Division that allows them to consolidate and concentrate many of their reentry programs and services. The Reentry Services Division is comprised of a national office, and both regional and institution-based Reentry Affairs Coordinators who coordinate efforts among bureau staff, community volunteers and program participants. A list of Institution Reentry Affairs Coordinators for each Federal Bureau of Prisons institution is available by visiting http://www.bop.gov/jobs/volunteer.jsp.

FEDERAL REENTRY SERVICES HOTLINE

In April 2016, the U.S. Department of Justice in collaboration with the Federal Bureau of Prisons launched a new reentry services hotline to provide assistance to recently released individuals. This hotline is staffed by inmates employed by Federal Prison Industries who are specially-trained to provide assistance to recently released federal inmates as they navigate various reentry challenges and seek community resources. For immediate assistance, please call 877.895.9196 to speak with a trained representative.

COMMUNITY CORRECTIONS

In an effort to provide offenders with enhanced opportunity for success, most federal offenders are eligible to serve a portion of their sentence in a community correctional facility as their term of imprisonment comes to an end. The Second Chance Act of 2008 provides that, "the Director of the Bureau of Prisons shall, to the extent practicable, ensure that a prisoner serving a term of imprisonment spends a portion of the final months of that term under conditions that will afford that prisoner a reasonable opportunity to adjust to and prepare for re-entry of that prisoner into the community. Such conditions may include a community correctional facility."

For a list of Federal Residential Reentry Centers (formerly known as halfway houses), please see Appendix 1-B: Federal Residential Reentry Centers.

National Contact:

Federal Bureau of Prisons
320 First Street, NW
Washington, DC 20534
P: 202.353.3598

Additional Resources:

Federal Bureau of Prisons, *A Directory of Bureau of Prisons' National Programs*
https://www.bop.gov/inmates/custody_and_care/docs/BOPNationalProgramCatalog.pdf

Federal Bureau of Prisons, *Inmate Occupational Training Directory*
https://www.bop.gov/inmates/custody_and_care/docs/inmate_occupational_training_directory.pdf

Federal Bureau of Prisons, *Making Changes*
https://www.bop.gov/resources/pdfs/bop_making_changes_4.15.2016_1.pdf

Federal Bureau of Prisons, *Reentering your Community - A Handbook*
https://www.bop.gov/resources/pdfs/reentry_handbook.pdf

Federal Bureau of Prisons, *Roadmap to Reentry*
https://www.justice.gov/reentry/file/844356/download

NATIONAL INSTITUTE OF CORRECTIONS | TRANSITION & OFFENDER WORKFORCE DEVELOPMENT DIVISION
http://www.nicic.gov/owd

The National Institute of Corrections is an agency within the U.S. Department of Justice, Federal Bureau of Prisons that provides training, technical assistance, information services, and policy/program development assistance to federal, state, and local corrections agencies. Through their Transition and Offender Workforce Development Division, the National Institute of Corrections coordinates the efforts of corrections agencies and their partnering agencies to improve employment programs for defendants and offenders by assisting professionals who provide employment services.

National Contact:

National Institute of Corrections
Transition and Offender Workforce Development Division
320 First Street, NW
Washington, DC 20534
P: 800.877.1461

FEDERAL PRISON INDUSTRIES | INMATE TRANSITION PROGRAM BRANCH

http://www.unicor.gov/about_fpi_programs.aspx

The Inmate Transition Program Branch, a division of Federal Prison Industries (UNICOR) serves to strengthen existing Federal Bureau of Prisons programs and to establish new ones designed to enhance the post release transition of federal prisoners.

National Contact:

Federal Bureau of Prisons
Inmate Transition Program Branch
320 First Street, NW
Washington, DC 20534
P: 202.305.3972

NATIONAL INSTITUTE OF JUSTICE

http://www.ojp.usdoj.gov/nij

The National Institute of Justice is the research, development, and evaluation agency of the U.S. Department of Justice and is dedicated to researching crime control and justice issues. The National Institution of Justice provides objective, independent, evidence-based knowledge and tools to meet the challenges of crime and justice, particularly at the state and local level.

National Contact:

National Institute of Justice
2277 Research Boulevard
Rockville, MD 20850
P: 304.519.6208

REENTRY LEGISLATION | SECOND CHANCE ACT OVERVIEW

Signed into law on April 9, 2008, the Second Chance Act was designed to improve outcomes for people returning to communities after incarceration. This first-of-its-kind legislation authorizes federal grants to government agencies and nonprofit organization to provide employment assistance, housing, substance abuse treatment, family programming, mentoring, victims support, and other services that help reduce recidivism. The Second Chance Act's grant programs are funded and administered by the Office of Justice Programs, a division of the U.S. Department of Justice.

The following is a list of specific Second Chance Act grant programs and priority areas of consideration:

- Demonstration grants provide funding to state and local government agencies and federally recognized Indian tribes to plan and implement comprehensive strategies that address the challenges faced by adults and youth returning to their communities after incarceration.
- Mentoring grants support nonprofit organizations and federally recognized Indian tribes that provide mentoring, case management, and other transitional services.
- Co-occurring treatment grants provide funding to state and local government agencies and federally recognized Indian tribes to implement or expand integrated treatment programs for individuals with co-occurring substance abuse and mental health disorders.
- Family-based substance abuse treatment grants support state and local government agencies and federally recognized Indian tribes in establishing or enhancing family-based residential substance abuse treatment programs in correctional facilities that include recovery and family supportive services.
- Reentry court grants help state and local government agencies and federally recognized Indian tribes establish state, local, and tribal reentry courts that monitor offenders and provide them with the treatment services necessary to establish a self-sustaining and law-abiding life.
- Technology career training grants help state and local government agencies and federally recognized Indian tribes to establish programs to train individuals in prisons, jails, or juvenile facilities for technology-based jobs and careers during the three-year period before their release.
- Recidivism reduction grants provide funding to state departments of correction to achieve reductions in recidivism rates through planning, capacity-building, and implementation of effective and evidence-based interventions.

Smart Probation grants provide funding to state and local government agencies and federally recognized Indian tribes to implement evidence-based supervision strategies to improve outcomes for probationers.

Beginning in 2012, Second Chance Act grant programs began providing priority consideration to agencies that propose a Pay for Success model. The Pay for Success concept was developed by the Nonprofit Finance Fund. Additional information on the Second Chance Act can be found at: http://csgjusticecenter.org/nrrc/projects/second-chance-act/.

REENTRY FACTS & TRENDS (1)

Each year, more than 600,000 men and women are released from state and federal prisons. Another 9 million cycle through local jails. When reentry fails, the cost – both societal and economic – are high. Statistics indicate that more than two-thirds of state prisoners are rearrested within 3 years of their release and half are reincarcerated. High rates of recidivism mean more crime, more victims, and more pressure on an already overburdened criminal justice system. The cost of imprisonment also wreaks havoc on state and municipal budgets. In the past 20 years, state spending on corrections has grown at a faster rate than nearly any other state budget item. The U.S. now spends more than $68 billion on federal, state and local corrections. Because reentry intersects with issues of health and housing, education and employment, family, faith, and community well-being, many agencies are focusing on the reentry population with initiatives that aim to improve outcomes in many areas.

---

1. Source: National Reentry Resource Center, Reentry Facts & Trends. Available online at, http://csgjusticecenter.org/nrrc/facts-and-trends.

GENERAL REENTRY FACTS

- State and federal prisons held approximately 1,598,780 prisoners at the end of 2011 - approximately one in every 107 U.S. citizens.
- At least 95 percent of state prisoners will be released back to their communities at some point.
- During 2011, 688,384 sentenced prisoners were released from state and federal prisons.
- Approximately 9 million individuals are released from jail each year.
- At the end of 2011, 4,814,200 adults — one in fifty U.S. adults — were on probation, parole, or other post-prison supervision. Approximately 853,900 were on parole.
- In a study that looked at recidivism in over 40 states, more than 4 in 10 offenders returned to state prison within three years of their release.
- In 2011, parole violators accounted for 30.8 percent of all prison admissions, 33 percent of state admissions, and 7.9 percent of federal admissions.
- In 2011, approximately 12% of parolees were re-incarcerated. Eight percent of parolees were re-incarcerated due to parole violations and revocations, and 3% of parolees were re-incarcerated for new offenses.

MENTAL HEALTH

- The incidence of serious mental illnesses is two to four times higher among prisoners than it is in the general population.
- In a study of more than 20,000 adults entering five local jails, researchers documented serious mental illnesses in 14.5 percent of the men and 31 percent of the women, which taken together, comprises 16.9 percent of those studied — rates in excess of three to six times those found in the general population.

SUBSTANCE ABUSE

- Three quarters of those returning from prison have a history of substance use disorders. Over 70 percent of prisoners with serious mental illnesses also have a substance use disorder.
- In 2004, 53 percent of state and 45 percent of federal prisoners met Diagnostic and Statistical Manual for Mental Disorders (DSM) criteria for drug abuse and dependence. Nearly a third of state and a quarter of federal prisoners committed their offense under the influence of drugs. Among state prisoners who were dependent on or abusing drugs, 53 percent had at least three prior sentences to probation or incarceration, compared to 32 percent of other inmates. At the time of their arrest, drug dependent or abusing state prisoners (48 percent) were also more likely than other inmates (37 percent) to have been on probation or incarceration sentences.
- In 2002, 68 percent of jail inmates met DSM criteria for drug abuse or dependence. Half of all convicted jail inmates were under the influence of drugs or alcohol at the time of offense. Inmates who met substance dependence/abuse criteria were twice as likely as other inmates to have three or more prior probation or incarceration sentences.
- Only 7 percent of prisoners who met DSM criteria for alcohol/drug dependence or abuse receive treatment in jail or prison.

HOUSING AND HOMELESSNESS

- More than 10 percent of those entering prisons and jails are homeless in the months before their incarceration. For those with mental illness, the rates are even higher — about 20 percent. Released prisoners with a history of shelter use were almost five times as likely to have a post-release shelter stay.
- According to a qualitative study by the Vera Institute of Justice, people released from prison and jail to parole who enter homeless shelters in New York City were seven times more likely to abscond during the first month after release than those who had some form of housing.

HEALTH

- The prevalence of chronic illnesses and communicable disease is far greater among people in jails and prisons.
- In 1997, individuals released from prison or jail accounted for nearly one-quarter of all people living with HIV or AIDS, almost one-third of those diagnosed with hepatitis C, and more than one-third of those diagnosed with tuberculosis.
- At year-end 2008, 1.5% (20,231) of male inmates and 1.9% (1,913) of female inmates held in state or federal prisons were HIV positive or had confirmed AIDS. Confirmed AIDS cases accounted for nearly a quarter (23%) of all HIV/AIDS cases in state and federal prisons. In 2007, the most recent year for which general population data are available, the overall rate of estimated confirmed AIDS among the state and federal prison population (0.43%) was 2.5 times the rate in the general population (0.17%).

FAMILIES

- An estimated 809,800 prisoners of the 1,518,535 held in the nation's prisons at midyear 2007 were parents of children under age 18. Parents held in the nation's prisons – 52 percent of state inmates and 63 percent of federal inmates – reported having an estimated 1,706,600 minor children, accounting for 2.3 percent of the U.S. resident population under age 18.
- Since 1991, the number of children with a mother in prison has more than doubled, up 131 percent. The number of children with a father in prison has grown by 77 percent.
- Twenty-two percent of the children of state inmates and 16 percent of the children of federal inmates were age 4 or younger. For both state (53 percent) and federal (50 percent) inmates, about half their children were age 9 or younger.

WOMEN AND REENTRY

- At the end of 2009, federal and state correctional facilities held 113,462 women, an increase of 22% since 2000.
- At least 712,000 women were on probation and 103,000 women were on parole at year end 2010.
- Compared to men, women are more likely to be incarcerated for drug and property crimes, and less likely to be incarcerated for violent crime. In 2008, 53.8% of sentenced male prisoners were convicted for violent offenses, compared to 35.6% of sentenced women prisoners. 29% of women were convicted of property crimes, compared to 17.7% of men. 26.9% of women prisoners were convicted of drug offenses, compared to 17.8% of men.

CHAPTER 2 | IDENTIFICATION & DOCUMENT RESOURCES

"All you need is the plan, the road map, and the courage to press on to your destination." ~ Earl Nightingale

Proper identification is an important component of any incarcerated individuals community reintegration plan. Identification is required to open a bank account, take a driver's test or apply for a job. For information about how to obtain proper government-issued identification upon release, contact any of the following agencies.

DRIVER'S LICENSE & IDENTIFICATION CARD

To apply for a current driver's license in your state of legal residence, an identification card, or an instruction permit, you may present a copy of an expired driver's license, instruction permit, or state identification card.

If you do not have an expired driver's license, instruction permit, or identification card, you may usually present one primary and one secondary document from your states approved document list. Pursuant to the REAL ID Act, the primary document must contain your full legal name (first, middle, and last) and the month, day and year of birth regardless of the state applying to. Each state has its own rules and regulations which can be learned by contacting them directly.

State Contact:

Please refer to Appendix 2-A: State Driver License & Identification Card Offices.

SOCIAL SECURITY CARD

Social security is part of almost everyone's life, no matter what your age or social standing. If you have never applied for a Social Security Card and are over the age of 12, you are required to apply in-person and provide at least two documents to prove age, identity, and U.S. citizenship or current lawful work-authorized immigration status. To apply for a replacement card, you are required to provide one document to prove your identity.

When completed, applicants are required to take (or mail) their applications and necessary documents to a local Social Security office. If you live or receive mail in Bronx, NY; Brooklyn, NY; Queens, NY; Orlando, FL; (Orange, Osceola and Seminole Counties); Sacramento County, CA; Phoenix, AZ (Maricopa County and Apache Junction Area); Las Vegas, NV; Philadelphia, PA; or Great Twin Cities Metropolitan Area, MN, you must apply in-person or by mail to a Social Security Card Center.

If you have additional questions or concerns regarding applying for a Social Security Card or the evidence documents required, please visit http://www.socialsecurity.gov or call the Social Security Administration directly at 800.772.1213 for assistance.

National Contact:

U.S. Social Security Administration
Office of Public Inquiry
6401 Security Boulevard
Baltimore, MD 21235
P: 800.772.1213

Additional Resources:

U.S. Social Security Administration, *Application for a Social Security Card – Form SS-5*
http://www.socialsecurity.gov/online/ss-5.pdf

U.S. Social Security Administration, *Consent for Release of Information – Form SSA-3288*
http://www.socialsecurity.gov/online/ssa-3288.pdf

U.S. Social Security Administration, *Your Social Security Number and Card*
http://ssa.gov/pubs/EN-05-10002.pdf

U.S. PASSPORT

Passports are issued by the U.S. Department of State to citizens and nationals of the United States to provide documentation for foreign travel.

For U.S. citizens traveling on business or as tourists, especially in Europe, a U.S. passport is often sufficient to gain admittance for a limited stay. For many countries, however, a visa must also be obtained before entering. It is the responsibility of the traveler to check in advance and obtain any required visas from the appropriate embassies or nearest consulates. Each country has its own specific guidelines concerning length of stay and purpose of visit, etc. Some may require visitors to display proof that they have 1) sufficient funds to stay for the intended time period, 2) onward/return tickets, and/or, 3) at least 6 months remaining validity on their U.S. passport.

New restrictions imposed by the U.S. Department of State require that all U.S. citizens returning to the United States or its territories after air, land, or sea travel anywhere outside the country – including, for the first time, Mexico, Canada, and the Caribbean – be required to have a valid passport to reenter the country.

For up-to-date passport and international travel information visit, http://www.travel.state.gov/passport or contact the National Passport Information Center at 877.487.2778 to speak with a trained specialist.

National Contact:

U.S. Department of State
Washington, DC 20520
P: 877.487.2778

Additional Resources:

U.S. Department of State, *U.S. Passport Application – Form DS-11*
http://www.state.gov/documents/organization/212239.pdf

Administration for Children and Families, *Office of Child Support Enforcement, Passport Denial*
http://www.acf.hhs.gov/programs/css/resource-library/search?topic[5319]=5319

VITAL RECORDS: BIRTH, DEATH, MARRIAGE & DIVORCE

Vital records are state-issued certificates of birth, death, marriage and divorce maintained within a central location. Each record provides proof of a particular life event and is usually considered valid for obtaining most major forms of identification at both the state and federal level. For example, a birth certificate provides proof of when and where you were born. An original or certified copy of a birth certificate can be useful when providing identity in certain situations, such as applying for a driver's license, social security card, health benefits, passport, or general assistance programs.

You may request an application form, fee schedule, and specific eligibility requirements from the Office of Vital Records and Statistics for the state where the event occurred.

State Contact:

Please refer to Appendix 2-B: State Vital Record Offices.

Additional Resources:

National Center for Health Statistics, *Where to Write for Vital Records*
http://www.cdc.gov/nchs/w2w/w2w.pdf

CHAPTER 3 | EMPLOYMENT & CAREER DEVELOPMENT RESOURCES

"Choose a job you love, and you will never have to work a day in your life."
~ Confucius

Today's job market is vast and forgiving. Individuals with criminal histories should be honest, realistic and focused when it comes to finding and securing employment upon release from incarceration. There are many employment related tools and resources available to those who wish to succeed. The following resources were selected as an introduction to the programs and services available to assist job seekers with obtaining gainful employment regardless of their background.

FEDERAL & STATE LABOR DEPARTMENTS

Federal and state labor departments are an unparalleled source of employment, training and career exploration information. For a listing of programs and services offered within a specific geographic area, please contact your state labor department or an American Job Center for additional information and/or referral.

National Contact:

U.S. Department of Labor
Francis Perkins Building
200 Constitution Avenue, NW
Washington, DC 20210
P: 866.4.USA.DOL
I: http://www.dol.gov

State Contact:

Please refer to Appendix 3-A: State Department of Labor Offices.

U.S. DEPARTMENT OF LABOR SPONSORED PROGRAMS

The mission of the U.S. Department of Labor is to foster, promote, and develop the welfare of the wage earners, job seekers, and retirees of the United States; improve working conditions; advance opportunities for profitable employment; and assure work-related benefits and rights.

EMPLOYMENT & TRAINING PROGRAMS
http://www.doleta.gov

The U.S. Department of Labor's Employment and Training Administration funds training programs that teach job skills and provide job placement services for adults who are at least 18 years of age or older. The programs are administered locally by American Job Centers, formerly known as One-Stop Career Centers. The types of training offered by local American Job Centers may vary depending on the job opportunities available in each individual community. As such, individuals are encouraged to contact their local American Job Center for a detailed listing of the programs and services offered within their local area.

ADULT TRAINING PROGRAMS
http://www.dol.gov/dol/topic/training/adulttraining.htm

The U.S. Department of Labor's Employment and Training Administration funds training programs that teach job skills and provide job placement services for adults who are at least 18 years of age. The programs are administered locally by American Job Centers. The types of training offered by a local training center can vary depending on the job opportunities in the community. To help locate training programs in your area, search for an American Job Center in your state, call 877.US-2JOBS.

APPRENTICESHIP
http://www.dol.gov/dol/topic/training/apprenticeship.htm

Apprenticeship is a combination of on-the-job training and related instruction in which workers learn the practical and theoretical aspects of a highly skilled occupation. Apprenticeship programs can be sponsored by individual employers, joint employer and labor groups, and/or employer associations.

The role of the U.S. Department of Labor is to safeguard the welfare of apprentices, ensure equality of access to apprenticeship programs, and provide integrated employment and training information to sponsors and the local employment and training community. Additional information regarding apprenticeship programs such as local program options may be identified by visiting the U.S. Department of Labor's Office of Apprenticeship website directly at http://www.doleta.gov/OA. A listing of state and regional apprenticeship offices is available in Appendix 3-B: State & Regional Offices of Apprenticeship.

DISLOCATED WORKERS
http://www.dol.gov/dol/topic/training/dislocatedworkers.htm

The U.S. Department of Labor's Employment and Training Administration provides information on training programs and other services that are available to assist workers who have been laid-off or are about to be laid-off. Services are designed to meet local needs and may vary from state to state. Some services for dislocated workers have eligibility requirements.

INDIAN & NATIVE AMERICANS
http://www.dol.gov/dol/topic/training/indianprograms.htm

The Workforce Investment Act contains provisions aimed at supporting employment and training activities for Indian, Alaska Native, and Native Hawaiian individuals. The U.S. Department of Labor's Indian and Native American Programs fund grant programs that provide training opportunities at the local level for this target population.

JOB CORPS
http://www.dol.gov/dol/topic/training/jobcorps.htm

Job Corps is the nation's largest and most comprehensive residential education and job training program for at-risk youth, ages 16 to 24. Job Corps combines classroom, practical, and work-based learning experiences to prepare youth for stable, long-term, high-paying jobs.

AMERICAN JOB CENTERS
http://www.dol.gov/dol/topic/training/onestop.htm

American Job Centers are designed to provide a full range of assistance to job seekers in one convenient location. Established under the Workforce Innovation and Opportunity Act (WIOA), the centers offer referrals, career counseling, job listings, and similar employment-related services. Customers can visit a center in-person or connect to the center's information through personal computer or kiosk remote access.

The American Job Center System is coordinated by the U.S. Department of Labor's Employment and Training Administration. The Employment and Training Administration website provides a clickable map of American Job Center websites for each state and a list of state, regional, and local center locations at http://www.doleta.gov/usworkforce/onestop/onestopmap.cfm. For added convenience, a list of State American Job Center websites is located in Appendix 3-C: American Job Center Websites.

PEOPLE WITH DISABILITIES
http://www.dol.gov/dol/topic/training/disabilitytraining.htm

The U.S. Department of Labor's Employment and Training Administration provides funds and administers grant programs that offer training and employment assistance to people with disabilities.

The U.S. Department of Labor's Employment and Training Administration is also responsible for enforcing parts of the Ticket to Work and Self-Sufficiency Program, which aims to provide greater access for people with disabilities to training services, vocational rehabilitation services, and other support services they need to obtain, regain, or maintain employment.

SAFETY & HEALTH

http://www.dol.gov/dol/topic/training/safety.htm

The U.S. Department of Labor's Occupational Safety and Health Administration funds grants to train workers and employers to recognize, avoid, and prevent safety and health hazards in their workplace.

The Occupational Safety and Health Administration's Outreach Training Program is the agency's primary way to train workers in the basics of occupational safety and health. Through the program, individuals who complete a one-week Occupational Safety and Health Administration trainer course are authorized to teach 10-hour or 30-hour courses in construction or general industry safety and health standards.

SENIORS

http://www.dol.gov/dol/topic/training/seniors.htm

The Senior Community Service Employment Program is a part-time employment program for low-income persons age 55 or over. Program participants work at community and government agencies and are paid the federal or state minimum wage, whichever is greater. They may also receive training and can use their participation as a bridge to other employment positions which are not supported with federal funds.

VETERANS

http://www.dol.gov/dol/topic/training/veterans.htm

The Veterans Employment and Training Service of the U.S. Department of Labor assists veterans, reservists, and National Guard members in securing employment. Employment and training assistance is also available from the Departments' Employment and Training Administration.

YOUTH PROGRAMS

http://www.dol.gov/dol/topic/training/youth.htm

The U.S. Department of Labor's Employment and Training Administration supports a wide variety of programs to ensure that all youth have the skills and training they need to successfully make the transition to adulthood and careers.

For additional information regarding any of the above Employment and Training Programs, contact the U.S. Department of Labor or your local American Job Center for assistance.

National Contact:

U.S. Department of Labor
Employment and Training Administration
200 Constitution Avenue, NW
Washington, DC 20210
P: 202.693.2796

LABOR MARKET INFORMATION, TRENDS & PROJECTIONS

http://www.bls.gov/emp

The U.S. Department of Labor's Bureau of Labor Statistics compiles, publishes and disseminates a wide range of labor market information, from regional wages for specific occupations to statistics on national, state and local area employment trends. Information on state occupational projections is available at http://www.projectionscentral.com.

National Contact:

U.S. Department of Labor
Bureau of Labor Statistics
200 Constitution Avenue, NW
Washington, DC 20210
P: 202.691.5262

State Contact:

Please refer to Appendix 3-D: State Labor Market Information Offices.

Additional Resources:

Occupational Outlook Quarterly, *The 2010-20 Job Outlook in Brief*
http://publications.usa.gov/USAPubs.php?PubID=569

UNEMPLOYMENT INSURANCE
http://www.workforcesecurity.doleta.gov

The Unemployment Insurance Program provides benefits to eligible workers who become unemployed through no fault of their own and who meet other eligibility requirements. Each state administers its own program under federal guidelines. Eligibility requirements, benefits, and length of benefits are determined by individual states in accordance with applicable law. For more information, visit http://www.dol.gov/dol/topic/unemployment-insurance or contact your local American Job Center for assistance.

National Contact:

U.S. Department of Labor
Employment and Training Administration
200 Constitution Avenue, NW
Washington, DC 20210
P: 202.693.3029

ELECTRONIC CAREER EXPLORATION & EMPLOYMENT TOOLS

CAREERONESTOP.ORG
http://www.careeronestop.org

CareerOneStop.org is a suite of web-based products funded and developed by the U.S. Department of Labor. CareerOneStop.org includes America's Service Locator, America's Career InfoNet, and the MySkillsMyFuture websites. Each product offers unique solutions for the increasing demand of today's labor market to meet the specialized needs of jobseekers, employers, and the workforce and educational communities alike.

CareerOneStop.org is...

- Your source for employment information and inspiration
- The place to manage your career
- Your pathway to career success
- Tools to help job seekers, students, businesses and career professionals
- Sponsored by the U.S. Department of Labor

CareerOneStop.org products include:

AMERICA'S SERVICE LOCATOR
http://www.servicelocator.org

America's Service Locator connects individuals to employment and training opportunities available at local American Job Centers. The website provides contact information for a range of local work-related services, including unemployment benefits, career development, and educational opportunities.

AMERICA'S CAREER INFONET
http://www.careerinfonet.org

America's Career InfoNet helps individuals explore career opportunities to make informed employment and education choices. This website features user-friendly occupational and industry information, salary data, career videos, education resources, self-assessment tools, and other resources that support talent development in today's fast-paced global marketplace.

MYSKILLS MYFUTURE
http://www.myskillsmyfuture.org

This website helps laid-off workers and other career changers find new occupations to explore. Users can identify occupations that require skills and knowledge similar to their current or previous job, learn more about these suggested matches, locate local training programs, and/or apply for jobs.

COMPETENCY MODEL CLEARINGHOUSE
http://www.careeronestop.org/competencymodel

The Competency Model Clearinghouse provides the business community with a means to communicate its skill needs to educators and the workforce system in a common industry-driven framework. The models and other competency-based resources support development of curriculum and increased awareness of careers in high-growth industries.

WORKER REEMPLOYMENT
http://www.careeronestop.org/reemployment

This website provides employment, training, and financial assistance for laid-off workers. The website includes a Job Search tool with job listings for all fifty states updated daily. Users will also find resources for getting immediate help with unemployment insurance, healthcare, and other financial needs; job searching and resume tips; changing careers and understanding transferable skills; and upgrading skills through education and training.

If you have additional questions and would like to contact CareerOneStop.org's Customer Service Center for guidance and assistance with any of the CareerOneStop.org products, please contact them by phone at 877.348.0502 between the hours of 7:00 am and 4:00 pm (CST), Monday through Friday.

Additional Resources:

CareerOneStop.org, *CareerOneStop Overview*
http://www.careeronestop.org/TridionMultimedia/CosOverview.pdf

CareerOneStop.org, *CareerOneStop PowerPoint*
http://www.careeronestop.org/TridionMultimedia/tcm24-22150_PPT_COSRedesign2015.pptx

CareerOneStop.org, *CareerOneStop Ex-Offender Overview*
http://www.careeronestop.org/TridionMultimedia/Exoffender.pdf

O*NET CAREER EXPLORATION TOOLS
http://www.onetcenter.org/dev_tools.html

The O*Net Career Exploration Tools are a suite of assessment tools designed for career counseling, career planning and exploration. The tools are designed to assist a wide variety of individuals to gain personal insight that will help them identify occupations that they might find satisfying.

Use of a variety of tools supports the whole-person approach to assessment, providing a firmer basis for individuals to make important career decisions. The O*Net Career Exploration Tools include:

- Ability Profiler
- Interest Profiler
- Computerized Interest Profiler
- Work Importance Locator
- Work Importance Profiler

For more information about these tools, including ordering information and available product downloads, please contact the National O*Net Center directly.

National Contact:

National O*Net Center
P.O. Box 27625
Raleigh, NC 27611
P: Not Provided

AMERICAN JOB CENTER NETWORK
http://jobcenter.usa.gov/

As the cornerstone of the American Job Center Network this website provides a single access point – open 24-7 – to key federal programs and critical local resources to help people find a job, identify training programs, and gain skills in growing industries. Connecting Americans to online resources from across the federal government, nearly 3,000 brick-and-mortar American Job Centers, and hundreds of local training programs and job resources funded through federal grants, the proud partners of the American Job Center Network provide an easily-identifiable source for the help and services individuals and businesses need. No matter what state you're in, whether you're online or visiting in person, when you see the American Job Center Network, take comfort knowing you're in the right place to jump start your job search, explore new career options, or tap into the most talented and dedicated workforce in the world.

WHAT ARE THE DIFFERENT TYPES OF AMERICAN JOB CENTERS?

Comprehensive American Job Centers: These centers provide a full array of employment and training-related services for workers, youth and businesses. These locations include the mandatory Workforce Innovation and Opportunity Act (WIOA) partners on-site.

Affiliate American Job Centers: These centers provide limited employment and training-related services for workers, youth, and businesses. These locations do not include all the mandatory Workforce Innovation and Opportunity Act (WIOA) partners (i.e., Veterans, Vocational Rehabilitation) on-site.

The American Job Center website is a diverse collection of job search tools. The American Job Center website includes the following sections:

- Job Search
- Resume and Interviewing
- Unemployment Insurance
- Skills Transferability Tool
- Networking
- Other Benefits and Income Support

Additionally, if you would like to locate your local American Job Center, please visit their convenient search tool at http://www.careeronestop.org/ExOffender/american-job-center-finder.aspx for access to over 3,000 American Job Centers nationwide.

OCCUPATIONAL INFORMATION RESOURCES

Like any major decision, selecting a career involves a lot of fact finding. Fortunately, some of the best informational resources are easily accessible through publications created by the U.S. Department of Labor's Bureau of Labor Statistics. The following publications are meant to be used in conjunction with traditional occupational exploration resources to ensure a comprehensive and successful approach to employment.

OCCUPATIONAL OUTLOOK HANDBOOK
http://www.bls.gov/ooh/

The Occupational Outlook Handbook is a nationally recognized source of career information, designed to provide valuable assistance to individuals making decisions about their future work lives. The roughly 334 occupational groupings covered in the Occupational Outlook Handbook accounted for about 84 percent of the jobs in the economy in 2015.

The Occupational Outlook Handbook is no longer available in print from the Government Printing Office. A print version of the Occupational Outlook Handbook is or will be available from the following private publishers:

- Bernan - http://www.bernan.com
- Claitor's Publishing - http://www.claitors.com
- JIST Publishing - http://www.jist.emco.com

CAREER GUIDE TO INDUSTRIES
The Bureau of Labor Statistics has discontinued publication of the Career Guide to Industries as an independent product. The Bureau of Labor Statistics website has data on current and projected occupational employment within industries and current and projected industry employment by occupation. The Career Outlook occasionally publishes articles on industries. Search the Career Outlook archive at
http://www.bls.gov/careeroutlook/articles.htm for industry-related information.

CAREER OUTLOOK
http://www.bls.gov/careeroutlook/

Career Outlook (formerly *Occupational Outlook Quarterly*) supplements the *Occupational Outlook Handbook* and is published by the Bureau of Labor Statistics of the U.S. Department of Labor.

Career Outlook articles provide data and information on a variety of topics — including occupations and industries, pay and benefits, and more. These articles are helpful for students, counselors, jobseekers, and others planning careers.

O*NET ONLINE
http://www.onetonline.org

O*Net Online is a comprehensive source of descriptions and skill sets for specific occupations. O*Net Online allows both the public and private sector to directly access key data for identifying and developing the skills of the American workforce. The O*Net system provides information about skills, knowledge, abilities, tasks and the context in which work is done.

STATE & LOCAL JOB BANKS

A job bank is a database of current job opportunities within a specific geographic area or occupational field. Most job banks are computer-based and job listings are posted and maintained by prospective employers. In addition, job banks allow job seekers to post electronic resumes and submit completed applications for job opportunities listed within their database. A listing of state sponsored job banks is available within Appendix 3-E: State Job Bank Websites.

EX-OFFENDER HIRING INCENTIVES

FEDERAL BONDING PROGRAM
http://www.bonds4jobs.com

The Federal Bonding Program is a unique job placement tool to help job applicants get and keep a job. The program issues Fidelity Bonds and is sponsored by the U.S. Department of Labor. A Fidelity Bond is a business insurance policy which protects employers in case of any loss of money or property due to employee dishonesty. Fidelity bond coverage is usually $5,000 with no deductible amount of liability for the employer. Higher amounts of coverage, up to $25,000, may be allowed if justified.

To be eligible for the bond, the employer must schedule a date to start work for the prospective employee. Bond coverage is provided for any at-risk applicant whose background usually leads employers to question their honesty and deny them employment. This includes people with criminal records, people in treatment or recovery for alcohol and/or other drug addictions, and people with little or no work history, including people transitioning from welfare to work. Upon request, a local American Job Center or Department of Labor representative requests the McLaughlin Company in Washington, D.C. to issue to the employer a Fidelity Bond insurance policy covering the worker. This policy is underwritten through the Travelers Property Casualty Insurance Company.

National Contact:

Federal Bonding Program
The McLaughlin Company
9210 Corporate Boulevard, Suite 250
Rockville, MD 20850
P: 202.293.5566

State Contact:

Please refer to Appendix 3-F: State Federal Bonding Program Coordinators.

Additional Resources:

U.S. Department of Labor, *Federal Bonding Program: Answers to Questions About Fidelity Bonding*
http://bonds4jobs.com/assets/brochure.pdf

U.S. Department of Labor, *Employment and Training Administration's Federal Bonding Training Video*
http://bonds4jobs.com/assets/content/FBPTool.mov

UNICOR BONDING PROGRAM
http://www.unicor.gov

Initiated in February, 2006 the UNICOR Bonding Program provides a $5,000 fidelity bond for employed ex-federal prisoners who worked in Federal Prison Industries (UNICOR) for at least six months during their incarceration. For additional information, contact the national UNICOR bonding specialist directly.

National Contact:

Federal Bureau of Prisons
Federal Prison Industries (UNICOR)
320 First Street, NW
Washington, DC 20534
P: 202.305.3972

Additional Resources:

U.S. Department of Justice, Federal Bureau of Prisons, *UNICOR's Federal Bonding Program Toolkit*
http://www.bop.gov/resources/pdfs/toolkit.pdf

WORK OPPORTUNITY TAX CREDIT

http://www.doleta.gov/business/incentives/opptax

The Work Opportunity Tax Credit is a federal tax credit incentive, which Congress provides to private-sector businesses for hiring individuals from nine target groups who have consistently faced significant barriers to employment. The main objective of this program is to enable the targeted employees to gradually move from economic dependency into self-sufficiency as they earn a steady income and become contributing taxpayers, while the participating employers are compensated by being able to reduce their federal income tax liability. The Work Opportunity Tax Credit joins other workforce programs that help incentivize workplace diversity and facilitate access to good jobs for all Americans.

WHAT DOES WOTC DO?

The Work Opportunity Tax Credit helps targeted workers move from economic dependency into self-sufficiency as they earn a steady income and become contributing taxpayers, while participating employers are able to reduce their income tax liability.

HOW LARGE IS THE TAX CREDIT?

The maximum tax credit ranges from $1,200 to $9,600, depending on the employee hired.

National Contact:

U.S. Department of Labor
Employment and Training Administration
200 Constitution Avenue, NW
Washington, DC 20210
P: 202.693.2786

State Contact:

Please refer to Appendix 3-G: State Work Opportunity Tax Credit Coordinators.

Additional Resources:

U.S. Department of Labor, *State Work Opportunity Tax Credit Coordinators*
http://www.doleta.gov/business/incentives/opptax/State_Contacts.cfm

U.S. Department of Labor, *National and Regional Work Opportunity Tax Credit Coordinators*
http://www.doleta.gov/business/incentives/opptax/Regional_Contacts.cfm

U.S. Department of Labor, *Tips for Applying*
http://www.doleta.gov/business/incentives/opptax/pdf/Tip_Submitting_Application.pdf

U.S. Department of Labor, *Work Opportunity Tax Credit Target Group Eligibility Chart*
http://www.doleta.gov/business/incentives/opptax/pdf/Target_Group_Eligibility.pdf

U.S. Department of Labor, *Work Opportunity Tax Credit Employer's Guide*
http://www.doleta.gov/business/incentives/opptax/pdf/WOTC_Employer_Guide.pdf

U.S. Department of Labor, *Work Opportunity Tax Credit Application Methods*
http://www.doleta.gov/business/incentives/opptax/PDF/WOTC_Submission_Processes_by_State.pdf

U.S. Department of Labor, *Work Opportunity Tax Credit Program Brochure*
http://www.doleta.gov/business/incentives/opptax/PDF/employers_wotc_program_brochure.pdf

MINIMUM WAGE LAWS

Minimum wage laws in the United States are complicated and have many exceptions and variations. There are both federal and state minimum wage laws, yet each state sets its own minimum wage level, which may be the same, higher or lower then the federal minimum wage. In general, where federal and state laws have different minimum wage rates, the higher standard applies.

FEDERAL & STATE MINIMUM WAGE

http://www.wagehour.dol.gov

The federal minimum wage provisions are contained in the Fair Labor Standards Act. The federal minimum wage is $7.25 per hour effective July 24, 2009. Many states also have minimum wage laws. Some state laws provide greater employee protections; employers must comply with both. State minimum wage data is available online at http://www.dol.gov/whd/minwage/america.htm.

Table 1: Summary of State Minimum Wage Rates Effective January 1, 2017										
AL: NONE	AK: $9.75	AZ: $8.05	AR: $8.00	CA: $10.00	CO:$ 8.31	CT: $9.60	DE: $8.25	DC: $11.50	FL: $8.05	
GA: $5.15	HI: $8.50	ID: $7.25	IL: $8.25	IN: $7.25	IA: $7.25	KS: $7.25	KY: $7.25	LA: NONE	ME: $7.50	
MA: $10.00	MD: $8.75	MI: $8.50	MN: $9.50	MS: NONE	MO: $7.65	MT: $8.05	NE: $9.00	NV: $8.25	NH: $7.25	
NJ: $8.38	NM: $7.50	NY: $9.00	NC: $7.25	ND: $7.25	OH: $8.10	OK: $7.25	OR: $9.75	PA: $7.25	PR: $7.25	
RI: $9.60	SC: NONE	SD: $8.55	TN: NONE	TX: $7.25	UT: $7.25	VT: $9.60	VA: $7.25	WA: $9.47	WV: $8.75	
WI: $7.25	WY: $5.15									

National Contact:

U.S. Department of Labor
Wage and Hour Division
200 Constitution Avenue, NW
Washington, DC 20210
P: 866.487.9243

Additional Resources:

U.S. Department of Labor, *Federal Minimum Wage Laws Website*
http://www.dol.gov/esa/whd/flsa/

CAREER RESOURCES FOR THE DISABLED

The following organizations provide information designed to help specific groups of people with overcoming disability challenges related to employability. Visit your local library or American Job Center for information on additional organizations associated with specific groups or needs.

AMERICAN COUNCIL OF THE BLIND

http://www.acb.org

The American Council of the Blind is a national membership organization established to promote the independence, dignity, and well-being of blind and visually impaired people in the United States. Through numerous programs and services, the American Council of the Blind enables blind people to live and work independently and to advocate for their rights.

National Contact:

American Council of the Blind
1155 15th Street, NW, Suite 1004
Washington, DC 20005
P: 202.467.5081

EQUAL EMPLOYMENT OPPORTUNITY COMMISSION

http://www.eeoc.gov

The Equal Employment Opportunity Commission enforces laws that make discrimination illegal in the workplace. The commission oversees all types of work situations including hiring, firing, promotions, harassment, training, wages, and benefits.

National Contact:

Equal Employment Opportunity Commission
131 M Street, NE
Washington, DC 20507
P: 202.663.4900

NATIONAL COUNCIL ON DISABILITY

http://www.ncd.gov

The National Council on Disability is an independent federal agency making recommendations to the President and Congress of the United States on policies affecting Americans with disabilities.

National Contact:

National Council on Disability
1331 F Street, NW, Suite 850
Washington, DC 20004
P: 202.272.2004

NATIONAL COUNCIL ON THE AGING

http://www.ncoa.org

The National Council on the Aging is a national voice for older adults – especially those who are vulnerable and disadvantaged – and the community organizations that serve them. The National Council on the Aging also provides resources and assistance to those individuals in need of referral.

National Contact:

National Council on the Aging
1901 L Street, NW, 4th Floor
Washington, DC 20036
P: 202.479.1200

NATIONAL FEDERATION OF THE BLIND

http://www.nfb.org

The National Federation of the Blind is a national organization that serves as an advocate for change and centralized repository and dissemination source of reference and referral information for the blind and those individuals and agencies assisting them.

National Contact:

National Federation of the Blind
1800 Johnson Street
Baltimore, MD 21230
P: 410.659.9314

NATIONAL ORGANIZATION ON DISABILITY

http://www.nod.org

The National Organization on Disability is a nonprofit organization dedicated to the advancement of resources and assistance for the disabled through legislative reform and information dissemination. The National Organization on Disability can provide assistance with obtaining information on employment opportunities, transportation, and other considerations for people with disabilities.

National Contact:

National Organization on Disability
910 Sixteenth Street, NW, Suite 600
Washington, DC 20006
P: 202.293.5960

U.S. DEPARTMENT OF JUSTICE | AMERICANS WITH DISABILITIES ACT INFORMATION LINE

http://www.ada.gov

The U.S. Department of Justice's Americans with Disabilities Act Information Line permits businesses, state and local governments, or others to call and ask questions about general or specific Americans with Disabilities Act requirements including questions about the Americans with Disabilities Act Standards for Accessible Design.

National Contact:

U.S. Department of Justice
Disability Rights Section
950 Pennsylvania Avenue, NW
Washington, DC 20530
P: 800.514.0301

U.S. DEPARTMENT OF LABOR | OFFICE OF DISABILITY EMPLOYMENT POLICY

http://www.dol.gov/odep

The U.S. Department of Labor's Office of Disability Employment Policy works to create policies to ensure that people with disabilities are fully integrated in the workforce.

National Contact:

U.S. Department of Labor
Office of Disability Employment Policy
200 Constitution Avenue, NW, Room S1303
Washington, DC 20004
P: 202.693.7880

STATE & FEDERAL GOVERNMENT EMPLOYMENT OPPORTUNITIES

Previously incarcerated individuals and those with criminal convictions receive no special consideration when applying for employment with state or federal governments. The application and selection procedures for state jobs follow state guidelines, while federal jobs are governed by the rules and guidelines of the Office of Personnel Management.

OFFICE OF PERSONNEL MANAGEMENT

http://www.opm.gov

The Office of Personnel Management manages the civil service of the federal government, coordinates recruiting of new government employees, and manages their health insurance and retirement benefits programs.

National Contact:

Office of Personnel Management
1900 E Street, NW
Washington, DC 20415
P: 202.606.1800

Additional Resources:

Occupational Outlook Quarterly, *How to Get a Job in the Federal Government*
http://publications.usa.gov/USAPubs.php?PubID=1338

EMPLOYMENT ELIGIBILITY CONSIDERATIONS

U.S. CITIZENSHIP AND IMMIGRATION SERVICES
http://www.uscis.gov

Citizens and non-citizens must be prepared to provide employers with documentation to verify identity and lawful employment authorization. U.S. Citizenship and Immigration Services of the U.S. Department of Homeland Security requires employers to complete Form I-9 to document verification of the identity and employment authorization of each new employee hired after November 6, 1986, to work in the United States.

National Contact:

U.S. Citizenship and Immigration Services
111 Massachusetts Avenue, NW
Washington, DC 20529
P: 800.375.5286

Additional Resources:

U.S. Citizenship and Immigration Services, *Employment Eligibility Verification - Form I-9 - English*
http://www.uscis.gov/files/form/i-9.pdf

U.S. Citizenship and Immigration Services, *Employment Eligibility Verification - Form I-9 - Spanish*
http://www.uscis.gov/files/form/i-9_spanish.pdf

COMPANIES WHO HIRE EX-OFFENDERS

Ex-offenders should assume that employers will hire them if they are a good match for their needs. Limiting a job search to employers that are perceived to hire ex-offenders can limit wages and job prospects. Ex-offenders should focus on finding employers who are a good match for their skills, experience, and career goals. Treating an employment search like a job and spending at least 8 hours a day at it are vital to any successful job search. A list of employers known to actively recruit and employ ex-offenders is available within Appendix 3-H: Companies Who Hire Ex-Offenders.

TEMPORARY EMPLOYMENT AGENCIES
Temporary employment agencies are a good way for anyone to quickly get employed and acquire work experience. With temporary employment agencies, individuals work for the agency which, in turn, places them on temporary assignments with their clients. While most companies primarily recruit individuals for temporary or part-time positions, many of them also have temporary-to-permanent programs. With most agencies, individuals work three or four months with one employer in the hopes of being hired for a full-time position once their contract expires and all of the performance expectations have been met. Some of the most prominent agencies are Kelly Services, Labor Finders, and Manpower.

National Contact:

Kelly Services
999 West Big Beaver Road
Troy, MI 48084
P: 248.362.4444
I: http://www.kellyservices.com

Labor Finders International, Inc.
11426 North Jog Road
Palm Beach Gardens, FL 33418
P: 561.627.6502
I: http://www.laborfinders.com

Manpower Group
100 Manpower Place
Milwaukee, WI 53212
P: 414.961.1000
I: http://www.manpower.com

NATIONAL EMPLOYMENT ADVOCACY/PRACTITIONER ORGANIZATIONS

NATIONAL CAREER DEVELOPMENT ASSOCIATION
http://www.ncda.org

The National Career Development Association (NCDA) provides professional development, publications, standards, and advocacy to practitioners and educators who inspire and empower individuals to achieve their career and life goals.

NCDA provides programs and services for career development professionals and for the public involved with or interested in career development, including, but not limited to, professional development activities, publications, research, general information, professional standards, advocacy, and recognition for achievement and service. NCDA provides a voice for thousands of members who deliver career services to diverse groups in a broad variety of settings and to their clients. NCDA maintains a comprehensive web site of information, resources and tools for career development professionals and the public through their website.

Additionally, the National Career Development Association maintains an excellent list of internet sites for career planning. This list is available in Appendix 3-I: Internet Sites for Career Planning or by visiting their website.

National Contact:

National Career Development Association
305 North Beech Circle
Broken Arrow, OK 74012
P: 866.367.6232

NATIONAL H.I.R.E. NETWORK
http://www.hirenetwork.org

Established by the Legal Action Center, the National Helping Individuals with Criminal Records Re-enter through Employment Network is both a national clearinghouse for information and an advocate for policy change. The goal of the National H.I.R.E. Network is to increase the number and quality of job opportunities available to people with criminal records by changing public policies, employment practices and public opinion. The National H.I.R.E. Network also provides training and technical assistance to agencies working to improve employment prospects for people with criminal histories.

National Contact:

National H.I.R.E. Network
Legal Action Center
225 Varick Street
New York, NY 10014
P: 212.243.1313

Additional Resources:

National H.I.R.E. Network, *Resources, Information & Assistance Clearinghouse*
http://www.hirenetwork.org/clearinghouse

National H.I.R.E. Network, *Publications Catalog*
http://www.hirenetwork.org/content/publications

VOLUNTEER OPPORTUNITIES

Networkforgood.org, 1-800-Volunteer.org, and VolunteerMatch.org are internet-based services that connect volunteers with nonprofit and public sector organizations around the country. Volunteers enter a zip code or indicate the geographic area in which they would like to work, and the programs list organizations that could use their help.

CORPORATION FOR NATIONAL AND COMMUNITY SERVICE
http://www.nationalservice.gov

The Corporation for National and Community Service is a government organization geared towards matching jobseekers and volunteers with community service jobs. The Corporation for National and Community Service organizes and oversees AmeriCorps, SeniorCorps, Learn and Serve America, Martin Luther King, Jr. Day events and many other programs designed to expand community service and volunteerism within the United States and around the world.

National Contact:

Corporation for National and Community Service
1201 New York Avenue, NW
Washington, DC 20525
P: 202.606.5000

CHAPTER 4 | ADVOCACY & LEGAL RESOURCES

"It is not the strongest of the species that survives, nor the most intelligent, but rather the one most adaptable to change." ~ Clarence Darrow

This section provides information for anyone interested in gaining a better understanding of their criminal history and how it will impact their life beyond incarceration. In addition, some agencies were selected for their ability to provide direct and/or indirect advocacy and assistance with navigating the criminal justice system and overcoming obstacles to successful community reintegration.

CRIMINAL RECORD REPOSITORIES

Federal and state law enforcement agencies maintain criminal record repositories of criminal arrests, arraignments and convictions within their specific jurisdictions. Criminal record repositories should be contacted to ensure the accuracy of the information contained within a record and to identify who is legally entitled to access such records.

FEDERAL CRIMINAL RECORD REPOSITORY
http://www.fbi.gov/about-us/cjis/background-checks

An F.B.I. Identification Record – often referred to as a criminal history or a "rap sheet" – is a listing of information taken from fingerprint submissions retained by the F.B.I. in connection with arrests and in some instances, federal employment, naturalization, or military service. The process of responding to an Identification Record request is generally known as a criminal background check.

If the fingerprints are related to an arrest, the Identification Record includes the name of the agency that submitted the fingerprints to the F.B.I., the date of the arrest, the arrest charge, and the disposition of the arrest, if known. All arrest data included in an Identification Record is obtained from fingerprint submissions, disposition reports, and other information submitted by agencies having criminal justice responsibilities.

Only the subject of an F.B.I. Identification Record can request a copy of their own record. Individuals typically make this request for personal review, to challenge the information on record, or to satisfy a requirement to live, work, or travel in a foreign country.

National Contact:

National Crime Information Center
1000 Custer Hollow Road
Clarksburg, WV 26306
P: 304.625.2000

Additional Resources:

U.S. Department of Justice, *Fingerprint Card – FD 258*
http://www.fbi.gov/about-us/cjis/background-checks/standard-fingerprint-form-fd-258

STATE CRIMINAL RECORD REPOSITORIES
State criminal record information is available by contacting the state criminal record repository for the state in which the event occurred. Individuals should contact the state agency regarding specific eligibility requirements before submitting a request for disclosure.

State Contact:

Please refer to Appendix 4-A: State Criminal Record Repositories.

LEGAL ASSISTANCE & INFORMATION

If you need an attorney to advise or represent you, ask friends and family for recommendations. You can also contact the Lawyer Referral Service of your state bar association. Websites such as http://www.abalawinfo.org and http://www.nolo.com can help with answers to general legal questions.

If you cannot afford a lawyer, you may qualify for free legal help from a Legal Aid or Legal Service Corporation office. These offices generally offer legal assistance for such things as landlord-tenant relations, family matters, Social Security, welfare, and workers' compensation. If the Legal Aid office in your area does not handle your type of case, it may refer you to other local, state, or national organizations that can provide help.

Free assistance may also be available from a law school program where students, supervised by attorneys, handle a variety of legal matters. Some of these programs are open to all; others limit their service to specific groups, such as low-income persons. Contact a local law school for availability.

National Contact:

National Legal Aid and Defender Association
1140 Connecticut Avenue, NW, Suite 900
Washington, DC 20036
P: 202.452.0620
I: http://www.nlada.org

Legal Services Corporation
333 K Street, NW, 3rd Floor
Washington, DC 20007
P: 202.295.1500
I: http://www.lsc.org

AMERICAN BAR ASSOCIATION
http://www.americanbar.org

The American Bar Association is an association of lawyers. The American Bar Association accredits law schools, and provides the public with information about the law, courts and resource guides for legal issues. Upon request, the American Bar Association may provide written assistance and referral information for those individuals who do not have access to their website or other publicly accessible legal resources.

National Contact:

American Bar Association
321 North Clark Street
Chicago, IL 60654
P: 312.988.5000

State Contact:

Please refer to Appendix 4-B: State Bar Associations.

Additional Resources:

American Bar Association, *State and Local Bar Associations*
http://shop.americanbar.org/ebus/ABAGroups/DivisionforBarServices/BarAssociationDirectories/StateLocalBar Associations.aspx

LAWHELP.ORG
http://www.lawhelp.org

LawHelp.org was created for people living on low-incomes, and the legal organizations that serve them. This website provides referrals to local legal aid and public interest law offices, basic information about legal rights, self-help information, court information, and links to social service agencies. LawHelp.org was built by Pro Bono Net, a nonprofit organization headquartered in New York, and by partnering legal aid organizations throughout the United States.

National Contact:

Pro Bono Net
151 West 30th Street, 10th Floor
New York, NY 10001
P: 212.760.2554

THE CENTER FOR CONSTITUTIONAL RIGHTS | JAILHOUSE LAWYER'S HANDBOOK
http://jailhouselaw.org

This Jailhouse Lawyer's Handbook is a resource for prisoners who wish to file federal lawsuits addressing poor conditions in prison or abuse by staff. It also contains limited general information about the American legal system. This handbook is available for free to anyone: prisoners, families, friends, activists, lawyers, and others.

The Center for Constitutional Rights hopes that you find the Handbook helpful, and that it provides some aid in protecting your rights behind bars.

For additional information, please write for the Jailhouse Lawyer's Handbook, 5th Edition at the address below.

National Contact:

The Center for Constitutional Rights
666 Broadway, 7th Floor
New York, NY 10012

Additional Resources:

The Center for Constitutional Rights, *Jailhouse Lawyer's Handbook*
http://ccrjustice.org/files/Report_JailhouseLawyersHandbook.pdf

The Center for Constitutional Rights, *Online Chapter Search*
http://jailhouselaw.org/about-this-handbook/

COLLATERAL CONSEQUENCES

Defined as penalties imposed automatically or authorized but not automatically required to be imposed, collateral consequences are laws and regulations that serve as barriers to employment, housing, and other services that are essential to an individual's stability in the community.

Additional Resources:

American Bar Association, *Internal Exile: Collateral Consequences of Conviction in Federal Laws and Regulations*
http://www.abanet.org/cecs/internalexile.pdf

American Bar Association, *National Inventory of the Collateral Consequences of Conviction*
http://www.abacollateralconsequences.org/

Legal Action Center, *After Prison: Roadblocks to Reentry*
http://www.lac.org/roadblocks-to-reentry/

VOTER FELONY DISENFRANCHISEMENT
http://www.sentencingproject.org

There are millions of Americans prohibited from voting due to laws that disenfranchise individuals convicted of felony offenses. Felony disenfranchisement rates vary by state, as states institute a wide range of disenfranchisement policies. The 11 most extreme states restrict individuals voting rights even after they have served their prison sentence and are no longer on probation or parole. Only two states, Maine and Vermont, do not restrict the voting rights of individuals with felony convictions, including those in prison.

If you are interested in identifying what the official voting policy is within a particular state, please contact the voting authority for that state or see the table below for more information.

State Contact:

Please refer to Appendix 4-C: State Voter Registration Authorities.

Table 2: Summary of Felony Disenfranchisement Restrictions in 2017

No Restriction	Prison	Prison & Parole	Prison, Parole & Probation	Prison, Parole, Probation & Post-Sentence – Some or All
Maine	District of Columbia	California	Alaska	Alabama
Vermont	Hawaii	Colorado	Arkansas	Arizona
	Illinois	Connecticut	Delaware	Florida
	Indiana	New York	Georgia	Iowa
	Massachusetts		Idaho	Kentucky
	Michigan		Kansas	Mississippi
	Montana		Louisiana	Nebraska
	New Hampshire		Maryland	Nevada
	North Dakota		Minnesota	Tennessee
	Ohio		Missouri	Virginia
	Oregon		New Jersey	Wyoming
	Pennsylvania		New Mexico	
	Rhode Island		North Carolina	
	Utah		South Dakota	
			Texas	
			Washington	
			West Virginia	
			Wisconsin	

CRIMINAL JUSTICE AGENCIES & ADVOCACY GROUPS

The following agencies and organizations are dedicated to ensuring the humane and fair treatment of the incarcerated and the rehabilitation of the criminal justice system within their respective areas of service.

AMERICAN CIVIL LIBERTIES UNION | NATIONAL HEADQUARTERS

http://www.aclu.org

The American Civil Liberties Union handles state and federal conditions of confinement claims affecting large numbers of prisoners.

National Contact:

American Civil Liberties Union
125 Broad Street
New York, NY 10004
P: 212.549.2500

AMERICAN CIVIL LIBERTIES UNION | CAPITAL PUNISHMENT PROJECT

http://www.aclu.org/capital

The Capital Punishment Project of the American Civil Liberties Union works towards the abolishment of the death penalty.

National Contact:

American Civil Liberties Union
Capital Punishment Project
201 West Main Street, Suite 402
Durham, NC 27701
P: 919.682.5659

AMERICAN CIVIL LIBERTIES UNION | CRIMINAL LAW REFORM PROJECT

http://www.aclu.org

The Criminal Law Reform Project of the American Civil Liberties Union seeks an end to excessively harsh crime policies that result in mass incarceration and stand in the way of a just and equal society.

National Contact:

American Civil Liberties Union
Criminal Law Reform Project
125 Broad Street, 18th Floor
New York, NY 10004
P: 212.284.7340

AMERICAN CIVIL LIBERTIES UNION | LESBIAN, GAY, TRANSGENDER, AND AIDS PROJECT

http://www.aclu.org/getequal

The Lesbian, Gay, Transgender, and AIDS Project of the American Civil Liberties Union fights discrimination and moves public opinions of Lesbian, Gay, Bisexual, and Transgender rights through the courts, legislature and public education on a national level.

National Contact:

American Civil Liberties Union
Lesbian, Gay, Transgender, and AIDS Project
125 Broad Street, 18th Floor
New York, NY 10004
P: 212.549.2627

AMERICAN CIVIL LIBERTIES UNION | NATIONAL IMMIGRANTS RIGHTS PROJECT

http://www.aclu.org

The National Immigrants Rights Project of the American Civil Liberties Union works to defend the civil and constitutional rights of immigrants through a comprehensive program of impact litigation and public education.

National Contact:

American Civil Liberties Union
National Immigrants Rights Project
405 14th Street, Suite 300
Oakland, CA 94612
P: 510.625.2010

AMERICAN CIVIL LIBERTIES UNION | NATIONAL WOMEN'S RIGHTS PROJECT

http://www.aclu.org/womensrights

The National Women's Rights Project of the American Civil Liberties Union works to empower poor women, women of color, and immigrant women who have been victimized by gender bias and face pervasive barriers to equality through litigation, community outreach, advocacy and public education.

National Contact:

American Civil Liberties Union
National Women's Rights Project
125 Broad Street, 18th Floor
New York, NY 10004
P: 212.549.2665

AMERICAN CIVIL LIBERTIES UNION | NATIONAL TECHNOLOGY AND LIBERTY PROGRAM

http://www.aclu.org/privacy

The National Technology and Liberty Program of the American Civil Liberties Union fights to preserve the American tradition that governments not use technology to track individual citizens or violate privacy unless there is evidence of wrongdoing.

> **National Contact:**
>
> American Civil Liberties Union
> National Technology and Liberty Program
> 915 15th Street, NW, 6th Floor
> Washington, DC 20005
> P: 202.715.0817

AMERICAN CIVIL LIBERTIES UNION | PROGRAM ON FREEDOM OF RELIGION AND BELIEF

http://www.aclu.org/religion

The Program on Freedom of Religion and Belief of the American Civil Liberties Union works to preserve freedom of speech and ensure that religious liberties are protected by keeping the government out of religious matters.

> **National Contact:**
>
> American Civil Liberties Union
> Program on Freedom of Religion and Belief
> 915 15th Street, NW, 2nd Floor
> Washington, DC 20005
> P: 202.675.2330

AMERICAN CIVIL LIBERTIES UNION | REPRODUCTIVE FREEDOM PROJECT

http://www.aclu.org

The Reproductive Freedom Project of the American Civil Liberties Union advocates for pregnant women while incarcerated to ensure the receipt of needed reproductive health services.

> **National Contact:**
>
> American Civil Liberties Union
> Reproductive Freedom Project
> 125 Broad Street, 18th Floor
> New York, NY 10004
> P: 212.549.2665

AMERICAN CIVIL LIBERTIES UNION | VOTING RIGHTS PROJECT

http://www.votingrights.org

The Voting Rights Project of the American Civil Liberties Union works to protect the gains in political participation won by minorities since passage of the 1965 Voting Rights Act, including felony disenfranchisement.

> **National Contact:**
>
> American Civil Liberties Union
> Voting Rights Project
> 2600 Marquis One Tower
> 245 Peachtree Center Avenue, NE
> Atlanta, GA 30303
> P: 404.523.2721

BATTERED WOMEN'S JUSTICE PROJECT

http://www.bwjp.org

The Battered Women's Justice Project provides assistance to battered women charged with crimes and to their defense but does not provide direct legal assistance.

National Contact:

Battered Women's Justice Project
1801 South Nicollet Avenue, Suite 102
Minneapolis, MN 55403
P: 800.903.0111

CAMPAIGN FOR THE FAIR SENTENCE OF YOUTH

http://www.fairsentencingofyouth.org

Campaign for the Fair Sentencing of Youth is a national coalition and clearinghouse that coordinates, develops and supports efforts to implement just alternatives to the extreme sentencing of America's youth with an emphasis on abolishing life without parole sentences for all youth.

National Contact:

Campaign for the Fair Sentencing of Youth
1090 Vermont Avenue, NW, Suite 400
Washington, DC 20005
P: 202.289.4673

CITIZENS UNITED FOR REHABILITATION OF ERRANTS | FEDERAL PRISON CHAPTER

http://www.fedcure.org

A special interest chapter of the National Citizens United for Rehabilitation of Errants (C.U.R.E.) organization, FedCURE advocates on behalf of the federal inmate population. Realizing that successful advocacy can only occur when society has been enlightened about federal prison realities, FedCURE seeks to create a paradigm where elected officials and American society have a clear understanding of the issues confronted by the federal inmate population.

National Contact:

Citizens United for Rehabilitation of Errants
Federal Prison Chapter
P.O. Box 15667
Plantation, FL 33318
P: 904.861.7659

CITIZENS UNITED FOR REHABILITATION OF ERRANTS | NATIONAL CHAPTER

http://www.curenational.org

Citizens United for Rehabilitation of Errants (C.U.R.E.) is a national organization with state and special interest chapters that advocate for rehabilitative opportunities for prisoners and less reliance on incarceration.

National Contact:

Citizens United for Rehabilitation of Errants
National Capitol Station
P.O. Box 2310
Washington, DC 20013
P: 202.789.2126

CRITICAL RESISTANCE | NATIONAL HEADQUARTERS

http://www.criticalresistance.org

Critical Resistance is a national nonprofit organization that works to end society's reliance on prisons, policing and other forms of social control as solutions to social problems. Critical Resistance challenges the prison industrial complex by organizing and building relationships with incarcerated men and women in an effort to effect change. Upon request, Critical Resistance will provide individuals access to multiple publications and toolkits.

National Contact:

Critical Resistance
1904 Franklin Street, Suite 504
Oakland, CA 94612
P: 510.444.0484

FAMILIES AGAINST MANDATORY MINIMUMS

http://www.famm.org

Families Against Mandatory Minimums publishes the FAMMGram three times a year, which includes information about injustices resulting from mandatory minimum sentencing laws with an emphasis on federal laws. Families Against Mandatory Minimums also serves as a national advocate against the use of mandatory minimum sentences within the judicial system.

National Contact:

Families Against Mandatory Minimums
1100 H Street, NW
Washington, DC 20005
P: 202.822.6700

GAY AND LESBIAN ADVOCATES AND DEFENDERS

http://www.glad.org

Gay and Lesbian Advocates and Defenders is a national nonprofit organization dedicated to impacting litigation on gay, lesbian, bisexual, transgender and HIV related civil rights and discrimination issues within the United States. Gay and Lesbian Advocates and Defenders do not provide direct legal representation and maintains a strong presence in the New England area.

National Contact:

Gay and Lesbian Advocates and Defenders
30 Winter Street, Suite 800
Boston, MA 02108
P: 617.426.1350

INNOCENCE PROJECT

http://www.innocenceproject.org

The Innocence Project is a national nonprofit legal clinic that handles cases where post conviction DNA testing can yield conclusive proof of innocence. Potential clients of the Innocence Project go through an extensive screening process to determine whether of not DNA testing of evidence could support their claim of innocence.

National Contact:

Innocence Project
55 5th Avenue, 11th Floor
New York, NY 10003
P: 212.364.5340

JUST DETENTION INTERNATIONAL

http://www.justdetention.org

Just Detention International seeks to end sexual violence against detainees in the United States and around the world. Just Detention International provides counseling resources for imprisoned and released rape survivors upon request. *Note:* Incarcerated individuals may communicate with Just Detention International using legal mail by addressing their correspondence to: Ms. Cynthia Totten, Esq. at the below address.

National Contact:

Just Detention International
3325 Wilshire Boulevard, Suite 340
Los Angeles, CA 90010
P: 213.384.1400

JUSTICE AND MERCY

http://www.justicemercy.org

Justice and Mercy is a nonprofit, volunteer organization dedicated to decreasing the effects of crime in communities, increasing public safety, and restoring both crime victims and offenders. Justice and Mercy achieves these goals by educating and informing the public at large, advocating cost-effective and practical reforms within the criminal justice system and by supporting and encouraging wise public policy.

National Contact:

Justice and Mercy
P.O. Box 223
Shillington, PA 19607
P: 610.208.0406

LEGAL ACTION CENTER
http://www.lac.org

The Legal Action Center is a national nonprofit organization that provides free legal services to formerly incarcerated people, recovering alcoholics, and substance abusers. The Legal Action Center provides services such as counseling to clients on unfair and discriminatory hiring practices and other legal problems for people with HIV infection and their families, past and current substance abusers, women and children. The Legal Action Center also serves as an advocate for change and reform in all aspects of the criminal justice system.

National Contact:

Legal Action Center
225 Varick Street
New York, NY 10014
P: 212.243.1313

NATIONAL ASSOCIATION FOR THE ADVANCEMENT OF COLORED PEOPLE | NATIONAL HEADQUARTERS
http://www.naacp.org

The National Association for the Advancement of Colored People is an African-American civil rights organization, formed in 1909. Its mission is "to ensure the political, educational, social, and economic equality of rights of all peoples and to eliminate racial hatred and racial discrimination".

National Contact:

National Association for the Advancement of Colored People
4805 Mt. Hope Drive
Baltimore, MD 21215
P: 410.580.5777

NATIONAL ASSOCIATION FOR THE ADVANCEMENT OF COLORED PEOPLE | NATIONAL PRISON PROJECT
http://www.naacp.org

The National Prison Project of the National Association for the Advancement of Colored People works on ex-offender re-enfranchisement and racial disparities within the criminal justice system as well as providing the incarcerated with a vehicle of empowerment through the formation of institution based branches and chapters.

National Contact:

National Association for the Advancement of Colored People
National Prison Project
8 West 26th Street
Baltimore, MD 21218
P: 410.358.8900

NATIONAL GAY & LESBIAN TASKFORCE
http://www.thetaskforce.org

The National Gay & Lesbian Taskforce seeks to combat all sexual orientation-based discrimination through extensive education and lobbying efforts. The National Gay & Lesbian Taskforce maintains and administers an information referral clearinghouse of over 4,000 organizations nationwide that provide assistance and guidance to those in need.

National Contact:

National Gay & Lesbian Taskforce
1824 14th Street, NW
Washington, DC 20009
P: 202.332.6482

NATIONAL LAWYERS GUILD

http://www.nlg.org

The National Lawyers Guild is an association dedicated to the need for basic change in the structure of our political and economic system. The National Lawyers Guild provides self-help law kits free of charge to assist offenders in representing themselves and their own cases or in assisting others. The self-help kits are written in an easy to use language that tells individuals how to file civil complaints, how to deal with grievances, and most other legal matters encountered during the course of being incarcerated.

National Contact:

National Lawyers Guild
132 Nassau Street, Room 922
New York, NY 10038
P: 212.679.5100

THE NATIONAL DEATH ROW ASSISTANCE NETWORK OF C.U.R.E.

http://www.ndran.org

The National Death Row Assistance Network of C.U.R.E. is an organization formed to help death row prisoners across the United States gain access to legal, financial, and community support and to assist individual efforts to act as self-advocates.

National Contact:

The National Death Row Assistance Network of C.U.R.E.
6 Tolman Road
Peaks Island, ME 04108
P: 888.255.6196

U.S. DEPARTMENT OF JUSTICE | CIVIL RIGHTS DIVISION

http://www.usdoj.gov/crt/split

The U.S Department of Justice, Civil Rights Division is charged with enforcing the Civil Rights of Institutionalized Persons Act, which authorizes the U.S. Attorney General to conduct investigations and initiate litigation relating to conditions of confinement in state or locally operated institutions. They are also responsible for the enforcement of Title III of the Civil Rights Act of 1964, the Religious Land Use and Institutionalized Persons Act, the Violent Crime Control and Law Enforcement Act of 1994, and the Safe Streets Act of 1968.

National Contact:

U.S. Department of Justice
Special Litigation Section, Civil Rights Division
950 Pennsylvania Avenue, NW
Washington, DC 20530
P: 202.514.6255

SEX OFFENDER REGISTRY & REFERRAL RESOURCES

THE DRU SJODIN NATIONAL SEX OFFENDER PUBLIC WEBSITE

http://www.nsopw.gov

The Dru Sjodin National Sex Offender Public Website (NSOPW) is an unprecedented public safety resource that provides the public with access to sex offender data nationwide. NSOPW is a partnership between the U.S. Department of Justice and state, territorial, and tribal governments, working together for the safety of adults and children.

First established in 2005 as the National Sex Offender Public Registry (NSOPR), NSOPW was renamed by the Adam Walsh Child Protection and Safety Act of 2006 in honor of 22-year-old college student Dru Sjodin of Grand Forks, North Dakota, a young woman who was kidnapped and murdered by a sex offender who was registered in Minnesota.

NSOPW is the only U.S. government website that links public state, territorial, and tribal sex offender registries from one national search site. Parents, employers, and other concerned residents can utilize the Website's search tool to identify location information on sex offenders residing, working, and attending school not only in their own neighborhoods but in other nearby states and communities. In addition, the Website provides visitors with information about sexual abuse and how to protect themselves and loved ones from potential victimization.

STATE SEX OFFENDER REGISTRIES

State sex offender registries maintain and coordinate the registration of individuals convicted of certain sexual offenses within their jurisdiction. They may also provide registered sex offenders with information regarding their legal obligations under applicable state law and assistance with understanding or addressing any issues related to offense classification. Each state maintains its own sex offender registry according to both state and federal law.

State Contact:

Please refer to Appendix 4-D: State Sexual Offender Registries.

ASSOCIATION FOR THE TREATMENT OF SEXUAL ABUSERS
http://www.atsa.com

The Association for the Treatment of Sexual Abusers is a nonprofit organization that serves as a national advocacy, research and referral center for the prevention and treatment of sexual abuse. The Association for the Treatment of Sexual Abusers maintains an extensive referral database of treatment providers, agencies and organizations willing to assist interested individuals with the treatment of sexually abusive behaviors.

National Contact:

Association for the Treatment of Sexual Abusers
4900 Southwest Griffith Drive, Suite 274
Beaverton, OR 97005
P: 503.643.1023

THE SAFER SOCIETY FOUNDATION
http://www.safersociety.org

The Safer Society Foundation is a national research, advocacy, and referral center on the prevention and treatment of sexual abuse. Individuals may write to receive referral information for treatment providers within their local community.

National Contact:

The Safer Society Foundation
P.O. Box 340
Brandon, VT 05733
P: 802.247.3132

CHAPTER 5 | VETERAN RESOURCES & ASSISTANCE

"Ability is what you're capable of doing. Motivation determines what you do. Attitude determines how well you do it." ~ Lou Holtz

eterans play a vital role in ensuring the strength of the United States by dedicating their lives to the safety and security of its citizens. Veterans and their dependents are entitled to a wide range of services and benefits based on their level and duration of service.

VETERANS SERVICES & BENEFITS

U.S. DEPARTMENT OF VETERANS AFFAIRS

http://www.va.gov

The U.S. Department of Veterans Affairs administers federal benefits for veterans and their families. Some programs include home loans, life insurance, financial assistance, job training, and health resources.

National Contact:

U.S. Department of Veterans Affairs
1722 I Street, NW
Washington, DC 20421
P: 800.827.1000

Additional Resources:

U.S. Department of Veterans Affairs, *Federal Benefits for Veterans, Dependents and Survivors*
http://publications.usa.gov/USAPubs.php?PubID=1050

U.S. DEPARTMENT OF VETERANS AFFAIRS | VETERANS BENEFITS ADMINISTRATION

http://www.vba.va.gov/VBA

The Veterans Benefits Administration within the U.S. Department of Veterans Affairs helps veterans receive benefits, such as educational and financial resources. For information regarding specific benefit eligibility, visit the Veterans Benefits Administration website at http://www.ebenefits.va.gov.

National Contact:

U.S. Department of Veterans Affairs
Veterans Benefits Administration
810 Vermont Avenue, NW
Washington, DC 20420
P: 800.827.1000

U.S. DEPARTMENT OF VETERANS AFFAIRS | VETERANS HEALTH ADMINISTRATION

http://www.va.gov/health

The Veterans Health Administration within the U.S. Department of Veterans Affairs serves the needs of America's veterans by providing primary care, specialized care, and related medical and social support services. For information regarding specific benefit eligibility, visit the Veterans Health Administration eligibility website at http://www.va.gov/healthbenefits.gov.

National Contact:

U.S. Department of Veterans Affairs
Veterans Health Administration
810 Vermont Avenue, NW
Washington, DC 20420
P: 877.222.8387

Additional Resources:

U.S. Department of Veterans Affairs, *Veterans Health Benefits Guide*
http://publications.usa.gov/USAPubs.php?PubID=861

U.S. DEPARTMENT OF LABOR | VETERANS EMPLOYMENT AND TRAINING SERVICE
http://www.dol.gov/vets

The Veterans Employment and Training Service of the U.S. Department of Labor, provides resources to prepare and assist veterans obtain meaningful careers and maximize their employment opportunities.

National Contact:

U.S. Department of Labor
Veteran's Employment and Training Service
200 Constitution Avenue, NW, Room S1325
Washington, DC 20210
P: 866.487.2365

THE AMERICAN LEGION
http://www.legion.org

The American Legion is a nonprofit organization dedicated to assisting veterans in obtaining benefits, including health care and compensation, from the U.S. Department of Veterans Affairs. The American Legion also provides assistance with locating employment and educational opportunities throughout the United States.

National Contact:

The American Legion
1608 K Street, NW
Washington, DC 20006
P: 202.861.2700

INCARCERATED & HOMELESS VETERAN ASSISTANCE

HEALTH CARE FOR RE-ENTRY VETERANS
http://www.va.gov/homeless/index.asp

The Health Care for Re-entry Veterans Program is designed to address the community reentry needs of incarcerated veterans.

The goals of the Health Care for Re-entry Veterans Program are to prevent homelessness, reduce the impact of medical, psychiatric, and substance abuse programs upon community re-adjustment, and decrease the likelihood of re-incarceration for those leaving prison. Health Care for Re-entry Veterans Programs services include:
- Outreach and pre-release assessment services for veterans in prison.
- Referrals and linkages to medical, psychiatric, and social services, including employment services upon release.
- Short term case management assistance upon release.

While the Veterans Health Administration may not provide medical services that are part of care to be provided by correctional institutions, the Veterans Health Administration may provide outreach and pre-release assessment.

Each Veterans Integrated Service Network has a Health Care for Re-entry Veterans Specialist who is the regional point-of-contact for incarcerated veteran services. Each state also has a Health Care for Re-entry Veterans Specialist who is the designated point-of-contact for incarcerated veteran services in the state.

A critical part of the Health Care for Re-entry Veterans Program is providing information to veterans while they are incarcerated so they may plan for reentry themselves. To support this, program administrators across the United States have developed state-specific resource guides which identify steps that veterans can take prior to their release.

National Contact:

U.S. Department of Veterans Affairs
Office of Public & Intergovernmental Affairs
Homeless Veterans Program
810 Vermont Avenue, NW
Washington, DC 20420
P: 202.461.7384

Additional Resources:

U.S. Department of Veterans Affairs, *Health Care for Re-entry Veterans Specialists*
http://www.va.gov/homeless/reentry.asp

U.S. Department of Veterans Affairs, *Health Care for Re-entry Veterans Guides*
http://www.va.gov/homeless/reentry_guides.asp

NATIONAL COALITION FOR HOMELESS VETERANS

http://www.nchv.org

The mission of the National Coalition for Homeless Veterans is to end homelessness among veterans by shaping public policy, promoting collaboration, and building the capacity of service providers.

The National Coalition for Homeless Veterans – a nonprofit organization governed by a 17-member board of directors – is the resource and technical assistance center for a national network of community-based service providers and local, state and federal agencies that provide emergency and supportive housing, food, health services, job training and placement assistance, legal aid and case management support for hundreds of thousands of homeless veterans each year.

The National Coalition for Homeless Veterans also serves as the primary liaison between the nation's care providers, Congress and the executive branch agencies charged with helping them succeed in their work. The National Coalition for Homeless Veteran's advocacy has strengthened and increased funding for virtually every federal homeless veterans assistance program in existence today.

For assistance with overcoming the challenges of homelessness or other related disabilities, contact the National Coalition for Homeless Veterans for direct assistance or referral to a service provider in your local area.

National Contact:

National Coalition for Homeless Veterans
333 ½ Pennsylvania Avenue, SE
Washington, DC 20003
P: 877.424.3838

Additional Resources:

National Coalition for Homeless Veterans, *Planning for Your Release: A Guide for Incarcerated Veterans*
http://www.nchv.org/images/uploads/Planning%20for%20Yr%20Release%20Dec%202012(1).pdf

VOCATIONAL REHABILITATION AND EMPLOYMENT | VETSUCCESS PROGRAM

http://www.vetsuccess.gov

The Vocational Rehabilitation and Employment VetSuccess Program assists veterans with service-connected disabilities to prepare for, find, and keep suitable jobs. Services that may be provided include: Comprehensive rehabilitation evaluation to determine abilities, skills and interests for employment; employment services; assistance finding and keeping a job; and on-the-job training, apprenticeship, and non-paid work experience. For information about possible employment services, contact the National Call Center for Homeless Veterans at 877.424.3838.

National Contact:

U.S. Department of Veterans Affairs
VetSuccess Program
810 Vermont Avenue, NW
Washington, DC 20420
P: 877.424.3838

MILITARY HANDBOOKS

MILITARY HANDBOOKS
http://militaryhandbooks.com

Military Handbooks was launched with one simple goal – to give the Military community the very best information available about pay, benefits, retirement planning, education benefits, career decisions, and much more! And to provide it in a series of straightforward, easy-to-understand handbooks – for free!

MILITARY SERVICE RECORDS

NATIONAL ARCHIVES AND RECORDS ADMINISTRATION
http://www.nara.gov

Service members who have been discharged from military service and certain other interested parties are entitled to request, obtain and review personnel files stored at the National Archives and Records Administration. Records contained at the National Archives and Records Administration are an excellent means of proving military service for government program eligibility and in many instances can be used as identification when proving identity.

National Contact:

National Personnel Records Center
Military Personnel Records
1 Archives Drive
St. Louis, MO 63138
P: 314.801.0800

Additional Resources:

National Personnel Records Center, *Request for Military Personnel Records - Standard Form 180*
http://www.archives.gov/research/order/standard-form-180.pdf

CHAPTER 6 | TRANSPORTATION RESOURCES

"Good fortune is what happens when opportunity meets with planning."
~ Thomas Edison

R eliable transportation is vital to any successful reintegration plan. Whether it's a personal vehicle that you own, public transportation, or carpooling with friends and colleagues, transportation plays an integral role in everyone's life. The resources within this section can assist with identifying and overcoming potential issues associated with obtaining a valid drivers license and provide extensive insight into what forms of public transportation may be available in a specific geographic area.

NATIONAL PROBLEM DRIVER STATUS CHECK

NATIONAL DRIVER REGISTER
http://www.nhtsa.gov

The National Driver Register was created to improve traffic and transportation safety by providing a nation-wide database of problem drivers that assists state driver licensing agencies in identifying these individuals and assists employers in making hiring and certification decisions.

The National Driver Register is a computerized database of information about drivers who have had their licenses revoked or suspended, or who have been convicted of serious traffic violations such as driving while impaired by alcohol or drugs. State motor vehicle agencies provide the National Driver Register with the names of individuals who have lost their privilege to drive or who have been convicted of a serious traffic violation.

When an individual applies for a driver's license, the state motor vehicle agency is obligated by law to check to see if the name is listed within the National Driver Register database. If an individual has been reported to the National Driver Register as a problem driver, their ability to obtain a driver's license may be denied.

What kind of information does the National Driver Register contain?

The National Driver Register is populated with the following "pointer" information:

- First, last and middle name, alias names;
- Date of birth, license number, and social security number;
- Sex, height, eye color;
- The agency that added the pointer, also referred to as the state-of-record.

This information is supplied and maintained by individual states as a result of convictions and license withdrawals pertaining to highway safety violations. No driver history information is maintained within the National Driver Register. The Problem Driver Pointer System "points" a state-of-inquiry to the state-of-record when probable identification is made through the National Driver Register.

How do I find out if I am listed in the National Driver Register?

Individuals are entitled, under provisions of the Privacy Act, to request a file search to see if they have a record on the National Driver Register. As a private citizen, you must send a notarized letter or "privacy act request" to the National Driver Register indicating that you would like a file check. Requests should be sent to the address below and include the individuals full legal name, date of birth, state and driver license number (if known), sex, height, weight, and eye color. In addition, a social security number is preferred but disclosure is optional. There is currently no fee for this service.

National Contact:

National Driver Register
1200 New Jersey Avenue, SE, Suite W55-123
Washington, DC 20590
P: 888.327.4236

Additional Resources:

National Driver Register, *Record Request Form*
http://jetcareers.com/forms/NDR.pdf

PUBLIC TRANSPORTATION OPTIONS

AMERICAN PUBLIC TRANSPORTATION ASSOCIATION

http://www.apta.com

The American Public Transportation Association is a membership organization, representing rapid rail and motor bus systems and manufacturers, suppliers, consulting firms and citizens. Through their extensive website, individuals can access detailed information regarding available public transportation systems and options within a particular service area. Additional information about public transportation options within a specific area can be found by visiting the "United States Local and State Transit Links" section of their website at http://www.apta.com/resources/links/Pages/default.aspx or see Appendix 6-A: State Public Transportation Websites.

National Contact:

American Public Transportation Association
1666 K Street, NW, Suite 1100
Washington, DC 20006
P: 202.496.4800

CHAPTER 7 | FAMILY & RELATIONSHIP RESOURCES

"It's never too late to be what you might have been." ~ George Eliot

Parenting is a life-transforming experience where personal responsibility takes priority over all other factors. Parenthood requires taking responsibility for loved ones and helping them to create an exciting and meaningful future. The resources listed within this section were chosen for their ability to provide individuals with the tools and resources necessary to ensure healthy and productive relationships. Time spent separated from loved ones should be utilized to strengthen and enhance the relationship.

CHILD SUPPORT ASSISTANCE

OFFICE OF CHILD SUPPORT ENFORCEMENT
http://www.acf.hhs.gov/programs/css/resource/reentry

The Child Support Enforcement Program is a federal, state, and local effort to locate parents, their employers and/or their assets; establish paternity if necessary; and establish and enforce child support orders. State and local Child Support Enforcement offices provide daily operation of the programs. The role of the federal government is to provide funding, issue policies, ensure that federal requirements are met, and interact with other federal agencies that help support the Child Support Enforcement Program.

The Office of Child Support Enforcement has created a series of printable resources on how to change a child support order in specific states and jurisdictions. To review these documents, please see Appendix 7-A: Changing a Child Support Order for the appropriate links.

National Contact:

Administration for Children and Families
Office of Child Support Enforcement
370 L'Enfant Promenade, SW
Washington, DC 20447
P: 202.401.9373

State Contact:

Please refer to Appendix 7-B: State Child Support Enforcement Offices.

Additional Resources:

Office of Child Support Enforcement, *Child Support Enforcement Handbook*
https://www.acf.hhs.gov/sites/default/files/programs/css/child_support_handbook_with_toc.pdf

Office of Child Support Enforcement, *Guide to Changing a Child Support Order*
https://www.acf.hhs.gov/sites/default/files/programs/css/changing_a_child_support_order.pdf

Office of Child Support Enforcement, *Frequently Asked Questions*
https://www.acf.hhs.gov/programs/css/faq

DOMESTIC VIOLENCE REDUCTION OPTIONS

HARM REDUCTION COALITION
http://www.harmreduction.org

The Harm Reduction Coalition is a national advocacy and capacity building organization dedicated to promoting the dignity of individuals impacted by drug use and other social stigmas. The Harm Reduction Coalition produces and disseminates a wide variety of brochures and manuals to educate and inform those most in need.

National Contact:

Harm Reduction Coalition
22 West 27th Street, 5th Floor
New York, NY 10001
P: 212.213.6376

NATIONAL COALITION AGAINST DOMESTIC VIOLENCE

http://www.ncadv.org

The National Coalition Against Domestic Violence is a nonprofit organization comprised of individuals concerned for the wellbeing of battered women and their families. This program supports and engages battered women of all racial, social, religious, economic groups, ages and lifestyles. The National Coalition Against Domestic Violence is opposed to the use of violence as a means of control over others and supports equality in relationships and the concept of helping women assert power over their lives.

National Contact:

National Coalition Against Domestic Violence
1 Broadway, Suite B210
Denver, CO 80203
P: 303.839.1852

Additional Resources:

U.S. Department of Health and Human Services, *Domestic Violence: Older Women Can be Victims Too*
https://publications.usa.gov/USAPubs.php?PubID=635

NATIONAL DOMESTIC VIOLENCE HOTLINE

http://www.ndvh.org

The National Domestic Violence Hotline is available in over 140 languages and operates 24 hours a day. For direct and confidential assistance call 800.799.7223 and speak to a trained specialist.

PARENTING RESOURCES & ADVOCACY AGENCIES

There are many organizations and agencies that provide services to incarcerated parents, children of incarcerated parents and their caregivers. By utilizing the resources and assistance provided through the following agencies, individuals are encouraged to build or rebuild the parent-child bond and address any issues that would preclude future involvement in the lives of those involved.

AID TO INCARCERATED MOTHERS

http://www.aim-ma.org

Aid to Incarcerated Mothers is a national nonprofit organization that provides help to incarcerated mothers with keeping their families together, obtaining support services and counseling for children, and locating assistance with transitional needs to ensure a safe and successful community reintegration.

National Contact:

Aid to Incarcerated Mothers
32 Rutland Street, 4th Floor
Boston, MA 02118
P: 617.536.0058

BIG BROTHERS/BIG SISTERS OF AMERICA

http://www.bbbsa.org

Big Brothers/Big Sisters of America provides volunteer and professional services to assist children and youth in achieving their highest potential as they grow. There are over 700 Big Brother/Big Sisters agencies nationwide where more than 75,000 children are matched with adult volunteers annually. The agency also provides counseling, referral, and family support services to more than 100,000 families each year. Additionally, some programs focus on children with special needs including physical or learning disabilities, as well as those who are abused, neglected or have dropped out of school.

National Contact:

Big Brothers/Big Sisters of America
230 North 13th Street
Philadelphia, PA 19107
P: 215.567.7000

BOYS & GIRLS CLUBS OF AMERICA

http://www.bgca.org

Boys & Girls Clubs of America is a private, nonprofit organization providing developmental programs for disadvantaged young people. Boys & Girls Clubs of America coordinates a national network of centers throughout the United States that provide programs and services designed to enhance the lives of disadvantaged young people and their families. Programs include after school activities, educational training and personal growth and development services for those most in need.

National Contact:

Boys & Girls Clubs of America
1275 Peachtree Street, NE
Atlanta, GA 30309
P: 404.487.5700

CENTER FOR CHILDREN OF INCARCERATED PARENTS

http://www.e-ccip.org

The Center for Children of Incarcerated Parent's mission is the prevention of intergenerational crime and incarceration. Their goals are met through the production of high quality documentation and the development of model services for children of criminal offenders and their families. The Center of Incarcerated Parents offers educational projects in three formats, 1) correspondence centers nationwide for incarcerated parents, 2) courses taught by trained staff regionally, and 3) training of instructors to teach approved curricula. Interested individuals are encouraged to write for a catalog of resources and materials available free of charge to incarcerated parents.

National Contact:

Center for Children of Incarcerated Parents
P.O. Box 41-286
Eagle Rock, CA 90041
P: 626.449.2470

CHILD WELFARE LEAGUE OF AMERICA

http://www.cwla.org

The Child Welfare League of America is a national nonprofit organization with over 800 affiliated public and private agencies that together serve more than 2 million children and families every year. The Child Welfare League of America and its agencies offer services for the many areas of child welfare including child protection, chemical dependency prevention and treatment, and housing and homelessness.

National Contact:

Child Welfare League of America
440 First Street, NW, 3rd Floor
Washington, DC 20001
P: 202.638.2952

THE NATIONAL RESOURCE CENTER ON CHILDREN AND FAMILIES OF THE INCARCERATED

http://www.nrccfi.camden.rutgers.edu

The National Resource Center on Children and Families of the Incarcerated became a part of the Rutgers University – Camden campus in October 2013.

NRCCFI began as the Family and Corrections Network (FCN), founded by Jim Mustin in 1983 as the first national organization in the United States focused on Families of the incarcerated. In 2006, the Federal Resource center on Children of Prisoners merged with FCN to create NRCCFI.

The mission of the National Resource Center on Children and Families of the Incarcerated at Rutgers Camden is to raise awareness about the needs and concerns of the children of the incarcerated and their families by:

- Disseminating accurate and relevant information and research
- Guide the development of family strengthening policy and practice
- Train, prepare, and inspire those working in the field, and
- Include the families in defining the issues and designing solutions

If you would like to learn more about the programs and services available in your area to assist children and families of the incarcerated, please see the Directory of Programs Serving Children and Families of the Incarcerated. The Directory of Programs Serving Children and Families of the Incarcerated is an update of the Directory of Programs Serving Families of Adult Offenders, dated October 2001.

National Contact:

The National Resource Center on Children and Families of the Incarcerated
405-7 Cooper Street, Room 103
Camden, NJ 08102
P: 856.225.2718

Additional Resources:

National Resource Center on Children and Families of the Incarcerated, *National Programs*
http://nrccfi.camden.rutgers.edu/resources/directory/national-programs/

National Resource Center on Children and Families of the Incarcerated, *Programs in States AL through MO*
http://nrccfi.camden.rutgers.edu/resources/directory/states-al-mo/

National Resource Center on Children and Families of the Incarcerated, *Programs in States MT through WY*
http://nrccfi.camden.rutgers.edu/resources/directory/states-mt-wy/

National Resource Center on Children and Families of the Incarcerated, *International Programs*
http://nrccfi.camden.rutgers.edu/resources/directory/international-programs/

NATIONAL FATHERHOOD INITIATIVE

http://www.fatherhood.org

The National Fatherhood Initiative's mission is to improve the well being of children by increasing the proportion of children growing up with involved, responsible and committed fathers. As part of the National Fatherhood Initiative's mission to disseminate educational materials to the public and to help men become better fathers, they have developed several informative resources that emphasize the importance of fathers in their children's life.

National Contact:

National Fatherhood Initiative
P.O. Box 126157
Harrisburg, PA 17112
P: 434.589.3036

NATIONAL INCARCERATED PARENTS AND FAMILIES NETWORK

http://www.incarceratedparents.org

The National Incarcerated Parents and Families Network is a national nonprofit, volunteer organization dedicated to decreasing the effects of crime on communities, increasing public safety, and ministering to and restoring both crime victims and offenders. The National Incarcerated Parents and Families Network achieves its goals by educating and informing the public at large, advocating cost-effective and practical reforms within the criminal justice system and by supporting and encouraging wise public policy.

National Contact:

National Incarcerated Parents and Families Network
P.O. Box 6745
Harrisburg, PA 6745
P: Not Provided

NATIONAL RUNAWAY SWITCHBOARD

http://www.1800runaway.org

The National Runaway Switchboard helps keep America's runaway and at-risk youth safe and off the streets. The organization serves as the federally designated national communication system for runaway and homeless youth. The National Runaway Switchboard is staffed by trained specialists who provide assistance and referral information to anyone without regard to age or circumstances. Assistance is available 24 hours a day by calling their hotline at 800.786.2929.

National Contact:

National Runaway Switchboard
3080 North Lincoln Avenue
Chicago, IL 60657
P: 773.880.9860

SESAMEWORKSHOP

http://www.sesameworkshop.org

Sesame Workshop is the nonprofit educational organization that revolutionized children's television programming with the landmark Sesame Street. Beyond television, the Workshop produces content for multiple media platforms on a wide range of issues including literacy, health, and military deployment. Initiatives meet specific needs to help young children and families develop critical skills, acquire healthy habits, and build emotional strength to prepare for lifelong learning.

Additional Resources:

SesameWorkshop, *Little Children BIG Challenges. Incarceration*
http://www.sesamestreet.org/incarceration

YMCA | YOUNG MEN'S CHRISTIAN ASSOCIATION

http://www.ymca.org

The YMCA is one of the nation's largest and most comprehensive nonprofit service organizations. YMCA provides health and fitness; social and personal development; sports and recreation; education and career development; and camps and conferences to children, young adults, the elderly, families, the disabled, refugees and foreign nationals, YMCA residents, and community residents, through a broad range of specific programs.

National Contact:

YMCA | Young Men's Christian Association
801 North Dearborn
Chicago, IL 60610
P: 312.932.1200

YWCA | YOUNG WOMEN'S CHRISTIAN ASSOCIATION

http://www.ywca.org

The YWCA is a nonprofit organization that represents more than 25 million women worldwide. YWCA is committed to empowering women to overcome racism and injustice. YWCA provides shelter to women and children who are homeless or have been victims of domestic violence. YWCA also offers employment training, GED and ESL courses, Welfare-to-Work programs, and career counseling workshops.

National Contact:

YWCA | Young Women's Christian Association
610 Lexington Avenue
New York, NY 10022
P: 212.755.4500

CHAPTER 8 | EDUCATIONAL PROGRAMS & RESOURCES

"To accomplish great things, we must not only act but also dream; not only plan but also believe." ~ Anatole France

The pursuit and completion of an academic course of study such as a high school diploma, General Educational Development diploma or post-secondary degree are important tools in the process of successfully reentering society and today's workforce. The information within this section was compiled for its ability to help individuals achieve their academic goals.

ACADEMIC PROGRAMS

Community colleges, four-year colleges, and universities provide individuals with the opportunity to pursue an academic course of study. Most academic programs don't prepare students for a specific job or profession. Instead, they are designed to provide a wide variety of skills to assist with succeeding in whichever career is chosen after graduation.

COMMUNITY COLLEGES

A community college is a public education institution that offers a wide variety of services which may include Literacy/Adult Basic Education programs, vocational programs, and two-year degree programs. Community colleges do not offer four-year or advanced degrees although some universities use community college campuses as sites to offer their advanced courses.

To locate a community college in your area visit the American Association of Community Colleges' website at http://www.aacc.nche.edu and select the heading entitled "Find Your Community College."

FOUR-YEAR COLLEGES & UNIVERSITIES

Four-year colleges and universities include both public and private institutions where individuals can earn a Bachelor of Science or a Bachelor of Arts degree upon completion. To earn a Bachelor's degree, individuals can begin their coursework at a community college and transfer to a four-year college or university, or apply directly once they earn a General Educational Development of high school diploma.

To locate a four-year college or university in your area, go to http://www.collegeboard.com and select the heading entitled "College Boards Free College Search Tool."

ADVANCED DEGREES

Some professions require an advanced degree (Master's degree or Ph.D.). Universities provide graduate programs for individuals interested in furthering their education beyond a Bachelor's degree or in pursuing a career in a field that requires an advanced degree. The Princeton Review provides information on graduate programs across the United States through their website at, http://www.princetonreview.com.

Additional Resources:

U.S. Department of Education, *Back to School: A Guide to Continuing Your Education After Prison*
http://www.edpubs.gov/document/ed005088p.pdf?ck=287

U.S. Department of Education, *Taking Charge of Your Future: Get the Education and Training You Need*
http://www.edpubs.gov/document/ed005354p.pdf?ck=450

HIGH SCHOOL EQUIVALENCY PROGRAM

GENERAL EDUCATIONAL DEVELOPMENT
http://www.gedtestingservice.com

The General Educational Development (GED) testing program was developed to give U.S. and Canadian citizens who have not graduated from high school the opportunity to demonstrate the level of achievement normally acquired through the completion of a traditional U.S./Canadian high school course of study. The five GED comprehensive examinations cover writing, social studies, science, interpreting literature and arts, and math.

Emphasis is on intellectual ability such as evaluating, analyzing, drawing conclusions and the ability to understand and apply information and concepts. The tests are administered in all 50 states, U.S. territories, and the 10 Canadian provinces.

For additional information about General Educational Development, call 800.626.9433 to find the nearest official GED Testing Center or locate your jurisdiction's GED testing administrator, please visit http://www.gedtestingservice.com/testers/ged-testing-administrator.

National Contact:

American Council on Education
General Educational Development Testing Service
One DuPont Circle, NW, Suite 250
Washington, DC 20036
P: 800.626.9433

State Contact:

Please refer to Appendix 8-A: State GED Administrative Offices.

REHABILITATIVE EDUCATION & TRAINING

VOCATIONAL REHABILITATION
http://www.jan.wva.edu/sbses/vocrehab.htm

Vocational Rehabilitation, a state-supported division of services, assists individuals with disabilities who are pursuing meaningful careers. Vocational Rehabilitation assists those individuals to secure gainful employment commensurate with their abilities and capabilities through local job searches and awareness of self-employment and telecommuting opportunities. In addition, to Vocational Rehabilitation, some states have separate agencies serving individuals who are blind and visually impaired.

National Contact:

U.S. Department of Education
Rehabilitation Services Administration
400 Maryland Avenue, SW
Washington, DC 20202
P: 202.245.7468

State Contact:

Please refer to Appendix 8-B: State Vocational Rehabilitation Agencies.

KNOWLEDGE-BASED COLLEGE CREDIT OPTIONS

COLLEGE-LEVEL EXAMINATION PROGRAM
http://www.collegeboard.com/student/testing/clep/about.htm

The College-Level Examination Program serves high school students, enrolled college students, international students, and adults returning to college. It is designed to allow students to get college credit for knowledge learned outside the classroom. The heart of CLEP is a series of computer-based examinations rewarding students for what they know, whether they've learned it in school, on the job, through reading, by observation, or in the course of their life experiences.

There are five general examinations and 30 subject-specific examinations. The general examinations are in English composition, humanities, college mathematics, natural sciences, and social sciences. The tests are at the level of courses taken in the first 2 years of college. Subject examinations include composition and literature, foreign languages, history and social science, mathematics and science, and business. The general and subject examinations are multiple choice questions limited to 90 minutes. The subject examinations, requiring a higher degree of specialized knowledge and training, demonstrate the specific knowledge and skills a student may have gained through job experience, outside course work, or independent reading.

The College-Level Examination Program is the most widely accepted credit-by-examination program in the United States. Nearly two-thirds of accredited institutions of higher education give credit for satisfactory scores on the examinations. Colleges have found that students who complete such exams are motivated, intellectually curious, and independent learners – qualities colleges look for and value in their students.

National Contact:

College Level Examination Board
45 Columbus Avenue
New York, NY 10023
P: 212.713.8000

DEFENSE ACTIVITY FOR NON-TRADITIONAL EDUCATION SUPPORT (DANTES) SUBJECT STANDARDIZED TESTS
http://www.GetCollegeCredit.com

There are 38 DANTES Subject Standardized Tests (DSSTs). Fact Sheets/Study Guides containing descriptions of the content of each exam, sample questions, and lists of approved texts are available at no charge from the below address.

National Contact:

Prometric: Attn DSST Program
1260 Energy Lane
St. Paul, MN 55108
P: 877.471.9860

FEDERAL & STATE STUDENT FINANCIAL ASSISTANCE

FEDERAL STUDENT FINANCIAL AID
http://www.studentaid.ed.gov

Federal student aid comes from the federal government – specifically, the U.S. Department of Education. Federal student aid is financial assistance for eligible students to pay for education expenses at an eligible postsecondary school (e.g. college, vocational school, and graduate school).

Federal student aid covers such expenses as tuition and fees, room and board, books and supplies, and transportation. Aid can also be used to help pay for a computer and for dependent care.

There are three main categories of federal student aid:

Grants – Unlike loans, grants are not repaid unless, for example, an individual is awarded funds incorrectly or they withdraw from school prior to the planned end of term or if they do not meet the terms of a stated agreement. Almost all federal grants are awarded to students with financial need.

Work Study – The federal Work-Study Program provides jobs for students demonstrating financial need and emphasizes employment in civic education and work related to a specific course of study, whenever possible.

Loans – Student loans, unlike grants and work-study, are borrowed money that must be repaid, with interest, just like an auto loan or home mortgage. Individuals cannot have these loans canceled because they didn't like the education they received, didn't get a job in their specified field of study, or they're having financial difficulty.

What are the eligibility requirements for federal student aid?

To receive aid from the federal student aid program, you must meet certain criteria. The most basic eligibility requirements are that individuals must:

- Be a U.S. citizen or eligible non-citizen;
- Have earned a GED or high school diploma or passed an approved ability-to-benefit test;
- Have registered with Selective Service;
- Have no defaulted student loans;
- Be enrolled in a degree or certificate program that participates in the federal student aid program;
- Be making satisfactory academic progress.

Am I eligible for federal student aid while incarcerated? (1)

Individuals who are currently incarcerated have limited eligibility for federal student aid. An individual is considered to be incarcerated if he or she is serving a criminal sentence in a penitentiary, prison, jail, reformatory, work farm, or similar correctional institution, whether it is operated by the government or by a contractor. An individual is not considered to be incarcerated if he or she is in a halfway house or on home detention or is sentenced to serve only on weekends.

Those individuals incarcerated in institutions other then federal or state institutions are eligible for Federal Pell Grants, Federal Supplemental Educational Opportunity Grants, and Federal Work-Study but not for federal student loans.

It is important to note that, upon an individual's release, most eligibility limitations will be removed. In addition, an individual may be eligible to apply for aid in anticipation of being released so that their aid is processed in time for them to start school.

I was convicted of drug possession and/or sale – am I eligible for federal student aid?

A federal or state drug conviction can disqualify an individual for federal student aid funds. Convictions only count if they were for an offense that occurred during a period of enrollment for which the individual was receiving Title IV funds. Also, a conviction that was reversed, or removed from the individuals record does not count, nor does one received while a juvenile, unless the individual was tried as an adult.

The chart below illustrates the period of ineligibility for federal student aid funds, depending on whether the conviction was for sale or possession and whether the student had previous offenses. (A conviction for sale of drugs includes convictions for conspiring to sell drugs.)

Table 3: Period of Ineligibility for Federal Student Aid		
	Possession Of Illegal Drugs	Sale Of Illegal Drugs
1st Offense	1 Year From Date Of Conviction	2 Years From Date Of Conviction
2nd Offense	2 Years From Date Of Conviction	Indefinite Period
3+ Offenses	Indefinite Period	

If an individual was convicted of both possession and selling illegal drugs, and the periods of ineligibility are different, the individual will be ineligible for the longer period. (2)

Individuals regain eligibility the day after the period of ineligibility ends or when they successfully complete a qualified drug rehabilitation program or, effective beginning with the 2010-2011 award year, passes two unannounced drug tests given by such a program. Further drug convictions will make an individual ineligible again.

Individuals denied eligibility for an indefinite period can regain it after successfully completing a rehabilitation program, passing two unannounced drug tests from such a program, or if a conviction is reversed, set aside, or removed from the individual's record so that fewer than two convictions for sale or three convictions for possession remain on the record. In such cases, the nature and dates of the remaining convictions will determine when the individual regains eligibility.

For additional information regarding eligibility for federal student aid or to request printed information such as brochures, fact sheets or booklets about federal student aid and related topics, contact the Federal Student Aid Information Center for assistance.

---

1. Incarcerated Students: HEA Sec. 401(b)(8) and 484(b)(5) 34 CFR 600.2 and 668.32(c)(2)
2. Drug Convictions: HEA Sec. 848(r) 34 CFR 668.40

National Contact:

Federal Student Aid Information Center
P.O. Box 84
Washington, DC 20044
P: 800.433.3243

Additional Resources:

U.S. Department of Education, *Funding Your Education: The Guide to Federal Student Aid*
http://publications.usa.gov/USAPubs.php?PubID=2274

U.S. Department of Education, *Federal Student Aid Grant Programs Fact Sheet*
http://publications.usa.gov/USAPubs.php?PubID=224

U.S. Department of Education, *Federal Student Aid Loan Programs Fact Sheet*
http://publications.usa.gov/USAPubs.php?PubID=225

U.S. Department of Education, *Federal Student Aid for Adult Students*
http://publications.usa.gov/USAPubs.php?PubID=930

U.S. Department of Education, *Federal Student Aid for Incarcerated Individuals*
http://www.studentaid.ed.gov/students/attachments/siteresources/IncarcFAQ.pdf

STATE FINANCIAL ASSISTANCE

Many state and local governments have student financial assistance options (scholarships, loans, and grants) that may be applied to reduce the overall financial burden to students within a specific community or geographic area. In addition, some institutions of higher education have direct financial assistance options designed to assist students and families. A list of state higher education agencies is located in Appendix 8-C: State Higher Education Agencies.

SELECTIVE SERVICE SYSTEM

http://www.sss.gov

Selective Service is the process by which the U.S. government administers involuntary military enrollment. Registration with the Selective Service is required for all males between the ages of 10 and 25.

Registration with the Selective Service is required to receive certain federal or state benefits, including federal student aid.

To register with Selective Service or verify prior registration, contact Selective Service directly to request a *"Registration Form"* or *"Status Information Letter"*.

National Contact:

Selective Service System, Registration Information Office
P.O. Box 94638
Palatino, IL 60094
P: 847.688.6888

SCHOLARSHIP, INTERNSHIP & FELLOWSHIP OPPORTUNITIES

There are many financial aid programs offered by charitable foundations and major corporations. Most of them provide scholarships, internships and fellowships to individuals based on their ethnic and social backgrounds among other criteria. Most organizations focus on applicants who show academic promise and the greatest level of need. The following list is a brief sampling of the many organizations available. For more detailed information visit your local public library or http://www.collegeboard.org.

AMERICAN INDIAN COLLEGE FUND

http://www.collegefund.org

The American Indian College Fund awards approximately 5,000 scholarships annually to students at tribal colleges and universities. The American Indian College Fund requires that each applicant demonstrate financial need and high academic achievement. In addition, applicants must be Alaskan Native or American Indian.

National Contact:

American Indian College Fund
8333 Greenwood Boulevard
Denver, CO 80221
P: 303.426.8900

ASIAN & PACIFIC ISLANDER AMERICAN SCHOLARSHIP FUND

http://www.apiasf.org

The Asian and Pacific Islander American Scholarship Fund has awarded more than $60 million to deserving students since 2003.

National Contact:

Asian and Pacific Islander American Scholarship Fund
2025 M Street, NW, Suite 610
Washington, DC 20036
P: 202.986.6892

GATES MILLENNIUM SCHOLARS PROGRAM

http://www.gmsp.org

Gates Millennium Scholars provides scholarships to African-American, American Indian/Alaskan-Native, Asia Pacific Islander-American, and Hispanic-American U.S. citizens and permanent residents enrolled full-time in a degree-granting college. Applicants must demonstrate financial need, high academic achievement, leadership and service orientation.

National Contact:

Gates Millennium Scholars
P.O. Box 10500
Fairfax, VA 22031
P: 877.690.4677

HISPANIC SCHOLARSHIP FUND

http://www.hsf.net

The Hispanic Scholarship Fund provides scholarships to Mexican American, Hispanic American, and Puerto Rican U.S. citizens and permanent residents enrolled full-time in a degree-granting college. In addition, applicants must demonstrate financial need and high academic achievement.

National Contact:

Hispanic Scholarship Fund
1411 West 190th Street, Suite 325
Gardena, CA 90248
P: 877.473.4636

UNITED NEGRO COLLEGE FUND

http://www.uncf.org

The United Negro College Fund awards 10,000 African American students from low and moderate income families each year with scholarships and internship programs so they can afford college tuition, books, and room and board. Applicants must demonstrate high academic achievement.

National Contact:

United Negro College Fund
1805 7th Street, NW
Washington, DC 20001
P: 800.331.2244

SPECIAL EDUCATION RESOURCES

U.S. DEPARTMENT OF EDUCATION | OFFICE OF SPECIAL EDUCATION & REHABILITATIVE SERVICES
http://www.ed.gov/about/offices/list/osers/osep/index

The Office of Special Education and Rehabilitative Services of the U.S. Department of Education provides support to parents and individuals, school districts and states in three main areas: 1) special education, 2) vocational rehabilitation, and 3) research. For assistance with locating and obtaining a referral to special education or vocational rehabilitation service providers within a specific geographic area, contact the Office of Special Education and Rehabilitative Services for assistance or visit your local American Job Center.

National Contact:

U.S. Department of Education
Office of Special Education & Rehabilitative Services
400 Maryland Avenue, SW
Washington, DC 20202
P: 202.245.7468

NATIONAL ASSOCIATION OF PRIVATE SPECIAL EDUCATION CENTERS
http://www.napsec.org

The National Association of Private Special Education Centers is a nonprofit association whose mission is to represent private special education programs and affiliated state associations and to ensure access for individuals to appropriate private special education programs and services.

National Contact:

National Association of Private Special Education Centers
1522 K Street, NW, Suite 1032
Washington, DC 20005
P: 202.434.8225

REGIONAL, STATE & SPECIALIZED ACCREDITATION AGENCIES

The accreditation status of a college, university or other educational program provides an indication of its general quality and reputation. The following accrediting bodies are recognized by the U.S. Department of Education or the Council for Higher Education Accreditation. Individuals who are interested in participating in an educational course of study should first ascertain the accreditation status of the institution applying to by contacting one of the following agencies.

MIDDLE STATES COMMISSION ON HIGHER EDUCATION | REGIONAL
http://www.msche.org

The Middle States Commission of Higher Education of the Middle States Association of Colleges and Schools is the regional accrediting body for Delaware, the District of Columbia, Maryland, New Jersey, New York, Pennsylvania, Puerto Rico, and the U.S. Virgin Islands.

National Contact:

Middle States Association of Colleges and Schools
Middle States Commission on Higher Education
3624 Market Street, 2nd Floor Annex
Philadelphia, PA 19104
P: 267.284.5000

NEW YORK STATE BOARD OF REGENTS | STATE
http://www.regents.nysed.gov

The New York State Board of Regents of the New York State Education Department is the general accrediting body for the State of New York. This agency oversees registration of degree-granting programs or curricula offered by institutions of higher education and of credit-bearing certificate and diploma programs offered by degree-granting institutions of higher education.

National Contact:

New York State Board of Regents
New York State Education Department
89 Washington Avenue, Room 110EB
Albany, NY 12234
P: 518.474.5889

COMMISSION ON INSTITUTIONS OF HIGHER EDUCATION | REGIONAL

http://www.neasc.org

The Commission on Institutions of Higher Education of the New England Association of Schools and Colleges is the regional accrediting body for Connecticut, Maine, Massachusetts, New Hampshire, Rhode Island, and Vermont.

National Contact:

New England Association of Schools and Colleges
Commission on Institutions of Higher Education
209 Burlington Road
Bedford, MA 01730
P: 781.271.0022

COMMISSION ON TECHNICAL AND CAREER INSTITUTIONS | REGIONAL

http://www.ctci.neasc.org

The Commission on Technical and Career Institutions of the New England Association of Schools and Colleges is the regional accrediting body for Connecticut, Maine, Massachusetts, New Hampshire, Rhode Island, and Vermont. This agency covers colleges and institutions that offer programs leading to an associate degree but do not offer programs leading to a degree in liberal arts or general studies.

National Contact:

New England Association of Schools and Colleges
Commission on Technical and Career Institutions
209 Burlington Road, Suite 201
Bedford, MA 01730
P: 781.541.5416

THE HIGHER LEARNING COMMISSION | REGIONAL

http://www.ncahigherlearningcommission.org

The Higher Learning Commission of the North Central Association of Colleges and Schools is the regional accrediting body for Arizona, Arkansas, Colorado, Illinois, Indiana, Iowa, Kansas, Michigan, Minnesota, Missouri, Nebraska, New Mexico, North Dakota, Ohio, Oklahoma, South Dakota, West Virginia, Wisconsin, and Wyoming.

National Contact:

North Central Association of Colleges and Schools
The Higher Learning Commission
30 North LaSalle Street, Suite 2400
Chicago, IL 60602
P: 312.263.0456

NORTHWEST COMMISSION ON COLLEGES AND UNIVERSITIES | REGIONAL

http://www.nwccu.org

The Northwest Commission on Colleges and Universities is the regional accrediting body for Alaska, Idaho, Montana, Nevada, Oregon, Utah, and Washington.

National Contact:

Northwest Commission on Colleges and Universities
8060 165th Avenue, NE, Suite 100
Redmond, WA 98052
P: 425.558.4224

SOUTHERN ASSOCIATION OF COLLEGES AND SCHOOLS | REGIONAL

http://www.sacscoc.org

The Commission on Colleges of the Southern Association of Colleges and Schools is the regional accrediting body for Alabama, Florida, Georgia, Kentucky, Louisiana, Mississippi, North Carolina, South Carolina, Tennessee, Texas, and Virginia.

National Contact:

Southern Association of Colleges and Schools
Commission on Colleges
1866 Southern Lane
Decatur, GA 30033
P: 404.679.4500

ACCREDITING COMMISSION FOR COMMUNITY AND JUNIOR COLLEGES | REGIONAL

http://www.accjc.org

The Accrediting Commission for Community and Junior Colleges of the Western Association of Schools and Colleges is the regional accrediting body for California, Hawaii, the U.S. Territories of Guam and American Samoa, the Commonwealth of the Northern Mariana Islands, the Republic of Palau, the Federated States of Micronesia, and the Republic of the Marshall Islands.

National Contact:

Western Association of Schools and Colleges
Accrediting Commission for Community and Junior Colleges
10 Commercial Boulevard, Suite 204
Novato, CA 94949
P: 415.506.0234

ACCREDITING COMMISSION FOR SENIOR COLLEGES AND UNIVERSITIES | REGIONAL

http://www.wascweb.org

The Accrediting Commission for Senior Colleges and Universities of the Western Association of Schools and Colleges is the regional accrediting body for California, Hawaii, the U.S. Territories of Guam and American Samoa, the Commonwealth of the Northern Mariana Islands, the Republic of Palau, the Federated States of Micronesia, and the Republic of the Marshall Islands.

National Contact:

Western Association of Schools and Colleges
Accrediting Commission for Senior Colleges and Universities
985 Atlantic Avenue, Suite 100
Alameda, CA 94501
P: 510.748.9001

DISTANCE EDUCATION AND TRAINING COUNCIL | SPECIALIZED

http://www.detc.org

The Distance Education and Training Council is a voluntary, non-governmental, educational organization that accredits distance education institutions.

National Contact:

Distance Education and Training Council
1601 18th Street, NW, Suite 2
Washington, DC 20009
P: 202.234.5100

OPEN EDUCATIONAL RESOURCES (OER)

Open educational resources (OER) are educational materials available for study at no cost on the web. Some are available for anyone to access any time; others, such as Massive Open Online Courses (MOOCs), require sign-up and are only available during certain times. Please note that some MOOC providers offer certificates of completion or other products or services for a fee; however, the MOOCs themselves are by definition free of charge and include access to the main body of learning materials.

CHOOSING OPEN EDUCATIONAL RESOURCES

Most sites for university-based OER can be searched through www.ocwconsortium.org and/or www.oercommons.org.

Sites that specialize in web courses designed by college professors under contract with the website sponsor, rather than in web versions of existing college courses, include:

- http://www.saylor.org
- http://www.education-portal.com
- http://www.opencourselibrary.com

CHAPTER 9 | GENERAL ASSISTANCE PROGRAMS

"I have not failed. I've just found 10,000 ways that won't work." ~ *Thomas Edison*

F ederal and state assistance programs are generally designed to assist people who need a job, housing, public assistance, and other services. Each program has different standards for participation with low income being the most common requirement. There are no government assistance programs exclusively for ex-offenders.

GOVERNMENT ASSISTANCE RESOURCES

BENEFITS.GOV

http://www.benefits.gov

Benefits.gov was launched in an effort to provide citizens with easy, online access to government benefit and assistance programs.

The site's core function is the eligibility prescreening questionnaire or "Benefit Finder." Answers to the questionnaire are used to evaluate a visitor's situation and compare it with the eligibility criteria for more then 1,000 federally-funded benefit and assistance programs representing 17 partner agencies. Each program description provides citizens with the next steps to apply for any benefit program of interest.

Benefits.gov is unable to respond to specific scenarios or provide personalized advice. For additional government information, individuals are encouraged to call USA.gov's National Contact Center at 800.333.4636, Monday through Friday, 8:00 am to 8:00 pm (EST), to speak with an information specialist, or visit them online at http://www.usa.gov.

CATALOG OF FEDERAL DOMESTIC ASSISTANCE

http://www.cfda.gov

The Catalog of Federal Domestic Assistance is a government-wide compendium of federal programs, projects, services, and activities that provide assistance or benefits to the American public. It contains financial and non-financial programs administered by departments and agencies of the federal government.

As a basic reference source of federal programs, the primary purpose of the Catalog of Federal Domestic Assistance is to assist users in identifying programs that meet specific objectives of the potential applicant, and to obtain general information on federal assistance programs.

The U.S. Government Printing Office prints and sells copies of the Catalog of Federal Domestic Assistance to interested parties. For purchasing information, contact them at 866.512.1800. You may also use the U.S. Government Printing Office's online bookstore at http://www.bookstore.gpo.gov.

National Contact:

U.S. Government Printing Office
P.O. Box 979050
St. Louis, MO 63197
P: 202.512.1800

Additional Resources:

Government Services Administration, *Catalog of Federal Domestic Assistance*
http://www.cfda.gov/downloads/CFDA_2016.pdf

GOVERNMENT-FUNDED FINANCIAL ASSISTANCE

TEMPORARY ASSISTANCE FOR NEEDY FAMILIES

Administered and coordinated at the federal level by the U.S. Department of Health and Human Services, Temporary Assistance for Needy Families is a federal assistance program that provides financial assistance and services to low-income individuals and families with children under the age of 18 who meet specific program eligibility requirements.

Eligible individuals and families are provided with supportive services including assistance with work and training related expenses, transportation, and childcare when needed. Financial assistance is provided on a rotating basis for families with children until they are able to support themselves. Recipients of aid are required to pursue employment, training and/or education that will lead to employment, participate in volunteer community service, or provide child care services to other program participants.

The Diversion Program within Temporary Assistance for Needy Families is designed to eliminate barriers to employment such as providing financial and direct assistance with car repairs, work clothing, or tools in an effort to ensure employability.

Individuals who have been convicted of a drug offense after January 1, 1989 and those currently on parole or probation are not eligible for assistance under the Temporary Assistance for Needy Families program. In addition, a conviction of Welfare fraud automatically results in a life-time denial of assistance.

Individuals who believe they may be eligible for services through Temporary Assistance for Needy Families are encouraged to contact their local American Job Center for additional information and eligibility requirements.

National Contact:

U.S. Department of Health and Human Services
200 Independence Avenue, SW
Washington, DC 20201
P: 877.696.6775

EMERGENCY RELIEF

There have been many changes in the welfare system and the availability of welfare from the federal government is severely limited. Emergency Relief programs are cash and in-kind assistance programs financed and administered entirely by the state, county, or locality in which they operate. Emergency Relief programs are likely to serve disabled, elderly, and otherwise unemployable individuals and children or families with children. There are no national laws that require state governments to provide Emergency Relief or to establish uniform rules across the state if Emergency Relief is provided. Individuals who believe they may be eligible for Emergency Relief are encouraged to contact their local American Job Center for additional information and eligibility requirements.

HUMAN SERVICE INFORMATION & REFERRAL

2-1-1 | UNITED WAY
http://www.211us.org

2-1-1 is the national abbreviated dialing code for free access to health and human service information and referral. 2-1-1 is an easy-to-remember and universally recognizable number that makes a critical connection between individuals and families seeking services or volunteer opportunities and the appropriate community-based organizations and government agencies. 2-1-1 makes it possible for people to navigate the complex and ever-growing maze of human service agencies and programs.

Every hour of every day, hundreds of people need human services – they are looking for training, employment, food pantries, help for an aging parent, addiction prevention programs for their teenage children, affordable housing options, support groups and ways of becoming part of their community. 2-1-1 allows people to give help and to get help.

As of February 2016, 2-1-1 serves over 283 million Americans (90.6% of the entire population) covering all 50 states including Washington, DC and Puerto Rico (39 states plus Washington, DC and Puerto Rico enjoy 100% coverage). (1) As of August 2012, more than 19 million Canadians – more than 56% of the population – have access to 2-1-1 services.

For additional information about the services offered by 2-1-1, please dial 211 from any telephone or visit them online at http://www.211us.org.

---

1. Coverage is defined as populations with landline telephone access to 2-1-1 dialing codes.

Additional Resources:

United Way | 2-1-1, *Nationwide Program Coverage & Status Website*
http://www.211us.org/status.htm

United Way | 2-1-1, *Reentry Webpage*
http://www.211.org/services/reentry

UNITED WAY OF AMERICA
http://www.unitedway.org

Through a network of volunteers and local charities, United Way organizations throughout America help meet the health and human care needs of millions of people. The United Way system includes over 1,900 community-based organizations. United Way volunteers raise funds that are used for human services ranging from disaster relief, emergency food and shelter, crisis intervention, and physical rehabilitation and youth development.

National Contact:

United Way of America
701 North Fairfax Street
Alexandria, VA 22314
P: 703.836.7112

SOCIAL SECURITY BENEFITS

U.S. SOCIAL SECURITY ADMINISTRATION
http://www.socialsecurity.gov

The U.S. Social Security Administration oversees a number of benefit programs, including retirement benefits, disability benefits, dependents benefits, and survivors benefits.

SOCIAL SECURITY DISABILITY BENEFITS
Social Security Disability benefits can be paid only to people who have recently worked and paid Social Security taxes, and who are unable to work because of a serious medical condition that is expected to last for at least a year or result in death. The fact that an individual is a recent parolee or is unemployed does not automatically qualify as a disability.

SUPPLEMENTAL SECURITY INCOME BENEFITS
Supplemental Security Income benefits can be paid to people who are 65 or older or blind or disabled and who have low income and limited resources. No Supplemental Security Income benefits are payable for any months that an individual resides in prison.

SOCIAL SECURITY RETIREMENT BENEFITS
Social Security Retirement benefits can be paid only to people who are 62 or older. Generally, an individual must have worked and paid taxes into Social Security for 10 years to be eligible.

TICKET TO WORK PROGRAM
The Ticket to Work Program is administered under the Ticket to Work and Work Incentive Improvement Act of 1999 and provides an opportunity for people who receive Social Security Disability benefits to work. It provides training and employment opportunities for disabled individuals while allowing them to continue to receive social security benefits. To learn more about programs and eligibility requirements, go to http://www.tickettowork.com.

Social Security and Supplemental Security Income benefits are not payable for the months that an individual is confined to a jail, prison, or certain other public institution for the commission of a crime. In addition, individuals are not automatically eligible for Social Security Disability or Social Security Income benefits when they are released.

National Contact:

U.S. Social Security Administration
Office of Public Inquiries
6401 Security Boulevard
Washington, DC 21235
P: 800.772.1213

Additional Resources:

U.S. Social Security Administration, *A "Snapshot"*
http://ssa.gov/pubs/EN-05_10006.pdf

U.S. Social Security Administration, *Understanding the Benefits*
http://ssa.gov/pubs/EN-05-10024.pdf

U.S. Social Security Administration, *How You Earn Credits*
http://ssa.gov/pubs/EN-05-10072.pdf

U.S. Social Security Administration, *How Work Affects Your Benefits*
http://ssa.gov/pubs/EN-05-10069.pdf

U.S. Social Security Administration, *Your Ticket to Work: What You Need to Know to Keep it Working for You*
http://ssa.gov/pubs/EN-05-10062.pdf

U.S. Social Security Administration, *What Prisoners Need To Know*
http://ssa.gov/pubs/EN-05-10133.pdf

U.S. Social Security Administration, *Entering the Community after Incarceration – How We Can Help*
http://ssa.gov/pubs/EN-05-10504.pdf

U.S. Social Security Administration, *How to Correct Your Social Security Earnings Statement*
http://ssa.gov/pubs/EN-05-10081.pdf

CHAPTER 10 | HOUSING ASSISTANCE RESOURCES

"Far and away the best prize that life offers is the chance to work hard
at work worth doing." ~ Theodore Roosevelt

Housing information may be obtained from the local Department of Housing for the community returning to upon release. For those individuals who do not have access to local information, contact any of the agencies listed below for assistance identifying appropriate housing options.

IMMEDIATE & SHORT TERM HOUSING

COMMUNITY ACTION PARTNERSHIP

http://www.communityactionpartnership.org

Community Action Agencies provide services to reduce the effects of poverty in many communities. Many provide energy assistance, winterization, housing, and emergency shelter services.

> **National Contact:**
>
> Community Action Partnership
> 1140 Connecticut Avenue, NW, Suite 1210
> Washington, DC 20036
> P: 202.265.7546

GOODWILL INDUSTRIES

http://www.goodwill.org

Goodwill Industries is a nonprofit organization with hundreds of locations nationwide that provide job training, housing assistance and shelter services to people who are trying to overcome physical, emotional and developmental disabilities, poverty and other challenges.

> **National Contact:**
>
> Goodwill Industries – National Headquarters
> 15810 Indianola Drive
> Rockville, MD 20855
> P: 800.644.3945

HOMELESS SHELTER DIRECTORY

http://www.homelessshelterdirectory.org

Homeless shelters are a form of temporary housing for homeless individuals and families. Homeless shelters sometimes provide other services, such as soup kitchens, and job skills training. The Homeless Shelter Directory is a web-based application with access to referral information nationwide.

SOBER HOUSING

http://www.soberhouses.com

Soberhouses.com is a quick and reliable source of information for referrals into treatment programs, detoxification centers, halfway houses, sober houses. The mission of Soberhouses.com is to provide a user friendly, free access site for professionals and individuals to locate much needed resources.

> **National Contact:**
>
> Soberhouses.com, Inc.
> 297 Northeast 6th Avenue
> Delray Beach, FL 33483
> P: 561.265.1564

THE SALVATION ARMY
http://www.salvationarmyusa.org

The Salvation Army through its many national locations provides shelter services and housing vouchers to individuals in need of assistance. They may also assist with meals and other needs. Adult Rehabilitation Centers, a service of the Salvation Army provide substance abuse treatment services within a structured therapeutic environment.

National Contact:

The Salvation Army - National Headquarters
615 Slaters Lane, P.O. Box 269
Alexandria, VA 22313
P: 800.728.7825

VOLUNTEERS OF AMERICA
http://www.volunteersofamerica.org

Volunteers of America is a nonprofit organization dedicated to helping those in need rebuild their lives and reach their full potential through providing emergency services and resources to ex-offenders and their families. Services include employment training, technical assistance, bus tokens, clothing, tools, food, and much more.

National Contact:

Volunteers of America
1660 Duke Street
Alexandria, VA 22314
P: 800.899.0089

PERMANENT & LONG TERM HOUSING

U.S. DEPARTMENT OF HOUSING AND URBAN DEVELOPMENT
http://www.hud.gov

The U.S. Department of Housing and Urban Development's public housing program was established to provide decent and safe rental housing for eligible low-income families, the elderly, and persons with disabilities. Public housing comes in all sizes and shapes, from scattered single family houses to high-rise apartments for elderly families. There are currently approximately 2.3 million households living in public housing units, managed by some 3,300 Housing Authorities. The U.S. Department of Housing and Urban Development administers federal aid to local housing agencies who manage the housing for low-income residents at rents they can afford. The U.S. Department of Housing and Urban Development furnishes technical and professional assistance in planning, developing and managing these developments but does not provide direct housing services.

Public housing is limited to low-income families and individuals. A housing agency determines program eligibility based on, 1) annual gross income; 2) whether you qualify as elderly, a person with a disability, or as a family; and 3) U.S. citizenship or immigration status. A criminal conviction does not automatically limit program eligibility.

HOUSING CHOICE VOUCHER PROGRAM
The Housing Choice Voucher program is the federal government's major program for assisting very low-income families, the elderly, and the disabled to afford decent, safe, and sanitary housing in the private market. Since housing assistance is provided on behalf of the family or individual, participants are able to find their own housing, including single-family homes, townhouses and apartments. The participant is free to choose any housing that meets the requirements of the program and is not limited to units located in subsidized housing projects.

Housing Choice Vouchers are administered locally by public housing agencies. The public housing agencies receive federal funds from the U.S. Department of Housing and Urban Development to administer the voucher program.

A housing subsidy is paid to the landlord directly by the public housing agencies on behalf of the participant. The participant then pays the difference between the actual rent charged by the landlord and the amount subsidized by the program. Under certain circumstances, if authorized by the public housing agencies, a participant may use its voucher to purchase a modest home.

The U.S. Department of Housing and Urban Development is an excellent source of housing information and should be used as a starting point for obtaining information on any type of housing. Whether you're looking for public housing options or are interested in purchasing your own home, the U.S. Department of Housing and Urban Development can help.

National Contact:

U.S. Department of Housing and Urban Development
415 7th Street, SW
Washington, DC 20410
P: 202.708.1112

State Contact:

Please refer to Appendix 10-A: HUD Field & Regional Offices.

Additional Resources:

U.S. Department of Housing and Urban Development, *HUD Home Buying Guide*
http://publications.usa.gov/USAPUBS.php?PubID=5459

U.S. Department of Housing and Urban Development, *A Guide for Making Housing Decisions*
http://publications.usa.gov/USAPUBS.php?PubID=781

U.S. Department of Housing and Urban Development, *Buying a Home: Settlement Costs and Information*
http://publications.usa.gov/USAPUBS.php?PubID=1096

U.S. Department of Housing and Urban Development, *How to Buy a Home with a Low Down Payment*
http://publications.usa.gov/USAPUBS.php?PubID=5399

U.S. Department of Housing and Urban Development, *Shopping for Your Home Loan*
http://publications.usa.gov/USAPUBS.php?PubID=286

U.S. DEPARTMENT OF AGRICULTURE | RURAL HOUSING SERVICE
http://www.rurdev.usda.gov

There are more then 2.5 million substandard housing units in rural America. Rural Housing Service programs help address this challenge by financing new or improved housing for over 65,000 low-to-moderate income families annually. Over 2 million families now own their homes as a result of Rural Housing Service homeownership programs.

The direct and indirect impact of housing development and rehabilitation reverberate through the nation. Residential construction and rehabilitation stimulate various manufacturing and trade industries and related professional services. Housing activities also benefit the larger economy as wages are earned and spent by those directly involved in housing development. Rural Housing Service has played a significant role in the National Partnership for Homeownership to help more women and minorities achieve their homeownership goals.

Rural Housing Service offers two types of homeownership loans – guaranteed and direct loans. The purpose is to provide financing – with no down payment and at favorable rates and terms – either through a direct loan with Rural Housing Service or with a loan from a private financial institution which is guaranteed by Rural Housing Service. These loans are for the purchase, construction, rehabilitation, or relocation of a dwelling and related facilities for low or moderate income rural persons.

SELF-HELP HOUSING
Self-Help Housing Loans help groups of 6 to 10 low-income families build their own homes by providing materials and the skilled labor they cannot furnish themselves. The families must agree to work together until all homes are furnished.

RURAL RENTAL HOUSING LOANS
Apartment living is often an alternative for people who cannot afford the purchase price and maintenance costs of their own individual house. Rural Rental Housing loans are made to finance building construction and site development of multi-family living quarters for people with low, very low and modest incomes. Some

units are reserved for people 62 years and older. Loans can be made in this program to construct housing that will be operated in cooperative form, but loan funds may not be used to finance individual units within a project.

HOME IMPROVEMENT LOANS & GRANT

Home Improvement and Repair Loans and Grants enable low-income rural homeowners to remove health and safety hazards from their homes and to make it accessible for people with disabilities. Grants are available for people 62 years and older who cannot afford to repay a loan.

The U.S. Department of Agriculture through its Rural Housing Service is one of the nation's leading funding sources for housing development in rural America.

National Contact:

U.S. Department of Agriculture
Rural Housing Service
1400 Independence Avenue, SW
Washington, DC 20250
P: 202.692.0090

State Contact:

Please refer to Appendix 10-B: USDA Rural Housing Service Offices.

HABITAT FOR HUMANITY INTERNATIONAL

http://www.habitat.org

The goal of Habitat for Humanity International is to build decent, adequate, and affordable homes in partnership with people in need. Through volunteer labor, management expertise, and tax-deductible donations of money and materials, Habitat for Humanity International builds and rehabilitates homes with the help of potential homeowners. Houses are sold at no profit to partner families, and no-interest mortgages are issued over a fixed period. Small monthly mortgage payments, including taxes and insurance, are repaid over 7 to 20 years and deposited into a revolving "Fund for Humanity" which supports the construction of more homes.

Habitat for Humanity International is not a "free" housing program. Each potential homeowner family is required to invest 500 hours of "sweat equity" actually working alongside Habitat for Humanity International volunteers to build their home, or another family's home. This reduces the cost of the home, increases the pride of ownership among family members, and fosters the development of positive relationships with other community members.

Interested individuals and families are encouraged to inquire with Habitat for Humanity International for referral to their local office.

National Contact:

Habitat for Humanity International
121 Habitat Street
Americus, GA 31709
P: 800.334.3308

NATIONAL HOUSING ADVOCACY AND SUPPORT RESOURCES

CORPORATION FOR SUPPORTIVE HOUSING

http://www.csh.org

The Corporation for Supportive Housing helps communities create permanent housing with services to prevent and end homelessness by bringing together people, skills, and resources; providing high-quality advice and development expertise; making loans and grants to supportive housing sponsors; strengthening the supportive housing industry; and reforming public policy to make it easier to create and operate supportive housing.

National Contact:

Corporation for Supportive Housing
50 Broadway, 17th Floor
New York, NY 10004
P: 212.986.2966

NATIONAL ASSOCIATION OF HOUSING AND REDEVELOPMENT OFFICIALS
http://www.nahro.org

The National Association of Housing and Redevelopment Officials is a professional membership organization comprised of 21,227 housing and community development agencies and officials throughout the US who administer a variety of affordable housing and community development programs at the local level. The National Association of Housing and Redevelopment Official's mission is to create affordable housing and safe, viable communities that enhance the quality of life for all Americans, especially those of low- and moderate-income, by ensuring that housing and community development professionals have the leadership skills, education, information and tools to serve communities in a rapidly changing environment; advocating for appropriate laws and policies which are sensitive to the needs of the people served, are financially and programmatically viable for the industry, are flexible, promote deregulation and local decision making; and fostering the highest standards of ethical behavior, service and accountability.

National Contact:

National Association of Housing and Redevelopment Officials
630 Eye Street, NW
Washington DC 20001
P: 202.289.3500

HOUSING DISCRIMINATION RESOURCES

OFFICE OF FAIR HOUSING AND EQUAL OPPORTUNITY
http://www.hud.gov/offices/fheo

The U.S. Department of Housing and Urban Development's Office of Fair Housing and Equal Opportunity enforces federal laws and establishes policies that ensure all Americans have equal access to the housing of their choice. Individuals who believe they have been the victim of housing discrimination are encouraged to file a complaint with this office.

National Contact:

U.S. Department of Housing and Urban Development
Office of Fair Housing and Equal Opportunity
451 7th Street, SW, Room 5204
Washington, DC 20410
P: 202.708.4252

State Contact:

Please refer to Appendix 10-C: HUD Regional Offices of Fair Housing & Equal Housing Opportunity.

CHAPTER 11 | APPEARANCE, CLOTHING & HOUSEWARES

"If you can dream it, you can do it." ~ Walt Disney

An individuals clothing, personal hygiene and overall appearance are often the first thing communicated to others and should be viewed as vital to successful community and social reintegration. The following organizations provide the tools and resources needed to ensure a strong, confident and professional first impression. Whether your involved in a job search, need clothing for work or are simply trying to situate yourself in the community, the following agencies can provide assistance with all aspects of personal appearance and hygiene.

EMPLOYMENT & PROFESSIONAL CLOTHING

CAREERGEAR
http://www.careergear.org

Since 1999, CareerGear has helped thousands of disconnected and under-served job-seeking men become self-sufficient members of their communities. By providing interview counseling and business attire, CareerGear offers vital services to men of all ages and ethnic backgrounds, as well as recipients of public assistance, the disabled, recovering addicts, Iraqi War Veterans, former foster care children, recent immigrants, and the formerly incarcerated. CareerGear invests in men who have begun to turn their lives around. Each program participant will have completed a job-training program and scheduled a job interview prior to graduating the program.

CareerGear's philosophy is simple but powerful: Successful employment is a catalyst towards men emerging as fathers and leaders within their communities.

The CareerGear team of assistant managers works one-on-one with men to help them select an appropriate outfit for their upcoming job interview. Professional clothing provided includes a suit, dress shirt, tie, belt, shoes, and overcoat.

Each participant receives one suit for an interview; once he is employed or actively seeking employment he is encouraged to become a member of the Professional Development Series. In 2012, 1,610 men received a business suit and career counseling at CareerGear's national headquarters in New York City while CareerGear affiliates suited another 2,200.

National Contact:

CareerGear National
120 Broadway, 36th Floor
New York, NY 10271
P: 212.577.6190

DRESS FOR SUCCESS
http://www.dressforsuccess.org

Dress for Success clients come from a continually expanding and diverse group of nonprofit and government agencies including homeless shelters, immigration services, and job training programs, educational institutions and domestic violence shelters, among many other organizations. More then 3,000 organizations throughout the world send women to Dress for Success for professional apparel and career development services.

On their initial visit, clients receive a suit appropriate for the industry in which she is interviewing and, if available, accessories. After a woman finds a job she can return to Dress for Success for additional clothing that can be mixed and matched to make several outfits, providing her with the foundation for a professional wardrobe. Dress for Success serves clients by referral only, and women must have an interview before receiving clothing.

National Contact:

Dress for Success
32 East 31st Street, 7th Floor
New York, NY 10016
P: 212.532.1922

SECOND HAND CLOTHING OPTIONS

There are many organizations and business that sell inexpensive clothing, furniture and household items to individuals and families with limited budgets. The following organizations have locations in many communities throughout the United States.

GOODWILL INDUSTRIES | OUTLET STORES
http://www.goodwill.org

Goodwill Industries operates an extensive network of thrift stores located throughout the United States. These stores provide clothing, house wares and other items to individuals and families in need at low prices. Most stores are run by individuals who participate in the Goodwill Industries occupational training programs and emergency shelter programs and serve as volunteers. Shopping for clothing in locations closer to affluent areas tends to garner a better quality selection.

National Contact:

Goodwill Industries – Thrift Stores
15810 Indianola Drive
Rockville, MD 20855
P: 800.644.3945

SALVATION ARMY | NATIONAL FAMILY STORES
http://www.salvationarmyusa.org

The Salvation Army operates an extensive network of thrift stores located throughout the United States. These stores provide clothing, house wares and other items to individuals and families in need at low prices. Most stores are run by individuals who participate in the Salvation Army's occupational training program, emergency shelter program or their substance abuse treatment program. Shopping for clothing in locations closer to affluent areas tends to garner a better quality selection. All proceeds from purchases are used to fund the Salvation Army Adult Rehabilitation Centers.

National Contact:

The Salvation Army – Family Stores
615 Slaters Lane, P.O. Box 269
Alexandria, VA 22313
P: 800.728.7825

TATTOO & BODY ART REMOVAL PROGRAMS

Removing visible tattoos, especially those that are antisocial or related to gangs, will improve an individual's chances of finding employment. Removing tattoos of victims of human trafficking can be a major step in the recovery process and can help restore dignity and self-esteem. But how do you do it, and how do you pay for it?

You can begin by using the Jails to Jobs Tattoo Removal Directory available at http://jailstojobs.org/wordpress/tattoo-removal/, which includes tattoo removal clinics across the United States. Some of them charge. Others are free but may have eligibility requirements. This directory is a work in progress and is by no means a complete list.

HOMEBOY INDUSTRIES
http://homeboyindustries.org/what-we-do/tattoo-removal/

No entity on the planet removes more tattoos than Homeboy Industries. At Homeboy Industries, laser tattoo removal is provided to individuals enrolled in the Homeboy program or walk-in community clients. This has proven to be a critical service for former gang members because the majority posses visible tattoos – a physical obstacle that makes it difficult for them to obtain secure employment.

National Contact:

Homeboy Industries
130 West Bruno Street
Los Angeles, CA 90012
P: 323.526.1254

FRESH START TATTOO REMOVAL

http://www.freshstarttattooremoval.org

The Fresh Start Tattoo Removal Program, Inc. (an official 501(c)3 organization) is a nationwide community program that removes visible gang and prison tattoos off of former gang members for free to help these people get jobs and improve the quality of their lives. With employment, there is a much lower return to prison rate.

National Contact:

Fresh Start Tattoo Removal Program, Inc.
189 East Second Street
New York, NY 10009
P: 917.723.4206

CHAPTER 12 | CONSUMER EDUCATION

"There are some people who live in a dream world, and there are some who face reality; and then there are those who turn one into the other." ~ Douglas H. Everett

Being released back into society after incarceration can be a stressful experience regardless of individual circumstances. The decisions made today about how to manage finances can effect ones ability to get credit, insurance, a place to live, and even a job. The resources listed in this section have the ability to help individuals understand and use a variety of consumer products and resources.

CONSUMER PROTECTION & EDUCATION PROGRAMS

CONSUMER PROTECTION OFFICES
http://www.usa.gov/consumer

Consumer Protection Offices offer a variety of important services. They mediate complaints, conduct investigations, license and regulate professionals, provide educational material, and advocate in the consumer interest.

Before sending a written complaint, call or write the office to confirm that it handles the type of complaint you have and determine whether complaint forms are provided. Many offices distribute consumer materials specifically geared to state and local issues. Ask whether any information is available regarding your problem.

For a listing of consumer protection offices in your area, please visit, http://www.usa.gov/consumer or request a free copy of the Consumer Action Handbook from the address below.

National Contact:

General Services Administration
Office of Citizen Services and Innovative Technologies
1800 F Street, NW, 2nd Floor
Washington, DC 20405
P: 202.501.1794

State Contact:

Please refer to Appendix 12-A: State Consumer Protection Offices.

FEDERAL CITIZEN INFORMATION CENTER
http://www.pueblo.gsa.gov

For more than 40 years, the Federal Citizen Information Center has been a trusted one-stop source for answers to questions about consumer problems and government services. Consumers can get the information they need in four ways: by calling 888.878.3256, through printed publications and online through various social media channels and the Federal Citizen Information Center's family of websites.

National Contact:

Federal Citizen Information Center
Pueblo, CO 81009
P: 800.878.3256

Additional Resources:

Federal Citizen Information Center, *Consumer Information Catalog*
http://publications.usa.gov/USAPubs.php?PubID=9801

Federal Citizen Information Center, *Consumer Action Handbook*
http://publications.usa.gov/USAPubs.php?PubID=5131

FEDERAL DEPOSIT INSURANCE CORPORATION

http://www.fdic.gov

The Federal Deposit Insurance Corporation is the independent deposit insurance agency created by Congress to maintain stability and public confidence in the nation's banking system. In its unique role as deposit insurer of banks and savings associations, and in cooperation with other federal and state regulatory agencies, the Federal Deposit Insurance Corporation seeks to promote the safety and soundness of insured depository institutions in the United States financial system by identifying, monitoring, and addressing risks to the deposit insurance funds. The Federal Deposit Insurance Corporation aims at promoting pubic understanding and sound public policies by providing financial and economic information and analysis. It seeks to minimize disruptive effects from the failure of banks and savings associations, and to ensure fairness in the sale of financial products and the provision of financial services.

National Contact:

Federal Deposit Insurance Corporation
Division of Depositor and Consumer Protection
1100 Walnut Street, Box 11
Kansas City, MO 64106
P: 877.275.3342

Additional Resources:

Federal Deposit Insurance Corporation, *Your Insured Deposit*
http://publications.usa.gov/USAPubs.php?PubID=5833

Federal Deposit Insurance Corporation, *FDIC Consumer News*
http://www.fdic.gov/consumernews

FEDERAL RESERVE SYSTEM

http://www.federalreserve.gov

The Federal Reserve System is the central bank of the United States. The system was established on December 23, 1913, originally to give the country an elastic currency, provide facilities for discounting commercial paper, and improve the supervision of banking. Since then, the system's responsibilities have been broadened. Over the years, stability and growth of the economy, a high level of employment, stability in the purchasing power of the dollar, and reasonable balance in transactions with other countries have come to be recognized as primary objectives of governmental economic policy.

The Federal Reserve System consists of the Board of Governors, the 12 District Reserve Banks and their branch offices, and the Federal Open Market Committee. Several advisory councils help the board meet its varied responsibilities.

The 12 District Reserve Banks and their branch offices serve as the decentralized portion of the system, carrying out day-to-day operations such as circulating currency and coin and providing fiscal agency functions and payment mechanism services. The 12 District Reserve Banks are located in Boston, New York, Philadelphia, Cleveland, Richmond, Atlanta, Chicago, St. Louis, Minneapolis, Kansas City, Dallas, and San Francisco.

National Contact:

Federal Reserve System – Consumer Help
P.O. Box 1200
Minneapolis, MN 55480
P: 888.851.1920

FEDERAL TRADE COMMISSION

http://www.ftc.gov

The Federal Trade Commission works for the consumer to prevent fraudulent, deceptive, and unfair business practices in the marketplace and to provide information to help consumers spot, stop, and avoid them. To file a complaint or to get free information on consumer issues, visit their website or call their toll-free number. The Federal Trade Commission records consumer complaints (Internet, telemarketing, identity theft, and other fraud-related complaints) into the Consumer Sentinel Network, a secure, online database and investigative tool available to hundreds of law enforcement agencies.

National Contact:

Federal Trade Commission
Bureau of Consumer Protection
600 Pennsylvania Avenue, NW
Washington, DC 20580
P: 877.382.4357

U.S. Consumer Financial Protection Bureau

http://www.consumerfinance.gov

The U.S. Consumer Financial Protection Bureau was established by Congress in 2012 as part of the Dodd-Frank Wall Street Reform and Consumer Protection Act. The core functions of the U.S. Consumer Financial Protection Bureau are to ensure that, 1) consumers get the information they need to make the financial decisions they believe are best for themselves and their families, 2) prices are clear up front, 3) that risks are visible, and 4) that nothing is buried in fine print. The U.S. Consumer Financial Protection Bureau believes that in a market that works, consumers should be able to make direct comparisons among products and no provider should be able to use unfair, deceptive, or abusive practices.

National Contact:

U.S. Consumer Financial Protection Bureau
1700 G Street, NW
Washington, DC 20552
P: 855.411.2372

Additional Resources:

U.S. Consumer Financial Protection Bureau, *Consumer Financial Protection Bureau Brochure*
http://publications.usa.gov/USAPubs.php?PubID=6105

National Do Not Call Registry

http://www.donotcall.gov

The National Do Not Call Registry allows consumers to permanently restrict telemarketing calls by registering their telephone number at http://www.donotcall.gov or by calling 888.382.1222. If consumers receive telemarketing calls after registering their telephone number with the National Do Not Call Registry, they can file a complaint using the same website and toll-free number.

Placing a telephone number on this national registry will stop most telemarketing calls, but not all of them. Calls that are still permitted include those from political organizations, charities, telephone surveyors, and some organizations with which consumers have an existing relationship.

National Contact:

National Do Not Call Registry
600 Pennsylvania Avenue, NW
Washington, DC 20580
P: 888.382.1222

Better Business Bureaus

http://www.bbb.org

Better Business Bureaus are nonprofit organizations that encourage honest advertising and selling practices and are supported primarily by local businesses. Better Business Bureaus offer a variety of consumer services, including consumer education materials; business reports, particularly unanswered or unsettled complaints or other problems; mediation and arbitration services; and information about charities and other organizations that are seeking public donations. They also provide ratings of local companies to express the Better Business Bureau's confidence that the company operates in a trustworthy manner and demonstrates a willingness to resolve customer concerns.

BBBOnline (http://www.bbb.org/online) provides internet users an easy way to verify the legitimacy of online businesses. Companies carrying the BBBOnline seal have been checked out by the Better Business Bureau and agree to resolve customer concerns in a timely and professional manner.

The Council of Better Business Bureaus, the umbrella organization of the Better Business Bureaus, can assist with complaints about the truthfulness and accuracy of national advertising claims, including children's advertising; and provides reports on national soliciting charities.

National Contact:

Council of Better Business Bureaus, Inc.
4200 Wilson Boulevard, 8th Floor
Arlington, VA 22203
P: 703.276.0100

State Contact:

Please refer to Appendix 12-B: Local Better Business Bureaus.

IDENTITY THEFT SOLUTIONS

FEDERAL TRADE COMMISSION | ID THEFT CLEARINGHOUSE
http://www.ftc.gov/idtheft

Each year millions of consumers have their identities stolen. In the course of a day, you may write a check at the grocery store, use your credit card to purchase tickets to a ball game or rent a car, change service providers for your cell phone, or apply for a credit card. These are all opportunities for identity theft.

According to the Federal Trade Commission, identity theft occurs when personal information is used, without an individual's permission, to commit fraud. The more you know about how to protect your identity by controlling your identifying information such as your Social Security number and what to do if a problem arises, the harder it is for identity thieves to make you a victim.

Identity theft is very serious and harms not only the victims, but also the companies (banks, credit unions, stores, medical services, etc.) that can't recover the money and ultimately, consumers assume the increased costs. Victims of identity theft spend months, sometimes years – and possibly thousands of dollars – cleaning up the damage the thieves have done to their good name and credit. Victims may lose job opportunities, be refused loans for education, housing, or cars, or even get arrested for crimes they did not commit.

What should you do if you are a victim of identity theft?
- Report incidents of identity theft to the Federal Trade Commission at http://www.ftc.gov/idtheft or contact the Federal Trade Commission's Identity Theft hotline at, 877.438.4338.
- File a report with the local police. Be sure to get a copy of the police report.
- Contact the fraud departments of the three major credit reporting agencies:
    Equifax – 800.525.6285, http://www.equifax.com
    Experian – 888.397.3742, http://www.experian.com
    TransUnion – 800.680.7289, http://www.transunion.com
- Report misuse of your Social Security number to the U.S. Social Security Administration.
- Close any accounts that have been tampered with or opened fraudulently.

If you have previously been in contact with the Internal Revenue Service and have not achieved a resolution, contact the Internal Revenue Service's Identity Theft Protection Unit at 800.908.4490.

National Contact:

Federal Trade Commission
ID Theft Clearinghouse
600 Pennsylvania Avenue, NW
Washington, DC 20580
P: 877.438.4338

Additional Resources:

Federal Trade Commission, *Identity Theft: What to Know, What to Do*
http://publications.usa.gov/USAPubs.php?PubID=645

Federal Trade Commission, *Taking Charge: What to Do If Your Identity Is Stolen*
http://publications.usa.gov/USAPubs.php?PubID=3326

CONSUMER REPORTING AGENCIES & CREDIT SCORES

CONSUMER CREDIT REPORTS

A consumer credit report contains information on where you work and live, how you pay your bills, and whether you've been sued or arrested, or have filed for bankruptcy. Consumer Reporting Agencies gather this information and sell it to creditors, employers, insurers, and others. The most common type of consumer reporting agency is the credit bureau. There are three major credit bureaus: Equifax: 800.685.1111 or http://www.equifax.com; Experian: 888.397.3742 or http://www.experian.com; and TransUnion: 800.888.4213 or http://www.transunion.com.

National Contact:

Equifax
Office of Consumer Affairs
P.O. Box 740241
Atlanta, GA 30374
P: 800.685.1111

TransUnion
Consumer Solutions
P.O. Box 2000
Chester, PA 19022
P. 800.888.4213

Experian
National Consumer Assistance Center
P.O. Box 2002
Allen, TX 75013
P: 888.397.3742

FREE ANNUAL CREDIT REPORT

http://www.annualcreditreport.com

The Fair Credit Reporting Act requires each of the three nationwide credit reporting companies – Equifax, Experian, and TransUnion – to provide consumers with a free copy of their consumer credit report, at their request, once every 12 months. The Fair Credit Reporting Act promotes the accuracy and privacy of information in the files of the nation's consumer credit reporting companies. The Federal Trade Commission, the nation's consumer protection agency, enforces the Fair Credit Reporting Act with respect to credit reporting companies.

Consumers may order their reports from each of the three nationwide credit reporting companies at the same time, or they can order their report from each of the company's one at a time. The law allows consumers to order one free copy of their report from each of the nationwide credit reporting companies every 12 months.

The three nationwide credit reporting companies have set up a central website, a toll-free telephone number, and a mailing address through which consumers can order their free annual report.

To order, visit http://www.annualcreditreport.com, call 877.322.8228, or complete the Annual Credit Report Request Form and mail it to the address below. Do not contact the three nationwide credit reporting companies individually as they are only providing free annual credit reports through this central processing center.

National Contact:

Annual Credit Report Request Service
P.O. Box 105281
Atlanta, GA 30348
P: 877.322.8228

Additional Resources:

Annual Credit Report Request Service, *Annual Credit Report Request Form*
http://annualcreditreport.com/manualRequestForm.action

Federal Trade Commission, *Your Access to Free Credit Reports*
http://www.ftc.gov/bcp/edu/pubs/consumer/credit/cre34.pdf

Federal Trade Commission, *Building a Better Credit Report*
http://publications.usa.gov/USAPubs.php?PubID=3116

Federal Trade Commission, *Disputing Errors on Credit Reports*
http://publications.usa.gov/USAPubs.php?PubID=3241

LexisNexis© Personal Report

https://personalreports.lexisnexis.com/access_your_full_file_disclosure.jsp

Through LexisNexis© Risk Solutions, you can order certain reports about yourself or certain reports on others such as prospective caretakers, contractors and doctors. These reports are made available through the LexisNexis© website for a small fee and are prepared by various LexisNexis© entities.

Access Your Full File Disclosure

See what information about you is maintained in the LexisNexis© files – order copies of the information that LexisNexis© may maintain and use to create consumer reports about you. This includes items such as real estate transactions and ownership data, lien, judgments, and bankruptcy records, professional license information, and historical addresses on file.

Once LexisNexis© has verified your identity, all information will be mailed to the address you provide on the request form. LexisNexis© will also include contact information in case you have questions about the information or feel there is an error in any of the reports.

To request a full file disclosure, complete the form below and mail it to the address listed. Please be sure to include all requested identifying data.

National Contact:

LexisNexis© Consumer Center
Attn: Full File Disclosure
P.O. Box 105108
Atlanta, GA 30348

Additional Resources:

LexisNexis©, *Full File Disclosure Request Form*
https://personalreports.lexisnexis.com/pdfs/CD107_CP-File-Disclosure-Request-Form_pg-3.pdf

LexisNexis©, *Full File Disclosure Instructions*
https://personalreports.lexisnexis.com/pdfs/CD107_CP-File-Disclosure-Request-Form_pg-1.pdf

Consumer Credit Scores

http://www.myFICO.com

The information in a credit report is used to calculate an individual's FICO score, a number generally between 300 and 850. The acronym stands for Fair, Isaac and Company. The higher a score, the less risk an individual poses to creditors. A high score, for example, makes it easier to obtain a loan, rent an apartment, or obtain a lower and more competitive insurance rate. Individual FICO scores are available from http://www.myFICO.com for a fee.

Free Annual Credit Reports do not contain a credit score, although individuals can purchase a copy of their credit score when they request their Free Annual Credit Report through http://www.annualcreditreport.com.

To build a better credit score individuals should consider the following, you don't rebuild a credit score; you rebuild a credit history. When trying to rebuild a credit history time's the single most important factor. There is no "quick fix" for a bad credit score, so individuals should be suspicious of deals offering a fast and easy solution to this problem.

National Contact:

Fair Isaac Corporation
2665 Long Lake Road, Building C
Saint Paul, MN 55113
P: 612.758.5200

Additional Resources:

Federal Citizen Information Service, *Your Credit Score*
http://publications.usa.gov/USAPubs.php?PubID=3379

CHEXSYSTEMS© CONSUMER ASSISTANCE

https://www.consumerdebit.com/consumerinfo/us/en/freereport.htm

Under the Fair and Accurate Credit Transaction Act amendments to the federal Fair Credit Reporting Act, consumers are entitled to a free copy of their consumer report upon request, once every 12 months.

You may order a copy of your consumer report by contacting the address below. ChexSystems© will send your report to you, free of charge, via U.S. mail within 5 business days of receiving your request.

National Contact:

ChexSystem, Inc.
Attn: Consumer Relations
7805 Hudson Road, Suite 100
Woodbury, MN 55125
P: 800.428.9623

Additional Resources:

ChexSystems© Consumer Assistance, *FACTA Free Annual Report Request Form*
http://www.chexsystems.com/web/chexsystems/consumerdebit/otherpage/FACTAFreeReport/

CONSUMER CREDIT COUNSELING SERVICES

Counseling services are available to help consumer's budget money and pay bills. Credit unions, extension offices, military family service centers, and religious organizations are among those that may offer free or low-cost credit counseling.

Local nonprofit agencies that provide educational programs on money management and help in developing debt payment plans operate under the name Consumer Credit Counseling Service. Make certain that the agency is accredited by the Council on Accreditation or the International Organization for Standards or registered with the Association of Independent Consumer Credit Counseling Agencies. The counselor should also be certified by the National Foundation for Credit Counseling, an organization that supports a national network of credit counselors.

Typically, a counseling service will negotiate lower payments with a creditor on behalf of their client and then make the payments using money provided by the client each month. The cost of setting up this debt-management plan is paid by the creditor, not the consumer.

If you would like to find an agency in your area, contact the National Foundation for Credit Counselors or the Association of Independent Consumer Credit Counseling Agencies for an affiliated financial counseling agency in your area.

National Contact:

Association of Independent Consumer Credit Counseling Agencies
11350 Random Hills Road, Suite 800
Fairfax, VA 22030
P: 866.703.8787

National Foundation for Credit Counselors
200 M Street, NW, Suite 505
Washington, DC 20036
P: 800.388.2227

Additional Resources:

Federal Trade Commission, *Choosing a Credit Counselor*
http://publications.usa.gov/USAPubs.php?PubID=3314

PRIVATE & NONPROFIT CONSUMER ADVOCACY AGENCIES

CONSUMER ACTION

http://www.consumer-action.org

An education and advocacy organization specializing in credit, finance, and telecommunications issues, Consumer Action offers a multi-lingual consumer complaint hotline and consumer education materials in as many as eight languages.

National Contact:

Consumer Action
221 Main Street, Suite 480
San Francisco, CA 94105
P: 415.777.9635

CONSUMER FEDERATION OF AMERICA

http://www.consumerfed.org

The Consumer Federation of America is a consumer advocacy and education organization that represents consumer interests on issues such as telephone service, insurance and financial services, product safety, indoor air pollution, health care, product liability, and utility rates. It develops and distributes studies of various consumer issues, as well as printed consumer guides and educational materials to interested individuals upon request or through their robust website.

National Contact:

Consumer Federation of America
1620 I Street, NW, Suite 200
Washington, DC 20006
P: 202.387.6121

FINANCIAL INDUSTRY REGULATORY AUTHORITY

http://www.finra.org

The Financial Industry Regulatory Authority is the largest non-governmental regulator for all securities firms doing business in the United States. Created in July 2007 through the consolidation of the National Association of Securities Dealers and the member regulation, enforcement, and arbitration functions of the New York Stock Exchange, the Financial Industry Regulatory Authority is dedicated to investor protection and market integrity through effective and efficient regulation and complementary compliance and technology-based services. The Financial Industry Regulatory Authority produces and disseminates a wide variety of consumer education materials.

National Contact:

Financial Industry Regulatory Authority
1736 K Street, NW
Washington, DC 20006
P: 301.590.6500

JUMP$TART COALITION FOR PERSONAL FINANCIAL LITERACY
http://www.jumpstart.org

Jump$tart is a national coalition of organizations dedicated to improving the financial literacy of pre-kindergarten through college-age youth and under-served populations by providing advocacy, research standards, and educational resources. Jump$tart strives to prepare youth for life-long successful financial decision-making.

National Contact:

Jump$tart Coalition
919 18th Street, NW, Suite 300
Washington, DC 20006
P: 202.466.8604

CREDIT CARD RATING SERVICE

CARDTRAK
http://www.creditcard.com

CardTrak publishes an extensive list of banks and credit unions offering credit cards with low finance charges, low or no annual fees, and full grace periods. Individuals interested in obtaining a copy of this valuable resource should contact CardTrak directly for current pricing and availability.

National Contact:

CardTrak.com, Inc.
P.O. Box 111678
Naples, FL 34108
P: 800.344.7714

TAXPAYER EDUCATION & ASSISTANCE

INTERNAL REVENUE SERVICE
http://www.irs.gov

The mission of the Internal Revenue Service is to provide America's taxpayers top quality service by helping them understand and meet their tax responsibilities while applying the tax law with integrity and fairness to all. Personal and business tax related issues may be addressed by contacting them directly.

National Contact:

Internal Revenue Service
1111 Constitution Avenue, NW
Washington, DC 20224
P: 800.829.1040

TAXPAYER ADVOCATE SERVICE
http://www.taxpayeradvocate.irs.gov

The Taxpayer Advocate Service was created to ensure that every taxpayer is treated fairly, and that they know and understand their rights. The Taxpayer Advocate Service offers free help to guide taxpayers through the often confusing process of resolving their tax problems. If a taxpayer is having tax problems and has not been able to resolve them on their own, the Taxpayer Advocate Service will help. Trained advocates will ensure that the best interests of any taxpayer are represented to the Internal Revenue Service.

National Contact:

Taxpayer Advocate Service
National Taxpayer Advocate
1111 Constitution Avenue, NW, Room 3031-TA
Washington, DC 20224
P: 877.777.4778

State Contact:

Please refer to Appendix 12-C: State Taxpayer Advocate Service Offices.

LOW INCOME TAXPAYER CLINICS

http://www.irs.gov

Low Income Taxpayer Clinics represent low income taxpayers before the Internal Revenue Service and assist taxpayers in audits, appeals and collection disputes. Low Income Taxpayer Clinics also help taxpayers respond to Internal Revenue Service notices and correct account problems.

Low income taxpayers who need assistance in resolving tax disputes with the Internal Revenue Service that can not afford representation may qualify for help from a Low Income Taxpayer Clinic that provides free and low cost assistance. Using poverty guidelines published annually by the U.S. Department of Health and Human Services, each clinic decides independently who meets the income eligibility guidelines and other criteria before agreeing to represent an individual. Eligible taxpayers must generally have incomes that do not exceed 250 percent of the poverty guidelines. The poverty guidelines can be found online at http://aspe.hhs.gov/poverty/index.shtml.

If you are interested in obtaining more information about Low Income Taxpayer Clinics or would like to locate a clinic in your local community, go to http://www.irs.gov/uac/Contact-a-Low-Income-Taxpayer-Clinic for the most recent information.

AUTOMOBILE, HEALTH, HOMEOWNERS & LIFE INSURANCE EDUCATION

INSURANCE INFORMATION INSTITUTE

http://www.iii.org

The Insurance Information Institute is a nonprofit, communications organization supported by the property/casualty insurance industry that works to improve public understanding of insurance. The Insurance Information Institute creates and disseminates a wide variety of resource materials to consumers about insurance related issues.

National Contact:

Insurance Information Institute
110 William Street
New York, NY 10038
P: 212.346.5500

CHAPTER 13 | HEALTH, WELLNESS & LEISURE-TIME RESOURCES

"Patience and perseverance have a magical effect before which difficulties disappear and obstacles vanish." ~ John Quincy Adams

T aking care of your personal health and wellness plays an important role in community reintegration. Making healthier and more educated choices about ones personal wellbeing can substantially improve how someone feels, reduce the risk of many diseases and ensure a long, active and fulfilled lifestyle.

HEALTH & WELLNESS RESOURCES

U.S. DEPARTMENT OF HEALTH AND HUMAN SERVICES
http://www.hhs.gov

The U.S. Department of Health and Human Services is the United States government's principal agency for protecting the health of all Americans and providing human services, especially for those who are least able to help themselves.

The U.S. Department of Health and Human Services represents almost a quarter of all federal outlays, and it administers more grant dollars then all other federal agencies combined. The U.S. Department of Health and Human Service's Medicare program is the nation's largest health insurer, handling more than 1 billion claims per year. Medicare and Medicaid together provide health care insurance for one in four Americans.

The U.S. Department of Health and Human Services works closely with state and local governments, and many agency funded services are provided at the local level by state or county agencies, or through private sector grantees. The Department's programs are administered by 11 operating divisions, including eight agencies in the U.S. Public Health Service and three human services agencies. The U.S. Department of Health and Human Services includes more than 300 programs, covering a wide spectrum of activities. In addition to the services they deliver, the U.S. Department of Health and Human Services programs provide equitable treatment of beneficiaries nationwide, and they enable the collection of national health and other data.

National Contact:

U.S. Department of Health and Human Services
200 Independence Avenue, SW
Washington, DC 20201
P: 877.696.6775

State Contact:

Please refer to Appendix 13-A: HHS Office of the Secretary Regional Offices.

FOOD & NUTRITION ASSISTANCE PROGRAMS

U.S. DEPARTMENT OF AGRICULTURE | FOOD AND NUTRITION SERVICE
http://www.fns.usda.gov

The Food and Nutrition Service, formerly known as the Food and Consumer Service, administers the nutrition assistance programs of the U.S. Department of Agriculture. The mission of the Food and Nutrition Service is to provide children and needy families with better access to food and a healthier diet through its food assistance programs and comprehensive nutrition education efforts.

The Food and Nutrition Service has elevated nutrition and nutrition education to a top priority in all its programs. In addition to providing access to nutritious food, the Food and Nutrition Service also works to empower program participants with knowledge of the link between diet and health.

The agency was established August 8, 1969, but many of the food programs originated long before the Food and Nutrition Service existed as a separate agency. The Supplemental Nutrition Assistance Program (formerly the Food Stamp Program), now the cornerstone of the U.S. Department of Agriculture's nutrition assistance, began in its modern form in 1961, but it had its origins in the Food Stamp Plan to help the needy in the 1930's.

The National School Lunch Program also has its roots in Depression-era efforts to help low-income children. The Needy Family Program, which has evolved into the Food Distribution Program on Indian Reservations, was the primary means of food assistance during the Great Depression.

The Food and Nutrition Service works in partnership with the States in all programs. States determine most administrative details regarding distribution of food benefits and eligibility of participants and the Food and Nutrition Service provides funding to cover most of the States' administrative costs.

Congress appropriated $82.7 billion for Food and Nutrition Service programs in Fiscal Year 2012. By comparison, Food and Nutrition Services programs cost $1.6 billion in 1970, the first full year of the agency's operation.

National Contact:

U.S. Department of Agriculture
Food and Nutrition Information Service
3101 Park Center Drive
Alexandria, VA 22302
P: 703.305.2064

Additional Resources:

Food and Nutrition Information Center, *How to Get Food Help Brochure*
http://publications.usa.gov/USAPubs.php?PubID=549

CHOOSEMYPLATE

http://www.choosemyplate.gov

MyPlate was developed as an effort to promote healthy eating to consumers. The MyPlate icon is easy to understand and it helps to promote messages based on the 2010 Dietary Guidelines for Americans. The new MyPlate icon builds on a familiar image – a plate – and is accompanied by messages to encourage consumers to make healthy choices.

ChooseMyPlate.gov is the consumer access point to the U.S. Department of Agriculture's guidance on food and nutrition and is updated and managed by the Center for Policy and Promotion.

National Contact:

National Agriculture Research Library
10301 Baltimore Avenue, Room 105
Beltsville, MD 20705
P: 301.504.5414

Additional Resources:

ChooseMyPlate.gov, *Let's Eat for the Health of It*
http://publications.usa.gov/USAPubs.php?PubID=1350

ChooseMyPlate.gov, *Focus on Fruits*
http://publications.usa.gov/USAPubs.php?PubID=649

ChooseMyPlate.gov, *Got Your Dairy Today?*
http://publications.usa.gov/USAPubs.php?PubID=653

ChooseMyPlate.gov, *Make Half Your Grains Whole*
http://publications.usa.gov/USAPubs.php?PubID=651

ChooseMyPlate.gov, *Sample Menus for a 2000 Calorie Food Pattern*
http://publications.usa.gov/USAPubs.php?PubID=648

FEEDING AMERICA

http://www.feedingamerica.org

Feeding America is a charitable hunger relief organization that feeds approximately 37 million people annually through a network of more than 200 food banks and 61,000 local charitable agencies including food pantries, soup kitchens, emergency shelters, after-school programs, Kids Cafes, Community Kitchens, and BackPack Programs.

National Contact:

Feeding America
35 East Wacker Drive, Suite 2000
Chicago, IL 60601
P: 800.771.2303

Additional Resources:

Feeding America, *Food Bank Locator*
http://feedingamerica.org/foodbank-results.aspx

MEALS ON WHEELS ASSOCIATION OF AMERICA
http://www.mowaa.org

Meals on Wheels Association of America is an association with programs throughout the United States that provide nutritious meals and other nutrition services to men and women who are elderly, homebound, disabled, frail, or at risk.

National Contact:

Meals on Wheels Association of America
203 South Union Street
Alexandria, VA 22314
P: 703.548.5558

Additional Resources:

Meals on Wheels Association of America, *"Find a Meal" Program Locator*
http://www.momaa.org/page.aspx?pid=253

THE CENTER FOR NUTRITION POLICY AND PROMOTION
http://www.cnpp.usda.gov

The Center for Nutrition Policy and Promotion, an organization of the U.S. Department of Agriculture, was established in 1994 to improve the nutrition and well-being of Americans. Towards this goal, the Center for Nutrition Policy and Promotion focuses its efforts on two primary objectives:

1. Advance and promote dietary guidance for all Americans, and
2. Conduct applied research and analysis in nutrition and consumer economics.

The Center for Nutrition Policy and Promotion's core projects to support its objectives is:

- Dietary Guidelines for Americans
- U.S.D.A. Food Guidance System (MyPlate, MyPyramid, Food Guide Pyramid)
- Expenditures on Children by Families

For additional information on the Center for Nutrition Policy and Promotion and its projects, visit http://www.cnpp.usda.gov or contact them directly.

National Contact:

U.S. Department of Agriculture
Center for Nutrition Policy and Promotion
3101 Park Center Drive, 10th Floor
Alexandria, VA 22302
P: 703.305.7600

SUPPLEMENTAL NUTRITION ASSISTANCE PROGRAM
http://www.fns.usda.gov/snap

The Supplemental Nutrition Assistance Program is the largest nutrition assistance program administered by the U.S. Department of Agriculture. The goal of the program is "to alleviate hunger and malnutrition by increasing food purchasing power of all eligible households who apply for participation" as stated in the Food Stamp Act of 1977, as amended (P.L. 108-269). The program provides monthly benefits to eligible low-income families which can be used to purchase food. As of October 1, 2008, SNAP is the new name for the Federal Food Stamp Program. It stands for the Supplemental Nutrition Assistance Program.

The amount of benefits a household gets is called an allotment. The net monthly income of the household multiplied by.3, and the result is subtracted from the maximum allotment for the household size to find the household's allotment. This is because Supplemental Nutrition Assistance Program households are expected to spend about 30 percent of their resources on food. The maximum monthly allotment for a single individual is $200.

To apply for benefits, or for information about the Supplemental Nutrition Assistance Program in your community, call the National Supplemental Nutrition Assistance Program hotline at 800.221.5689 or contact your local American Job Center for additional information.

State Contact:

Please refer to Appendix 13-B: SNAP Application and Local Office Locator Links.

Additional Resources:

Food and Nutrition Information Center, *Food Stamp Pre-Screening Tool*
http://www.foodstamps-step1.usda.gov

Food and Nutrition Information Center, *Supplemental Nutrition Assistance Program Brochure*
http://publications.usa.gov/USAPubs.php?PubID=551

HEALTH INFORMATION, CENTERS AND CLEARINGHOUSES

CDC NATIONAL PREVENTION INFORMATION NETWORK
http://www.cdcnpin.org

The Centers for Disease Control and Prevention's National Prevention Information Network is the United States reference, referral and distribution service for information on HIV/AIDS, sexually transmitted diseases, and tuberculosis. The National Prevention Information Network produces and disseminates materials and information on HIV/AIDS, sexually transmitted diseases and tuberculosis to organizations and people working in those disease fields in international, national, state and local settings.

National Contact:
CDC National Prevention Information Network
P.O. Box 6003
Rockville, MD 20849
P: 800.458.5231

CENTER FOR HEALTH JUSTICE
http://www.centerforhealthjustice.org

Formerly Correct Help, Center for Health Justice provides information related to HIV in prison. Individuals are encouraged to contact them if they do not receive proper medical assistance or are denied access to programs as a result of HIV status.

National Contact:
Center for Health Justice
900 Avila Street, Suite 102
Los Angeles, CA 90012
P: 213.229.0979

CLEARINGHOUSE ON DISABILITY INFORMATION
http://www.ed.gov/about/offices/list/osers

The Clearinghouse on Disability Information provides assistance to people with disabilities, or anyone requesting information, by doing research and providing documents in response to inquiries. Information provided includes areas of federal funding for disability-related programs. The Clearinghouse on Disability Information staff is trained to refer requests to other sources of disability-related information, if necessary. Information provided may be useful to individuals with disabilities, their families, schools and universities; teacher's and/or school administrators, and organizations that have persons with disabilities as clients.

National Contact:

U.S. Department of Education
Office of Special Education and Rehabilitative Services
550 12th Street, SW, Room 5133
Washington, DC 20202
P: 202.245.7307

NATIONAL ALLIANCE FOR THE MENTALLY ILL

http://www.nami.org

The National Alliance for the Mentally Ill provides a wide range of services to individuals and families living with mental illness including support groups and special interest networks; up-to-date, scientific information through publications; a toll-free helpline; annual Mental Illness Awareness Week campaigns; advocacy for services; and support for research.

National Contact:

National Alliance for the Mentally Ill
2107 Wilson Boulevard, Suite 300
Arlington, VA 22201
P: 703.524.7600

Additional Resources:

U.S. Department of Health and Human Services, *Mental Health Medications*
http://publications.usa.gov/USAPubs.php?PubID=696

NATIONAL ASSOCIATION OF STATE ALCOHOL/DRUG PROGRAM DIRECTORS

http://www.nasadad.org

The National Association of State Alcohol/Drug Program Directors is a private, not-for-profit educational, scientific, and informational organization whose basic purpose is to foster and support the development of effective alcohol and other drug abuse prevention and treatment programs throughout every State. The National Association of State Alcohol/Drug Program Directors serves as a focal point for the examination of alcohol and other drug related issues of common interest to both other national organizations and federal agencies by conducting research, fostering collaboration, providing training and cross-training, providing technical assistance, promoting national standards, shaping policy, and ensuring stable funding.

National Contact:

National Association of State Alcohol/Drug Abuse Directors
808 17th Street NW, Suite 410
Washington, DC 20006
P: 202. 293.0090

NATIONAL ASSOCIATION OF STATE MENTAL HEALTH PROGRAM DIRECTORS

http://www.nasmhpd.org

The National Association of State Mental Health Program Directors is an organization that advocates for the collective interests of state mental health authorities and their directors at the national level. The National Association of State Mental Health Program Directors analyzes trends in the delivery and financing of mental health services and identifies public mental health policy issues and best practices in the delivery of mental health services. The association apprises its members of research findings and best practices in the delivery of mental health services, fosters collaboration, provides consultation and technical assistance, and promotes effective management practices and financing mechanisms adequate to sustain the mission.

National Contact:

National Association of State Mental Health Program Directors
66 Canal Center Plaza, Suite 302
Alexandria, VA 22314
P: 703.739.9333

NATIONAL CENTER FOR COMPLEMENTARY AND INTEGRATIVE HEALTH

http://www.nccam.nih.gov

The National Center for Complementary and Integrative Health Information Clearinghouse operates a toll-free telephone service through which information specialists search National Center for Complementary and Integrative Health databases for scientific information on complementary and alternative medicine therapies or conditions and can answer inquiries in English and Spanish. The Fax-on-Demand service, with fact sheets and other information, is also available through the toll-free number. National Center for Complementary and Integrative Health services and materials are provided at no cost. The clearinghouse does not provide medical referrals, medical advice, or recommendations for specific complementary and alternative medicine therapies

National Contact:

National Center for Complementary and Integrative Health
P.O. Box 7923
Gaithersburg, MD 20898
P: 888.644.6226

NATIONAL CRIMINAL JUSTICE REFERENCE CENTER

http://www.ncjrs.gov

The National Criminal Justice Reference Service was established in 1972 as a centralized information services for criminal justice practitioners and researchers. The National Criminal Justice Reference Service provides reference services; distributes publications of the U.S. Department of Justice, Office of Justice Programs; acquires publications for its collection; and provides other services, such as document loan and information dissemination, via the internet. A computerized database includes abstracts of all materials in The National Criminal Justice Reference Service collection. (The database is available on CD-ROM and on DIALOG.) Health issues covered by The National Criminal Justice Reference Service includes violence prevention; mental health illness and crime; victimization; human development and criminal behavior; family violence and child abuse; health care fraud; substance abuse and treatment; and correctional health care, including AIDS and tuberculosis.

National Contact:

National Criminal Justice Reference Service
P.O. Box 6000
Rockville, MD 20849
P: 800.851.3420

NATIONAL HEALTH INFORMATION CENTER

http://www.health.gov/nhic

The National Health Information Center helps the public and health professionals locate health information through identification of health information resources, an information and referral system, and publications. The National Health Information Center uses a database containing descriptions of health-related organizations to refer inquiries to the most appropriate resources. The National Health Information Center does not diagnose medical conditions or give medical advice. The National Health Information Center prepares publications and directories on health promotion and disease prevention topics.

National Contact:

National Health Information Center
P.O. Box 1133
Washington, DC 20013
P: 800.336.4797

NATIONAL INSTITUTE ON DRUG ABUSE VIRTUAL INFORMATION CENTER

http://www.nida.nih.gov

The National Institute on Drug Abuse Virtual Information Center responds to inquiries sent by the public, medical and health professionals, educators, researchers, people in the substance abuse field, and the media. Information is provided on the common drugs of abuse and a variety of topics related to drug abuse and addiction. The National Institute on Drug Abuse Research Dissemination Center distributes publications for the National Institute on Drug Abuse. To order free print copies of publications, call the National Institute on Drug Abuse Virtual Information Center at 877.643.2644, send them a fax at 240.645.0227, or e-mail them at drugpubs@nida.nih.gov.

National Contact:

National Institute of Drug Abuse
Office of Science Policy and Promotion
6001 Executive Boulevard, Room 5213
Bethesda, MD 20892
P: 301.443.1124

NATIONAL INSTITUTE OF MENTAL HEALTH

http://www.nimh.nih.gov

The National Institute of Mental Health makes available a variety of brochures on mental disorders free of charge by contacting them directly. Their pamphlets offer the latest information about symptoms, diagnoses, and treatment of various mental illnesses. Easy-to-read materials on topics such as bipolar disorder, depression, post-traumatic stress disorder, schizophrenia and psychiatric medications are available.

National Contact:

National Institute of Mental Health
Office of Information and Publications
6001 Executive Boulevard, Room 8184, MSC 9663
Bethesda, MD 20892
P: 866.615.6464

Additional Resources:

U.S. Department of Health and Human Services, *Depression*
http://publications.usa.gov/USAPubs.php?PubID=442

U.S. Department of Health and Human Services, *Depression in Women*
http://publications.usa.gov/USAPubs.php?PubID=708

SAMHSA's HEALTH INFORMATION NETWORK

http://www.samhsa.gov/shin

The Substance Abuse and Mental Health Services Administration's Health Information Network is central to SAMHSA's mission to disseminate information and products to promote the adoption of effective prevention, intervention, and treatment policies, programs, and practices; provide access to scientific research on substance abuse and mental health issues; and serve as a first point of contact for individuals seeking information on the prevention and treatment of mental and substance use disorders.

National Contact:

SAMHSAs Health Information Network
P.O. Box 2345
Rockville, MD 20847
P: 877.726.4727

SAMHSA's HOMELESSNESS RESOURCE CENTER

http://www.homeless.samhsa.gov

The Substance Abuse and Mental Health Services Administration's Homelessness Resource Center, seeks to improve the daily lives of people affected by homelessness and who have mental health, substance use problems and trauma histories. The Homelessness Resource Center does this through training and technical assistance, online learning opportunities, and publications for homeless service providers. The Homelessness Resource Center also maintains an extensive knowledge database of studies, papers, and reports related to homelessness.

National Contact:

SAMHSA's Homelessness Resource Center
Center for Social Innovation
200 Reservoir Street, Suite 202
Needham, MA 02494
P: 617.467.6014

HEALTH INSURANCE ASSISTANCE & COVERAGE

For information about government supported medical assistance and insurance coverage, individuals are encouraged to contact the U.S. Department of Health and Human Services. The U.S. Department of Health and Human Services is the primary funding source for all government medical assistance programs and is the administrator for the 2010 Affordable Care Act, and both Medicare and Medicaid at the federal level. For more detailed information, visit http://www.cms.gov.

2010 AFFORDABLE CARE ACT
http://www.healthcare.gov

The 2010 Affordable Care Act puts in place comprehensive health insurance reforms that will roll out over several years. Most provisions will take effect by early 2014; a timeline is available at http://www.healthcare.gov/law/timeline. The law is intended to lower health care costs, provide more health care choices, and enhance the quality of health care for all Americans. Major provisions effecting consumers include:

- Coverage for seniors who hit the Medicare Prescription Drug "donut hole," including a rebate for those who reach the gap in drug coverage.
- Expanded coverage for young adults, allowing them to stay on their parents' plan until they are 26 years old.
- Providing access to insurance for uninsured Americans with pre-existing conditions.
- Expanded preventative care (e.g. wellness visits and mammograms) to Medicare and Medicaid participants.
- Medical coverage to children not eligible for care under Medicaid.
- In 2013, consumers can set aside up to $2,500 in a flexible spending account for medical expenses that aren't covered by insurance.

The Affordable Care Act also requires states to establish online "Health Insurance Marketplaces" to facilitate the comparison of available insurance options and ultimately subscriber enrollment in the program of their choice.

The following levels of coverage are designed to enable individuals to select the most comprehensive and financially appropriate option for their circumstances:

- Bronze – 60% insurance coverage with 40% responsibility of the subscriber
- Silver – 70% insurance coverage with 30% responsibility of the subscriber
- Gold – 80% insurance coverage with 20% responsibility of the subscriber
- Platinum – 90% insurance coverage with 10% responsibility of the subscriber

Individual subscribers may qualify for a health insurance premium subsidy based on income and household size to reduce the out-of-pocket expenses associated with coverage.

For additional information about the Affordable Care Act and how it can best serve you and your health insurance coverage needs, contact the national toll-free enrollment hotline at 800.318.2596 or visit their website at http://www.healthcare.gov.

National Contact:

U.S. Department of Health and Human Services
200 Independence Avenue, SW
Washington, DC 20201
P: 877.696.6775

Additional Resources:

U.S. Department of Health and Human Services, *About the Health Insurance Marketplace*
http://publications.usa.gov/USAPubs.php?PubID=971

U.S. Department of Health and Human Services, *Get Ready to Enroll in the Marketplace*
http://publications.usa.gov/USAPubs.php?PubID=973

U.S. Department of Health and Human Services, *The Affordable Care Act and Women*
http://publications.usa.gov/USAPubs.php?PubID=661

MEDICAID

http://www.medicaid.gov

Medicaid is available only to certain low-income individuals and families who fit into an eligibility group that is recognized by federal and state law. Medicaid does not pay money to eligible participants; it sends payments directly to a specified health care provider. Depending on state rules, participants may also be asked to pay a small part (co-pay) of the cost for some medical services. Medicaid is a state administered program and each state sets its own program guidelines regarding eligibility and level of service. Medicaid is administered federally by the Centers for Medicare and Medicaid Services, a division of the U.S. Department of Health and Human Services.

National Contact:

Centers for Medicare and Medicaid Services
Office of External Affairs
7500 Security Boulevard
Baltimore, MD 21244
P: 877.267.2323

MEDICARE

http://www.medicare.gov

Medicare is a government sponsored health care program for people 65 years of age or older, some younger people with disabilities, and those with permanent kidney failure. Medicare is administered federally by the Centers for Medicare and Medicaid Services, a division of the U.S. Department of Health and Human Services.

National Contact:

Centers for Medicare and Medicaid Services
Office of External Affairs
7500 Security Boulevard
Baltimore, MD 21244
P: 800.633.4227

Additional Resources:

U.S. Department of Health and Human Services, *Welcome to Medicare*
http://publications.usa.gov/USAPubs.php?PubID=573

U.S. Department of Health and Human Services, *A Quick Look at Medicare*
http://publications.usa.gov/USAPubs.php?PubID=577

U.S. Department of Health and Human Services, *Medicare Basics: A Guide for Families and Friends with Medicare*
http://publications.usa.gov/USAPubs.php?PubID=6039

U.S. Department of Health and Human Services, *Enrolling in Medicare Part A & Part B*
http://publications.usa.gov/USAPubs.php?PubID=2120

U.S. Department of Health and Human Services, *MyMedicare.gov – Free and Secure Online Account Access*
http://www.mymedicare.gov

THE MEDICARE RIGHTS CENTER
http://www.medicarerights.org

The Medicare Rights Center works to ensure access to affordable health care for older adults and people with disabilities through counseling, advocacy, and educational programs. It works with clients nationwide through a telephone hotline, internet services, a large volunteer network and community programs. The Medicare Rights Center also produces and disseminates a wide variety of consumer education materials to those looking for accurate and reliable information.

National Contact:

The Medicare Rights Center
520 8th Avenue, North Wing, 3rd Floor
New York, NY 10018
P: 800.333.4114

ONLINE HEALTH INFORMATION

There are many online resources available to help those looking for health information make educated and informed health care decisions. Individuals should be wary of websites sponsored by companies that are trying to sell a particular treatment or product. It's better to contact reputable associations or visit sites run by government agencies and recognized organizations such as the Centers for Disease Control and Prevention (http://www.cdc.gov), Food and Drug Administration (http://www.fda.gov/consumer), National Cancer Institute (http://www.cancer.gov), National Institute on Aging (http://www.nia.nih.gov), National Women's Health Information Center (http://www.womenshealth.gov), the Mayo Clinic (http://www.mayoclinic.com) or the American Medical Association (http://www.ama.org). This information should complement, not replace, what is received from a doctor or other medical professional. MedlinePlus and HealthFinder.gov are sites that are generally recognized as reliable and definitive information sources.

MEDLINEPLUS
http://www.medlineplus.gov

Look up a condition or disease at MedlinePlus, and you'll find a page organized to make it easy to find the information you're looking for. Sponsored by the National Library of Medicine — part of the National Institute of Health — the website draws from the National Library of Medicine, National Institute of Health, other government agencies, and health-related organizations. Other MedlinePlus features include a drug and supplement look-up, an illustrated medical encyclopedia, and current health news headlines and links.

HEALTHFINDER.GOV
http://www.healthfinder.gov

A one-stop-shop for finding reliable health information online, HealthFinder.gov draws on more than 1,600 government and nonprofit organizations to point you to current information. The site — a product of the Office of Disease Prevention and Health Promotion in the U.S. Department of Health and Human Services — also offers consumer health guides, recent health news by topic, and a directory of health-related organizations.

FREE OR LOW-COST CLINICS

As a result of the 2010 Affordable Care Act, consumers have many options when choosing a health care provider regardless of their income or social standing. However, there are still many free or low cost clinics that focus on the needs of under-served populations throughout the United States. Finding a free or low-cost clinic is as easy as visiting http://www.findhealthcenter.hrsa.gov and entering the zip code for the area in which you would like service.

ADDICTION RESOURCES

ALCOHOLICS ANONYMOUS
http://www.aa.org

Alcoholics Anonymous is a fellowship of men and women who share their experiences, strength and hope with each other that they may solve their common problem and help others to recover from alcoholism. The primary purpose of Alcoholics Anonymous membership is to stay sober and help other alcoholics to achieve sobriety. Alcoholics Anonymous produces and disseminates a wide variety of informational brochures and literature to help individuals understand and overcome alcoholism. Informational resources are available in printed format for those individuals who are unable to actively participate in meetings by contacting Alcoholics Anonymous, Inc. directly.

National Contact:

Alcoholics Anonymous, Inc.
Grand Central Station
P.O. Box 459
New York, NY 10163
P: 212.870.3400

AL-ANON & AL-ATEEN
http://www.al-anon.org

Since its founding in 1951, Al-Anon Family Groups has pursued its mission to help family and friends recover from the effects of someone else's drinking. The mission of Al-Anon Family Groups is advanced through the creation and dissemination of educational books and pamphlets to assist individuals to understand and overcome the challenges of addiction and through community-based meetings designed to help in the healing process by bringing individuals with similar issues and circumstances together to discuss and share their experiences.

National Contact:

Al-Anon Family Group, Inc.
1600 Corporate Landing Parkway
Virginia Beach, VA 23454
P: 757.563.1600

NARCOTICS ANONYMOUS
http://www.na.org

The Narcotics Anonymous program started as a small movement within the United States, which has grown into one of the world's oldest and largest organizations of its type. Narcotics Anonymous offers recovery to addicts around the world by focusing on the disease of addiction rather than any particular drug. Narcotics Anonymous meetings are a place to share recovery with other addicts.

National Contact:

Narcotics Anonymous, Inc.
P.O. Box 9999
Van Nuys, CA 91409
P: 818.773.9999

NATIONAL ASSOCIATION FOR SHOPLIFTING PREVENTION
http://www.shopliftingprevention.org

The National Association for Shoplifting Prevention is the nationwide leader in shoplifting prevention efforts. The National Association for Shoplifting Prevention's unparalleled shoplifter research and ongoing collaboration with community stakeholders — from crime prevention, to law enforcement, to retailers, to criminal and juvenile justice — has been the basis for all its organizational activities and the foundation for its programs and services.

National Contact:

National Association for Shoplifting Prevention
225 Broadhollow Road, Suite 400E
Melville, NY 11747
P: 631.923.2737

SEX ADDICTS ANONYMOUS

http://www.sexaa.org

Sex Addicts Anonymous is a national nonprofit organization committed to the treatment of individuals who have an addiction to sex. Sex Addicts Anonymous coordinates meetings in local communities to encourage open and honest discussion of related issues among its members.

National Contact:

Sex Addicts Anonymous
P.O. Box 70949
Houston, TX 77270
P: 800.477.8191

CHAPTER 14 | BUSINESS & ENTREPRENEURIAL RESOURCES

*"An inner quality that many entrepreneurs say helps them
survive is optimism." ~ Jean Chatzky*

T here is no way to eliminate all the risks associated with starting a small business, but it is possible to improve one's chances of success with good planning, preparation and insight. The resources listed in this section are a good starting point for any entrepreneur and will provide assistance and guidance in all aspects of forming, starting and expanding a small business. Individuals reentering society after a term of incarceration should be wary about starting a small business as 56% of new businesses fail within 4 years of operation. (1)

WRITING A BUSINESS PLAN

Entrepreneurs should think about what type of business they want to start and after deciding on a particular business, the next step should be to develop a business plan. A business plan should be thought of as a roadmap with milestones for the business. A business plan usually begins as a pre-assessment tool to determine profitability and market share, and then expands into an in-business assessment tool to determine success, obtain financing and determine repayment ability, among other factors.

Creating a comprehensive business plan can be a long process, and should be taken seriously as it is often times your first impression on a potential investor or collaborator. In general, a good business plan contains:

- Introduction
- Marketing
- Financial Management
- Operations
- Concluding Statement

A business plan is a flexible document that should change as businesses grow and adapt to reflect the changing business environment.

Additional Resources:

MasterCard International, *Business Planning Tools*
http://www.mastercardbusiness.com/apmea/en/smallbiz/businessplanning/businessplanning.html

FORMS OF BUSINESS

The most common forms of business are the sole proprietorship, partnership, and corporation. When beginning a business, entrepreneurs must decide which form of business to use. Legal and tax considerations enter heavily into these decisions.

SOLE PROPRIETORSHIP

A sole proprietorship is an unincorporated business that is owned by one individual. It is the simplest form of business organization to start and maintain. The business has no existence apart from the owner. Its liabilities are personally tied to the owner. The owner undertakes the risks of the business for all assets owned, whether or not used in the business. Income and expenses of the business are included on the owners' personal tax return.

PARTNERSHIP

A partnership is the relationship existing between two or more persons who join to carry on a trade or business. Each person contributes money, property, labor, or skill, and expects to share in the profits and losses of the business.

A partnership must file an annual information return to report income, deductions, gains, losses, etc., from its operations, but it does not pay income tax. Instead, it "passes through" any profits or losses to its partners. Each partner includes his or her share of the partnership's items on his or her tax return.

---

1. Rob Hurtt, "Thinking Big For Your Small Business," *St. Louis Business Journal*, May 9, 2008

CORPORATION

In forming a corporation, prospective shareholders exchange money, property, or both, for the corporation's capital stock. A corporation generally takes the same deductions as a sole proprietorship to figure its taxable income. A corporation can also take special deductions.

The profit of a corporation is taxed to the corporation when earned, and then taxed to the shareholders when distributed as dividends. However, shareholders cannot deduct any loss of the corporation.

S CORPORATION

An eligible domestic corporation can avoid double taxation (once to the corporation and again to the shareholders) by electing to be treated as an S corporation. Generally, an S corporation is exempt from federal income tax other than tax on certain capital gains and passive income. On their tax returns, the S corporation's shareholders include their share of the corporation's separately stated items of income, deduction, loss, and credit, and their share of non-separately stated income or loss.

LIMITED LIABILITY COMPANY

A limited liability company is an entity formed under state law by filing articles of organization as a limited liability company. None of the members filing articles of organization are personally liable for its debts. A limited liability company may be classified for federal income tax purposes as a partnership, a corporation, or an entity disregarded as an entity separate from its owner by applying Internal Revenue Service regulations.

ARTICLES OF INCORPORATION

The process of forming a corporation varies somewhat from state to state. The articles of incorporation are usually filed with the secretary of state's office in the state in which the company incorporates. The articles contain:

- The corporation's name.
- The names of the people who incorporated it.
- Its purpose.
- Its duration (usually perpetual).
- The number of shares that can be issued, their voting rights, and any other rights the shareholders have.
- The corporation's minimum capital.
- The address of the corporation's office.
- The name and address of the person responsible for the corporation's legal service.
- The names and addresses of the first directors.

In addition to the articles of incorporation, a corporation has bylaws. Bylaws describe how the firm is to be operated from both a legal and managerial perspective. The bylaws include:

- How, when, and where shareholders' and directors' meetings are held.
- Directors' authority.
- Duties and responsibilities of officers, and the length of their appointment.

Additional Resources:

U.S. Small Business Administration, *Record Keeping in a Small Business*
http://publications.usa.gov/USAPubs.php?PubID=178

BUSINESS IDENTIFICATION NUMBERS

Business owners must have a taxpayer identification number so the Internal Revenue Service can process relevant business tax returns. The two most common kinds of taxpayer identification numbers are the social security number and the employer identification number.

- A social security number is issued to individuals by the Social Security Administration.
- An employer identification number is issued to individuals (sole proprietors), partnerships, corporations, and other entities by the Internal Revenue Service.

Business owners must include their taxpayer identification number on all returns and other documents sent to the Internal Revenue Service. A taxpayer identification number may also be required by other persons who use it in the preparation of returns or other documents being sent to the Internal Revenue Service.

EMPLOYER IDENTIFICATION NUMBER
http://www.irs.gov/businesses/small/article/0,,id-102767,00.html

Employer Identification Numbers are used to identify the tax accounts of employers, certain sole proprietors, corporations, partnerships, estates, trusts, and other entities.

Business owners who don't already have an Employer Identification Number should get one if they:

1. Have employees,
2. Have a qualified retirement plan,
3. Operate their business as a corporation or partnership, or
4. File returns for:
   a. Employment taxes, or
   b. Excise taxes.

Applying for an Employer Identification Number can be done quickly and efficiently using the Internal Revenue Service's online application at http://www.irs.gov/businesses/small. Applications are also accepted over the telephone by calling 800.829.4933 between the hours of 7:00 am and 10:00 pm in the applicant's local time zone.

GENERAL BUSINESS DEVELOPMENT & FUNDING RESOURCES

U.S. SMALL BUSINESS ADMINISTRATION
http://www.sba.gov

Every year, the U.S. Small Business Administration and its nationwide network of resource partners help millions of potential and existing small business owners start, grow and succeed.

If you're just starting, the U.S. Small Business Administration and its resources can help you with loans and business management skills. If you're already in business, you can use the U.S. Small Business Administration's resources to help manage and expand your business, obtain government contracts, recover from disaster, find foreign markets, and make your voice heard in the federal government.

The U.S. Small Business Administration restricts the loan eligibility of firms where a principle, owner, officer, director, key employee or principle of an affiliated business are incarcerated, on parole or probation, or have been indicted for a felony or a crime of moral turpitude. However, this does not preclude ineligible individuals or businesses from receiving training or counseling through U.S. Small Business Administration sponsored or supported programs.

National Contact:

U.S. Small Business Administration
409 3rd Street, SW, Suite 7600
Washington, DC 20416
P: 800.827.5722

State Contact:

Please refer to <u>Appendix 14-A: U.S. Small Business Administration District & Branch Offices</u>.

Additional Resources:

U.S. Small Business Administration, *SBA Small Business Advantage Brochure*
<u>http://publications.usa.gov/USAPubs.php?PubID=179</u>

U.S. SMALL BUSINESS ADMINISTRATION'S RESOURCE PARTNERS

<u>http://www.sba.gov/sba-direct</u>

In addition to district offices which serve every state and territory, the U.S. Small Business Administration works with a variety of local resource partners to meet the needs of small businesses everywhere. These professionals can help with writing a formal business plan, locating sources of financial assistance, managing and expanding a business, finding opportunities to sell goods or services to the government, and recovering from disaster.

SERVICE CORPS OF RETIRED EXECUTIVES

<u>http://www.score.org</u>

Service Corps of Retired Executives is a national network of nearly 14,000 entrepreneurs, business leaders and executives who volunteer as mentors to America's small businesses. The Service Corps of Retired Executives has helped more than 8.5 million entrepreneurs nationwide by leveraging decades of expertise from seasoned business professionals to help entrepreneurs start businesses, grow companies and create jobs in local communities.

With more than 370 offices throughout the country, Service Corps of Retired Executives matches entrepreneurs with a mentor whose personality, experience, and skills are a good fit for your business needs. Whether you are a start-up business or growing company, Service Corps of Retired Executives mentors can offer free and confidential advice. As members of your community, Service Corps of Retired Executives mentors understand local business licensing rules, economic conditions and lending standards. Service Corps of Retired Executives also offers local small business workshops at modest fees on popular topics such as increasing sales, managing cash flow and marketing your business.

You can count on Service Corps of Retired Executives as a trusted resource to offer in-depth mentoring, sound advice and guidance, and tools and resources that can help you succeed as a business owner. For 24/7 access to advice and online webinars on topics such as staring, growing, marketing and e-commerce for small business, visit Service Corps of Retired Executives online at <u>http://www.score.org</u> or call them at 800.624.0245.

National Contact:

Service Corps of Retired Executives
1175 Herndon Parkway, Suite 900
Herndon, VA 20170
P: 800.624.0245

SMALL BUSINESS DEVELOPMENT CENTERS

<u>http://www.sba.gov/sbdc</u>

The Small Business Development Center program has been vital to the U.S. Small Business Administration's entrepreneurial outreach for more than 30 years. It had become one of the largest professional small business management and technical assistance networks in the nation. With nearly 900 locations across the country, Small Business Development Center's offer free one-on-one expert business advice and low-cost training by qualified small business professionals to existing and future entrepreneurs.

The Small Business Development Center program includes special focus areas such as, green business technology, disaster recovery and preparedness, import and export assistance, veteran's assistance, electronic commerce, technology transfer and regulatory compliance.

Through federal grants, Small Business Development Center's in every state and territory provide the foundation for the economic growth of small businesses. These small businesses, in turn, advance local and regional economic development through the generation of business revenues, job creation and job retention. This return on investment is demonstrated by fiscal 2013 outcomes, where Small Business Development Center's:

- Assisted more than 13,000 entrepreneurs to start new businesses – an estimated 37 new business starts per day.
- Provided counseling services to over 107,000 emerging entrepreneurs and nearly 102,000 existing businesses.
- Provided training services to approximately 380,000 clients.

The efficacy of the Small Business Development Center program has been validated by a nationwide impact study. Of the clients surveyed, more than 80 percent reported that the business assistance they received from the Small Business Development Center counselor was worthwhile. Similarly, more than 50 percent reported that Small Business Development Center guidance was beneficial in making the decision to start a business. More than 40 percent of long-term clients, those receiving 5 hours or more of counseling, reported an increase in sales and 38 percent reported an increase in profit margins. For information regarding Small Business Development Center programs visit http://www.sba.gov/sbdc.

National Contact:

U.S. Small Business Administration
Small Business Development Centers
409 3rd Street, SW, Suite 7600
Washington, DC 20416
P: 800.827.5722

ONLINE TOOLS & TRAINING

U.S. SMALL BUSINESS ADMINISTRATION'S ONLINE TOOLS & TRAINING
http://www.sba.gov/training

The Small Business Administration's Small Business Training Network is a virtual campus complete with free online courses, workshops, podcasts, learning tools and business-readiness assessments.

Key features of the Small Business Training Network include:

- Training is available anytime and anywhere – all you need is a computer with internet access.
- More than 30 free online courses and workshops available.
- Templates and samples to get your business planning underway.
- Online, interactive assessment tools are featured and used to direct clients to appropriate training.

Course topics include a financial primer keyed around the U.S. Small Business Administration's loan-guarantee programs, a course on exporting, and courses for Veterans and women seeking federal contracting opportunities, as well as an online library of podcasts, business publications, templates and articles.

SMALL BUSINESS RESOURCE MAGAZINE
http://www.sbaguides.com/magazine/download/

The Small Business Resource Magazine is the most complete guide to starting and expanding a business. Entrepreneurs can find information on local regulations, government loans, training and assistance, and business advocacy.

Additional Resources:

U.S. Small Business Administration, *National Resource Magazine – English*
http://www.sbaguides.com/pdf/english/national.pdf

U.S. Small Business Administration, *National Resource Magazine – Spanish*
http://www.sbaguides.com/wp-content/uploads/national-spanish.pdf

GRANTS FOR SMALL BUSINESSES

The U.S. Small Business Administration does not provide grants for starting and expanding a business. Government grants are funded by tax dollars and, therefore, require very stringent compliance and reporting measures to ensure the money is well spent. As you can imagine, grants are not given away indiscriminately.

Grants from the federal government are authorized and appropriated through bills by Congress and signed by the President. The grant authority varies widely among agencies. The U.S. Small Business Administration has authority to make grants to nonprofit and educational organizations in many of its counseling and training programs, but does not have the authority to make grants to small businesses. The announcements for the counseling and training grants will appear on http://www.grants.gov. If Congress authorizes Specific Initiative Grants, organizations receiving such grants will receive individual notification.

Some business grants are available through state and local programs, nonprofit organizations and other groups. For example, some states provide grants for expanding child care centers; creating energy efficient technology; and developing marketing campaigns for tourism. These grants are not necessarily free money, and usually require the recipient to match funds or combine the grant with other forms of financing such as loans. The amount of the grant money available varies with each business and each grantor.

If you are not one of these specialized businesses, both federal and state government agencies provide financial assistance programs that help small business owners obtain loans and venture capital financing from commercial lenders.

REENTRY SOURCEBOOK

APPENDICIES

APPENDIX 1-A: LOCAL REENTRY SERVICE PROVIDERS

There are many local agencies that provide services to assist individuals, families and communities with navigating the challenges of community reintegration. Services offered vary by agency and the availability of funding resources. If an agency does not provide the specific services or assistance you're looking for, request a referral to another agency that may be better equipped to meet your specific needs.

ALABAMA

ACLU of Alabama

http://www.aclualabama.org

Local chapters of the American Civil Liberties Union provide advocacy and legal assistance on a limited basis to concerned individuals and groups impacted by the criminal justice system - emphasis on prison conditions and civil liberties. Contact directly for specific areas of service.

> **Local Contact:**
>
> ACLU of Alabama
> 207 Montgomery Street, Suite 910
> Montgomery, AL 36104
> P: 334.262.0304

Aid to Inmate Mothers

http://www.inmatemoms.org

Aid to Inmate Mothers provides transitional programs for mothers who are between 18 and 24 months of their release date. They also offer educational programs for women prisoners, release planning, and follow-up case management for one year after release.

> **Local Contact:**
>
> Aid to Inmate Mothers
> P.O. Box 986
> Montgomery, AL 36101
> P: 334.262.2245

Citizens United for Rehabilitation of Errants

http://www.curenational.org

CURE, Citizens United for Rehabilitation of Errants is a national nonprofit prison advocacy organization with state and special interest chapters throughout the United States. Local and special interest chapters provide assistance to ex-offenders on a limited basis within their respective service areas.

> **Local Contact:**
>
> Citizens United for Rehabilitation of Errants
> P.O. Box 190504
> Birmingham, AL 35219
> P: 205.481.3781

Equal Justice Initiative

http://www.eji.org

The Equal Justice Initiative represents death-row prisoners in direct appeals to the appellate courts in Alabama and in post-conviction challenges in state and federal courts.

> **Local Contact:**
>
> Equal Justice Initiative
> 122 Commerce Street
> Montgomery, AL 36104
> P: 334.269.1803

Re-Entry Ministries, Inc.

Re-Entry Ministries, Inc. is a nonprofit organization that offers a variety of post-release services to previously incarcerated individuals in Alabama. Programs include support groups for people with criminal records and families of currently and previously incarcerated men and women, church services, job readiness and placement assistance, and Alcoholics Anonymous meeting.

> **Local Contact:**
>
> Re-Entry Ministries, Inc.
> P.O. Box 100461
> Birmingham, AL 35219
> P: 205.320.2101

Renascence, Inc.

Renascence, Inc. assists in the transition of non-violent, male ex-offenders from prison to steady employment and responsible living. Renascence, Inc. provides housing, appropriate monitoring, interpersonal and life skills programs, recovery support groups, as well as access to employment, health, and educational services and opportunities.

> **Local Contact:**
>
> Renascence, Inc.
> 215 Clayton Street
> Montgomery, AL 36104
> P: 334.832.1402

The Ordinary People Society

http://www.wearetops.org

The Ordinary People Society is a faith-based nonprofit organization that offers hope, without regard to race, sex, creed, color or social status, to individuals and their families who suffer the effects of drug addiction, incarceration, homelessness, unemployment, hunger and illness, through comprehensive faith-based programs that provide a continuum of unconditional acceptance and care.

Local Contact:

The Ordinary People Society
403 West Powell Street
Dothan, AL 36303
P: 334.671.2882

ALASKA

ACLU of Alaska
http://www.akclu.org

Local chapters of the American Civil Liberties Union provide advocacy and legal assistance on a limited basis to concerned individuals and groups impacted by the criminal justice system - emphasis on prison conditions and civil liberties. Contact directly for specific areas of service.

Local Contact:

ACLU of Alaska
1057 West Firewood Lane, Suite 111
Anchorage, AK 99503
P: 907.276.2258

Citizens United for Rehabilitation of Errants
http://www.alaskacure.org

CURE, Citizens United for Rehabilitation of Errants is a national nonprofit prison advocacy organization with state and special interest chapters throughout the United States. Local and special interest chapters provide assistance to ex-offenders on a limited basis within their respective service areas.

Local Contact:

Citizens United for Rehabilitation of Errants
P.O. Box 84
Willow, AK 99688
P: 907.841.1686

New Life Development, Inc.
http://www.newlifedevelopmentinc.com

New Life Development, Inc. is an agency committed to helping ex-offenders live lives of purpose and passion. It provides transitional supportive housing programs for men, women, and women with children who have had involvement with the criminal justice system; homeless prevention services; chemical dependency education; and employment services that include on-the-job training, resume preparation, interviewing skills, and collaboration with partnering employment specialists and job developers to assist program participants.

Local Contact:

New Life Development, Inc.
1231 Gambell Street, Suite 200
Anchorage, AK 99501
P: 907.868.8090

ARIZONA

ACLU of Arizona
http://www.acluaz.org

Local chapters of the American Civil Liberties Union provide advocacy and legal assistance on a limited basis to concerned individuals and groups impacted by the criminal justice system - emphasis on prison conditions and civil liberties. Contact directly for specific areas of service.

Local Contact:

ACLU of Arizona
P.O. Box 17148
Phoenix, AZ 85011
P: 602.650.1854

American Friends Service Committee
http://www.afsc.org

American Friends Service Committee serves as a resource for prisoners, ex-offenders, and their families to find information and resources to address their questions and needs, and a place to get involved in bringing their voices to the seats of power in Arizona

Local Contact:

American Friends Service Committee
103 North Park Avenue, Suite 111
Tucson, AZ 85719
P: 520.623.9141

Citizens United for Rehabilitation of Errants
http://www.middlegroundprisonreform.org

CURE, Citizens United for Rehabilitation of Errants is a national nonprofit prison advocacy organization with state and special interest chapters throughout the United States. Local and special interest chapters provide assistance to ex-offenders on a limited basis within their respective service areas.

Local Contact:

Citizens United for Rehabilitation of Errants
Affiliate
139 East Encanto Drive
Tempe, AZ 85281
P: 480.966.8116

JobPath, Inc.
http://www.jobpath.net

JobPath, Inc. is an employment training program run by a community-based non-profit that specializes in assisting individuals with criminal records. Referrals for program participation come from recruitment in the community, churches, schools, neighborhood centers and by "word of mouth". Soft skills, including resume preparation, interviewing techniques and job readiness are offered. Using labor market trends, individuals are directed to appropriate training programs at the local community college.

Local Contact:

JobPath, Inc.
924 North Aluernon Way
Tucson, AZ 85711
P: 520.324.0402

Middle Ground Prison Reform, Inc.

http://www.middlegroundprisonreform.org

Middle Ground Prison Reform, Inc. offers counseling, education, employment readiness training programs, and referrals to social service agencies upon request.

Local Contact:

Middle Ground Prison Reform, Inc.
139 East Encanto Drive
Tempe, AZ 85281
P: 480.966.8116

Tetra Services of Phoenix

http://www.thebeacongroup.org

Tetra Services of Phoenix is a private, non-profit rehabilitation agency that is part of the Tucson-based Beacon Group dedicated to providing vocational rehabilitation services to individuals with disabilities in the Phoenix area. Services include job development, job coaching, and training that promotes self-sufficiency and independence. Their Community Re-Integration Services program is designed for anyone with a disability who has a criminal background history that has proven to be a barrier to employment. Entry into the program is through a 2-day employment skills building workshop that is designed specifically for ex-offenders. Job development and placement services are provided after successful completion of the workshop.

Local Contact:

Tetra Services of Phoenix
ReIntegration Services
2222 North 24th Street
Phoenix, AZ 85008
P: 602.685.9703

Women Living Free

Women Living Free is an educational and support program that assists women with criminal records returning to the community by working in collaboration with community agencies. Services offered include job interview techniques, resume writing, and job search and placement services.

Local Contact:

Women Living Free
9220 West Coolidge Street
Phoenix, AZ 85037
P: 623.206.2823

ARKANSAS

ACLU of Arkansas

http://www.acluarkansas.org

Local chapters of the American Civil Liberties Union provide advocacy and legal assistance on a limited basis to concerned individuals and groups impacted by the criminal justice system - emphasis on prison conditions and civil liberties. Contact directly for specific areas of service.

Local Contact:

ACLU of Arkansas
904 West Second Street, Suite 1
Little Rock, AR 72201
P: 501.374.2660

Arkansas Enterprise Group

http://www.southerngoodfaithfund.org

Arkansas Enterprise Group is a nonprofit organization funded by the Southern Good Faith Fund. The Arkansas Enterprise Group offers job training and placement upon completion of their daily curriculum which includes extensive training in education, job readiness skills, personal development, and work experience.

Local Contact:

Arkansas Enterprise Group
2304 West 29th Avenue
Pine Bluff, AR 71603
P: 870.535.6233

Arkansas Voices for Children Left Behind

http://www.arkansasvoices.com

Arkansas Voices for Children Left Behind is an advocacy group providing assistance and advocacy to families and children affected by the criminal justice system.

Local Contact:

Arkansas Voices for Children Left Behind
2715 Marshfield Court
Wrightsville, AR 72206
P: 501.897.0809

Center for Youth and Family Prison Project

The Center for Youth and Family Prison Project serves individuals during and after incarceration, their children and the children's caretakers. Services offered include mental health and substance abuse counseling, family crisis intervention, literacy programs, housing assistance, and employment services.

Local Contact:

Center for Youth and Family Prison Project
5905 Forest Place, Suite 202
Little Rock, AR 72207
P: 501.660.6886

Citizens United for Rehabilitation of Errants
http://www.curenational.org

CURE, Citizens United for Rehabilitation of Errants is a national nonprofit prison advocacy organization with state and special interest chapters throughout the United States. Local and special interest chapters provide assistance to ex-offenders on a limited basis within their respective service areas.

Local Contact:

Citizens United for Rehabilitation of Errants
P.O. Box 56001
Little Rock, AR 72215
P: 501.223.2620

Ramoth, Inc.
www.ramothinc.com

Ramoth, Inc. is a staffing agency that helps former offenders coming out of prison to find gainful employment.

Local Contact:

Ramoth, Inc.
P.O. Box 4934
Little Rock, AR 72214
P: 501.615.1090

CALIFORNIA

Abram Friedman Occupational Center
The Abram Friedman Occupational Center is a vocational training program offering training in more then 23 different vocations. Program applicants must be 18 years of age or older and functionally literate.

Local Contact:

Abram Friedman Occupational Center
1646 South Olive Street
Los Angeles, CA 90015
P: 213.745.2013

Academic Achievement Center | Educational Opportunity Program
http://www.csus.edu/eop

A system wide program of California State University, the Educational Opportunity Program provides admission, counseling services, academic advising, financial assistance, and retention services to students with low-incomes. Participants must be residents of California.

Local Contact:

Academic Achievement Center | Educational Opportunity Program
6000 J Street, Lassen Hall 2205
Sacramento, CA 95819
P: 916.278.6183

ACLU of San Diego and Imperial Counties
http://www.aclusandiego.org

Local chapters of the American Civil Liberties Union provide advocacy and legal assistance on a limited basis to concerned individuals and groups impacted by the criminal justice system - emphasis on prison conditions and civil liberties. Contact directly for specific areas of service.

Local Contact:

ACLU of San Diego and Imperial Counties
P.O. Box 87131
San Diego, CA 92138
P: 619.232.2121

Allied Fellowship Services
Allied Fellowship Services provides employment services to previously incarcerated individuals including employment workshops, health education, and drug counseling. Allied Fellowship Services also operates a residential home for men that can accommodate 30 residents.

Local Contact:

Allied Fellowship Services
1524 29th Avenue
Oakland, CA 94601
P: 510.535.1236

Arriba Juntos
www.arribajuntos.org

Arriba Juntos, a community-based organization, has been operating for over 37 years, serving a diverse population in San Francisco. In addition to an employment program for individuals with criminal histories, it offers youth programming and ESL classes to over 2,000 clients each year. Arriba Juntos has direct placement for clients who have job skills. Training is available in computer technology, including Microsoft Office Suite, and certified nurse assistance with the ability to obtain California Licensing. In addition, they work in collaboration with the San Francisco Municipal Railway (MUNI) to offer a driver training course through which clients may obtain their Commercial Driving License and consideration for employment with MUNI as bus drivers. Additional training programs include life skills, job interview technique, resume writing, and daily survival skills components. Arriba Juntos has a subsidized on-the-job training program that is used as an incentive to employers to hire individuals with criminal records.

Local Contact:

Arriba Juntos
1850 Mission Street
San Francisco, CA 94103
P: 415.487.3240

Beil T'Shuvah | House of Return

http://www.beittshuvahia.org

Beil T'Shuvah operates House of Return, a residential reentry facility for Jewish men and woman who have been recently released from a term of incarceration. Services offered for House of Return residents include drug counseling, education, and employment services.

Local Contact:

Beil T'Shuvah | House of Return
8831 Venice Boulevard
Los Angeles, CA 90034
P: 310.204.5200

Berkeley Oakland Support Services

http://www.self-sufficiency.org

The Berkeley Oakland Support Services (BOSS) program offers pre-release and parole planning assistance to incarcerated and recently released individuals.

Local Contact:

Berkeley Oakland Support Services
P.O. Box 1996
Berkeley, CA 94701
P: 510.649.1930

Bethesda Family Ministries International

http://www.bethesdafamily.org

Bethesda Family Ministries International is a ministry that ministers to currently and previously incarcerated individuals and their families in the Sacramento area.

Local Contact:

Bethesda Family Ministries International
3882 Stillman Park Circle, Suite 19A
Sacramento, CA 95824
P: 877.492.0115

California Food Policy Advocates

http://www.cfpa.net

California Food Policy Advocates provide pre-release and parole planning services in the San Francisco Bay Area. Also provides information on welfare, social security, food stamps, and agencies that provide emergency aid.

Local Contact:

California Food Policy Advocates
116 New Montgomery Street, Suite 633
San Francisco, CA 94105
P: 415.777.4422

Casa Libre | Freedom House

http://www.casa-libre.org

The Freedom House of Casa Libre offers a transitional living program for homeless youth under the age of 18.

Local Contact:

Casa Libre | Freedom House
845 South Lake Street
Los Angeles, CA 90057
P: 213.637.5614

Center for Children of Incarcerated Parents

http://www.e-ccip.org

The Center for Children of Incarcerated Parents mission is the prevention of intergenerational crime and prevention. Its goals are met through the production of high quality documentation on the development of model services for children of criminal offenders and their families. The Center for Children of Incarcerated Parents provides research and resources information in four pivotal areas: education, family reunification, therapeutic services and information.

Local Contact:

Center for Children of Incarcerated Parents
P.O. Box 41-286
Eagle Rock, CA 90041
P: 626.449.2470

Centerforce | Division of Health Services

http://www.centerforce.org

In addition to coordinating HIV prevention programs in several California State Prisons, Centerforce provides case management, literacy, family support services, health education, parenting policy, research, training, consultation, and educational development services to currently and previously incarcerated individuals.

Local Contact:

Centerforce | Division of Health Services
2955 Kerner Boulevard, 2nd Floor
San Rafael, CA 94901
P: 415.458.9980

Central City Hospitality House

http://www.hospitalityhouse.org

Central City Hospitality House is a nonprofit organization that offers an emergency shelter, drop-in center, mail and message service, job referrals and placement, free clothing and counseling to those in need.

Local Contact:

Central City Hospitality House
290 Turk Street
San Francisco, CA 94102
P: 415.749.2119

Community Connection Resource Center

The Community Connection Resource Center offers comprehensive services for recently released offenders. These services include drug counseling, sober living houses, vocational training assistance, job development and placement, social services assistance, one-on-one counseling. It provides referrals for housing, as well as transitional housing for six months. It also has a youth program available. It is necessary to call for an interview/appointment. Community Connection Resource has centers located throughout the state where 3,000 to 3,500 recently released offenders are serviced annually.

> **Local Contact:**
>
> Community Connection Resource Center
> 4080 Centre Street, Suite 104
> San Diego, CA 92103
> P: 619.294.3900

Community Construction Training Center

The Community Construction Training Center works with low-income individuals and the formerly incarcerated to provide job development and vocational training services.

> **Local Contact:**
>
> Community Construction Training Center
> 250 West 85th Street
> Los Angeles, CA 90003
> P: 323.753.6211

Community Information Center

Community Information Center provides a public information and referral service to the community of Sacramento. Through their referral service, individuals may receive referrals to more than 1,400 community programs and services in the local area.

> **Local Contact:**
>
> Community Information Center
> P.O. Box 1834
> Sacramento, CA 95812
> P: 800.510.2020

CRASH | Community Resources and Self-Help
http://www.crashinc.org

This organization offers daily out-patient treatment services and long-term residential programs. Services provided include individual and group counseling, vocational and educational services, socialism skills, recovery planning, and release preparation.

> **Local Contact:**
>
> CRASH | Community Resources and Self-Help
> Information and Intake
> 927 24th Street
> San Diego, CA 92102
> P: 619.233.8054

Delancey Street Foundation

Delancey Street Foundation is based on the principle of self motivation. Through multiple locations around the United States, they provide a reintegration program that offers counseling and training in moving and trucking, para-transit services, a restaurant and catering services, a print and copy shop, retail and wholesale sales, advertising specialty sales, and an automotive service center.

> **Local Contact:**
>
> Delancey Street Foundation
> 400 North Vermont Avenue
> Los Angeles, CA 90004
> P: 323.644.4122

Delancey Street Foundation
http://www.eisenhowerfoundation.org

Delancey Street Foundation is based on the principle of self motivation. Success in the program is based on "pulling yourself up the bootstraps." Program capacity is 450 persons at the San Francisco facility. A two-year commitment is required of all participants; however participants may stay longer in the program if needed. Walk-ins are accepted for interviews; offenders may be interviewed while incarcerated. To be placed on a waiting list, individuals must write a letter requesting an interview. Recently released offenders must be able to transfer their parole/probation supervision to San Francisco. Residents learn not only academic and vocational skills, but also the interpersonal, social survival skills, along with the attitudes, values, sense of responsibility, and self-reliance necessary to live in the mainstream of society drug-free, successful and legitimately. Delancey Street owns and operates several commercial businesses staffed by its residents. Individuals receive training in different vocational, business skills as well as managerial skills in the different aspects of business, and skills in owning and operating a business.

> **Local Contact:**
>
> Delancey Street Foundation
> 600 Embarcadero
> San Francisco, CA 94107
> P: 415.957.9800

East Los Angeles Skills Center
http://www.elasc.adultinstruction.org

The East Los Angeles Skills Center offers a unique program for pre-release individuals, incorporating both academic study and employment training.

> **Local Contact:**
>
> East Los Angeles Skills Center
> 3921 Selig Place
> Los Angeles, CA 90031
> P: 323.227.0018

Friends Outside
http://www.friendsoutside.org

Friends Outside provides various social services to state and county prisoners and their families in California and Nevada.

> **Local Contact:**
>
> Friends Outside
> 620 North Aurora Street
> Stockton, CA 95202
> P: 209.955.0701

Haight Ashbury Free Medical Clinic

http://www.hafci.org

The Haight Ashbury Free Medical Clinic provides free healthcare to those in need, including substance abuse programs, HIV treatment, and care for the homeless.

> **Local Contact:**
>
> Haight Ashbury Free Medical Clinic
> 558 Clayton Street
> San Francisco, CA 94117
> P: 415.487.5632

JobTrain

http://www.jobtrainworks.org

JobTrain is a non-profit vocational training school that provides low or no-cost entry level training. As an American Job Center, it services walk-in clients in collaboration with other agencies. At its location are offices of the Department of Social Services, a local community college board and a local adult school. It also provides youth services in the form of after-school programs for drop-outs or potential drop-outs. Training classes run from six weeks to six months. Training is available in construction trades, hazardous material removal, culinary arts, clerical, certified nurse assistant, desktop publishing and A+ Certification (computer technician), including the Oracle system.

> **Local Contact:**
>
> JobTrain
> 1200 O'Brien Drive
> Menlo Park, CA 94025
> P: 650.330.6429

Loaves and Fishes of Sacramento

http://www.sacramentoloavesandfishes.org

Loaves and Fishes of Sacramento provides free noon meals, daytime hospitality shelter, health clinic, AIDS hospice, legal services, housing resources, emergency school for homeless children, and overnight shelter for women and children.

> **Local Contact:**
>
> Loaves and Fishes of Sacramento
> 1321 North C Street
> Sacramento, CA 95814
> P: 916.446.0874

Los Angeles Free Clinic

http://www.lafreeclinic.org

The Los Angeles Free Clinic offers medical, dental, legal, and counseling services to those in need.

> **Local Contact:**
>
> Los Angeles Free Clinic
> 8405 Beverly Boulevard
> Los Angeles, CA 90048
> P: 323.653.1990

Los Angeles Mission

The Los Angeles Mission provides emergency housing for 4 nights (every 10 days), two meals, free clothing, shower and shoes to those in need.

> **Local Contact:**
>
> Los Angeles Mission
> 303 East 5th Street
> Los Angeles, CA 90013
> P: 213.629.1227

Metropolitan Skills Center

The Metropolitan Skills Center offers vocational training, English as a second Language classes, high school diploma and GED classes to individuals in need.

> **Local Contact:**
>
> Metropolitan Skills Center
> 2801 West 6th Street
> Los Angeles, CA 90057
> P: 213.386.7269

Mexican American Opportunity Foundation

http://www.maof.org

The Mexican American Opportunity Foundation provides training and subsequent job placement, counseling, emergency shelter, legal assistance, food, clothing, and medical care, at a number of California locations.

> **Local Contact:**
>
> Mexican American Opportunity Foundation
> 401 North Garfield Avenue
> Montebello, CA 90640
> P: 323.890.9600

Mothers Reclaiming Our Children

Mothers Reclaiming Our Children is a nonprofit organization working to create a nationwide program to provide support to families, attend court hearings and trials, and work with attorneys. Provides advocacy work for prisoners and their families.

> **Local Contact:**
>
> Mothers Reclaiming Our Children
> 4167 Normandies Avenue
> Los Angeles, CA 90037
> P: Not Provided

Northern California Service League

http://www.norcalserviceleague.org

The Northern California Service League offers pre-release services on the county level. A 40-hour core program I life skills is given. The Northern California Service League also provides social services to assist families of offenders during their loved one's incarceration, substance abuse counseling, GED tutoring, parenting skills, and counseling on domestic violence issues. In addition, they provide a 30-

day shelter program and help with obtaining public assistance.

Local Contact:

Northern California Service League
Post Release Services
28 Boardman Place
San Francisco, CA 94103
P: 415.863.2323

Northern California Service League
http://www.norcalserviceleague.org

The Northern California Service League offers pre-release services on the county level. A 40-hour core program I life skills is given. The Northern California Service League also provides social services to assist families of offenders during their loved one's incarceration, substance abuse counseling, GED tutoring, parenting skills, and counseling on domestic violence issues. In addition, they provide a 30-day shelter program and help with obtaining public assistance.

Local Contact:

Northern California Service League
San Francisco Hall of Justice, Room 116
850 Bryant Street
San Francisco, CA 94103
P: 415.552.9250

Northern California Service League
http://www.norcalserviceleague.org

The Northern California Service League offers pre-release services on the county level. A 40-hour core program I life skills is given. The Northern California Service League also provides social services to assist families of offenders during their loved one's incarceration, substance abuse counseling, GED tutoring, parenting skills, and counseling on domestic violence issues. In addition, they provide a 30-day shelter program and help with obtaining public assistance.

Local Contact:

Northern California Service League
598 North First Street, Suite 202
San Jose, CA 95112
P: 408.297.9601

Playa Vista Job Opportunities and Business Service
http://www.pvjobs.org

Playa Vista is a construction development, non-profit organization located in Los Angeles. The company allots 10% of all jobs at the construction site to at-risk people, including individuals with criminal histories. Assessment of math and reading skills is done, as well as assistance with job resumes and job placement. Clients must be referred from an American Job Center or a community-based organization. From information received through the assessment and job skills, an employment profile is developed and entered into the

Playa Vista database. Both union and non-union contractors work on the development site. Clients are eligible to become members of the different trade unions where applicable.

Local Contact:

Playa Vista Job Opportunities and Business Service
4112 South Main Street
Los Angeles, CA 90037
P: 323.432.3955

Prison Law Office
http://www.prisonlaw.com

The Prison Law Office provides direct legal assistance for the range of problems encountered by California prisoners, excluding challenges to criminal convictions. The Prison Law Office dedicated most of its resources on conditions of confinement.

Local Contact:

Prison Law Office
General Delivery
San Quentin, CA 94964
P: 415.457.9144

Private Industry Council of San Francisco
http://www.oaklandpic.org

Private Industry Council of San Francisco is a non-profit organization that provides employment, training a research services to employers and job seekers in San Francisco. The Private Industry Council of San Francisco is a public and private collaboration for workforce development. This program contracts with over 60 community-based organizations to provide training and employment services. Private Industry Council of San Francisco also has a program that serves recently release offenders among other populations. It provides GED preparation, basic literacy assistance, job development, job counseling and on-the-job training.

Local Contact:

Private Industry Council of San Francisco
1650 Mission Street, Suite 300
San Francisco, CA 94103
P: 415.431.8700

Project Rebound
http://www.sfsu.edu/-rebound

Project Rebound is a special admissions program for formerly incarcerated individuals wanting to enter San Francisco State University. Project rebound offers special guidelines concerning admissions and academic tutoring to new students.

Local Contact:

Project Rebound
Associated Students, Inc.
1650 Holloway Avenue, T-138
San Francisco, CA 94132
P: 415.405.0954

Proteus, Inc.
http://www.proteusinc.org

Proteus, Inc. participates in a statewide Jobs Plus program to assist individuals in securing employment in Fresno, Tulare, Kings, and Kern Counties and provide employment counseling, job skills, and job placement services.

Local Contact:

Proteus, Inc.
1830 North Dinuba Boulevard
Visalia, CA 93291
P: 559.733.5423

Rubicon Programs, Inc.
http:///www.rubiconprograms.org

Rubicon Programs serves a diverse population that includes low income, disabled, non-custodial fathers and the homeless. Its programs offer a myriad of services ranging from basic pre-employment skills, job search assistance, life skills, on-the-job paid training and experience at Rubicon Program headquarters to job retention support services. Approximately 2,500 clients undergo the intake process each year.

Local Contact:

Rubicon Programs, Inc.
2500 Bissell Avenue
Richmond, CA 94804
P: 510.235.1516

San Francisco Works
http://www.sfworks.org

San Francisco Works offers life skills training, case management services, and job training and placement to those individuals in need of employment.

Local Contact:

San Francisco Works
235 Montgomery Street, 12th Floor
San Francisco, CA 94104
P: 415.217.5193

Second Chance | STRIVE
http://www.secondchanceprogram.org

Second Chance serves individuals with a criminal history, long-term unemployment and/or underemployment, or homeless people. Using the STRIVE model; Second Chance encompasses a three-week job readiness program. In addition to assistance with resume writing, clothing and interview techniques, soft skills such as eye contact and hand shaking are taught. Upon completion of the three-week program, graduates of the program attend a job fair. STRIVE program graduates have a 95% employment rate.

Local Contact:

Second Chance | STRIVE
6145 Imperial Avenue
San Diego, CA 92114
P: 619.234.8888

Seventh Step Foundation | East Bay Chapter
The Seventh Step Foundation is a nonprofit organization that facilitates a re-entry program called Freedom House. Freedom House provides parolees with housing, meals, clothing and employment services.

Local Contact:

Seventh Step Foundation | East Bay Chapter
475 Medford Avenue
Hayward, CA 94541
P: 510.278.8031

South Bay Regional Center
The South Bay Regional Center of Episcopal Community Services, offers a 3 and 6 month program for individuals referred by the court or probation for misdemeanor, non-violent, or low-violence drug charges. AIDS education classes are also required for those referred for convictions on possession of narcotics and prostitution.

Local Contact:

South Bay Regional Center
3954 Murphy Canyon Road, Suite D-202
San Diego, CA 92123
P: 888.505.8031

The Insight Prison Project
http://www.insightprisonproject.org

The Insight Prison Project provides communication training in nonviolence within correctional facilities; expanding to include post-release training as well.

Local Contact:

The Insight Prison Project
805 Fourth Street, Suite 3
San Rafael, CA 94901
P: 415.459.9800

The WorkPlace CA
http://www.theworkplaceca.com

The WorkPlace CA is a private-for-profit company that specializes in serving the parolee population. It has six offices in the San Fernando Valley, Orange County, and Los Angeles County. The agency has a contract with the California Department of Corrections. Job specialists assist clients with developing resumes, completing job applications, and acquiring interview skills prior to developing job opportunities. Job specialists enroll clients in vocational training and coordinate efforts with One-Stop Centers. Clients must call to schedule and appointment; walk-in appointments are not accepted.

Local Contact:

The WorkPlace CA
3407 West 6th Street, Suite 705
Los Angeles, CA 90020
P: 213.386.1994

Time for Change Foundation
http://www.timeforchangefoundation.org

Since 2002, Time for Change Foundation's main objective has been to help homeless women with children achieve self-sufficiency by using a strength-based approach to address their individual needs. Through its programs and services they provide their clients with every opportunity to develop the skills necessary to become independent, community leaders and positive role models for their children and others. Direct services offered include emergency shelter, transitional housing, comprehensive case management, nutrition, wellness and smoking cessation education, independent living skills, leadership development, family reunification, fitness education, money management and certified substance abuse counselor programs.

Local Contact:

Time for Change Foundation
P.O. Box 5753
San Bernardino, CA 92412
P: 909.886.2994

Welcome Home Ministries
http://www.welcomehomeint.org

Welcome Home Ministries is a nationally recognized program that provides holistic faith-based, peer-driven supportive services for women in transition form incarceration into the community including helping participants to regain citizenship, return to school, acquire jobs and, most importantly, be reunited with their children.

Local Contact:

Welcome Home Ministries
1701 Mission Avenue, Trailer A
Oceanside, CA 92054
P: 760.439.1136

Youth Opportunities for San Francisco

Youth Opportunity for San Francisco is a new program offering employment and development services to youths, ages 14-21 years, who are transitioning out of the California Juvenile Justice system's youth ranches and guidance centers.

Local Contact:

Youth Opportunities for San Francisco
1850 Mission Street
San Francisco, CA 94103
P: 415.487.3912

COLORADO

Center for Spirituality at Work
http://www.cfsaw.org

The Center for Spirituality at Work provides mentoring and life skills services to incarcerated and formerly incarcerated women.

Local Contact:

Center for Spirituality at Work
P.O. Box 102168
Denver, CO 80250
P: Not Provided

Citizens United for Rehabilitation of Errants
http://www.coloradocure.org

CURE, Citizens United for Rehabilitation of Errants is a national nonprofit prison advocacy organization with state and special interest chapters throughout the United States. Local and special interest chapters provide assistance to ex-offenders on a limited basis within their respective service areas.

Local Contact:

Citizens United for Rehabilitation of Errants
3470 South Poplar Street, #406
Denver, CO 80224
P: 303.758.3390

Colorado Criminal Justice Reform Coalition
http://www.ccjrc.org

The Colorado Criminal Justice Reform Coalition is a network of organizations, faith communities, and individuals working to reverse the trend of mass incarceration in Colorado. The Colorado Criminal Justice Reform Coalition also coordinates and provides a reentry guide for returning offenders and their families. Also provides specific referral information upon request.

Local Contact:

Colorado Criminal Justice Reform Coalition
1212 Mariposa Street, #6
Denver, CO 80204
P: 303.825.0122

Colorado Prison Association | Volunteers of America

The Colorado Prison Association, a service of Volunteers of America, provides referral information for emergency financial assistance to recently released individuals.

Local Contact:

Colorado Prison Association | Volunteers of America
2660 Larimer Street
Denver, CO 80205
P: 303.297.0408

The Empowerment Program
http://www.empowermentprogram.org

The Empowerment Program offers transportation, case management, housing, employment, health and education services to recently released female offenders who are returning to the Denver area.

Local Contact:

The Empowerment Program
1600 York Street
Denver, CO 80206
P: 303.320.1989

Turnabout, Inc.
http://www.turnaboutprogram.org

Turnabout, Inc. is a non-profit employment, career and education service agency that provides access to a fully-stocked computer lab, daily job leads, transportation assistance, subsidized work skills training, and job search assistance to former offenders in the Metro Denver area.

Local Contact:

Turnabout, Inc.
1630 East 14th Avenue
Denver, CO 80218
P: 303.813.0005

CONNECTICUT

Career Resources, Inc.
http://www.careerresources.org

Career Resources is a non-profit workforce development organization that has achieved recognition for preparing youth and adults in Southwestern Connecticut to gain employment and progress in their careers. It also publishes a local directory of workforce development organizations in the Bridgeport area that provide employment services to people with criminal records.

Local Contact:

Career Resources, Inc.
350 Fairfield Avenue
Bridgeport, CT 06604
P: 203.333.5129

Community Partners in Action
http://www.cpa-ct.org

Community Partners in Action is a nonprofit organization that provides a variety of post-release services to formerly incarcerated individuals within Connecticut.

Local Contact:

Community Partners in Action
110 Bartholomew Avenue, Suite 3010
Hartford, CT 06106
P: 860.566.2030

Community Renewal Team, Inc.
Community Renewal Team, Inc. offers a broad selection of services for individually recently released from a term of incarceration.

Local Contact:

Community Renewal Team, Inc.
555 Windsor Street
Hartford, CT 06120
P: 860.560.5471

Families in Crisis, Inc. | New Haven
Families in Crisis, Inc. provides counseling and support services to individual offenders and their families. They also provide crisis intervention, case management, court management, transportation, childcare and other support services to those in need.

Local Contact:

Families in Crisis, Inc. | New Haven
48 Howe Street
New Haven, CT 06511
P: 203.498.7790

Families in Crisis, Inc. | Waterbury
Families in Crisis, Inc. provides counseling and support services to individual offenders and their families. They also provide crisis intervention, case management, court management, transportation, childcare and other support services to those in need.

Local Contact:

Families in Crisis, Inc. | Waterbury
232 North Elm Street
Waterbury, CT 06702
P: 203.573.8656

Family Re-Entry of Connecticut
Family Re-Entry of Connecticut provides counseling and therapy services, parental education, information, referrals, mentoring and gifts for children across a variety of sites.

Local Contact:

Family Re-Entry of Connecticut
9 Mott Avenue, Suite 104
Norwalk, CT 06850
P: 203.838.0496

People Empowering People
People Empowering People, a service of the University of Connecticut, provides life skills and leadership training,

mentoring, and support to families and friends of offenders.

Local Contact:

People Empowering People
UConn Cooperative Extension Service
UConn Box 70
Haddam, CT 06438
P: Not Provided

Perception Programs, Inc.

Perception Programs serves substance abusers, offenders, and people living with HIV in Connecticut. Programs include residential work release and treatment programs for men and women, short term substance abuse treatment for male offenders in transition, outpatient substance abuse treatment, and residential treatment and education programs that act as alternatives to incarceration for adults and adolescents. Program fees may apply.

Local Contact:

Perception Programs, Inc.
54 North Street, Box 407
Willimantic, CT 06226
P: 860.450.7122

STRIVE | New Haven

http://www.strivenewhaven.com

The STRIVE program provides job training and job retention skills, and assists program participants in their job search.

Local Contact:

STRIVE | New Haven
904 Howard Avenue, 2nd Floor
New Haven, CT 06511
P: 203.777.1720

STRIVE | South Arsenal Neighborhood Development

http://www.sandcorporation.com

The STRIVE program provides job training and job retention skills, and assists program participants in their job search.

Local Contact:

STRIVE | South Arsenal Neighborhood Development
1500 Main Street
Hartford, CT 06120
P: 860.278.8460

DELAWARE

Citizens United for Rehabilitation of Errants

CURE, Citizens United for Rehabilitation of Errants is a national nonprofit prison advocacy organization with state and special interest chapters throughout the United States. Local and special interest chapters provide assistance to ex-offenders on a limited basis within their respective service areas.

Local Contact:

Citizens United for Rehabilitation of Errants
P.O. Box 542
New Castle, DE 19720
P: Not Provided

Delaware Center for Justice

http://www.dcjustice.org

The Delaware Center for Justice's Community Reentry Services program implements a Prison-to-Work initiative that provides case management support and other crucial services that foster successful reentry. Services include housing assistance, job search assistance, identification acquisition, educational/vocational placement, life skills and social support, as well as post-employment follow-up.

Local Contact:

Delaware Center for Justice
100 West 10th Street, Suite 905
Wilmington, DE 19801
P: Not Provided

The Way Home, Inc.

http://www.thewayhomeprogram.org

The Way Home, Inc. provides participants with critical supplies and assists them with securing safe and stable housing. Case management services include job search assistance, transportation to probation and other necessary appointments, support groups, mentoring and referrals to various social services. The Way Home, Inc. currently manages one transitional home for male ex-offenders in Millsboro, Delaware.

Local Contact:

The Way Home, Inc.
P.O. Box 1103
Georgetown, DE 19947
P: 302.856.9870

DISTRICT OF COLUMBIA

Access Housing, Inc.

http://www.accesshousinginc.org

Access Housing, Inc. is a nonprofit community-based organization committed and dedicated to the principle that everyone, regardless of income or socio-economic status, has a right to decent, safe and affordable housing. The mission is achieved through high-quality, supportive services and property management. Access Housing, Inc. offers many programs designed to afford all eligible individuals with access to housing resources in the Washington, DC area.

Local Contact:

Access Housing, Inc.
8280-840 Chesapeake Street, SE
Washington, DC 20032
P: 202.561.8387

Altar of ED Ministries

Alter of ED Ministries provides recently released offenders and their families with transitional services.

Local Contact:

Altar of ED Ministries
2800 Ontario Road, NW, Suite 506
Washington, DC 20009
P: 202.232.0866

Center for Neighborhood Enterprise

http://www.cneonline.org

The Center for Neighborhood Enterprise's mission is to empower neighborhood leaders to promote solutions that reduce crime and violence, restore families, revitalize low-income communities, and create economic enterprise.

Local Contact:

Center for Neighborhood Enterprise
1625 K Street, NW, Suite 1200
Washington, DC 20006
P: 202.518.6500

Citizens United for Rehabilitation of Errants

http://www.curenational.org

CURE, Citizens United for Rehabilitation of Errants is a national nonprofit prison advocacy organization with state and special interest chapters throughout the United States. Local and special interest chapters provide assistance to ex-offenders on a limited basis within their respective service areas.

Local Contact:

Citizens United for Rehabilitation of Errants
P.O. Box 84724
Washington, DC 20002
P: Not Provided

DC Central Kitchen

http://www.dccentralkitchen.org

Through culinary job training, meal distribution, and supporting local food systems, DC Central Kitchen provides life skills, employment skills, and personal development to its consumers by building long-term solutions to the interconnected problems of poverty, hunger, and homelessness.

Local Contact:

DC Central Kitchen
425 2nd Street, NW
Washington, DC 20001
P: 202.234.0707

GSA Building Futures

http://www.dclabor.org

The GSA Building Futures project seeks to prepare and provide qualified candidates for entry-level work and apprenticeships in the construction industry. The six-week pre-apprenticeship training program is complimented by a vigorous screening process, case management, and job placement support and follow-up.

Local Contact:

GSA Building Futures
888 16th Street, NW, Suite 520
Washington, DC 20006
P: 202.974.8157

Jobs Partnership of Greater Washington

The Jobs Partnership of Greater Washington is a nonprofit ministry that provides pre-employment training, mentoring, and support classes for the chronically unemployed and underemployed.

Local Contact:

Jobs Partnership of Greater Washington
633 Park Road, NW
Washington, DC 20010
P: 202.726.7400

Jubilee Housing

http://www.jubileehousing.org

Jubilee Housing is a faith-based nonprofit organization founded in 1973 to provide affordable housing and supportive services to economically disadvantaged residents of Washington, DC.

Local Contact:

Jubilee Housing
1640 Columbia Road, NW, 2nd Floor
Washington, DC 20009
P: 202.299.1240

Jubilee Jobs

http://www.jubileejobs.org

Jubilee Jobs provides job training, job placement, resume writing workshops, and career planning assistance to those most in need.

Local Contact:

Jubilee Jobs
2712 Ontario Road, NW
Washington, DC 20009
P: 202.667.8970

Marshall Heights Community Development Organization

The Marshall Heights Community Development Organization provides career assessment, pre-employment skills training, job placement and monitoring and both individual and peer group counseling to those in need.

Local Contact:

Marshall Heights Community Development Organization
3939 Benning Road, NE
Washington, DC 20019
P: 202.396.1200

Office of Returning Citizen Affairs
http://www.orca.dc.gov/oeoa/site/default.asp

The Office of Returning Citizen Affairs provides useful information for the empowerment of previously incarcerated persons in order to create a productive and supportive environment where persons may thrive, prosper and contribute to the social, political and economic development of self, family, and community.

Local Contact:

Office of Returning Citizen Affairs
2100 Martin Luther King Jr. Avenue, SE, Suite 301
Washington, DC 20020
P: 202.715.7670

Our Place, DC
http://www.ourplacedc.org

Our Place DC provides post-release services to the recently released. Services include a support center offering employment and housing resources, a safe and nurturing environment, and referrals to other support services necessary to obtain and retain employment.

Local Contact:

Our Place, DC
801 Pennsylvania Avenue, SE, Suite 460
Washington, DC 20003
P: 202.548.2400

Project Empowerment

Project Empowerment provides supportive services, adult basic education, job counseling, employability, life skills and limited vocational training, and job search assistance to District of Columbia residents living in areas with high unemployment and/or poverty levels. Project Empowerment seeks to help elevate widespread joblessness among hard-to-serve populations with multiple employment barriers and successfully move them into the workforce.

Local Contact:

Project Empowerment
4058 Minnesota Avenue, NE
Washington, DC 20099
P: 202.698.5599

SOME's Center for Employment Training
http://www.some.org

The Mission of SOME's (So Others Might Eat) Center for Employment Training is to empower people out of poverty and into living wage careers through marketable skills training, human development, basic education and job development.

Local Contact:

SOME's Center for Employment Training
2815 O Street, SE
Washington, DC 20020
P: 202.583.4655

STRIVE | DC
The STRIVE program provides job training and job retention skills, and assists program participants in their job search.

Local Contact:

STRIVE | DC
715 I Street, NE
Washington, DC 20002
P: 202.484.1264

FLORIDA

Citizens United for Rehabilitation of Errants
http://www.flcure.org

CURE, Citizens United for Rehabilitation of Errants is a national nonprofit prison advocacy organization with state and special interest chapters throughout the United States. Local and special interest chapters provide assistance to ex-offenders on a limited basis within their respective service areas.

Local Contact:

Citizens United for Rehabilitation of Errants
P.O. Box 40934
Jacksonville, FL 32203
P: 904.861.7659

Free Inside Ministries
http://www.freeinside.org

Free Inside Ministries collaborates with Christian and community-oriented organizations to evangelize, disciple, and assist in the complete recovery of individuals impacted by substance abuse and incarceration.

Local Contact:

Free Inside Ministries
11225 U.S. Highway 19 North
Clearwater, FL 33764
P: 727.467.4333

House of Hope
http://www.hohinfo.org

The House of Hope, a faith-based organization, offers shelter and job placement services to recently released people with criminal records. Substance abuse, anger management and spiritual counseling are also available. Participants apply through the correctional facility chaplains' department six months before their anticipated release date. Program capacity is five residents. House of Hope staff utilizes American Job Centers and program contacts to obtain employment for its participants. Residency time ranges from three to six months.

Local Contact:

House of Hope
P.O. Box 12113
Gainesville, FL 32604
P: 352.376.3964

Operation New Hope Community Development Corporation

Operation New Hope Community Development Corporation rebuilds low-income communities by offering training and employment to neighborhood residents, 60% of whom are people with criminal records. Operation New Hope works with area churches to provide building/construction skills as well as mentors for each participant. Participation in the program ranges from three months to one year, after which time graduates may be placed in private construction industry jobs. Operation New Hope evaluates applicants before release for incarceration and works closely with the Florida Department of Corrections.

Local Contact:

Operation New Hope Community Development Corporation
Community Development Corporation
1321 North Main Street
Jacksonville, FL 32206
P: 904.354.4673

Pinellas Ex-Offender Re-Entry Coalition

http://www.exoffender.org

The Pinellas Ex-Offender Re-Entry Coalition is a coalition of more than 40 churches, agencies and organizations working t promote services to individuals with criminal records and their families. The Pinellas Ex-Offender Re-Entry Coalition utilizes existing agencies within the public and private sectors to provide services such as temporary housing, clothing, food, resume writing expertise, job interview techniques and employment services.

Local Contact:

Pinellas Ex-Offender Re-Entry Coalition
P.O. Box 15936
St. Petersburg, FL 33733
P: 727.538.4191

Tampa Crossroads, Inc.

http://www.tampacrossroads.com

Tampa Crossroads offers comprehensive residential and non-residential services to non-violent offenders and individuals with criminal histories. Defendants may be court mandated to Crossroads as an alternative to incarceration. Services include residential housing, case management, individual, group and family therapy, employability skills training, substance abuse therapy, and educational and transitional housing assistance.

Local Contact:

Tampa Crossroads, Inc.
5120 North Nebraska Avenue
Tampa, FL 33603
P: 812.238.8557

Time for Freedom, Inc.

http://www.thefreedomhouse.org

Time for Freedom, Inc. offers transitional housing and support for recently released men and women with criminal histories. Time for Freedom mandates attendance at four programs, Alcoholics Anonymous, Narcotics Anonymous, cognitive thinking, bible study and life skills. Al residents are expected to work, with limited job referrals available. Future plans include expansion of cottages industries to generate operational funds as well as teaching vocational skills. Graphic arts and printing is operational at present.

Local Contact:

Time for Freedom, Inc.
2006 NE 8th Road
Ocala, FL 34470
P. 352.351.1280

Urban League of Broward County

The Urban League of Broward County offers an employment skill-building program to assist low-income hard-to-employ individuals, including those with criminal histories, overcome obstacles to obtaining and maintaining a job. Included in the program are training workshops, job coaching and assistance with childcare and transportation needs. Families can also receive assistance in becoming homeowners.

Local Contact:

Urban League of Broward County
11 NW 36th Avenue
Fort Lauderdale, FL 33311
P: 954.584.0777

GEORGIA

Citizens United for Rehabilitation of Errants

CURE, Citizens United for Rehabilitation of Errants is a national nonprofit prison advocacy organization with state and special interest chapters throughout the United States. Local and special interest chapters provide assistance to ex-offenders on a limited basis within their respective service areas.

Local Contact:

Citizens United for Rehabilitation of Errants
2173 Waterway Lane
Snellville, GA 30078
P: 678.252.8256

Crison Ministries with Women

Crison Ministries with Women, a nonprofit organization, provides transitional housing, counseling, job training and support services to those most in need.

Local Contact:

Crison Ministries with Women
465 Boulevard, SE, Suite 205
Atlanta, GA 30312
P: 404.622.4314

Epiphany Ministry

http://www.epiphanyministry.org

Epiphany Ministry provides small group and one-on-one follow up in juvenile prisons and promotes the involvement of volunteers in on-going juvenile prison ministry. They also offer juveniles an opportunity to change their lives and value systems through a three-day short course in Christianity.

Local Contact:

Epiphany Ministry
P.O. Box 192
Danville, GA 31017
P: 478.962.0794

Friends of Prison Families

The Friends of Prison Families program works in three areas. They help families maintain contact with their family members who are incarcerated by arranging monthly visits, phone calls, etc. The second are is an educational program. Inmates are enrolled in a program where workshops that address issues such as, drug abuse, psychological problems, social aspects of returning to family/society, are given. The third area is a pre-release planning program in which family members are enlisted to help develop job and housing packages for release planning.

Local Contact:

Friends of Prison Families
1020 DeKalb Avenue, NE, Suite 18
Atlanta, GA 30306
P: 404.523.7110

Georgia Justice Project

http://www.gjp.org

The Georgia Justice Project combines legal aid and social services. Staff attorneys and social workers develop long-term relationships with clients who must make a commitment to rehabilitation before being accepted as clients. The Georgia Justice Project remains committed to clients during incarceration via visits and advocacy work for release on parole supervision. Individuals with criminal records receive assistance transitioning from prison to society and may be employed in the landscaping business owned and operated by The Georgia Justice Project. Drug testing is a component of The Georgia Justice Project program and, if necessary, clients are assisted in obtaining drug treatment.

Local Contact:

Georgia Justice Project
438 Edgewood Avenue
Atlanta, GA 30312
P: 404.827.0027

Goodwill Industries

Goodwill Industries offers a program for people with disabilities who have barriers to employment, including those with criminal records. Goodwill offers vocational evaluation and a psychometric assessment, as well as vocational training. It also offers workshops in social adjustment, including independent living and utilizing community resources. The complete evaluation takes two or three weeks and costs $720.00, which must be paid by the participant, Goodwill suggests that interested people try to find a sponsor to pay the cost of the evaluation.

Local Contact:

Goodwill Industries
P.O. Box 15007
Savannah, GA 31416
P: 912.354.6611

Goodwill Industries of North Georgia

http://www.ging.org

Goodwill of North Georgia, a non-profit corporation, provides job training and employment services to people who are having trouble finding work, want to change careers, or start their own business. With the agency's support, Goodwill participants overcome employment hurdles causes by physical, emotional and developmental disabilities, limited job skills, poverty and other challenges.

Local Contact:

Goodwill Industries of North Georgia
235 Peachtree Street
North Tower, Suite 2300
Atlanta, GA 30303
P: 404.728.8600

National Association of Previous Prisoners, Inc.

The National Association of Previous Prisoners, Inc. functions as a clearinghouse of information and support group provider for individuals with criminal histories. The National Association of Previous Prisoners collaborates with community and faith-based organizations to make referrals and obtain services for individuals with criminal histories in the transition from incarceration to living in society.

Local Contact:

National Association of Previous Prisoners, Inc.
P.O. Box 82
Stone Mountain, GA 30086
P: Not Provided

Project Welcome Home

Project Welcome Home provides women and youth with assistance such as literacy motivation, agency referrals, housing assistance, and mentoring to those in need.

Local Contact:

Project Welcome Home
P.O. Box 61660
Savannah, GA 31420
P: 914.351.1661

The Offender Probationer Parolee State Training Employment Program

The Offender Probationer Parolee State Training Employment Program (TOPSTEP) is a collaborative effort between the Georgia Departments of Labor and Corrections and the Georgia Board of Pardons and Paroles. All agencies work together to help people with criminal records find employment in Georgia. The Department of Corrections provides academic and vocational instruction, on-the-job training, counseling and substance abuse treatment. Sixty days before an inmate is scheduled to be released, he or she attends a pre-release readiness program. All inmates attend this transitional program except for those inmates who are releasing from prison with no supervision and/or follow-up. Those who will be released to parole supervision or probation, regardless of the crime of conviction or time served, are enrolled in the transitional program. All three agencies are involved in this program, but each agency administers its own portion of the program.

Local Contact:

The Offender Probationer Parolee State Training Employment Program
Georgia Department of Labor
148 Andrew Young International Boulevard, NE
Suite 426
Atlanta, GA 30303
P: 404.232.3540

The Open Door Community

http://www.opendoorcommunity.org

The Open Door Community is a nonprofit organization that serves meals, provides shower and change of clothing services as well as access to a free medical clinic.

Local Contact:

The Open Door Community
910 Ponce de Leon Avenue, NE
Atlanta, GA 30306
P: 404.974.9652

HAWAII

Central Oahu Youth Services Association, Inc.

The Central Oahu Youth Services Association, Inc. provides services to youth ages 12-17 through an Emergency Shelter Program and Wilderness Oceans Experience Program.

Services include individual group skill-building, social recreation, tutoring, and parent support groups for both programs. Those served include runaways, abused, neglected, homeless, and youth at-risk and those already on probation for minor violations.

Local Contact:

Central Oahu Youth Services Association, Inc.
66-528 Haleiwa Road
Haleiwa, HI 96712
P: 808.637.9344

Community Assistance Center | John Howard Association

http://www.cachawaii.org

The Community Assistance Center, a project of the John Howard Association, provides counseling and related services for individuals involved in the criminal justice system, individuals with criminal records, delinquents, at-risk youth, and adjudicated youthful offenders and their families; half-way houses for female offenders; transitional residence for adjudicated youth; anger management programs for juvenile offenders; and public education on corrections, crime prevention and alternatives to incarceration.

Local Contact:

Community Assistance Center | John Howard Association
200 North Vineyard Boulevard, Suite 330
Honolulu, HI 96817
P: 808.537.2917

Goodwill Industries of Hawaii, Inc.

http://www.higoodwill.org

Goodwill Industries of Hawaii, Inc. provides occupational skills training, job placement, and support services to people with various barriers to employment.

Local Contact:

Goodwill Industries of Hawaii, Inc.
2610 Kilihau Street
Honolulu, HI 96819
P: 808.836.0313

Network Enterprises, Inc.

http://www.networkenterprises.org

Network Enterprises, Inc. is a nonprofit organization established in 1985 to provide vocational rehabilitation, job training and placement and support services to persons in Hawaii with physical, social, economic and/or intellectual and cognitive challenges. Network Enterprises, Inc's mission is to assist clients in building and enhancing self-esteem and self-confidence and to motivate them to obtain and maintain successful, competitive employment.

Local Contact:

Network Enterprises, Inc.
680 Iwilei Road, Suite 695
Honolulu, HI 96817
P: 808.521.7774

YWCA of Oahu

http://www.ywca.org

Y.W.C.A. of Oahu provides programs in the areas of social development, job readiness and skills training, aquatics, wellness, childcare, youth services, arts and ceramics, camp and conference activities, and transitional housing.

Local Contact:

YWCA of Oahu
1040 Richards Street
Honolulu, HI 96813
P: 808.538.7061

ILLINOIS

Association House of Chicago

http://www.associationhouse.org

Association House of Chicago's Community Center integrates the basic needs of its participants such as, employment, career-oriented adult education and sector training programs into a Career Center where all participants have access to the resources they need to stabilize their lives, improve their skills, create individualized career plans and find employment linked to training.

Local Contact:

Association House of Chicago
Community Center
116 North Kedzie Avenue
Chicago, IL 60651
P: 773.772.7170

Career Advancement Network, Inc.

http://www.canchicago.org

Career Advancement Network's "Career Passport" is a therapeutic model of job training for at-risk populations that allows instructors or counselors to combine proven business tools with work related counseling and psycho-education.

Local Contact:

Career Advancement Network, Inc.
20 East Jackson, Suite 1000
Chicago, IL 60604
P: 312.356.9159

Chicago Jobs Council

http://www.cjc.net

The Chicago Jobs Council is an organization of over 100 community-based organizations, civic groups, businesses and individuals. The Chicago Jobs Council works with its members to ensure access to employment and career advancement opportunities for people in poverty. The Chicago Jobs Council pursues its goals through advocacy, applied research, public education and capacity-building initiatives focused on influencing the development or reform of public policies and programs.

Local Contact:

Chicago Jobs Council
29 East Madison Street, Suite 1700
Chicago, IL 60602
P: 312.252.0460

Chicago Legal Advocates for Incarcerated Mothers

Chicago Legal Advocates for Incarcerated Mothers provides legal and educational services to strengthen the bond between imprisoned mothers and their children.

Local Contact:

Chicago Legal Advocates for Incarcerated Mothers
70 East Lake Street
Chicago, IL 60601
P: 312.675.0912

Citizens United for Rehabilitation of Errants

CURE, Citizens United for Rehabilitation of Errants is a national nonprofit prison advocacy organization with state and special interest chapters throughout the United States. Local and special interest chapters provide assistance to ex-offenders on a limited basis within their respective service areas.

Local Contact:

Citizens United for Rehabilitation of Errants
1911 South Clark, Unit D
Chicago, IL 60616
P: 312.600.7455

Community Assistance Programs

http://www.capsinc.org

Community Assistance Programs (CAPs) is a not-for-profit employment agency that provides employment training and job placement services. Services include: interviewing techniques to help with a job interview; transportation assistance and other allowable work-related expenses for those who qualify; paid work for on-the-job training; caseworker assistance; and methods to help participants get and keep a job.

Local Contact:

Community Assistance Programs
11715 South Halsted Street
Chicago, IL 60628
P: 773.468.1993

Heartland Alliance for Human Needs and Human Rights
http://www.heartlandalliance.org

The Transitional Jobs – Re-Entry program places participants in subsidized employment for 20-30 hours per week at the minimum wage over a 3 to 6 month period. The program combines skill building and meaningful work experience with supportive services to successfully transition participants with felony convictions into the workforce. The program includes job readiness training to assist in resume preparation, interviewing skills, job leads, and a core curriculum to review job expectations.

Local Contact:

Heartland Alliance for Human Needs and Human Rights
1525 East Hyde Park Boulevard
Chicago, IL 60615
P: 773.624.6148

Howard Area Community Center
http://www.howardarea.org

The Howard Area Community Center sponsors an education and employment program dedicated to helping adults acquire the academic, employability, and life skills they need to achieve meaningful employment and economic self-sufficiency. The program offers adult education classes and operates an Employment Resource Center that assists people with their employment needs.

Local Contact:

Howard Area Community Center
7648 North Paulina Street
Chicago, IL 60626
P: 773.262.6622

Inspiration Corporation
http://www.inspirationcorp.org

Inspiration Corporation's employment project offers career services, employment preparation training, tuition subsidies, employer outreach, and job placement and retention services throughout Chicago.

Local Contact:

Inspiration Corporation
4554 North Broadway, Suite 207
Chicago, IL 60640
P: 773.878.0981

North Lawndale Employment Network
http://www.nlen.org

The North Lawndale Employment Network Resource Center provides participants with tools and information that allow them to conduct a comprehensive employment search using Internet access, fax and photocopy machines, and voicemail boxes. The North Lawndale Employment Network also participates in the transitional jobs program.

Local Contact:

North Lawndale Employment Network Resource Center
3726 West Flournoy
Chicago, IL 60624
P: 773.638.1825

Phalanx Family Services
http://www.phalanxgrpservices.org

Phalanx helps people with criminal records developing marketable skills through on-the-job work experience, vocational training, and work and life readiness classes. They provide exclusive job development, placement, and retention services to help secure and maintain employment. They also encourage GED, ABE and/or Literacy Education as important keys to employability and success.

Local Contact:

Phalanx Family Services
4628 West Washington
Chicago, IL 60644
P: 773.261.5100

Prison Action Committee | Community Re-Entry Project
http://www.members.tripod.com/thefreedomtrain

Prison Action Committee/Community Re-Entry Program is dedicated to assisting returned offenders in making successful transitions back into family and community life. The Community Re-Entry Program will create training and job opportunities for returning offenders, based upon their knowledge and skills. The program structure of the Community Re-Entry Program consists of four components: Mental health Development; GED/Vocational Training; Job Creation/Business Ventures; and Low-Income Housing Development.

Local Contact:

Prison Action Committee | Community Re-Entry Project
661 East 79th Street
Chicago, IL 60619
P: 773.874.7390

Rita's Ministry
http://www.ritasministry.org

Rita's Ministry is a nonprofit organization dedicated to restoring offenders to society by providing transitional assistance to individuals and their families.

Local Contact:

Rita's Ministry
P.O. Box 248
Aurora, IL 60507
P: 630.966.0252

Safer Foundation
http://www.saferfoundation.org

The Safer Foundation is a non-profit community-based organization that works with incarcerated offenders, parolees and individuals with criminal histories to ensure their successful rehabilitation and return to the community. The Safer Foundation offers peer-centered teaching that focuses on education, job training, social skills, and job placement support. It also offers specialized case management and post placement support for a full year following job placement.

Local Contact:

Safer Foundation
Educational Services
609 West Adams
Chicago, IL 60661
P: 312.575.3271

STRIVE Chicago Employment Services, Inc. – North

STRIVE provides the following programs: 1) Job Readiness Training Program, a free four-week training that prepares individuals to enter the workforce and build stable work histories; 2) Job Training and Economic Development Health Care Industry, in which participants receive paid on-the-job training, certificate of completion, state certification and employee benefits (this program is not available to people with felony convictions and current drug use); 3) Fathers at Work Initiative, designed to assist non-custodial fathers with placement assistance, post-placement services, support services, and career advancement services; 4) Food Placement, a free four-week training program with Eurest Dining Services located at Roosevelt University, during which clients receive experience in Food Service, and receive a certificate of completion for each component successfully completed; 5) Hospitality Academy, a free high quality employment training to career oriented individuals who are seeking employment within the hospitality industry; 6) Women Focus Groups; and 7) a Walgreen's Training Program, a partnership between STRIVE and Walgreen's drug stores to provide on-site customer service/retail training.

Local Contact:

STRIVE Chicago Employment Services, Inc. – North
1927 West Howard Street
Chicago, IL 60626
P: 312.465.5900

STRIVE Chicago Employment Services, Inc. – South

STRIVE provides the following programs: 1) Job Readiness Training Program, a free four-week training that prepares individuals to enter the workforce and build stable work histories; 2) Job Training and Economic Development Health Care Industry, in which participants receive paid on-the-job training, certificate of completion, state certification and employee benefits (this program is not available to people with felony convictions and current drug use); 3) Fathers at Work Initiative, designed to assist non-custodial fathers

with placement assistance, post-placement services, support services, and career advancement services; 4) Food Placement, a free four-week training program with Eurest Dining Services located at Roosevelt University, during which clients receive experience in Food Service, and receive a certificate of completion for each component successfully completed; 5) Hospitality Academy, a free high quality employment training to career oriented individuals who are seeking employment within the hospitality industry; 6) Women Focus Groups; and 7) a Walgreen's Training Program, a partnership between STRIVE and Walgreen's drug stores to provide on-site customer service/retail training.

Local Contact:

STRIVE Chicago Employment Services, Inc. – South
4910 South King Drive
Chicago, IL 60615
P: 312.624.9700

STRIVE Chicago Employment Services, Inc. – West

STRIVE provides the following programs: 1) Job Readiness Training Program, a free four-week training that prepares individuals to enter the workforce and build stable work histories; 2) Job Training and Economic Development Health Care Industry, in which participants receive paid on-the-job training, certificate of completion, state certification and employee benefits (this program is not available to people with felony convictions and current drug use); 3) Fathers at Work Initiative, designed to assist non-custodial fathers with placement assistance, post-placement services, support services, and career advancement services; 4) Food Placement, a free four-week training program with Eurest Dining Services located at Roosevelt University, during which clients receive experience in Food Service, and receive a certificate of completion for each component successfully completed; 5) Hospitality Academy, a free high quality employment training to career oriented individuals who are seeking employment within the hospitality industry; 6) Women Focus Groups; and 7) a Walgreen's Training Program, a partnership between STRIVE and Walgreen's drug stores to provide on-site customer service/retail training.

Local Contact:

STRIVE Chicago Employment Services, Inc. – West
1116 North Kedzie Avenue
Chicago, IL 60651
P: 312.645.7300

St. Leonard's Ministries
http://www.slministries.org

St. Leonard's Ministries developed the Michael Barlow Center to provide education, training, and job placement services for formerly incarcerated men and women.

Local Contact:

St. Leonard's Ministries
Michael Barlow Center
2120 West Warren Boulevard
Chicago, IL 60612
P: 312.738.1414

The Cara Program

http://www.thecaraprogram.org

The Cara Program has evolved as not only a best-in-class job training and placement provider for individuals affected by homelessness and poverty, but also a vehicle for true life transformation.

Local Contact:

The Cara Program
237 South Desplaines
Chicago, IL 60661
P: 312.798.3300

Westside Health Authority

Westside Health Authority's Community Reentry and Employment Services Program helps the formerly incarcerated residents of Chicago successfully reintegrate back into their community by offering a family-like environment that provides assistance with the supportive service, training and employment. Services include job placement, readiness training, and voicemail boxes.

Local Contact:

Westside Health Authority
5814-16 West Division Street
Chicago, IL 60651
P: 773.786.0226

Women's Self-Employment Project

http://www.wsep.net

The Women's Self-Employment Project provides entrepreneurial training to low-income women on how to start their own business.

Local Contact:

Women's Self-Employment Project
South Lasalle Street, Suite 1850
Chicago, IL 60603
P: 312.606.8255

INDIANA

Blue Jacket, Inc.

http://www.bluejacketinc.org

Blue Jacket, Inc. was launched in 2005 to: 1) fill the gap between the pre-employment training provided by Allen County Community Corrections and actual employment; 2) provide services to people with criminal records not active in the adult justice system; and 3) provide real transitional job opportunities. It provides vocational training and employment placement services and works to meet other reentry needs of formerly incarcerated individuals.

Local Contact:

Blue Jacket, Inc.
3702 South Clinton Street
Fort Wayne, IN 46806
P: 260.744.1900

Citizens United for Rehabilitation of Errants

http://www.incure.org

CURE, Citizens United for Rehabilitation of Errants is a national nonprofit prison advocacy organization with state and special interest chapters throughout the United States. Local and special interest chapters provide assistance to ex-offenders on a limited basis within their respective service areas.

Local Contact:

Citizens United for Rehabilitation of Errants
P.O. Box 61
Camby, IN 46113
P: 317.831.0765

Community Action Program | Public Action in Correctional Effort

The Community Action Program is a collaborative effort of Public Action in Correctional Effort and Offender Aid Restoration. The Community Action Program works within neighborhoods to identify resources for individuals with criminal records. Their goal is to coordinate efforts and maximize resources for community and faith-based organizations, as well as to identify businesses that are willing to employ individuals with criminal records. In addition to direct job placement, the Community Action Program assists clients in obtaining clothing, enrolling in training programs, obtaining housing and securing transportation.

Local Contact:

Community Action Program | Public Action in Correctional Effort
Offender Aid Restoration
3214 Hovey Street
Indianapolis, IN 46218
P: 317.283.5979

Companions on the Journey

http://www.in.gov/idoc/

Companions on the Journey are an interfaith network providing practical, spiritual and emotional support to individuals returning to St. Joseph County, Indiana from incarceration. Volunteer faith teams are matched with a prisoner from four to six months before release to develop an action plan for release. Volunteers are required to make a one or two year commitments to assist recently released prisoners reenter society.

Local Contact:

Companions on the Journey
Central United Methodist Church
1920 South Michigan Street
South Bend, IN 46613
P: 574.289.9130

Dismas House of Michiana

http://www.dismas.org

Dismas House of Michiana provides transitional housing and support services to recently release men and women. Services provided include room and board, transportation, job referrals, life skills, counseling and drug/alcohol counseling referrals. All residents pay program fees and are expected to gain employment within two weeks of arrival at Dismas House.

Local Contact:

Dismas House of Michiana
P.O. Box 4571
South Bend, IN 46634
P: 574.233.8522

Next Step Programs | The Adult Center for Education

http://www.doe.in.gov/adulted/welcome.html

Next Step Programs is a division of the Fletcher Place Ministry. The first program, Survival Skills, is a ten-week series of seminars that teach basic day-to-day life skills. Upon graduation from Survival Skills, computer training, writing workshops and job placement assistance are available. Each series of seminars can accommodate a total of 15 participants.

Local Contact:

Next Step Programs | The Adult Center for Education
Fletcher Place Ministry
1831 East Prospect Avenue
Indianapolis, IN 46203
P: 317.916.1427

Offender Aid and Restoration of Indianapolis

Offender Aid and Restoration assists those individuals who have been recently released from a term of incarceration by providing substance abuse therapy information and referral to needed services and placement in job training programs.

Local Contact:

Offender Aid and Restoration of Indianapolis
1426 West 29th Street, Suite 101
Indianapolis, IN 46208
P: 317.612.6804

Prison Ministries of Indiana

Prison Ministries of Indiana provides assistance to recently released inmates in the form of information and referral to needed services, placement in job training programs, as well as providing assistance in obtaining housing, food and clothing.

Local Contact:

Prison Ministries of Indiana
1205 East New York Street
Indianapolis, IN 46202
P: 317.964.1622

Public Action in Correctional Effort

Public Action in Correctional Effort serves as counselors to offenders seeking assistance with employment, housing, food, clothing, and personal problems. Job search and retention services are taught and referrals are maintained for client use.

Local Contact:

Public Action in Correctional Effort
1426 West 29th Street, Suite 204
Indianapolis, IN 46208
P: 317.612.6800

Public Advocates in Community Re-Entry

http://www.paceindy.org

The Community Action Program is a collaborative effort of Public Action in Correctional Efforts and Offender Aid Restoration. The Community Action Program works within neighborhoods to identify resources for individuals with criminal records. Their goal is to coordinate efforts and maximize resources for community and faith-based organizations, as well as to identify businesses that are willing to employ individuals with criminal records. In addition, to direct job placement, the Community Action Program assists clients in obtaining clothing, enrolling in training programs, obtaining housing and securing transportation.

Local Contact:

Public Advocates in Community Re-Entry
2855 North Keystone Avenue, Suite 110
Indianapolis, IN 46218
P: 317.612.6800

Salvation Army Adult Rehabilitation Center

The Salvation Army Adult Rehabilitation Center provides counseling and work therapy as part of a residential rehabilitation program for offenders, alcoholics, and drug abusers. Services are provided to adult males at least 21 years and older.

Local Contact:

Salvation Army Adult Rehabilitation Center
711 Washington Street
Indianapolis, IN 46202
P: 317.638.6585

IOWA

Citizens United for Rehabilitation of Errants

CURE, Citizens United for Rehabilitation of Errants is a national nonprofit prison advocacy organization with state and special interest chapters throughout the United States. Local and special interest chapters provide assistance to ex-offenders on a limited basis within their respective service areas.

Local Contact:

Citizens United for Rehabilitation of Errants
P.O. Box 41005
Des Moines, IA 50311
P: 515.277.6296

Microenterprise Training for Women in Corrections

http://www.ised.org/economicdevelopment.asp

Microenterprise Training for Women in Corrections, part of the Institute for Social and Economic Development, provides entrepreneurial training to women in prison. The program focuses on helping women utilize their talents and skills upon release from incarceration in starting small businesses, obtain quality jobs and build financial assets.

Local Contact:

Microenterprise Training for Women in Corrections
Institute for Social and Economic Development
910 23rd Avenue
Coralville, IA 52241
P: 319.338.2331

Safer Foundation – Iowa

http://www.saferfoundation.org

The safer Foundation whose headquarters are in Chicago, Illinois operates a program in Davenport, Iowa. An individualized approach to each client is utilized assisting with employment services, substance abuse treatment when necessary, education, case management and/or other support services, as needed. Contacts outside the organization are made when necessary. A job counselor is assigned to each client for at least one year post-job placement.

Local Contact:

Safer Foundation – Iowa
Davenport Iowa Adult Program
131 West 3rd Street
Davenport, IA 52801
P: 563.322.7974

KANSAS

Citizens United for Rehabilitation of Errants

CURE, Citizens United for Rehabilitation of Errants is a national nonprofit prison advocacy organization with state and special interest chapters throughout the United States. Local and special interest chapters provide assistance to ex-offenders on a limited basis within their respective service areas.

Local Contact:

Citizens United for Rehabilitation of Errants
2137 North Battin
Wichita, KS 67208
P: 316.618.8652

Forever Crowned Outreach Ministries

http://www.forevercrowned.org

Forever Crowned Outreach Ministries, a faith-based organization, offers job search assistance, job mediation, job readiness training, resume assistance and basic computer skills, as well as mentoring, counseling and life skills training to individuals with criminal histories.

Local Contact:

Forever Crowned Outreach Ministries
2046 East 9th Street, North
Wichita, KS 67214
P: 316.267.1244

Legal Services of Kansas

http://www.kansaslegalservices.org

Kansas Legal Services, in addition to legal assistance, provides employment and life-skills training to low-income Kansans to help them acquire and maintain employment in seven locations across Kansas. The following programs are offered: 1) individual case management; 2) job success, life skills and job readiness programs are offered; 3) WORKs (to help farmers and ranchers transition to non-farm employment); 4) custom computer training (individual or group classes); and 5) office training and assessment program.

Local Contact:

Legal Services of Kansas
712 South Kansas Avenue, Suite 200
Topeka, KS 66603
P: 785.233.7252

KENTUCKY

Citizens United for Rehabilitation of Errants

CURE, Citizens United for Rehabilitation of Errants is a national nonprofit prison advocacy organization with state and special interest chapters throughout the United States. Local and special interest chapters provide assistance to ex-offenders on a limited basis within their respective service areas.

Local Contact:

Citizens United for Rehabilitation of Errants
P.O. Box 221481
Louisville, KY 40252
P: Not Provided

LOUISIANA

Catholic Charities of the Archdiocese of New Orleans

Catholic Charities Archdiocese of New Orleans assists clients in developing employment skills to seek and retain jobs.

Local Contact:

Catholic Charities of the Archdiocese of New Orleans
Goodwill Industries Rehabilitation Center, Inc.
800 West 70th Street, Suite 1200
Shreveport, LA 71106
P: 318.869.2575

Citizens United for Rehabilitation of Errants

http://www.curelouisiana.org

CURE, Citizens United for Rehabilitation of Errants is a national nonprofit prison advocacy organization with state and special interest chapters throughout the United States. Local and special interest chapters provide assistance to ex-offenders on a limited basis within their respective service areas.

Local Contact:

Citizens United for Rehabilitation of Errants
P.O. Box 181
Baton Rouge, LA 70821
P: 225.270.5245

Communities Industrialization Center, Inc.

Communities Industrialization Center provides job training and placement to the unemployed and under-employed into unsubsidized job sin the New Orleans area.

Local Contact:

Communities Industrialization Center, Inc.
2701 Piety Street
New Orleans, LA 70126
P: 504.949.4421

Enhanced Job Skills Program

The Enhanced Job Skills Program, operated by the Lafayette Parish Correctional Center, assists individuals who are incarcerated for drug-related charges in preparing for employment upon release. The four-phase program begins with assessment and career selection, progressing to computer-based skills program that teaches basic skills for over 200 types of career categories. Phase III involves job search and interview techniques. Phase IV begins two months prior to release with assistance in job placement. The agency maintains contact with participants for six months following release.

Local Contact:

Enhanced Job Skills Program
Lafayette Parish Correctional Center
P.O. Box 3508
Lafayette, LA 70502
P: 337.236.5494

Goodwill Industries – Lafayette

http://www.lagoodwill.com

Goodwill Industries provides training, skill development and work opportunities for people with disabilities and other barriers to employment.

Local Contact:

Goodwill Industries – Lafayette
Goodwill Industries Acadiana, Inc.
5720 Cameron Street
Lafayette, LA 70596
P: 337.261.5811

Goodwill Industries – New Orleans

http://www.lagoodwill.com

Goodwill Industries provides training, skill development and work opportunities for people with disabilities and other barriers to employment.

Local Contact:

Goodwill Industries – New Orleans
Goodwill Industries of Southeastern Louisiana, Inc.
1000 South Jefferson Davis Parkway
New Orleans, LA 70185
P: 504.482.4173

Goodwill Industries – Shreveport

http://www.volunteermatch.org/orgs/org21350.html

Goodwill Industries provides training, skill development and work opportunities for people with disabilities and other barriers to employment.

Local Contact:

Goodwill Industries – Shreveport
Goodwill Industries Rehabilitation Center, Inc.
800 West 70th Street, Suite 1200
Shreveport, LA 71106
P: 318.869.2575

Project Return

Project Return offers the following services to individuals with criminal records: case management, including referrals to appropriate agencies as needed; addiction education and relapse prevention; remediation through college preparation education courses; basic computer skills; life skills, including family and parental relationship and post-prison issues; and employment planning. Employment planning involves resume preparation and job search assistance.

Local Contact:

Project Return
2703 General de Gaulle Drive
New Orleans, LA 70114
P: 504.988.1000

Total Community Action, Inc.
http://www.tca-nola.org

Total Community Action is a community-based organization that offers a variety of services including childhood development, job counseling and guidance, transportation for the elderly and disabled, youth work experience, and other services that address the needs of the disadvantaged. There are currently seven centers in operation.

Local Contact:

Total Community Action, Inc.
1420 South Jefferson Davis Parkway
New Orleans, LA 70125
P: 504.827.2200

MAINE

Citizens United for Rehabilitation of Errants

CURE, Citizens United for Rehabilitation of Errants is a national nonprofit prison advocacy organization with state and special interest chapters throughout the United States. Local and special interest chapters provide assistance to ex-offenders on a limited basis within their respective service areas.

Local Contact:

Citizens United for Rehabilitation of Errants
23 Washington Street
Sanford, ME 04073
P: Not Provided

Cumberland County Jail Pre-Release Program
http://www.cumberlandso.org

Cumberland County Jail has a work release/pre-release program for those individuals serving probation violations or time for felony convictions in the county jail. The jail offers a food service/culinary arts program, as well as a GED program. To be eligible for work release, participants must have a GED, no history of disciplinary reports, minimum-security level classification, and be in the last third of their sentence. There is also a ten-week life skills and employability seminar class that all participants are enrolled in prior to their release on work release. Dealing with one's criminal history is also part of the seminar. Assistance is given in job placement.

Local Contact:

Cumberland County Jail Pre-Release Program
50 County Way
Portland, ME 04102
P: 207.774.5939

Set Free in Maine

Set Free in Maine is a 10-year-old faith-based organization. Employment and life skills training are offered to former offenders upon release. Set Free in Maine has a working woodshop that employs former prisoners. Income generated from the sale of furniture is the funding mechanism for the program. Referrals to the program are made by religious organizations that operate within the prison system. Individual mentoring begins three to six months prior to release. Inmates are matched with a mentor in the area where the inmate is going to return. Set Free in Maine tries to meet individual needs such as housing and offering anger management groups.

Local Contact:

Set Free in Maine
Rural Route 1, 674 Riverside Road
Augusta, ME 04330
P: 207.622.4709

MARYLAND

American Correctional Association
http://www.aca.org

The American Correctional Association is a national membership organization dedicated to the safe and secure operation of correctional facilities. The American Correctional Association is comprised primarily of law enforcement and correctional personal.

Local Contact:

American Correctional Association
4380 Forbes Boulevard
Lanham, MD 20706
P: 301.918.1800

Citizens United for Rehabilitation of Errants
http://www.marylandcure.webs.com

CURE, Citizens United for Rehabilitation of Errants is a national nonprofit prison advocacy organization with state and special interest chapters throughout the United States. Local and special interest chapters provide assistance to ex-offenders on a limited basis within their respective service areas.

Local Contact:

Citizens United for Rehabilitation of Errants
P.O. Box 23
Simpsonville, MD 21150
P: 206.202.4872

Job Opportunities Taskforce
http://www.jotf.org

Job Opportunities Taskforce is a non-profit organization that advocates on a state level for re-entry workforce policies specific to the Baltimore area. Job Opportunities Taskforce is a network of workforce development providers, human services organizations, advocacy groups, and funders in the Baltimore region. It does not provide direct services.

> **Local Contact:**
>
> Job Opportunities Taskforce
> 2 East Read Street, 6th Floor
> Baltimore, MD 21202
> P: 410.234.8046

National Women's Prison Project, Inc.
http://www.nwpp-inc.com

The National Woman's Prison Project is a re-entry program that begins at the pre-release level and continues through re-entry to the community. Services offered include support and motivational groups, assistance with job training and housing, a clothing closet for job apparel, and mentoring services. The National Women's Prison Project collaborates with other programs in the Baltimore area to offer wraparound services to meet individual needs as they arise.

> **Local Contact:**
>
> National Women's Prison Project, Inc.
> 1701 Madison Avenue, Suite 505
> Baltimore, MD 21217
> P: 410.233.3385

Supporting Ex-Offenders in Employment Training and Transitional Services
http://www.goodwillches.org

Supporting Ex-Offenders in Employment Training and Transitional Services is a program of Goodwill Industries of the Chesapeake, Inc. to serve formerly incarcerated individuals. One of two major components, seven weeks of job readiness training, takes place at the Metropolitan Transition Center located in Baltimore, and with the coordination of the prison's administration, social work staff and transition coordinators. Baltimore City Community College provides pre-GED and GED instructors. The second component takes place at Goodwill's Career Center located in Baltimore and involves final job preparation and placement. The community component serves men and women who are on parole supervision or probation regardless of previous program involvement. Individuals who did not participate in the first component are required to participate in five to seven weeks of employment preparation.

> **Local Contact:**
>
> Supporting Ex-Offenders in Employment Training and Transitional Services
> Goodwill Industries of the Chesapeake, Inc.
> 222 East Redwood Street
> Baltimore, MD 21202
> P: 410.837.1800

MASSACHUSETTS

Aid to Incarcerated Mothers
Aid to Incarcerated Mothers provides services to incarcerated mothers and their children, as well as women who have had trouble with the law in the past and are trying to improve their lives upon reentering the community.

> **Local Contact:**
>
> Aid to Incarcerated Mothers
> 434 Massachusetts Avenue, Suite 503
> Boston, MA 02118
> P: 617.536.0058

American Friends Service Committee | Criminal Justice Program
http://www.afsc.org

The American Friends Service Committee Criminal Justice Program provides individuals with referrals for available legal help and assistance to prisoner organizations and community organizations working on prison related issues.

> **Local Contact:**
>
> American Friends Service Committee | Criminal Justice Program
> 2161 Massachusetts Avenue
> Cambridge, MA 02140
> P: 617.661.6130

Citizens United for Rehabilitation of Errants
CURE, Citizens United for Rehabilitation of Errants is a national nonprofit prison advocacy organization with state and special interest chapters throughout the United States. Local and special interest chapters provide assistance to ex-offenders on a limited basis within their respective service areas.

> **Local Contact:**
>
> Citizens United for Rehabilitation of Errants
> 670 Washington Street
> Dorchester, MA 02124
> P: 617.697.4149

Community Resources for Justice
http://www.crjustice.org

Community Resources for Justice offers programs including education, counseling, assistance with employment and housing, and substance abuse treatment.

> **Local Contact:**
>
> Community Resources for Justice
> 355 Boylston Street
> Boston, MA 02116
> P: 617.482.0520

Dismas House

http://www.dismashouse.org

Dismas House is a supportive community providing transitional housing and other support services to people with criminal histories. Staff and community programs assist residents to develop and achieve employment, educational and housing goals. Employment is a priority goal for all residents with a criminal history. There is a $75.00 fee per week. For people with criminal histories who arrive from prison the fee is waived for two weeks. Failure to pay the required program fees constitutes grounds for dismissal from the house.

Local Contact:

Dismas House
P.O. Box 30125
Worcester, MA 01603
P: 508.799.9389

First Incorporated

First Incorporated is a nonprofit organization that provides services for men who have been released from incarceration and have substance abuse and/or mental health concerns. The program is geared towards behavior modification through counseling and building structured living situations.

Local Contact:

First Incorporated
167 Centre Street
Roxbury, MA 02119
P: 617.427.1588

First Incorporated

First Incorporated is a nonprofit organization that provides services for men who have been released from incarceration and have substance abuse and/or mental health concerns. The program is geared towards behavior modification through counseling and building structured living situations.

Local Contact:

First Incorporated
37 Intercale Street
Roxbury, MA 02119
P: 617.445.2291

IMPACT | The Friends of Shattuck Shelter

http://www.shattuckshelter.org

IMPACT Employment Services, a project of The Friends of the Shattuck Shelter, is Greater Boston's largest employment services for individuals and families facing homelessness, including individuals with criminal histories. IMPACT counselors work with clients both before and after they are released to provide individual employment counseling and job search planning, referrals and assistance to help find and enroll in educational and job-skills training programs and much more. Based in downtown Boston, IMPACT's professional staff of employment counselors, job developers and educational and training specialists speaks a variety of languages and represent diverse cultural and economic backgrounds.

Local Contact:

IMPACT | The Friends of Shattuck Shelter
105 Chauncy Street
Boston, MA 02111
P: 617.542.3388

MASS Community Resource Center | Boston

Community Resource Centers are state-funded multi-service centers for offenders and ex-offenders. Services include work readiness classes, sex offender referral and support, thinking for a change classes, reintegration counseling groups, transitional intervention, transitional housing, and housing research assistance.

Local Contact:

MASS Community Resource Center | Boston
110 Arlington Street
Boston, MA 02116
P: 617.423.0750

MASS Community Resource Center | Fall River

Community Resource Centers are state-funded multi-service centers for offenders and ex-offenders. Services include work readiness classes, sex offender referral and support, thinking for a change classes, reintegration counseling groups, transitional intervention, transitional housing, and housing research assistance.

Local Contact:

MASS Community Resource Center | Fall River
186 South Main Street
Fall River, MA 02721
P: 508.676.3729

MASS Community Resource Center | Lowell

Community Resource Centers are state-funded multi-service centers for offenders and ex-offenders. Services include work readiness classes, sex offender referral and support, thinking for a change classes, reintegration counseling groups, transitional intervention, transitional housing, and housing research assistance.

Local Contact:

MASS Community Resource Center | Lowell
45 Merrimack Street, Suite 500
Lowell, MA 01852
P: 978.458.4286

MASS Community Resource Center | Springfield

Community Resource Centers are state-funded multi-service centers for offenders and ex-offenders. Services include work readiness classes, sex offender referral and support, thinking for a change classes, reintegration counseling groups, transitional intervention, transitional housing, and housing research assistance.

Local Contact:

MASS Community Resource Center | Springfield
136 Williams Street
Springfield, MA 01105
P: 413.737.9544

MASS Community Resource Center | Worcester

Community Resource Centers are state-funded multi-service centers for offenders and ex-offenders. Services include work readiness classes, sex offender referral and support, thinking for a change classes, reintegration counseling groups, transitional intervention, transitional housing, and housing research assistance.

Local Contact:

MASS Community Resource Center | Worcester
324 Grove Street
Worcester, MA 01605
P: 508.831.0050

SPAN, Inc.

SPAN. Inc. is a reintegration counseling program for individuals with criminal histories who are being released from or are post-release from a state or county correctional facility. Assistance is offered in the areas of housing, employment and health. Job development and placement services are available on a limited basis, as well as employment skills such as resume writing and soft skills development.

Local Contact:

SPAN, Inc.
110 Arlington Street
Boston, MA 02116
P: 617.423.0750

Spectrum Health Systems

Spectrum Health Systems operates five major programs in behavioral health, correctional treatment services, adolescent services, women's services and prevention services.

Local Contact:

Spectrum Health Systems
10 Mechanic Street, Suite 302
Worcester, MA 01608
P: 508.792.5400

The Neil J. Houston House

The Neil J. Houston House is a residential pre-release substance abuse treatment program. This program offers incarcerated pregnant women an alternative to incarceration, pre and post-natal medical services and early intervention services to their infants.

Local Contact:

The Neil J. Houston House
9 Notre Dame Street
Roxbury, MA 02119
P: 617.445.3066

The Salvation Army Harbor Light Center

Harbor Lights Center, a service of Salvation Army, provides both short-term and longer residential substance abuse treatment programs for individuals in transition from prison to community. Programs include daily meals, one-on-one counseling, structured classes on behavior and life-decisions, referrals and assistance making community contacts.

Local Contact:

The Salvation Army Harbor Light Center
83 Brookline Street
Boston, MA 02118
P: 617.536.7469

TIP Health and Education Services

This program helps HIV positive offenders make the transition back into the community by providing advocacy, counseling, crisis intervention and transportation services. They also provide information and referrals in the areas of medical care, housing and benefits, etc. to those in need of additional assistance.

Local Contact:

TIP Health and Education Services
60 Merrimack Street
Haverhill, MA 01830
P: Not Provided

MICHIGAN

Citizens United for Rehabilitation of Errants

CURE, Citizens United for Rehabilitation of Errants is a national nonprofit prison advocacy organization with state and special interest chapters throughout the United States. Local and special interest chapters provide assistance to ex-offenders on a limited basis within their respective service areas.

Local Contact:

Citizens United for Rehabilitation of Errants
P.O. Box 2736
Kalamazoo, MI 49003
P: 269.383.0028

Goodwill Industries of Greater Detroit

http://www.goodwilldetroit.org

Goodwill Industries of Greater Detroit provides services to individuals who are serving probation or have been recently released from a county or state correctional facility for a non-violent offense. Services include job readiness training, paid transitional work experience, basic academic and remedial training to improve math or reading skills and job placement. Employment follow-up/retention ser vices are also provided.

Local Contact:

Goodwill Industries of Greater Detroit
Employment Development Services
3111 Grand River Avenue
Detroit, MI 48208
P: 313.964.3900

MCM Ministries

http://www.newcreationsmin.net

MCM Ministries is dedicated to the spiritual needs of incarcerated men and women and at risk youth.

Local Contact:

MCM Ministries
1260 28th, SE
Grand Rapids, MI 49508
P: 616.475.5787

Project Transition | Matrix Human Services

Project Transition is part of Matrix Human Services, a multi-service social service agency. It is a residential treatment program that is mandated by the court or parole. An individual with a criminal history mat stay from 90 to 180 days. There is a mandatory 12-week outpatient component as well. Participants receive various forms of counseling ranging from substance abuse, mental illness, domestic violence, and anger management. Workshops are presented on resume writing, dressing for work and how to find and retain employment. There is no job placement available.

Local Contact:

Project Transition | Matrix Human Services
16260 Dexter
Detroit, MI 48221
P: 313.862.3400

Transition of Prisoners, Inc.

http://www.topinc.net

Transition of Prisoners, Inc. is a program that accepts people with criminal histories who have been released from incarceration 30 days or less. Transition of Prisoners, Inc. utilizes the services of area churches, community agencies and social service agencies to offer assistance to its clients. After attending four weekly group sessions a client is matched with an area church as a mentor. A case manager develops a transition plan with the client to meet their individual needs. The assigned mentor assists the client in completing the transition plan. Referrals for basic s, food, clothing, shelter, and help to arrange for job training and/or job development is provided. Workshops on developing cognitive skills and conflict resolution are conducted in-house.

Local Contact:

Transition of Prisoners, Inc.
P.O. Box 02938
Detroit, MI 48244
P: 313.875.3883

Volunteers in Prevention, Probation, and Prison, Inc.

Volunteers in Prevention, Probation, and Prison, Inc., helps with effective transition back into the community for ex-offenders through a series of programs and services.

Local Contact:

Volunteers in Prevention, Probation, and Prison, Inc.
163 Madison Avenue
Detroit, MI 48226
P: 313.964.1110

Women Arise – PROVE Project

PROVE (Post-Release Opportunities for Vocational Education) was created by a community-based program with funds from a federal lawsuit brought by women prisoners in Michigan. The participants, formerly incarcerated women, receive educational/vocational assessment, assistance in meeting educational and/or vocational goals and obtaining employment. PROVE provides monthly peer meetings, counseling, parenting classes, tutoring, grade monitoring, educational advice and application assistance.

Local Contact:

Women Arise – PROVE Project
13100 Averhill
Detroit, MI 48215
P: 313.331.1800

MINNESOTA

AMICUS, Inc.

http://www.amicus.org

AMICUS, Inc. is a Minnesota non-profit organization that offers a variety of programs designed to assist recently released individuals with criminal records in building new lives, both before and after release. Its Reconnect project provides re-entry services that help inmates prepare for release and gives recently released individuals much needed resources in their search for jobs, housing, clothing, family services, and more. Clients must cal for an appointment.

Local Contact:

AMICUS, Inc.
15 South 5th Street, Suite 1100
Minneapolis, MN 55402
P: 612.348.8570

Families & Offender United Project

http://www.crimeandjustice.org

Families & Offender United Project is a demonstration project of the Council of Crime and Justice. Phase one is a Reunification Class which is completed within three months of a participant's release on parole supervision. Phase two is post-release paid job training and support service. Phase two lasts for up to three months and consists mainly of janitorial/maintenance work. Workshops offered include life skills training, cognitive skills, job readiness, basic computer training, educational assessment and guidance, and community parenting classes. Community mentoring is available as is help in obtaining housing. Residents are referred to outside sources fro substance abuse counseling. Enrollment is limited at this time to men without a history of sex abuse convictions.

Local Contact:

Families & Offender United Project
Council of Crime and Justice
822 South 3rd Street, Suite 100
Minneapolis, MN 55415
P: 612.348.7874

Grace Prison Ministry

Grace Prison Ministry provides mentors to inmates and helps recently released individuals with criminal histories establish aftercare and support by re-establishing them in their communities with jobs, housing and other needs.

Local Contact:

Grace Prison Ministry
AMICUS, Inc.
15 South 5th Street, Suite 1100
Minneapolis, MN 55402
P: 612.348.8570

Minneapolis American Indian Center

http://www.maicnet.org

Minneapolis American Indian Center serves the needs of American Indian people in Minnesota by promoting self-sufficiency through education, employment assistance, and life-skills training. It has been designated an Indian and Native American Employment and Training site to provide employment and training services to the unemployed, under-employed and economically disadvantaged American Indian population residing in 71 county designated areas.

Local Contact:

Minneapolis American Indian Center
1530 East Franklin Avenue
Minneapolis, MN 55404
P: 612.879.1700

Project for Pride in Living, Inc.

http://www.ppl-inc.org

Project for Pride in Living, Inc. is a non-profit organization assisting low and moderate income people to become self-sufficient by addressing their job, affordable housing and neighborhood needs. Project for Pride in Living, Inc. provides work-readiness programs, paid training, and job placement.

Local Contact:

Project for Pride in Living, Inc.
2516 Chicago Avenue
Minneapolis, MN 55404
P: 612.874.8511

Project Re-Entry

http://www.gmcc.org

Project re-entry is a program sponsored by the Greater Minneapolis Council of Churches. Its mission is to recruit and assist congregations in developing housing, employment programs, mentoring and support groups for newly released prisoners in Hennepin County, Minnesota.

Local Contact:

Project Re-Entry
Greater Minneapolis Council of Churches
1001 East Lake Street
Minneapolis, MN 55407
P: 612.721.8687

Wilder Foundation

http://www.wilder.org

The Wilder Foundation offers two programs to assist individuals with criminal records. The Community Transition Center provides a community-based Job Club which helps participants overcome barriers to employment. Participants receive assistance with Adult Basic Education and GED preparation and a range of job readiness and placement services. In partnership with Ramsey County Community Corrections, the Community Transition Center also offers a community-based cognitive skills program which helps participants examine their lifestyles and the impact they have on the community.

Local Contact:

Wilder Foundation
919 Lafond Avenue
St, Paul, MN 55104
P: 651.917.6225

MISSISSIPPI

Citizens United for Rehabilitation of Errants

http://www.mississippicure.org

CURE, Citizens United for Rehabilitation of Errants is a national nonprofit prison advocacy organization with state and special interest chapters throughout the United States.

Local and special interest chapters provide assistance to ex-offenders on a limited basis within their respective service areas.

> **Local Contact:**
>
> Citizens United for Rehabilitation of Errants
> P.O. Box 97175
> Pearl, MS 39288
> P: 601.914.5658

Goodwill Industries of South Mississippi, Inc.

http://www.goodwillsms.org

Goodwill Industries provide training, skill development and work opportunities for people with disabilities and other barriers to employment.

> **Local Contact:**
>
> Goodwill Industries of South Mississippi, Inc.
> 2407 31st Street
> Gulfport, MS 39501
> P: 228.863.2323

Goodwill Industries of South Mississippi, Inc.

http://www.goodwillsms.org

Goodwill Industries provide training, skill development and work opportunities for people with disabilities and other barriers to employment.

> **Local Contact:**
>
> Goodwill Industries of South Mississippi, Inc.
> 104 East State Street
> Ridgeland, MS 39157
> P: 601.853.8110

MISSOURI

Association of Gospel Rescue Missions

The Association of Gospel Rescue Missions provides residential programs in some cities within Missouri.

> **Local Contact:**
>
> Association of Gospel Rescue Missions
> 1045 Swift Street
> North Kansas City, MO 64116
> P: 816.471.8020

Bishop Sullivan Center

Bishop Sullivan Center is a social service agency serving low-income and no-income individuals in Kansas City, Missouri. Bishop Sullivan Center does not have programs designed uniquely for clients with criminal records, but rather, serves all low-income individuals. The Bishop Sullivan Center provides emergency assistance such as food, clothing, rent, utility, and medication assistance. In addition, they provide social and economic advocacy, tutoring for youth, and free legal advice. These services are free and not referral is required.

> **Local Contact:**
>
> Bishop Sullivan Center
> 6435 Truman Road
> Kansas City, MO 64126
> P: 816.231.0984

Center for Women in Transition

http://www.cwitstl.org

The Center for Women in Transition is a mentoring program. Women with criminal histories are matched with a volunteer mentor for at least a year and receive assistance in identifying and locating community resources. The Center for Women in Transition also provides referrals for employment assistance and counseling.

> **Local Contact:**
>
> Center for Women in Transition
> 7529 South Broadway
> St. Louis, MO 63111
> P: 314.771.5207

Citizens United for Rehabilitation of Errants

http://www.mocure.org

CURE, Citizens United for Rehabilitation of Errants is a national nonprofit prison advocacy organization with state and special interest chapters throughout the United States. Local and special interest chapters provide assistance to ex-offenders on a limited basis within their respective service areas.

> **Local Contact:**
>
> Citizens United for Rehabilitation of Errants
> P.O. Box 1245
> Cape Girardeau, MO 63702
> P: 877.525.2873

Connections to Success

http://www.connectionstosuccess.org

Connections to Success acts as an intermediary, training and fostering collaborative efforts among area service providers and faith-based organizations in Kansas City to provide services through a holistic model that emphasizes faith-based mentoring. Connections to Success partners with faith-based organizations, employers, and others interested parties to reduce recidivism rates.

> **Local Contact:**
>
> Connections to Success
> 109 Archibauld
> Kansas City, MO 64111
> P: 816.561.5115

Employment Connection

http://www.employmentstl.org

The Employment Connection serves people with criminal histories, substance abusers, welfare recipients and others with barriers to employment. Services offered include a two-day employment-readiness training, one-on-one job placement and information on career development. Employment Connection also educates employers on the benefits and methods of employing persons with criminal histories. Clients are referred to Employment Connection from probation and/or parole officers and other agencies.

Local Contact:

Employment Connection
400 Laclede Avenue
St. Louis, MO 63108
P: 314.652.0360

Jail Ministry Outreach

Jail Ministry Outreach provides restorative justice through community services. This program was built around love, resource awareness for a positive reentry, and individual and group support sessions.

Local Contact:

Jail Ministry Outreach
8631 Delmar, Suite 306
St. Louis, MO 63124
P: 314.754.2821

Our Savior Lutheran Prison Ministry Service Group

Our Savior Lutheran Prison Ministry Service Group networks with other agencies to provide jobs, clothing, food and housing for recently released offenders.

Local Contact:

Our Savior Lutheran Prison Ministry Service Group
1500 San Simeon Way
Fenton, MO 63026
P: 636.343.2192

Project COPE

http://www.projcope.org

Project COPE (Congregation-Offender Partnership Enterprise) provides selected ex-offenders with community reentry support by partnering them for one year with faith-based volunteer teams. Through close personal relationships, these partnerships offer assistance in basic needs, job search, housing, health-care, counseling, substance abuse treatment and prevention, and financial counseling. Transitional housing is available for ex-offenders with no other housing options.

Local Contact:

Project COPE
3529 Marcus Avenue
St. Louis, MO 63115
P: 314.389.4804

NEBRASKA

CEGA Services | Offender Referral

CEGA Services offers pre-release referrals for housing, employment, and substance abuse treatment programs through the Offender Referral service.

Local Contact:

CEGA Services | Offender Referral
P.O. Box 81826
Lincoln, NE 68501
P: 402.464.0602

Central Nebraska Goodwill Industries, Inc.

http://www.goodwill.org

Goodwill Industries, Inc. prepares people for jobs and matches them with local employers. Services range from personal evaluation and office skills training to career counseling, childcare and transportation. Because each local community has different needs, programs and services vary from location to location.

Local Contact:

Central Nebraska Goodwill Industries, Inc.
1804 South Eddy Street
Grand Island, NE 68802
P: 308.384.7896

Goodwill Industries, Inc. Serving Eastern Nebraska & Southwest

http://www.goodwillomaha.com

Goodwill Industries, Inc. prepares people for jobs and matches them with local employers. Services range from personal evaluation and office skills training to career counseling, childcare and transportation. Because each local community has different needs, programs and services vary from location to location.

Local Contact:

Goodwill Industries, Inc. Serving Eastern Nebraska & Southwest
1111 South 41st Street
Omaha, NE 68105
P: 402.341.4609

Goodwill Industries, Inc. Serving Southeast Nebraska, Inc.

http://www.lincolngoodwill.org

Goodwill Industries, Inc. prepares people for jobs and matches them with local employers. Services range from personal evaluation and office skills training to career counseling, childcare and transportation. Because each local community has different needs, programs and services vary from location to location.

Local Contact:

Goodwill Industries, Inc. Serving Southeast Nebraska, Inc.
2100 Judson Street
Lincoln, NE 68521
P: 402.438.2022

Omaha Con-nections

http://www.omahacon-nections.com

Omaha Con-nections offers instruction in job readiness skills, survival skills and services for Veterans who have criminal histories. They offer written/visual materials for use with pre-release populations. In addition, job development services are available. Referrals came from direct service providers as well as direct contact from prison visits. Staff is also available for training criminal justice programs on how to prepare individuals for community reintegration.

Local Contact:

Omaha Con-nections
4140 North 42nd Street
Omaha, NE 68111
P: 402.451.1100

NEVADA

Citizens United for Rehabilitation of Errants

CURE, Citizens United for Rehabilitation of Errants is a national nonprofit prison advocacy organization with state and special interest chapters throughout the United States. Local and special interest chapters provide assistance to ex-offenders on a limited basis within their respective service areas.

Local Contact:

Citizens United for Rehabilitation of Errants
540 East St. Louis Avenue
Las Vegas, NV 89104
P: 702.347.1731

EVOLVE

EVOLVE (Educational and Vocational Opportunities Leading to Valuable Experience) offers motivational counseling, case management, vocational education and job placement to individuals with criminal histories. Services available include resume preparation, interview techniques and mentorship.

Local Contact:

EVOLVE
1971 Stella Lake Drive
Las Vegas, NV 89106
P: 702.638.6371

Las Vegas Reentry Program

The Las Vegas Reentry Program assists participating inmates in Nevada correctional facilities who are three to six months from release through referrals from criminal justice agencies, including the District Attorney, police, probation and parole, and walk-ins. Participants are provided with a psychological assessment, a life skills program, transitional assistance, and a variety of other services including employment service referrals to other agencies.

Local Contact:

Las Vegas Reentry Program
930 West Owens Avenue
Las Vegas, NV 89106
P: Not Provided

Nevada AIDS Foundation

The Nevada AIDS Foundation attempts to find housing for prisoners upon release and maintains a food bank to assist HIV positive formerly incarcerated individuals.

Local Contact:

Nevada AIDS Foundation
900 West 1st, Suite 200
Reno, NV 89503
P: 775.348.9888

Ridge House, Inc.

Ridge House offers a three-month residential substance abuse treatment program and an outpatient program that solely serves individuals with criminal histories and parolees recently released from prison. The residential program includes a six-week career-counseling program taught by an expert. The course involves an assessment process to help participants determine their strengths, role-playing to help raise self-confidence, classes on computers, resume writing, life skills training, and guidance on appropriate dress. Most program participants are referred to the program by caseworkers in the facilities or by parole officers. The program also offers applications in the facilities and does other outreach. At present, Ridge House, Inc. operates facilities in seven locations, four in northern Nevada and three in the south.

Local Contact:

Ridge House, Inc.
275 Hill Street, Suite 281
Reno, NV 89501
P: 775.322.8941

Transitional Living Communities

Transitional Living Communities has a variety of locations that assist clients with substance abuse problems, including one location, V2, which serves as a halfway house for individuals on parole, probation, and minimum supervision. Transitional Living Communities provides a 90-day substance abuse program that participants, other than those at V2, are free to leave at any time. Participants are provided with inexpensive, transitional housing (negotiable at $90.00 a month and no cost up-front). Transitional Living Communities also offers job-seeking assistance.

Local Contact:

Transitional Living Communities
210 North 10th Street
Las Vegas, NV 89101
P: 702.387.3131

NEW HAMPSHIRE

Transformations Program
http://www.laconia.tec.nh.us

The Transformations Program is offered by the New Hampshire Community Technical College and has a mission to assist recently released offenders with obtaining employment by providing life skills, employment skills, and job placement services.

Local Contact:

Transformations Program
New Hampshire Community Technical College
379 Belmont Road
Laconia, NH 03246
P: 603.524.3207

NEW JERSEY

American Friends Service Committee | Criminal Justice Program
http://www.afsc.org

The American Friends Service Committee Criminal Justice Program provides individuals with referrals for available legal help and assistance to prisoner organizations and community organizations working on prison related issues.

Local Contact:

American Friends Service Committee | Criminal Justice Program
89 Market Street, 6th Floor
Newark, NJ 07102
P: 973.643.2205

Citizens United for Rehabilitation of Errants
http://www.gardenstatecure.org

CURE, Citizens United for Rehabilitation of Errants is a national nonprofit prison advocacy organization with state and special interest chapters throughout the United States. Local and special interest chapters provide assistance to ex-offenders on a limited basis within their respective service areas.

Local Contact:

Citizens United for Rehabilitation of Errants
P.O. Box 1215
Willow Grove, PA 19090
P: 215.892.8796

Offender Aid and Restoration of Essex County

Offender Aid and Restoration of Essex County assists people with criminal records re-enter the community. In addition to helping clients acquire current forms of identification, Offender Aid and Restoration provide job development and placement services. Other services include transportation support and referrals for substance abuse treatment.

Local Contact:

Offender Aid and Restoration of Essex County
164 Clinton Avenue, Suite 170
Irvington, NJ 07111
P: 973.373.0100

The New Jersey Association on Correction

The New Jersey Association on Correction runs a number of criminal justice-focused residential facilities and resource centers. It also runs a number of residential facilities and community programs, some of which are focused on helping women and children, while others are intended to assist people with HIV and AIDS. These programs are located throughout the state.

Local Contact:

The New Jersey Association on Correction
986 South Broad Street
Trenton, NJ 08611
P: 609.396.8900

NEW MEXICO

Citizens United for Rehabilitation of Errants

CURE, Citizens United for Rehabilitation of Errants is a national nonprofit prison advocacy organization with state and special interest chapters throughout the United States. Local and special interest chapters provide assistance to ex-offenders on a limited basis within their respective service areas.

Local Contact:

Citizens United for Rehabilitation of Errants
P.O. Box 543
Deming, NM 88031
P: 575.546.9003

Coalition for Prisoner's Rights

The Coalition for Prisoner's Rights is a nonprofit organization that provides referral services to offenders and their families.

Local Contact:

Coalition for Prisoner's Rights
Prison Project of Santa Fe
P.O. Box 1911
Santa Fe, NM 87504
P: 505.982.9520

Delancey Street Foundation

Delancey Street Foundation is based on the principle of self motivation. Through multiple locations around the United States, they provide a reintegration program that offers counseling and training in moving and trucking, para-transit services, a restaurant and catering services, a print and copy shop, retail and wholesale sales, advertising specialty sales, and an automotive service center.

Local Contact:

Delancey Street Foundation
P.O. Box 1240
San Juan Pueblo, NM 87566
P: 505.852.4291

Dismas House

http://www.dismashousenewmexico.org

Dismas House offers transitional housing for recently released offenders, both male and female. A total of twenty one residents, fifteen male and six female, may be accommodated at any given time. Dismas House has no direct services but provides an environment that is emotionally supportive and encouraging to recently released offenders. Residents are encouraged to find employment and/or training as soon as possible. The cost, $400.00 per month, self-pay or otherwise contracted by the Department of Corrections (includes room and board).

Local Contact:

Dismas House
4514 Central South East
Albuquerque, NM 87107
P: 505.343.0746

Learn, Earn and Develop Success

Learn, Earn and Develop Success, a project of Families and Youth, Inc., works with adjudicated youth 16 to 21 years of age to provide job training and work experience. Referrals are received from the Probation Department and juvenile centers. The program consists of 180 hours paid work experience leading to permanent job placement, as well as assistance in setting educational and/or technical training goals.

Local Contact:

Learn, Earn and Develop Success
Families and Youth, Inc.
1320 South Solano, Box 1868
Las Cruces, NM 88001
P: 505.556.1627

Project IMPACT

http://www.pbjfamilyservices.org

Project IMPACT, a service of PBJ Family Services, Inc., offers a variety of services to reconnect incarcerated parents with their children and ease former prisoner's transition back into daily family life.

Local Contact:

Project IMPACT
1101 Lopez Road, SW
Albuquerque, NM 87105
P: 505.877.7060

Wings Ministry

http://www.wingsministry.org

Wings Ministry is a nonprofit organization designed for family members of incarcerated individuals. Their goal is to connect spouses, caregivers, and children of offenders with the nurturing and supporting relationships of Christian people in local churches.

Local Contact:

Wings Ministry
2270 D Wyoming Boulevard, NE, #130
Albuquerque, NM 87112
P: 505.291.6412

NEW YORK

AIDS in Prison Project | Osborne Association

http://www.osborneny.org

AIDS in Prison Project of the Osborne Association assists pre-release HIV positive men and women that intend to parole to New York with discharge planning.

Local Contact:

AIDS in Prison Project | Osborne Association
809 Westchester Avenue
Bronx, NY 10455
P: 718.378.7022

America Works, Inc. | Criminal Justice Program

http://www.americaworks.com

America Works, a for-profit job placement agency, assists hard-to-serve clients obtain employment in the private sector. In addition to addressing issues such as criminal records as a barrier to employment, America Works utilizes a supportive model including: job readiness; job placement; supportive and/or unsubsidized work experience; case management; job retention services or at least 6 months in unsubsidized jobs; supportive services; and advancement services.

Local Contact:

America Works, Inc. | Criminal Justice Program
575 8th Avenue, 14th Floor
New York, NY 10018
P: 212.244.5627

Catholic Charities of New York

http://www.catholiccharitiesny.org

Catholic Charities of New York offers a comprehensive series of programs to provide clothing, bail funds, referrals and many other services to those in need.

Local Contact:

Catholic Charities of New York
1011 First Avenue
New York, NY 10022
P: 888.744.7900

Center for Employment Opportunities
http://www.ceoworks.org

The Center for Employment Opportunities provides rigorous pre-employment training, short-term work crew experience, and long-term job development services to prepare clients with criminal records entering permanent employment. Services are provided to people with non-violent criminal histories who have completed New York State's Shock Incarceration program or who are on work release, parole, or probation.

Local Contact:

Center for Employment Opportunities
32 Broadway
New York, NY 10001
P: 212.422.4430

Citizens United for Rehabilitation of Errants
http://www.bestweb.net/~cureny

CURE, Citizens United for Rehabilitation of Errants is a national nonprofit prison advocacy organization with state and special interest chapters throughout the United States. Local and special interest chapters provide assistance to ex-offenders on a limited basis within their respective service areas.

Local Contact:

Citizens United for Rehabilitation of Errants
207 Riverside
Scotia, NY 12302
P: Not Provided

ComALERT
http://www.brooklynda.org/ca/comalert.htm

ComALERT is a project of the Office of the District Attorney of Kings County. ComALERT acts in several capacities. One is a service broker, referring clients to various community partners for services such as employment/job development, vocational training; second it monitors the progress of clients in the program; third it acts in a mediation role between probation and social service agencies. It actively works in the community to enhance relationships between the community and the criminal justice system.

Local Contact:

ComALERT
Office of the District Attorney, Kings County
350 Jay Street
Brooklyn, NY 11201
P: 718.250.2665

Delancey Street Foundation

Delancey Street Foundation is based on the principle of self motivation. Through multiple locations around the United States, they provide a reintegration program that offers counseling and training in moving and trucking, para-transit services, a restaurant and catering services, a print and copy shop, retail and wholesale sales, advertising specialty sales, and an automotive service center.

Local Contact:

Delancey Street Foundation
100 Turk Hill Road
Brewster, NY 10609
P: 845.278.6181

Developing Justice Project | Fifth Avenue Committee
http://www.fifthave.org

Developing Justice Project is a project of the Fifth Avenue Committee, a community-based non-profit organization that promotes social and economic justice in South Brooklyn, New York. In addition to promoting criminal justice reform, the Developing Justice Project offers walk-in support to individuals with criminal histories. Transitional supportive services in the areas of housing, permanent employment, education and skill development are available through individual case management services.

Local Contact:

Developing Justice Project | Fifth Avenue Committee
141 Fifth Avenue
Brooklyn, NY 11217
P: 718.237.2017

Exodus Transitional Community
http://www.etcny.org

Exodus Transitional Community directly serves recently released people with criminal records and makes referrals for programs not offered in-house. Services offered include career counseling, employment workshops including interview techniques; resume writing, job referrals, housing referrals, mental health counseling, substance abuse treatment referrals and Alternatives to Violence workshops.

Local Contact:

Exodus Transitional Community
161 East 104th Street, 4th Floor
New York, NY 10029
P: 917.492.0990

Exponents, Inc.
http://www.exponents.org

Exponents, Inc. offers a long-term case management program for HIV positive individuals who are in transition back into communities after a term of incarceration.

Local Contact:

Exponents, Inc.
Case Management Connection
151 West 26th Street, 3rd Floor
New York, NY 10001
P: 212.243.3434

Fast Forward

Fast Forward is designed especially for persons releasing from correctional institutions in the New York City area. Fast Forward offers vocational and education assessment programs, counseling, job placement, and individual counseling to those in need.

Local Contact:

Fast Forward
500 8th Avenue, Suite 1207
New York, NY 10018
P: 212.714.0600

Good Help Brooklyn

http://www.ibrooklyn.com/site/chamberdirect/goodhelp

The Brooklyn Chamber of Commerce is a business-driven employment service designed to help Brooklyn businesses and unemployed residents in Brooklyn. The organization works with employers to find job openings, screen potential employees, check references, and follow up with placements.

Local Contact:

Good Help Brooklyn
Brooklyn Chamber of Commerce
25 Elm Place, Suite 200
Brooklyn, NY 11201
P: 718.875.1000

Harlem Restoration Project, Inc.

Harlem Restoration Project, Inc. is a nonprofit organization that coordinates numerous building renovation projects within their area of service. Preference is given to ex-offenders when openings are available within any of its building renovation projects. All level of applicants are hired, from laborers to administrators. On occasion, housing is available to ex-offenders and their families.

Local Contact:

Harlem Restoration Project, Inc.
461 West 124th
New York, NY 10027
P: 212.622.8186

Judicial Process Commission

The Judicial Process Commission offers a mentoring program for individuals with criminal records in Monroe County, New York. Working with county inmates prior to release, Judicial Process Commission addresses concerns about re-entering society and offers job readiness training, including resume writing, interview techniques, a Job Club and assistance in networking to find employment.

Local Contact:

Judicial Process Commission
121 North Fitzhugh Street
Rochester, NY 14614
P: 585.325.7727

Making Career Connections

Making Career Connections is a supportive employment program for low or no-income persons, including individuals with criminal histories, who face barriers to employment. Services include barrier assessment and removal, job readiness training, job placement assistance and post-employment follow-up. Referrals are provided to external agencies to help provide stability for clients.

Local Contact:

Making Career Connections
278 Clinton Avenue
Albany, NY 12210
P: 518.432.0499

New York Public Library

http://www.nypl.org

The New York Public Library, Correctional Library Services publishes Connections, a directory of organizations in New York City that assist people with criminal records with various services. The guide also includes a guide of necessary information for assisting individuals with criminal records find employment. The guide is regularly updated and can be ordered from the New York Public Library. A copy of Connections is available to anyone releasing to the New York City area upon written request. Non-New York State residents are asked to send $15.00 per copy to defray mailing costs.

Local Contact:

New York Public Library
Correctional Services Librarian
455 Fifth Avenue
New York, NY 10016
P: 212.340.0971

Osborne Association

http://www.osborneny.org

The Osborne Association assists individuals with criminal records, defendants, people on probation or parole, prisoners and their families by offering a range of educational, vocational, support and health services, including defender-based advocacy, day reporting drug treatment and walk-in harm reduction services, acupuncture on demand for detoxification, and intensive AIDS/HIV case management. Also available are primary health care referrals, regular support groups, weekly AA and NA meetings, a Brooklyn-based youth entrepreneurship program, and an AIDS in Prison Hotline for prisoners. The Employment and Training Division of the Osborne Association provides comprehensive vocational services including assessment, testing, career and educational counseling, job-readiness workshops, job training and post-employment support in adjusting to the demands of the workplace and staying employed. Clients are encouraged to return for referrals for additional services or better jobs after working successfully at their first placement.

Local Contact:

Osborne Association
Employment and Training Division
36-31 38th Street
Long Island City, NY 11101
P: 718.707.2600

Palladia, Inc.

http://www.projectreturn.org

Paladia, Inc. helps parolees with employment readiness, job placement, individual and family counseling, as well as recreational and community service activities.

Local Contact:

Palladia, Inc.
2006 Madison Avenue
New York, NY 10035
P: 212.979.8600

Project Green Hope | Services for Women

Project Green Hope oversees residences for women which offer personal counseling, individual and group therapy, vocational workshops, assistance in vocational placement, substance abuse support groups, parenting information and advocacy in areas such as foster care.

Local Contact:

Project Green Hope | Services for Women
448 East 119th Street
New York, NY 10035
P: 212.369.5100

Providence House | Transitional Housing Program

http://www.providencehouse.org

Providence House is a community-based residential program for women who are on New York State parole and who cannot return to their place of residence after they are released from custody. Providence House has locations in Brooklyn and Queens that are staffed by a core community of volunteers and paid personnel.

Local Contact:

Providence House | Transitional Housing Program
703 Lexington Avenue
Brooklyn, NY 11221
P: 718.455.0197

Reentry Columbia

www.reentrycolumbia.org

Reentry Columbia provides pre-release planning in the Columbia County Jail to those who will be returning to Columbia County, New York. This includes visits with individ-

uals and weekly group classes. Additionally, Reentry Columbia provides post-release assessment and planning for all formerly incarcerated individuals returning to Columbia County, which includes referrals to service agencies that provide support with employment, housing, substance abuse treatment, and other needs.

Local Contact:

Reentry Columbia
First Reformed Church
52 Green Street
Hudson, NY 12534
P: 518.288.7996

St. Patrick Friary

St. Patrick Friary provides group counseling at many New York State Correctional Facilities and post-release assistance with housing, educational attainment, transportation, job training and placement.

Local Contact:

St. Patrick Friary
102 Seymore Street
Buffalo, NY 14210
P: 716.856.6131

Stand Up! Harlem

Stand Up! Harlem has emergency overnight accommodations, transitional housing for HIV positive individuals, case management, and health and holistic services for those in need. Stand Up! Harlem also coordinates a support group for ex-offenders.

Local Contact:

Stand Up! Harlem
145 West 130th Street
New York, NY 10027
P: 212.926.4072

STRIVE

http://www.strivenewyork.org

The core program at STRIVE consists of an intensive three-week attitude adjustment workshop. Emphasis is placed on the development of "soft skills" (e.g., work ethic, verbal and non-verbal communication techniques, appropriate attire for the workplace, and the spirit of cooperation and teamwork, etc.). Participants in STRIVE must undergo a lengthy intake procedure that includes a personal interview before they are admitted. Although there are very few restrictions on who may apply for the program, many factors are taken into consideration before an individual is selected. Once participants have completed their training, STRIVE's job developers endeavor to match employers with the individuals in the graduate pool. Although placement opportunities are sought for graduates that offer benefits, skill development, and room for career advancement wherever possible, the main focus is to provide graduates with the beginning of a stable work history that can be built upon.

Once an individual is placed, STRIVE offers follow-up services fro two years. Lastly, STRIVE's On-Site Social Services Program (OSSP) provides a comprehensive social service program that offers case management, short-term counseling, crisis intervention, advocacy, information and referrals.

Local Contact:
STRIVE
240 East 123rd Street, 3rd Floor
New York, NY 10035
P: 212.360.1100

The Fortune Society

http://www.fortunesociety.org

The Fortune Society is a self-help organization for individuals with criminal records. Membership extends on a national level. The Fortune Society offers counseling, referrals to vocational training, job placement, tutoring in preparation for the High School Equivalency Diploma, Basic Adult Literacy, English as a Second Language, and substance abuse treatment. It also offers a wide variety of alternatives to incarceration services for jail-bound defendants. The Fortune Society provides discharge planning, case management and support groups for individuals with HIV/AIDS.

Local Contact:
The Fortune Society
29-76 Northern Boulevard
Long Island City, NY 11101
P: 212.691.7554

The Verite Program

The Verite Program offers an ex-offender support group and groups surrounding the issues of substance abuse, relapse and recovery, HIV/AIDS, men's sexuality, stress and anger management. Provides limited mental health therapy as needed.

Local Contact:
The Verite Program
810 Classon Avenue
Brooklyn, NY 11238
P: 718.230.5100

Urban Pathways, Inc.

http://www.urbanpathways.org

Urban Pathways provides shelter and support services to homeless men and women in New York. In addition to providing housing programs and services to chemically addicted homeless individuals, Urban Pathways offers the ESTEEM (Employment Skills, Training, Education, Employment, Motivation) program. Services of ESTEEM include vocational and educational opportunities (e.g. counseling, job placement, and GED preparation and testing). The vocational program includes job training, coaching, and development in the areas of administration, messenger services, food service, etc.

Local Contact:
Urban Pathways, Inc.
575 8th Avenue, 9th Floor
New York, NY 10018
P: 212.736.7385

Wildcat Service Corporation

http://www.wildcatnyc.org

Wildcat Service Corporation provides counseling and work programs for the hard-core unemployed, especially ex-addicts, individuals with criminal records, welfare mothers, and out of-school youth. The three major work categories are clerical, construction, and maintenance. Jobs last up to 12 months. Clients must be referred by a correctional program or legal service provider.

Local Contact:
Wildcat Service Corporation
17 Battery Place
New York, NY 10004
P: 212.209.6000

WomenCare, Inc.

WomenCare, Inc. provides mentoring services for women making the transition from prison back to the community. WomenCare, Inc. provides access to resource and referrals in many areas such as, housing, employment, and parenting issues.

Local Contact:
WomenCare, Inc.
105 Chambers Street, 2nd Floor
New York, NY 10007
P: 212.463.9500

Women's Prisons Association

http://www.wpaonline.org

The Women's Prison Association works with women in county, state, and federal institutions throughout New York to provide a variety of services to help women transition back into the community.

Local Contact:
Women's Prisons Association
110 Second Avenue
New York, NY 10027
P: 212.674.1163

NORTH CAROLINA

Citizens United for Rehabilitation of Errants

CURE, Citizens United for Rehabilitation of Errants is a national nonprofit prison advocacy organization with state and special interest chapters throughout the United States. Local and special interest chapters provide assistance to ex-offenders on a limited basis within their respective service areas.

Local Contact:

Citizens United for Rehabilitation of Errants
P.O. Box 49572
Charlotte, NC 28277
P: 252.722.3414

Delancey Street Foundation

Delancey Street Foundation is based on the principle of self motivation. Through multiple locations around the United States, they provide a reintegration program that offers counseling and training in moving and trucking, para-transit services, a restaurant and catering services, a print and copy shop, retail and wholesale sales, advertising specialty sales, and an automotive service center.

Local Contact:

Delancey Street Foundation
811 North Elm Street
Greensboro, NC 27401
P: 336.379.8477

Energy Committed to Offenders

http://www.ecocharlotte.org

Energy Committed to Offenders is a community-based organization that begins working with offenders, located in either county or state facilities, during their incarceration. Presentations on employment topics are given prior to release. Energy Committed to Offenders assists recently released offenders as well. It offers transportation for job searches and provides transportation to and from new jobs. Energy Committed to Offenders also provides housing and clothing referrals for those recently released prisoners. Energy Committed to Offenders maintains a 20-bed live-in transitional canter where recently released female prisoners are encouraged to reconnect with their children and participate in parenting classes.

Local Contact:

Energy Committed to Offenders
P.O. Box 33533
Charlotte, NC 28233
P: 704.374.0762

Urban Ministries Center

http://www.urbanministrycenter.org

Urban Ministries Center is an intercept organization that offers food, laundry facilities, referrals, and employment counseling to those in need.

Local Contact:

Urban Ministries Center
945 North College Street
Charlotte, NC 28206
P: 704.347.0278

OHIO

AGAP Community Reentry Program

The Community Reentry Program is an outgrowth of the AGAP prison ministries program. Both programs are part of Christians in the Hood, a faith-based organization. Transition planning begins during incarceration focusing on developing life plans and identifying goals and issues that will be faced upon release. When an individual is released from prison, a needs assessment is done to determine the appropriate level of assistance required. Linkages are made with community agencies to further individual goals. Employment resources, accountability group counseling and educational services are all provided.

Local Contact:

AGAP Community Reentry Program
1378 Loretta Avenue
Columbus, OH 43211
P: 614.477.4931

Akron Urban League | Transitions Program

http://www.akronul.org

The Akron Urban League's Transition Program assists individuals with non-violent misdemeanors and felony convictions. The program offers job placement assistance and three weeks of job readiness training, including workshops in preparing a resume and increasing interviewing skills.

Local Contact:

Akron Urban League | Transitions Program
250 East Market Street
Akron, OH 44308
P: 330.434.3101

Citizens United for Rehabilitation of Errants

http://www.cure-ohio.org

CURE, Citizens United for Rehabilitation of Errants is a national nonprofit prison advocacy organization with state and special interest chapters throughout the United States. Local and special interest chapters provide assistance to ex-offenders on a limited basis within their respective service areas.

Local Contact:

Citizens United for Rehabilitation of Errants
P.O. Box 14808
Columbus, OH 43214
P: 877.826.8504

Community Connections

http://www.communityconnectionohio.com

Community Connections focuses on helping recently released inmates prepare fro and find employment. Case managers begin by ascertaining and addressing basic needs, including transportation, housing, and identification, which might create barriers in allowing participants to find or maintain employment. They then carry out an in house employment assessment which is used both to identify training needs and as a marketing tool to help market participants to employers by providing them with a full source of information.

Local Contact:

Community Connections
993 East Main Street
Columbus, OH 43205
P: 614.252.0660

Community Linkage

Community Linkage's main focus is on assisting anyone returning to the Hamilton area in finding employment, while simultaneously providing social services to try to meet the clients other needs, including shelter, food, transportation, identification, and other barriers that might prevent the individual from finding or keeping employment. The program also offers employment readiness and life skills classes.

Local Contact:

Community Linkage
116 South 2nd Street
Hamilton, OH 48011
P: 513.785.7546

Community Reentry

Community Reentry oversees 16 programs, each targeted towards assisting different populations in preparing for and finding employment following release from incarceration. Services include job placement and readiness and case management. Clients are also referred to assistance with emergency housing, job training, and substance abuse problems.

Local Contact:

Community Reentry
1468 West 25th Street
Cleveland, OH 44113
P: 216.696.2717

Community Shelter Board

http://www.csb.org

Community Shelter Board is an organization that offers an Internet-equipped emergency shelter, telephone access, employment leads, job training resources, and other community services to those in need.

Local Contact:

Community Shelter Board
115 West Main Street
Columbus, OH 43215
P: 614.221.9195

Goodwill Industries of Cleveland, Inc.

http://www.goodwill-cleveland.org

Goodwill Industries of Cleveland, Inc. has a Post-Release Service Center which offers individualized services to help clients overcome personal barriers to employment, including assistance with substance abuse, anger management, financial management, job seeking, clothing, housing, and food. Each client undergoes an initial evaluation upon intake to identify individual needs. Goodwill Industries of Cleveland, Inc. has a database of employers with whom it has long relationships, who know that all clients have criminal records and who let the organization know when they have possible openings. Staff then alerts their clients to the opening, select a group to send over for interviews, and send a member of staff as support. Goodwill Industries of Cleveland, Inc. asks that clients remain a minimum of 30 days in placement, so that they can get familiar with a job and the requirements of the working environment. Additionally, clients are followed for a year after placement in case any problems arise, and the organization has an open-door policy for former clients. Individuals with three failed placements are reevaluated and the process begins again.

Local Contact:

Goodwill Industries of Cleveland, Inc.
2295 East 55th Street
Cleveland, OH 44103
P: 216.431.8300

Opening Doors of Ohio, Inc.

http://www.openingmoredoors.org

Opening Doors of Ohio, Inc. is an inter-faith ministry that provides services to ex-offenders and their families.

Local Contact:

Opening Doors of Ohio, Inc.
1689 Haridin Lane
Powell, OH 43065
P: 614.543.0417

Providing Real Opportunities for Ex-Offenders to Succeed

Providing Real Opportunities for Ex-Offenders to Succeed (PROES) is a project of the Cleveland American Job Center. The program focuses on immediate employment augmented with support services. Providing Real Opportunities for Ex-Offenders to Succeed works in conjunction with the Employment Solutions Program of Alternatives Agency Inc., a halfway house for formerly incarcerated individuals. The intensive two-week program includes life skills training, communication skills, and job readiness preparation.

Local Contact:

Providing Real Opportunities for Ex-Offenders to Succeed
1020 Bolivar Road
Cleveland, OH 44115
P: 216.664.4673

Solid Opportunities for Advancement and Retention

http://www.gcul.org

Solid Opportunity for Advancement and Retention (SOAR), a project of the Greater Cincinnati Urban League, provides a combination of short0term education and training services with job placement assistance for African-American and Appalachian males and females. This six-week pre-employment training provides job readiness skills for people who may have employment barriers due to lack of work experience, lack of education/training, or criminal backgrounds. Solid Opportunity for Advancement and Retention accepts walk-in applicants.

Local Contact:

Solid Opportunities for Advancement and Retention
Greater Cincinnati Urban League
3458 Reading Road
Cincinnati, OH 45229
P: 513.281.9955

The Missing Link

Missing Link provides links between troubled youth and ex-offenders and life changing programs including Christian residential programs.

Local Contact:

The Missing Link
P.O. Box 40031
Cleveland, OH 44140
P: 440.282.1683

Towards Employment

http://www.towardsemployment.org

Towards Employment supports individuals in making the transition into the workplace. In addition to supportive services, the agency offers job readiness and life skills workshops, GED preparation, and computer skills instruction. Job placement and job retention support is offered to participants. Towards Employment has offered its services to low-income individuals and recently assumed management and delivery of the "Ex-offenders and Legal Services" programs formerly offered by Cleveland Works.

Local Contact:

Towards Employment
1224 Huron Road, 2nd Floor
Cleveland, OH 44115
P: 216.696.5750

Women's Re-Entry Network

The Women's Re-Entry Network is a program within Community Reentry that focuses entirely on women with criminal records. Services include assessment, intensive case management, individual and group counseling, and parenting classes. The Women's Re-Entry Network also offers information and referrals for housing, employment and other needs. It has offices in the county jail and local women's prison offering support groups and case management. The Women's Re-Entry Network acts as a bridge to services on the outside for women who are being released.

Local Contact:

Women's Re-Entry Network
1468 West 25th Street
Cleveland, OH 44113
P: 216.696.7535

OKLAHOMA

Big Five Community Services

http://www.bigfive.org

Big Five Community Services has job training opportunities to fit the needs of most workers while providing many other services. Their workforce development programs offer on-the-job training, work experience or classroom training. In addition, Big Five helps clients overcome other barriers to employment while they are pursuing a new job or training opportunities.

Local Contact:

Big Five Community Services
1502 North 1st Street, P.O. Box 1577
Durant, OK 74703
P: 580.924.5331

Case Recovery Ministry

Case Recovery Ministry provides services for ex-offenders and their families.

Local Contact:

Case Recovery Ministry
New Starts Prison Ministry
P.O. Box 19352
Oklahoma City, OK 73144
P: 405.420.3192

Citizens United for Rehabilitation of Errants

http://www.okcure.org

CURE, Citizens United for Rehabilitation of Errants is a national nonprofit prison advocacy organization with state and special interest chapters throughout the United States. Local and special interest chapters provide assistance to ex-offenders on a limited basis within their respective service areas.

Local Contact:

Citizens United for Rehabilitation of Errants
P.O. Box 9741
Tulsa, OK 74157
P: 918.744.9857

Community Action Project of Tulsa County

http://www.freetaxes.net

Community Action Project of Tulsa County is designed to assist those with modest incomes to obtain basic necessities, including a home, food, quality education, childcare, school supplies, health care and economic security for the future. Currently, Community Action Project of Tulsa County offers programs that provide support I housing, employment, education, childcare, tax preparation assistance, social services, emergency aid, medical services, and advocacy.

Local Contact:

Community Action Project of Tulsa County
717 South Houston, Suite 200
Tulsa, OK 74127
P: 918.382.3200

Criminal Justice and Mercy Ministry

Criminal Justice and Mercy Ministry provides services to ex-offenders and their families.

Local Contact:

Criminal Justice and Mercy Ministry
Oklahoma Methodist Conference
1501 Northwest 24th Street
Oklahoma City, OK 73106
P: 405.530.2015

Exodus House of Oklahoma City

Exodus House is a program administered by the United Methodist Church that provides transitional housing for recently released individuals and their children. Services offered include on-site substance abuse treatment, referrals for mental health counseling, and anger management counseling, and computer instruction. Job referrals are made, although no formal job development is available. Individuals with a history of sexual offenses or a tendency towards violence are not eligible for residency within Exodus House.

Local Contact:

Exodus House of Oklahoma City
433 Northwest 26th Street
Oklahoma City, OK 73103
P: 405.525.2300

Exodus House of Tulsa

Exodus House provides transitional housing for recently released individuals with criminal records as well as their children. It is administered by the United Methodist Church. Services provided include on-site substance abuse treatment, referrals for mental hygiene counseling, anger management group counseling and computer instruction. Job referrals are made, although no formal job development is available. People with a history of sexual offenses or a tendency towards violence are not accepted for residency at exodus House. Participants are picked up from a correctional facility by facility personnel. Average length of stay is six months; rent is not charged, however after employment is obtained the utility bill becomes the responsibility of the resident.

Local Contact:

Exodus House of Tulsa
2624 East Newton Street
Tulsa, OK 74110
P: 918.382.0905

Female Offenders Committed to Ultimate Success

Female Offenders Committed to Ultimate Success (FOCUS) is a pilot project of Resonance Women's Center that has been operational for over two years. Participants must be convicted only of a non-violent crime and have received a community sentence. During the first four weeks of the program, clients are housed at the local correctional facility, for the second four weeks, clients return home or go to transitional housing while suitable permanent housing is found. For the remaining 18 weeks clients attend daily programming including group and individuals counseling, case management, substance abuse treatment, and job skills training consisting of career readiness and job development. Clients are monitored and assessed by the court, parole/probation officers and social workers.

Local Contact:

Female Offenders Committed to Ultimate Success
Resonance Women's Center
1608 South Elwood Avenue
Tulsa, OK 74119
P: 918.587.3088

OREGON

ARCHES Project
http://www.committed.to/arches

The ARCHES Project is located on the campus of the Marion County jail. It functions as a central social service center for recently released individuals with criminal records who have no housing plan. On-site services include mental health counseling and substance abuse treatment. A tenant rent assistance program helps find and pay for permanent housing for up to two years. A One-Stop job service center at the project offers employment specialist counseling, intake and assessment services, pre-employment workshops as well as employment referrals.

Local Contact:

ARCHES Project
3950 Aumsville Highway, SE
Salem, OR 97301
P: 503.566.6927

Better People
http://www.betterpeople.org

Better People is an employment and counseling program solely dedicated to helping individuals with criminal histories find, keep and excel in good paying hobs with fair, decent employers. Better People is the first program in the country to combine job placement and retention services with a therapeutic approach called Moral Recognition Therapy. Better People costs only $25.00.

Local Contact:

Better People
4310 Northeast Martin Luther King Jr. Boulevard
Portland, OR 97211
P: 503.281.2663

Citizens United for Rehabilitation of Errants

http://www.oregoncure.org

CURE, Citizens United for Rehabilitation of Errants is a national nonprofit prison advocacy organization with state and special interest chapters throughout the United States. Local and special interest chapters provide assistance to ex-offenders on a limited basis within their respective service areas.

Local Contact:

Citizens United for Rehabilitation of Errants
1631 Northeast Broadway, #460
Portland, OR 97232
P: 503.977.9979

Steps to Success East

http://www.steps-2-success.org

Steps to Success East is a program designed to provide comprehensive educational, social, and employment services to enable job seekers to gain the skills and qualifications necessary to obtain permanent jobs or to transition into a new career. This program is a collaborative partnership between Mt. Hood and Portland Community Colleges, Oregon Adult and Family Services, Oregon Employment Department, Work Systems, Inc., Human Solutions, numerous employers in the Portland Metro Workforce, and state and local community action organizations. Steps to Success East is a "One-Stop" affiliate for East Multnomah County.

Local Contact:

Steps to Success East
1415 Southeast 122nd Avenue
Portland, OR 97233
P: 503.256.0432

PENNSYLVANIA

Baker Industries, Inc.

http://www.bakerindustries.org

Baker Industries employs hard to place individuals including those serving parole sentences. Baker Industries performs outsourcing services. The agency serves as a transitional step towards unsubsidized employment by emphasizing soft skills like being on time for work, good attendance, and productive interactions with co-workers and supervisors.

Local Contact:

Baker Industries, Inc.
184 Pennsylvania Avenue
Malvern, PA 19355
P: 610.296.9795

Bebashi | Care Outreach

http://www.bebashi.org/

Bebashi is a nonprofit organization that offers referrals, counseling, and HIV testing for people recently released from a term of incarceration.

Local Contact:

Bebashi | Care Outreach
1217 Spring Garden Street, 1st Floor
Philadelphia, PA 19123
P: 215.769.3561

Career & Workforce Development Center East

http://www.ymcaofpittsburgh.org

The Career & Workforce Development Center East of the YMCA of Greater Pittsburgh provides services to unemployed and underemployed residents of the East End and surrounding areas of Allegheny County, specializing in helping people with criminal records. In collaboration with the State Board of Parole and Probation, Career & Workforce Development Center East hosts the annual Get Back to Work Help Fair, a two-day program of workshops and a service provider and employer fair. Career & Workforce Development Center East also provides a three-day Basic Foundation Skills Work-Ready Training. The Board of Probation and Parole provides recently released individuals weekly ASCRA meetings at various YMCA locations. The Career & Workforce Development Center East also hosts a weekly employment group, providing assistance with resume writing, job search and interview techniques, and basic computer skills.

Local Contact:

Career & Workforce Development Center East
YMCA of Greater Pittsburgh – Homewood Branch
7140 Bennett Street
Pittsburgh, PA 15208
P: 412.241.2811

Carnegie Library of Pittsburgh

http://www.carnegielibrary.org/locations/jcec

The Carnegie Library provides generalized employment preparation and job-finding services, but does not provide any specialized services for individuals with criminal records. Among the services provided is assistance with resume preparation, GED and other educational assistance, guidance in selecting a college, providing test booklets for test preparation, descriptions of the various types of jobs available, assistance with setting up e-mail accounts, and classes on Internet and computer program usage.

Local Contact:

Carnegie Library of Pittsburgh
Job & Career Education Center
4400 Forbes Avenue
Pittsburgh, PA 15213
P: 412.622.3133

Christian Recovery Aftercare Ministry

http://www.craminc.org

Christian Recovery Aftercare Ministry is a faith-based organization that provides direct aftercare services to individuals recently released from a term of incarceration and those individuals who face barriers to successful community reintegration.

Local Contact:

Christian Recovery Aftercare Ministry
509 Division Street
Harrisburg, PA 17110
P: 717.234.3664

Citizens United for Rehabilitation of Errants

http://www.pacure.org

CURE, Citizens United for Rehabilitation of Errants is a national nonprofit prison advocacy organization with state and special interest chapters throughout the United States. Local and special interest chapters provide assistance to ex-offenders on a limited basis within their respective service areas.

Local Contact:

Citizens United for Rehabilitation of Errants
P.O. Box 8601
Philadelphia, PA 19101
P: 215.820.7001

Firm Foundation of Pennsylvania

http://www.firmfoundation.org

The Firm Foundation of Pennsylvania, a faith-based organization, offers a variety of services to adult men and women with drug/alcohol addiction histories and those who have had contact with the criminal justice system. General reentry services include mentoring, case management and career/job development. In addition, transitional housing for men and fatherhood enrichment services are also available.

Local Contact:

Firm Foundation of Pennsylvania
28 North 19th Street
Harrisburg, PA 17103
P: 717.233.6133

Goodwill Industries of Pittsburgh, Inc.

http://www.goodwillpitt.org

Goodwill Industries of Pittsburgh runs a Team Pennsylvania CareerLink site, which provides computer skills and job search services to the public. Any further services require that the individual be recommended to the organization and that the recommending party provide payment. However, these services are provided to all types of people, including those with criminal records and other significant barriers to employment including developmental and other disabilities. These further services begin with a one to four-day assessment, depending on needs, in which the individual is evaluated for skill level, job interests and other necessary information. Participants are then given job training, educational assistance, computer-based training, drier training, on-the-job paid work training and placement in the community. Goodwill Industries of Pittsburgh also offers different workshops focused on employment and provides referrals for any other requirements. Goodwill Industries of Pittsburgh offers 18 months of follow-up services, including intervention at job sites and other support services.

Local Contact:

Goodwill Industries of Pittsburgh, Inc.
2600 East Carson Street
Pittsburgh, PA 15203
P: 412.390.2327

Higher Ground Foundation

The Higher Ground Foundation is a nonprofit ministry that focuses on helping prisoners, ex-offenders, and others experience a life-changing transformation through seminars and workshops.

Local Contact:

Higher Ground Foundation
P.O. Box 1602
Altoona, PA 16603
P: 814.742.7500

Jewish Employment and Vocational Service

http://www.jevs.org

The Jewish Employment and Vocational Service is a nonprofit social service agency that focuses on enhancing the employability and self-sufficiency of clients through a broad range of education, training, health and rehabilitation programs. The Jewish Employment and Vocational Service's Prison Program provides vocational training and vocational assessment services to the inmates of the Philadelphia prison system by offering hands-on skills training to increase employability once individuals return to society. Inmates may participate in a wide range of vocational classes, including: welding; building maintenance; horticulture; word processing; desktop publishing; and environmental maintenance. In addition, the "World of Work" program emphasizes the steps involved in seeking and retaining employment, including completing job applications, writing resumes, preparing for job interviews, coping with pressure of the workplace and achieving a positive work ethic. The Jewish Employment and Vocational Service works in conjunction with the Pennsylvania Prison Society to provide re-entry and other services to the prison population, as well as the growing Adopt-a-Program where public/private sector partnerships are established to help prisoners secure employment or appropriate programs upon their re-entry to the community.

Local Contact:

Jewish Employment and Vocational Service
Philadelphia Industrial Correctional Center
8301 State Road
Philadelphia, PA 19136
P: 215.685.7114

Jubilee Ministries
http://www.jub.org

Jubilee Ministries strives to demonstrate the love of God to the economically disadvantaged by helping to meet their physical, emotional, and material needs regardless of race, color, creed, age, or gender.

Local Contact:

Jubilee Ministries
235 South 12th Street
Lebanon, PA 17042
P: 717.274.7528

Justice and Mercy
http://www.justicemercy.org

Justice and Mercy is a nonprofit, volunteer organization dedicated to decreasing the effects of crime in communities, increasing public safety, and ministering to and restoring both crime victims and offenders. Justice and Mercy achieves these goals by educating and informing the public at large, advocating cost-effective and practical reforms within the criminal justice system and by supporting and encouraging wise public policy.

Local Contact:

Justice and Mercy
P.O. Box 223
Shillington, PA 19607
P: 610.208.0406

Methodist Union of Social Agencies
http://www.musa.org

Methodist Union of Social Agencies runs a program for single parents that provides hob readiness, life skills, job search, job placement, and job retention assistance and other follow-up services to clients from Homestead, the Steel Valley, and Pittsburgh (95% of whom are people with criminal records) through a Welfare-to-Work grant from the county and the Pennsylvania Department of Labor and Industry. Clients begin by undergoing a full one-on-one

assessment to determine their needs. There is also a six-month follow-up period following successful job placement, in which full services, including any vocational training, continue to be available.

Local Contact:

Methodist Union of Social Agencies
131 East 9th Avenue
Homestead, PA 15120
P: 412.461.1800

Pennsylvania Prison Society
http://www.prisonsociety.org

The Pennsylvania Prison Society offers re-entry services to recently released people with criminal records and to those transitioning from welfare to work who also have a criminal record. Life skills workshops, job development and employment services are available. The Pennsylvania Prison Society also offers inmate family services, elder prisoner services, restorative justice programs, advocacy efforts and community outreach and education.

Local Contact:

Pennsylvania Prison Society
2000 Spring Garden Street
Philadelphia, PA 19130
P: 215.564.4775

Philadelphia Workforce Development Corporation
http://www.owdc.org

With more than 20 years' experience, Philadelphia Workforce Development Corporation is the region's premier workforce development agency, serving more than 10,000 job seekers every year. Whether you're looking for your first job, or a new career, Philadelphia Workforce Development Corporation, in partnership with the Pennsylvania CareerLink system and Department of Public Welfare has the ability to deliver a comprehensive set of services to make you the right person for the job. Philadelphia Workforce Development Corporation offers the Fresh New Start program, which is designed for Pennsylvania CareerLink members with criminal backgrounds who face challenges in obtaining employment.

Local Contact:

Philadelphia Workforce Development Corporation
1617 John F. Kennedy Boulevard, 13th Floor
Philadelphia, PA 19103
P: 215.557.2625

Philadelphia Youth Network
The Philadelphia Youth Network runs Youth Opportunity centers for out-of-school youth under the age of 21 living in the Empowerment Zone. The centers offer services to youth with criminal records and work with the juvenile justice system. However, there are no specialized services directed towards this population, and there are no focused efforts to gather specific information on clients with criminal records.

The centers provide a number of services including re-engagement, job readiness, education services, and referrals to other needed services. Clients receive follow-up services two years following job placement.

Local Contact:

Philadelphia Youth Network
John F. Kennedy Center, Room 681
734 Schuylkill Avenue
Philadelphia, PA 19146
P: 215.875.3823

Program for Female Offenders

http://www.stophiv.com/details.asp?id=2074

The Program for Female Offenders is a free program that provides a variety of services to adult women who either have a drug or alcohol abuse problem or who have had some contact with the criminal justice system. The services provided by the organization include drug education and prevention programs, screening, case management (i.e. life skills programs), financial assistance, employment assistance, GED courses, counseling, nutrition and other services.

Local Contact:

Program for Female Offenders
1515 Derry Street
Harrisburg, PA 17104
P: 717.238.9950

Ramsey Education and Development Institute

Ramsey Education and Development Institute provides a number of educational and job-preparation services to any Pennsylvania resident over the age of 18 (approximately 25% of clients served have criminal records). The services provided include GED classes at a variety of levels, basic and advanced computer skills classes, assistance in preparing job applications and a Welfare-to-Work program for unemployed and underemployed mothers. The Ramsey Education and Development Institute also have a network of referrals to address clients; other needs.

Local Contact:

Ramsey Education and Development Institute
17 West Airy
Norristown, PA 19401
P: 610.279.0301

Reading-Berks Emergency Shelter

http://www.rbes.org

Reading-Berks Emergency Shelter provides a number of services, including around-the-clock childcare services; job-readiness and placement through the Reading-Berks Emergency Shelter Job Quest; primary health care services through the Reading Health Dispensary; shelter services that include case management, goal-planning, life skills instruction and aftercare services as well as a safe place to sleep, eat and shower for families and individuals; and transitional and permanent housing programs for families and individuals.

Local Contact:

Reading-Berks Emergency Shelter
430 North 2nd Street
Reading, PA 19601
P: 610.374.4696

Southwestern Pennsylvania Reentry Project

A coalition of nonprofit organizations formed in 2001-2002, the Southwestern Pennsylvania Reentry Project aims to provide a whole range of services, including job readiness preparation, as well as trying to organize a smooth transition from incarceration back into the community, by making people coming out aware of the resources available to them. The Southwestern Pennsylvania Reentry Project has begun forming relationships with local correctional institutions. Members of the Southwestern Pennsylvania Reentry Project plan to offer a matrix of services to anyone in the local area with a criminal record, including housing opportunities, drug and alcohol treatment, mental health services, transportation, childcare, family support, etc. People coming out of prison or jail can come to any member organization and will be referred to other agencies that can provide needed services not provided by that organization.

Local Contact:

Southwestern Pennsylvania Reentry Project
Mon Valley Initiative
303 East 8th Avenue
Homestead, PA 15120
P: 412.464.4000

STRIVE Philadelphia | Metropolitan Career Center

http://www.strivecentral.com/sites/national/mcc.htm

Metropolitan Career Center is a private, nonprofit accredited school that serves under-skilled and economically disadvantaged Philadelphia youth and adults, enabling them to find and keep jobs. The Metropolitan Career Center offers five roads to employment, ranging from STRIVE, a four-week quick "attachment to the workforce" program, to a 60-week training course in computer hardware and software support that confers an Associate Degree in Specialized Technology Training and is provided free of charge to qualified students. The Metropolitan Career Center, STRIVE is an intensive four-week program. The program stresses the development of interpersonal skills, team building, and employment readiness. Through structured classes and group interaction, students develop job application skills, including resume writing, interviewing, and telephone usage. Students also receive individual counseling to help them address personal and family issues or other barriers. Referrals to outside agencies for assistance with housing, childcare, and other needs are made as necessary. Formal collaborations have been developed with Children's Aid Society of Pennsylvania and the Tenant Action Group to facilitate students' easy access to these supplemental services. Additionally, STRIVE staff maintain an active job bank and refer students to appropriate interviews. After students graduate from STRIVE, they can take advantage of these services and participate in Job Club activities until they are employed.

In addition, Metropolitan Career Center instituted a pilot program in 2002, an enhancement to STRIVE called Employment Plus in which STRIVE graduates receive more intensive follow-up and support services for 12-months after graduation to encourage and support long-term job retention and skill upgrading. These services focus on helping participants to overcome problems in the workplace and in their personal lives that could lead to their termination or resignation. Lastly, GED and computer classes offered on Saturdays are geared towards helping graduates gain advancement in the workplace.

Local Contact:

STRIVE Philadelphia | Metropolitan Career Center
162 West Chelten Avenue
Philadelphia, PA 19144
P: 215.843.6615

PUERTO RICO

RHODE ISLAND

CrossRd.s

The CrossRd.s program assists ex-offenders in job development, including case management, counseling, respite services and information and referral, along with other programs.

Local Contact:

CrossRd.s
160 Broad Street
Providence, RI 02903
P: 401.521.2255

Family Resource Community Action

Family Resource Center Action provides services that include classroom training, as well as opportunities to practice job skills in a professional environment. Additional benefits include intensive case management and job placement assistance for those who complete the program. For individuals who meet certain income requirements, there is no cost; services are available to others at various fees. Programs include: Making It Work which helps low-income clients prepare for employment and find a job; it then provides case management for six months following placement employment. Career Connections is designed to help individuals receive public assistance to become self-sufficient. Participants have four weeks of job readiness training, volunteer work experience, and then six months of case management following job placement. The Summer Youth Employment Training Program helps participants 14 to 21 years old

develop job and interpersonal skills, and encourages completion of high school. Family Resource Community Action also provides referral to GED, literacy and other programs or services.

Local Contact:

Family Resource Community Action
245 Main Street
Woonsocket, RI 02895
P: 401.766.0900

Family Resource Community Action

Family Resource Center Action provides services that include classroom training, as well as opportunities to practice job skills in a professional environment. Additional benefits include intensive case management and job placement assistance for those who complete the program. For individuals who meet certain income requirements, there is no cost; services are available to others at various fees. Programs include: Making It Work which helps low-income clients prepare for employment and find a job; it then provides case management for six months following placement employment. Career Connections is designed to help individuals receive public assistance to become self-sufficient. Participants have four weeks of job readiness training, volunteer work experience, and then six months of case management following job placement. The Summer Youth Employment Training Program helps participants 14 to 21 years old develop job and interpersonal skills, and encourages completion of high school. Family Resource Community Action also provides referral to GED, literacy and other programs or services.

Local Contact:

Family Resource Community Action
800 Clinton Street
Woonsocket, RI 02895
P: 401.765.5797

RI Network Center of Pawtucket

RI Network Centers provide educational training, and employment assistance to ex-offenders throughout Rhode Island.

Local Contact:

RI Network Center of Pawtucket
175 Main Street
Pawtucket, RI 02860
P: 401.721.1800

RI Network Center of Providence

RI Network Centers provide educational training, and employment assistance to ex-offenders throughout Rhode Island.

Local Contact:

RI Network Center of Providence
1 Reservoir Avenue
Providence, RI 02907
P: 401.462.8900

RI Network Center of West Warwick

RI Network Centers provide educational training, and employment assistance to ex-offenders throughout Rhode Island.

Local Contact:

RI Network Center of West Warwick
1330 Main Street
West Warwick, RI 02893
P: 401.828.8382

RI Network Center of Woonsocket

RI Network Centers provide educational training, and employment assistance to ex-offenders throughout Rhode Island.

Local Contact:

RI Network Center of Woonsocket
219 Pond Street
Woonsocket, RI 02895
P: 401.235.1201

Travelers Aid Society of Rhode Island

The Travelers Aid Society of Rhode Island assists ex-offenders in job development. Originally and on-site program at the Rhode Island Adult Correctional Institute called Making it Work, the program continues to help prisoners make the transition from prison to community life, specifically through employment services.

Local Contact:

Travelers Aid Society of Rhode Island
Justice Services Program
177 Union Street
Providence, RI 02903
P: 401.521.2255

Women in Transition, Inc.

The Women in Transition program is a resource for women who are beginning to transition back into community life. Women in Transition provides case management, counseling, life skills training, parenting classes, job development and housing assistance to those in need.

Local Contact:

Women in Transition, Inc.
P.O. Box 20135
Cranston, RI 02920
P: 401.462.1767

SOUTH CAROLINA

Alston Wilkes Society

http://www.alstonwilkessociety.org

The Alston Wilkes Society is a nonprofit organization that offers a variety of post-release services to formerly incarcerated individuals. They operate two co-ed facilities that house inmates from the Federal Bureau of Prisons. These facilities are located in Columbia and Greenville, South Carolina.

Local Contact:

Alston Wilkes Society
3519 Medical Drive
Columbia, SC 29203
P: 803.799.2490

Citizens United for Rehabilitation of Errants

CURE, Citizens United for Rehabilitation of Errants is a national nonprofit prison advocacy organization with state and special interest chapters throughout the United States. Local and special interest chapters provide assistance to ex-offenders on a limited basis within their respective service areas.

Local Contact:

Citizens United for Rehabilitation of Errants
P.O. Box 421
Green Pond, SC 29446
P: Not Provided

SOUTH DAKOTA

Citizens United for Rehabilitation of Errants

CURE, Citizens United for Rehabilitation of Errants is a national nonprofit prison advocacy organization with state and special interest chapters throughout the United States. Local and special interest chapters provide assistance to ex-offenders on a limited basis within their respective service areas.

Local Contact:

Citizens United for Rehabilitation of Errants
804 Nunda Place
Sioux Falls, SD 57107
P: 605.334.5472

South Dakota Prisoner Support Group

The South Dakota Prisoner Support Group was formed to support people on the inside, ex-offenders, family, and friends, and to draw attention to racist injustices, medical neglect, and illegal conditions inside South Dakota prisons and jails.

Local Contact:

South Dakota Prisoner Support Group
P.O. Box 3285
Rapid City, SD 57709
P: 605.399.7830

TENNESSEE

Breakaway Outreach

http://www.breakawayoutreach.com

Breakaway Outreach is a faith-based organization dedicated to helping kids Break-away from a troubled past by communicating the life-changing message of Jesus Christ so that every juvenile offender, and young person at-risk of delinquency, has the opportunity to hear and respond to that message.

Local Contact:

Breakaway Outreach
P.O. Box 3452
Cleveland, TN 37320
P: 423.559.9649

Chattanooga Endeavors

http://www.chattanoogaendeavors.com

Chattanooga Endeavors assists recently released individuals through a number of services, including preparation for employment. Assistance includes assessment, re-socialization, soft skills training, skill acquisition, extensive case management, group sessions and positive reinforcement. Computerized software is used to increase job skills and for educational purposes.

Local Contact:

Chattanooga Endeavors
P.O. Box 3351
Chattanooga, TN 37404
P: 423.266.1888

Citizens United for Rehabilitation of Errants

CURE, Citizens United for Rehabilitation of Errants is a national nonprofit prison advocacy organization with state and special interest chapters throughout the United States. Local and special interest chapters provide assistance to ex-offenders on a limited basis within their respective service areas.

Local Contact:

Citizens United for Rehabilitation of Errants
3850 Dunbar Drive
Nashville, TN 37207
P: Not Provided

Dismas House of Nashville

http://www.dismas.org

Dismas House is a supportive community shared by recently released offenders, college students, and local volunteers.

Typical length of stay is four to six months. Residents are expected to find employment and leave the community with a stable income, sense of self-worth and hope for a sober and productive future.

Local Contact:

Dismas House of Nashville
1513 16th Avenue
Nashville, TN 37212
P: 615.297.9287

Dismas House of Cooksville

http://www.dismas.org

Dismas House is a supportive community shared by recently released offenders, college students, and local volunteers. Typical length of stay is four to six months. Residents are expected to find employment and leave the community with a stable income, sense of self-worth and hope for a sober and productive future.

Local Contact:

Dismas House of Cooksville
1226 Byrne Avenue
Cooksville, TN 38502
P: 931.520.8448

Dismas House of Knoxville

Dismas House is a supportive community shared by recently released inmates, college students, and local volunteers. Typical length of stay is four to six months. Residents are expected to find employment and leave the community with a stable income, sense of self-worth and hope for a sober and productive future.

Local Contact:

Dismas House of Knoxville
1316 Forest Avenue
Knoxville, TN 37923
P: 931.520.8448

Dismas House of Memphis

http://www.dismas.org

Dismas House is a supportive community shared by recently released offenders, college students, and local volunteers. Typical length of stay is four to six months. Residents are expected to find employment and leave the community with a stable income, sense of self-worth and hope for a sober and productive future.

Local Contact:

Dismas House of Memphis
320 East Street
Memphis, TN 37212
P: 901.526.3701

Free-Enterprise Program
http://www.tricor.org

The Free-Enterprise program was established in 1994 for skilled workers who have served their sentences and can no longer work for TRICOR Industries. The program utilizes the Work Opportunity Tax Credit program and information about the federal Bonding Program as incentives to for-profit businesses to hire individuals with criminal records. Job placement coordinators cover the entire state. Workers must meet the following eligibility criteria: complete at least one year of successful training in a TRICOR program within three years of release; be within six weeks of release if the sentence does not involve parole; be approved by the Board of Probation and Parole and the employment requirement is the only factor that prevents release; have a high school diploma or GED; completed a TRICOR Life Skills program prior to release; completed a TRICOR Date Sheet and Resume indicating skills acquired and the number of years in training; and, agree to communicate with TRICOR staff regarding employment status after release for a period not to exceed three years.

Local Contact:

Free-Enterprise Program
TRICOR Industries
240 Great Circle Road, Suite 310
Nashville, TN 37228
P: 615.741.5705

Karat Place

Karat Place provides transitional housing for homeless women and women who have recently been released from incarceration. Karat Place can house up to 12 women and their children (no boys over the age of 12 years old are permitted to live in the units). Rent is free until employment is secured and then the rate is 30% of the resident's earned wages. Women may stay up to two years. There is limited job development and placement assistance, though Karat House staff work with local companies that are willing to hire individuals with criminal histories.

Local Contact:

Karat Place
829 North Parkway
Memphis, TN 38105
P: 901.525.4055

Project Return, Inc.
http://www.projectreturninc.org

Project Return provides a number of programs that assist individuals with criminal histories. The Jobs & Futures Program is available to any adult who has been incarcerated or is currently incarcerated and is planning for release by providing: life skills and job readiness training; employment placement services; direct aid (bus passes, emergency food boxes, etc.); and information and referral to support services, as well as on-going follow-up and job counseling.

Pre-Release Activities/Job Readiness Program is an intensive four-week program that prepares inmates for a productive job search. The curriculum includes instruction in the application process, want ads, networking, interviewing skills, attitude and job retention. Survival Skills aims to empower clients to effectively manage their family and employment responsibilities. During the 10 three-hour workshops, participants have the opportunity to learn and practice skills including money management, problem solving, family development, goal setting and conflict resolution.

Local Contact:

Project Return, Inc.
1200 Division Street, Suite 200
Nashville, TN 37203
P: 615.327.9654

Second Chance | YO! Memphis
http://www.yomemphis.org

The Second Chance program is a private/public partnership between the city of Memphis and local businesses designed to connect people with criminal histories looking for work with employers who are willing to hire them. To graduate from the program an applicant must keep a job for six months to a year, maintain a good work record and remain drug free. This program is open to those people who have only on felony conviction and is run under the umbrella of YO! Memphis, a youth workforce development program.

Local Contact:

Second Chance | YO! Memphis
444 North Main Street
Memphis, TN 38103
P: 901.545.0343

TEXAS

Association of X-Offenders, Inc.
http://www.xoffenders.org

The Association of X-Offenders, Inc. provides self-help support groups, information, referrals, mentoring, and religious ministry.

Local Contact:

Association of X-Offenders, Inc.
219 East William Joel Bryan Parkway, P.O. Box 3785
Bryan, TX 77805
P: 979.775.9200

Bridging the Gap Ministries
http://www.bridgingthegap.com

Bridging the Gap Ministries if a nonprofit organization that provides multiple services to the previously incarcerated and their families.

Local Contact:

Bridging the Gap Ministries
P.O. Box 131747
Tyler, TX 75713
P: 903.539.6797

Citizens United for Rehabilitation of Errants

CURE, Citizens United for Rehabilitation of Errants is a national nonprofit prison advocacy organization with state and special interest chapters throughout the United States. Local and special interest chapters provide assistance to ex-offenders on a limited basis within their respective service areas.

Local Contact:

Citizens United for Rehabilitation of Errants
P.O. Box 372
Burleson, TX 76097
P: Not Provided

Crime Prevention Institute

The Crime Prevention Institute provides post-release services including supportive resources, job placement services, employment monitoring and incentives, follow-up and information and referral services.

Local Contact:

Crime Prevention Institute
Targeted Project Re-Enterprise
8401 Shoal Creek Boulevard
Austin, TX 78763
P: 512.502.9704

Diocese of Beaumont Criminal Justice Ministry

http://www.dioceseofbmt.org

The Diocese of Beaumont offers an extensive selection of programs and services to recently released ex-offenders and their families through their Criminal Justice Ministry.

Local Contact:

Diocese of Beaumont Criminal Justice Ministry
P.O. Box 3948
Beaumont, TX 77704
P: 409.838.0451

Encompassing Reentry Ministries and Outreach

http://www.prisonministry.net

The Encompassing Reentry Ministry and Outreach program provides services to previously incarcerated individuals and their families.

Local Contact:

Encompassing Reentry Ministries and Outreach
P.O. Box 851587
Mesquite, TX 75185
P: Not Provided

Exodus Ministries, Inc.

http://www.exodusministry.4t.com

Exodus Ministries, Inc. provides aftercare and transitional services to people with criminal records by providing a place to live, employment training and placement, life skills and transportation.

Local Contact:

Exodus Ministries, Inc.
4630 Munger Avenue, #10
Dallas, TX 75204
P: 214.827.3772

Goodwill Industries of Dallas

http://www.goodwilldallas.org

Goodwill Industries provides training, skill development and work opportunities for people with disabilities and other barriers to employment.

Local Contact:

Goodwill Industries of Dallas
2800 North Hampton Road
Dallas, TX 75112
P: 214.638.2800

Goodwill Industries of Houston

http://www.goodwillhouston.org

Goodwill Industries of Houston offers assistance to individuals with criminal records who are referred to them by the Texas Rehabilitation Commission or Texas Workforce Commission. Instruction in soft skills, such as resume writing, interview techniques, and workplace responsibilities is given. Basic computer skills as well as basic accounting and finance techniques are taught. Job training for employment at Jiffy Lube is also available.

Local Contact:

Goodwill Industries of Houston
2030 Westheimer
Houston, TX 77098
P: 713.699.6311

Goodwill Industries of Southeast Texas and Southwest Louisiana

http://www.goodwillbmt.org

Goodwill Industries provides training, skill development and work opportunities for people with disabilities and other barriers to employment.

Local Contact:

Goodwill Industries of Southeast Texas and Southwest Louisiana
460 Wall Street
Beaumont, TX 77701
P: 409.838.9911

HoustonWorks USA

http://www.houstonworks.com

HoustonWorks USA is the largest operator of workforce centers in the Houston and greater Harris County region. These centers provide local access to job search and programs for adults 18 years and older. Three youth centers have been established within the Fifth Ward, Third Ward, and East End communities to address the unique job search concerns of youth between the ages of 14 and 25. Training is available in career fields such as healthcare, business, computers and education.

> **Local Contact:**
>
> HoustonWorks USA
> 600 Jefferson, Suite 900
> Houston, TX 77002
> P: 713.654.1919

MASS | (Mothers [Fathers]) for the Advancement of Social Systems, Inc.

http://www.massjab.org

Mothers [Fathers] for the Advancement of Social Systems, Inc. is a nonprofit organization that provides support services for individuals released from Texas State Prison. Services include, but are not limited to, assisting individuals in securing housing, employment, counseling, and any necessary support that eases reentry transition. In addition, Mothers [Fathers] for the Advancement of Social Systems, Inc. provides help with freeing innocent individuals who have been imprisoned.

> **Local Contact:**
>
> MASS | (Mothers [Fathers]) for the Advancement of Social Systems, Inc.
> 3737 Atlanta Street
> Dallas, TX 75215
> P: 214.421.0303

Mercy Heart

http://www.mercyheart.org

Mercy heart is a faith-based organization that assists families and children of the confined through and beyond the transition of incarceration towards mental, emotional, material and spiritual well-being.

> **Local Contact:**
>
> Mercy Heart
> 4805 Northeast Loop 820
> Fort Worth, TX 76137
> P: 817.514.0290

Morning Star Jail & Prison Ministry

http://www.morningstar-baptist.org

The Morning Star Jail & Prison Ministry is a service of Morning Star Baptist Church dedicated to providing services for previously incarcerated individuals and their families.

> **Local Contact:**
>
> Morning Star Jail & Prison Ministry
> 2251 El Paso
> Grand Prairie, TX 75051
> P: Not Provided

Saints of Christ Prison Ministry

The Saints of Christ Ministry is faith-based program that offers services to recently released offenders and their families.

> **Local Contact:**
>
> Saints of Christ Prison Ministry
> P.O. Box 111275
> Houston, TX 77293
> P: 281.449.2703

Welcome Home House

Welcome Home House is a recovery program for parolees that includes a structured drug free environment.

> **Local Contact:**
>
> Welcome Home House
> 921 North Peak Street
> Dallas, TX 75204
> P: 214.887.5204

UTAH

Behind the Wire Prisoner Information Network

Behind the Wire Prisoner Information Network is a resource organization for individuals incarcerated in Utah and their families.

> **Local Contact:**
>
> Behind the Wire Prisoner Information Network
> 235 West 100 South
> Salt Lake City, UT 84101
> P: 801.335.0234

VERMONT

Citizens United for Rehabilitation of Errants

CURE, Citizens United for Rehabilitation of Errants is a national nonprofit prison advocacy organization with state and special interest chapters throughout the United States. Local and special interest chapters provide assistance to ex-offenders on a limited basis within their respective service areas.

> **Local Contact:**
>
> Citizens United for Rehabilitation of Errants
> P.O. Box 484
> Montpelier, VT 05601
> P: 802.371.9932

Vermont Catholic Charities

http://www.vermontcatholic.org

Vermont Catholic Charities provides a wide variety of programs and services to previously incarcerated men and women including employment and transitional housing assistance.

Local Contact:

Vermont Catholic Charities
351 North Avenue
Burlington, VT 05401
P: 802.658.6110

Vermont Works for Women

http://www.vtworksforwomen.org

In addition to their Modular Home Program, Vermont Works for Women offers a Transitional Jobs program for women who are transitioning out of incarceration or off of public assistance. The transitional jobs program is a 10-week "soft skills" job readiness course, combined with short-term (3 months) job placement with area employers.

Local Contact:

Vermont Works for Women
Transitional Jobs Program
51 Park Street
Essex Junction, VT 05401
P: 802.655.8900

Vermont Works for Women

http://www.vtworksforwomen.org

Vermont Works for Women works to address the needs of women in Vermont to earn a livable wage and to succeed despite numerous personal, educational and economic barriers to employment. Vermont Works for Women currently offers and Modular Home project in the Northwest State Correctional Facility, in which female inmates build a modular home from start to finish, thereby learning carpentry, wiring, and plumbing. Once completed, the home is sold as low-income housing.

Local Contact:

Vermont Works for Women
Vocational Training for Incarcerated Women
51 Park Street
Essex Junction, VT 05401
P: 802.655.8900

VIRGINIA

Caregivers Choice

http://www.mentoring.org

Caregivers Choice is an innovative project that connects children of incarcerated parents to quality mentoring programs.

Local Contact:

Caregivers Choice
1600 Duke Street, Suite 300
Alexandria, VA 22314
P: 703.224.2200

Citizens United for Rehabilitation of Errants

http://www.vacure.org

CURE, Citizens United for Rehabilitation of Errants is a national nonprofit prison advocacy organization with state and special interest chapters throughout the United States. Local and special interest chapters provide assistance to ex-offenders on a limited basis within their respective service areas.

Local Contact:

Citizens United for Rehabilitation of Errants
P.O. Box 2310
Vienna, VA 22183
P: 703.272.3624

Offender Aid and Restoration of Arlington

Offender Aid and Restoration provides direct referrals, employment and vocational guidance, skills training, job placement, and counseling services to previously incarcerated individuals and the disadvantaged.

Local Contact:

Offender Aid and Restoration of Arlington
1400 Uhle Street, Suite 704
Arlington, VA 22201
P: 703.228.7030

Offender Aid and Restoration of Charlottesville & Albemarle

Offender Aid and Restoration provides direct referrals, employment and vocational guidance, skills training, job placement, and counseling services to previously incarcerated individuals and the disadvantaged.

Local Contact:

Offender Aid and Restoration of Charlottesville & Albemarle
750 Harris Street, Suite 207
Charlottesville, VA 22903
P: 434.296.2441

Offender Aid and Restoration of Richmond

http://www.oarric.org

Offender Aid and Restoration provides direct referrals, employment and vocational guidance, skills training, job placement, and counseling services to previously incarcerated individuals and the disadvantaged.

Local Contact:

Offender Aid and Restoration of Richmond
1 North 3rd Street, Suite 200
Richmond, VA 23219
P: 804.643.2746

Richmond Community Action Program, Inc.

http://www.rcapva.org

The Richmond Community Action Program provides post-release services including life skills training, consumer education, social skills and family relationship workshops, and emergency assistance in locating counseling, housing, employment, clothing, and transportation.

Local Contact:

Richmond Community Action Program, Inc.
1021 Oliver Hill Way
Richmond, VA 23219
P: 804.788.0050

TAP Virginia CARES (Community Action Program)

http://www.tapintohope.org

The TAP Virginia CARES (Community Action Re-entry System) program facilitates the return of people with criminal records to their communities and society. They provide basic needs assessment and support services, including employment counseling, assistance with job leads, transportation, resume and application assistance, peer support groups, civil rights restoration assistance, and referrals to appropriate agencies to people with criminal records and their families.

Local Contact:

TAP Virginia CARES (Community Action Program)
141 Campbell Avenue, SW, TAP Room 147
Roanoke, VA 24016
P: 540.342.9344

WASHINGTON

Central Area Motivation Program Reentry Services

http://www.campseattle.org

The Reentry Services Program of the Central Area Motivational Program offers ex-offenders programs designed to transition clients back into the workforce.

Local Contact:

Central Area Motivation Program Reentry Services
722 18th Avenue
Seattle, WA 98122
P: 206.812.4940

Citizens United for Rehabilitation of Errants

CURE, Citizens United for Rehabilitation of Errants is a national nonprofit prison advocacy organization with state and special interest chapters throughout the United States. Local and special interest chapters provide assistance to ex-offenders on a limited basis within their respective service areas.

Local Contact:

Citizens United for Rehabilitation of Errants
P.O. Box 515
Longview, WA 98632
P: Not Provided

Compass Center

http://www.compasscenter.org

The Compass Center is a Lutheran organization comprised of four shelters for those in immediate need, a transitional center for women, and transitional housing, Services provided include, mail services, the Compass center Bank, hygiene center, and chaplaincy.

Local Contact:

Compass Center
77 South Washington Street
Seattle, WA 98104
P: 206.357.3100

Crossways Ministries

http://www.crosswaysministries.com

Crossways Ministries, a faith-based organization, provides a two year interactive program in 11 facilities promoting responsible living to achieve freedom. Services provided include housing placement, employment, counseling/mentoring and fellowship. Crossways Ministries collaborates with other agencies to better serve individuals with criminal histories.

Local Contact:

Crossways Ministries
P.O. Box 1954
Auburn, WA 98071
P: Not Provided

Downtown Emergency Service Center

The Downtown Emergency Shelter gives priority to women, men over 60, mentally ill, physically or developmentally disabled and chemically dependent people in need of shelter services.

Local Contact:

Downtown Emergency Service Center
517 Third Avenue
Seattle, WA 98104
P: 206.464.1570

Goodwill Industries Inland Northwest

http://www.giin.org

Goodwill Industries Inland Northwest offers employment resources to individuals with criminal histories who have been released from custody within the previous year. Services include resume writing, counseling in how to address one's conviction history, interview skills and job development. Goodwill Industries relies on employer incentives, including the Federal Bonding Program and the Work Opportunity Tax Credit. Clients are followed for a one-year period, including re-employment, if necessary, as well as upgrading job levels.

Local Contact:

Goodwill Industries Inland Northwest
130 East 3rd Avenue
Spokane, WA 99202
P: 509.444.4319

Interaction Transition Program

Interactive Transition assists ex-offenders who are serious about making a successful transition from life in prison t life in the community. Interactive Transition operates a low-cost housing facility with transitioning support services.

Local Contact:

Interaction Transition Program
935 16th Avenue
Seattle, WA 98122
P: 206.324.3932

M-2 Job Therapy

M-2 Job Therapy provides a wide range of employment services for ex-offenders, including job referrals and resume assistance.

Local Contact:

M-2 Job Therapy
205 Avenue C
Snohomish, WA 96291
P: 877.625.6214

People for People
http://www.pfp.org

People for People is a nonprofit organization committed to serving people throughout Washington with employment and training needs.

Local Contact:

People for People
401 East Mt. View
Ellensburg, WA 98926
P: 509.925.5311

Pioneer Human Services
http://www.pioneerhumanserv.com

The mission of Pioneer Human Services is to create opportunities for clients to realize personal, economic, and social development through participating in an integrated array of training, employment, housing, and rehabilitation services.

Local Contact:

Pioneer Human Services
7440 West Marginal Way South
Seattle, WA 98108
P: 206.768.1990

Salvation Army Northwest Divisional Headquarters
http://www.nwarmy.org

The Salvation Army Northwest Divisional Headquarters oversees a wide range of service programs including support services for offenders and their families, coordinates shelter beds for ex-offenders and much more.

Local Contact:

Salvation Army Northwest Divisional Headquarters
P.O. Box 9219
Seattle, WA 98109
P: 206.587.0503

Salvation Army William Booth Center

The Salvation Army William Booth Center provides dormitory shelter space for Department of Corrections male inmates and a limited number of sex offenders.

Local Contact:

Salvation Army William Booth Center
811 Maynard Avenue South
Seattle, WA 98134
P: 206.287.0125

Seattle Goodwill | STRIVE Seattle
http://www.seattlegoodwill.org

Seattle Goodwill offers three programs: the Adult Basic Education Program, the Employment and Training Program, and STRIVE. The Adult Basic Education Program offers people aged 16 and over the opportunity to participate in classes to improve basic skills in subjects such as reading, writing, math, and computers. Adult Basic Education also offers basic life skills, English for speakers of other languages, citizenship, and GED preparation courses, as well as specialized programs such as the External Diploma Program, the Workplace Education Program and Sound-Waves. Each course is free and open to anyone who wants to participate. The Employment and Training Program is designed especially for individuals with barriers to employment such as a lack of education and work experience or limited English speaking ability. The Employment and Training Program combines classroom instruction with hands on job site experience, career planning, and job placement. STRIVE is a privately funded, nonprofit employment training and placement program. STRIVE provides training and placement services for participants and ongoing support to employers and employees. STRIVE provides intensive training that focuses largely on developing and reinforcing the workplace behaviors, attitudes and skills that are necessary to get and keep a good job.

Local Contact:

Seattle Goodwill | STRIVE Seattle
1400 South Lane Street
Seattle, WA 98144
P: 206.860.5767

WEST VIRGINIA

Citizens United for Rehabilitation of Errants

CURE, Citizens United for Rehabilitation of Errants is a national nonprofit prison advocacy organization with state and special interest chapters throughout the United States. Local and special interest chapters provide assistance to ex-offenders on a limited basis within their respective service areas.

> **Local Contact:**
>
> Citizens United for Rehabilitation of Errants
> P.O. Box 421
> Linn, WV 26384
> P: Not Provided

WISCONSIN

Citizens United for Rehabilitation of Errants

CURE, Citizens United for Rehabilitation of Errants is a national nonprofit prison advocacy organization with state and special interest chapters throughout the United States. Local and special interest chapters provide assistance to ex-offenders on a limited basis within their respective service areas.

> **Local Contact:**
>
> Citizens United for Rehabilitation of Errants
> P.O. Box 183
> Greendale, WI 53129
> P: 414.409.7028

Madison Urban Ministries

http://www.emum.org

Madison Urban Ministries, an interfaith organization, has a restorative justice project that supports people with criminal histories in their attempts to reenter society. Four to five volunteers form a "circle of support" to assist program participants with problems that arise upon their release from incarceration. Areas addressed are housing, transportation, employment referrals, counseling, substance/alcohol treatment, family reunification, and child support issues. People with criminal histories may be core members of the support circles and also form a speakers' bureau to address community groups.

> **Local Contact:**
>
> Madison Urban Ministries
> 2300 South Park Street, Suite 5
> Madison, WI 53713
> P: 608.256.0906

Milwaukee Transitional Jobs Reentry Project

The Milwaukee Transitional Jobs Project is a demonstration project funded by the Joyce Foundation to study the effectiveness of Transitional Jobs as a bridge to permanent employment for ex-offenders reentering the community after a period of incarceration. The goal of the Milwaukee Transitional Jobs Reentry Project is to provide qualified employees to Milwaukee area businesses while reducing the rate of recidivism among Wisconsin's ex-offender population creating a successful match between businesses and job seekers.

> **Local Contact:**
>
> Milwaukee Transitional Jobs Reentry Project
> 2821 North 4th Street, Suite 211
> Milwaukee, WI 53212
> P: 414.267.6020

WYOMING

Community Action of Laramie County

http://www.calc.net

Community Action of Laramie County provides workshops that address self-sufficiency issues including: self-image and performance; conflict and stress management; assertiveness training; career choices; and budgeting. It also provides housing assistance.

> **Local Contact:**
>
> Community Action of Laramie County
> 1620 Central Avenue, Suite 300
> Cheyenne, WY 82001
> P: 307.635.9291

Human Services Commission of Natrona County

http://www.hscnc.org

Human Services Commission of Natrona County provides outreach, advocacy, emergency services, self-sufficiency services, employment and training, housing, and volunteer services.

> **Local Contact:**
>
> Human Services Commission of Natrona County
> 800 Werner Court, Suite 201
> Casper, WY 82601
> P: 307.232.0124

APPENDIX 1-B: FEDERAL RESIDENTIAL REENTRY CENTERS

Residential Reentry Centers, formerly known as Community Confinement Centers are the Federal Bureau of Prisons means of transitioning prisoners back into society. The general purpose of Residential Reentry Center placement is to assist those with transitioning needs in establishing a foothold in the community before being discharged from custody.

ALASKA
Cordova Center
130 Cordova Street
Anchorage, AK 99501
P: 907.274.1022

Northstar Center
Mile 353.5 Parks Highway
Fairbanks, AK 99707
P: 907.474.4955

ALABAMA
Birmingham Community Services
1609 7th Street North
Birmingham, Al 35204
P: 205.324.8015

Bannum Place Of Montgomery
540 Sayre Street
Montgomery, Al 36104
P: 334.262.0227

Mobile Community Service
4901 Battleship Parkway
Spanish Fort, Al 36527
P: 251.626.5094

ARKANSAS
City Of Faith Community Corrections Center
1401 South Garfield Drive
Little Rock, AR 72204
P: 501.615.1090

ARIZONA
Behavioral Systems Southwest
950 East Diversion Dam Road
Florence, AZ 85232
P: 520.868.0880

BSS-CSC
2846 East Roosevelt Road
Phoenix, AZ 85008
P: 602.273.6293

BSSW-CSC (Pregnant Offender)
2846 East Roosevelt Road
Phoenix, AZ 85008
P: 602.273.6293

Behavioral Systems Southwest
6420 South Park Avenue
Tucson, AZ 85706
P: 520.573.3111

New Beginnings Treatment Center
2445 North Oracle Road
Tucson, AZ 85705
P: 520.624.0075

CALIFORNIA
Turning Point CCC-Bakersfield
1101 Union Avenue
Bakersfield, CA 93385
P: 661.325.5774

Western Care Centers, Inc.
11675 East End Avenue
Chino, CA 91710
P: 909.591.8538

Cornell Corrections – El Monte
11750 Ramona Boulevard
El Monte, CA 91732
P: 626.454.4593

Turning Point CCC – Fresno
3547 South Golden State Boulevard
Fresno, CA 93725
P: 559.442.8075

Garden Grove CCCC
11112 Barclay Drive
Garden Grove, CA 92641
P: 714.537.3607

Cornell Corrections, Inc. – Santa Barbara
6575 Trigo Road
Goleta, CA 93117
P: 805.968.6066

Working Alternatives
4026 West Century Boulevard
Inglewood, CA 90304
P: 310.671.3629

Gateways CCC
1801 Lakeshore Drive
Los Angeles, CA 90026
P: 323.644.2020

Vinewood Re-Entry CCC
5520 Harold Way
Los Angeles, CA 90028
P: 323.464.0817

Cornell Corrections – Oakland
205 Mac Arthur Boulevard
Oakland, CA 94610
P: 510.839.9051

Rubidoux Re-Entry CCC
3263 Rubidoux Boulevard
Rubidoux, CA 92509
P: 909.684.4840

Turning Point CCC – Salinas
116 East San Luis
Salinas, CA 93901
P: 831.422.9171

Correctional Alternatives, Inc.
551 South 35th Street
San Diego, CA 92113
P: 619.232.8600

Pacific Furlough Facility
2727 Boston Avenue
San Diego, CA 92113
P: 619.232.1066

CCI Mother w/Infant Program
111 Taylor Street
San Francisco, CA 94102
P: 415.346.9769

Cornell Correctional – San Francisco
111 Taylor Street
San Francisco, CA 94102
P: 415.346.9769

Turning Point CCC – Visalia
1845 South Court Street
Visalia, CA 93277
P: 559.732.5550

COLORADO
Comcor, Inc.
5250 North Nevada Street
Colorado Spring, CO 80918
P: 719.590.7600

Independence House
2765 South Federal Boulevard
Denver, CO 80236
P: 303.936.2035

Independence House
1479 Fillmore Street
Denver, CO 80206
P: 303.321.1718

Hilltop House Community Corrections
1050 Avenida Del Sol
Durango, CO 81301
P: 970.382.8406

Mesa County Criminal Justice Services
559 Pitkin Avenue
Grand Junction, CO 81501
P: 970.244.3303

CONNECTICUT
Cheyney House
155 Weathersfield Avenue
Hartford, CT 06106
P: 860.524.1774

Hartford House
10 Irving Street
Hartford, CT 06112
P: 860.547.1313

Watkinson House
136 Collins Street
Hartford, CT 06105
P: 860.524.1898

DISTRICT OF COLUMBIA
Community Care
3301 16th Street, NW
Washington, DC 20010
P: 202.842.7046

D.C. Department Corrections
1514 8th Street, NW
Washington, DC 20001
P: 202.232.1932

Fairview CSC
1430 G Street, NE
Washington, DC 20002
P: 202.396.8982

Hope Village CSC/CCC
2840 Langston Place, SE
Washington, DC 20020
P: 202.678.1551

Shaw Residence
1740 Park Road, NW
Washington, DC 20010
P: 202.842.7043

DELAWARE
Sussex Work Release Center
Road 6, Box 700
Georgetown, DE 19947
P: 302.856.5790

Plummer Community Corrections Center
38 Todds Lane
Wilmington, DE 19802
P: 302.577.3039

FLORIDA
Dismas House Charities, Inc.
141 NW 1st Avenue
Dania, FL 33004
P: 954.920.6558

Salvation Army
2400 Edison Avenue
Ft. Myers, FL 33902
P: 941.332.0140

Riverside House
968 NW 2nd Street
Miami, Fl 33128
P: 305.545.0926

Spectrum Programs, Inc.
101 NW 59th Street
Miami, FL 33127
P: 305.758.3634

Ocala Community Services Center
3820 NE 41st Street
Ocala, FL 34479
P: 352.368.2127

Bannum Place Of Orlando
2041 Mercy Drive
Orlando, FL 32808
P: 407.522.6200

Pensacola Community Services Center
5445-A Duval Street
Pensacola, FL 32503
P: 850.474.1991

Bannum of Tallahassee
1818 South Monroe Street
Tallahassee, FL 32303
P: 850.521.3431

Hillsborough Correctional CSC
4102 West Hillsborough Avenue
Tampa, FL 33614
P: 813.877.2257

The Salvation Army
1577 North Military Trail
West Palm Beach, FL 33409
P: 561.689.1212

GEORGIA
CCC – Dismas Charities of Atlanta
1010 West Peachtree Street, NE
Atlanta, GA 30309
P: 404.876.4690

CSC – Dismas House Of Atlanta
300 Wendell Court
Atlanta, GA 30336
P: 404.691.1425

CSC – Dismas House Of Macon
742-744 Second Street
Macon, GA 31201
P: 478.745.8733

CCC – Bannum, Incorporated
804 L.P. Owens Drive #1010
Savannah, GA 31408
P: 912.963.0032

HAWAII
Miller Hale
1547 Miller Street
Honolulu, HI 96813
P: 808.524.5888

IOWA

2nd – Curt Forbes Residential Center
111 Sherman Avenue
Ames, IA 50010
P: 515.232.3774

6th – Community Corrections Center
1051 29th Avenue, SW
Cedar Rapids, IA 52404
P: 319.398.3668

6th – Community Corrections Center
2501 Holiday Road
Coralville, IA 52241
P: 319.625.2202

Comp Sanctions Center
1228 South Main
Council Bluffs, IA 51503
P: 712.325.9306

7th - Davenport Work Release Center
605 Main, Box 2A
Davenport, IA 52803
P: 563.322.7986

5th – Des Moines Women Facility
1917 Hickman Road
Des Moines, IA 50314
P: 515.242.6325

5th – Ft. Des Moines Residential facility
70 Thayer Avenue & Hancock Boulevard
Des Moines, IA 50315
P: 515.242.6956

1st – Dubuque Residential Facility
1494 Elm Street
Dubuque, IA 52001
P: 563.556.6196

2nd – Ft. Dodge Residential Facility
703 1st Avenue North
Ft. Dodge, IA 50501
P: 515.955.6393

2nd – Beje Clark Residential Facility
P.O. Box 1226
Mason City, IA 50402
P: 641.424.3817

1st -Waterloo Res. Wrk/Rls Cent
314 E 6th Street, P.O. Box 4030
Waterloo, Ia 50703
P: 563.291.2015

1st -West Union Residential Facility
500 South Pine
West Union, IA 52175
P: 319.422.5758

IDAHO

Port of Hope Coeur D'alene Residential Center
218 North 23rd Street
Coeur D'alene, ID 83814
P: 208.664.3300

Port of Hope Nampa Residential
508 East Florida
Nampa, ID 83686
P: 208.463.0118

ILLINOIS

Prairie Center
122 West Hill Street
Champaign, IL 61820
P: 217.356.7576

Salvation Army Freedom Center
105 South Ashland
Chicago, IL 60607
P: 312.421.2406

Substance Abuse Services
1307 West Main Street
Marion, IL 62959
P: 618.997.5336

Residents In Transition
711 North East Monroe
Peoria, IL 61603
P: 309.671.8966

Triangle Center Mint Program
120 North 11th Street
Springfield, IL 62703
P: 217.544.9858

Triangle Center
120 North 11th Street
Springfield, IL 62703
P: 217.544.9858

INDIANA
Allen County Jail
12103 Lima Road
Ft Wayne, IN 46818
P: 219.449.7450

Volunteers of America - Indiana CSC
611 North Capitol
Indianapolis, IN 46204
P: 317.686.9841

Pact – Bradley House
132 East 6th Street
Michigan City, IN 46360
P: 219.872.9139

KANSAS
Community Correctional Center
4715 Brewer Place
Leavenworth, KS 66048
P: 913.351.0728

Community Correctional Center
1301 North Duncan
P.O. Box 711
Newton, KS 67114
P: 316.283.7829

Community Correctional Center
236 South Pattie
Wichita, KS 67214
P: 316.264.5999

Halfway House for Adults
1137 North Broadway
Wichita, KS 67214
P: 316.263.3243

KENTUCKY
Ashland House CCC
455 29th Street
Ashland, KY 41101
P: 606.324.4572

Warren County Regional Jail
920 Kentucky Street
Bowling Green, KY 42101
P: 270.843.4606

Dismas of Lexington
909 Georgetown Pike
Lexington, KY 40511
P: 859.231.8448

Laurel County Work Release Center
206 West Fourth Street
London, KY 40741
P: 606.878.9431

Dismas Charities of Louisville
124 West Oak Street
Louisville, KY 40203
P: 502.634.3608

Community Services Center
P.O. Box 2541, 621 South 7th Street
Paducah, KY 42001
P: 270.442.6251

Big Sandy Regional Jail
P.O. Box 1388
Panitsville, KY 41240
P: 606.297.5245

Pike County Detention Center
172 Division Street, Suite 103
Pikeville, KY 41501
P: 606.432.6291

Pulaski County Detention Center
300 Hail Knob Road
Somerset, KY 42501
P: 606.678.4315

LOUISIANA
Ecumenical House
6753 Cezanne Avenue
Baton Rouge, LA 70806
P: 225.924.5757

City of Faith Community Correctional Center
251 La Rue France
Lafayette, LA 70501
P: 337.261.3345

City of Faith Ministries, Inc.
3581 East Prien Lake Road
Lake Charles, LA 70601
P: 337.562.9893

Volunteers Of America, CSC
2929 St. Anthony Street
New Orleans, LA 70112
P: 504.944.5678

City of Faith Ministries, Inc.
752 Austin Place
Shreveport, LA 71101
P: 318.424.2701

MASSACHUSETTS
Barnstable County Work Release Center
Route 6A – Main Street
Barnstable, MA 02630
P: 508.375.6163

Barnstable County - Electric Monitoring
Route 6A – Main Street
Barnstable, MA 02630
P: 508.375.6160

Coolidge House
307 Huntington Avenue
Boston, MA 02115
P: 617.424.1390

Hampden County Pre-Release Center
325 Alabama Street
Ludlow, MA 01056
P: 413.547.8000

Hampden County Electric Monitor Program
311 State Street
Springfield, MA 01105
P: 413.547.8000

MARYLAND
Volunteers of America CSC
4601 East Monument Street
Baltimore, MD 21205
P: 410.276.5880

Montgomery County Pre-Release
11651 Nebel Street
Rockville, MD 20852
P: 301.468.4200

MAINE
Pharos House
5 Grant Street
Portland, ME 04101
P: 207.774.6021

MICHIGAN
Genesis Community Correctional Center
3875 Lillibridge
Detroit, MI 48214
P: 313.822.4060

Heartline, Inc.
8201 Sylvester
Detroit, MI 48214
P: 313.923.4200

Monica House Community Correctional Center
15380 Monica
Detroit, MI 48238
P: 313.345.3600

Renaissance SCS
11105 East Jefferson Avenue
Detroit, MI 48214
P: 313.822.2021

Community Alternatives
801 College, SE
Grand Rapids, MI 49507
P: 616.988.2553

Great Lakes Recovery Center
241 Wright Street
Marquette, MI 49855
P: 906.228.7611

Arete Center
709 Lapeer Avenue
Saginaw, MI 48607
P: 989.754.3361

Grand Traverse County Jail
320 Washington Street
Traverse City, MI 49684
P: 231.922.4530

MINNESOTA
Douglas County Jail/Work Release
8th and Elm Street
Alexandria, MN 56308
P: 320.762.8151

N.W. Regional Corrections
Box 624 600 Bruce Street
Crookston, MN 56716
P: 218.281.6363

Bethel Work Release Program
23 Mesaba Avenue
Duluth, MN 55806
P: 218.727.3828

Benton County Jail
581 Highway 23 NE
Foley, MN 56329
P: 320.968.8263

Volunteers of America (Male)
2825 East Lake Street
Minneapolis, MN 55406
P: 612.721.6327

Renville County Jail
500 East Depue Courthouse Annex
Olivia, MN 56277
P: 320.523.1161

Volunteers Of America (Female)
1771 Kent Street
Roseville, MN 55113
P: 651.488.2073

MISSOURI
Southeast Missouri Center
Highway 32 East, P.O. Drawer 459
Farmington, MO 63640
P: 573.756.5749

Westwood Treatment Center
3150 Warrior Lane
Poplar Bluff, MO 63901
P: 573.785.5333

Alpha House
MPO# 852, 2300 East Division
Springfield, MO 65801
P: 417.831.3033

Dismas House
5025 Cote Brilliante
St. Louis, MO 63113
P: 314.361.2802

Metro Employment/Training Program
1727 Locust Street
St. Louis, MO 63103
P: 314.241.1133

MISSISSIPPI
Bannum Place of Jackson
1031 Wholesale Row
Jackson, MS 39201
P: 601.949.7888

Bannum Place of Tupelo
630 A and D Street
Tupelo, MS 38801
P: 662.841.7888

MONTANA
Alpha House
3109 1st Avenue, North
Billings, MT 59101
P: 406.259.9695

Butte Pre-Release Center
62 West Broadway
Butte, MT 59701
P: 406.782.2316

Great Falls Pre-Release Center
1019 15th Street, North
Great Falls, MT 59401
P: 406.727.0944

NORTH CAROLINA
Salvation Army CCC
204 Haywood Street
Asheville, NC 28802
P: 828.253.4723

McLeod Comprehensive Sanction Center
145 Remount Road
Charlotte, NC 28203
P: 704.332.3180

Troy House CCC
1101 North Mangum Street
Durham, NC 27701
P: 919.683.8331

Bannum Place of Fayetteville
952 Bragg Boulevard
Fayetteville, NC 28301
P: 910.484.6442

Gaston County Work Release Center
475 North Marietta Street
Gastonia, NC 28052
P: 704.866.3550

Bannum Place of Greensboro
131 Manley Avenue
Greensboro, NC 27407
P: 336.852.7700

Cavalcorp Community Sanctions Center
312 Tryon Road
Raleigh, NC 27603
P: 919.773.1834

Bannum Place of Wilmington
716 Princess Street
Wilmington, NC 28401
P: 910.762.4235

Salvation Army CCC
1255 North Trade Street, POB 1205
Winston-Salem, NC 27102
P: 336.722.8721

NORTH DAKOTA
Centre, Inc.
315 West Indiana Avenue
Bismarck, ND 58502
P: 701.222.4966

Centre, Inc.
123 15th Street, North
Fargo, ND 58102
P: 701.237.9340

NEVADA
Clark Center
320 South First Street
Las Vegas, NV 89101
P: 702.385.9895

Bannum Place of Reno
245 Gentry Way
Reno, NV 89502
P: 775.829.4547

NEW JERSEY
Comprehensive Sanction Center
50 Fenwick Street
Newark, NJ 07114
P: 973.622.1400

NEW MEXICO
Dismas Charities, CSC
1595 West Picacho
Las Cruces, NM 88005
P: 505.647.1447

NEW YORK
Horizon Center CCC
35 Elizabeth Street
Albany, NY 12202
P: 518.465.3215

Volunteers of America
295 Clinton Street
Binghamton, NY 13902
P: 607.797.2258

Community Corrections Center
2534 Creston Avenue
Bronx, NY 10468
P: 718.561.4155

Brooklyn CC
988 Myrtle Avenue
Brooklyn, NY 11206
P: 718.574.4886

Buffalo Halfway House
115 Glenwood Avenue
Buffalo, NY 14209
P: 716.882.0027

Volunteers of America
175 Ward Street
Rochester, NY 14605
P: Not Provided

OHIO
Oriana House For Men
40 East Glenwood Avenue
Akron, OH 44309
P: 330.996.2222

Oriana House For Women
222 Power Street
Akron, OH 44304
P: 330.996.7595

Talbert House For Men
2216 Vine Street
Cincinnati, OH 45219
P: 513.684.7965

Talbert House For Women
1616 Harrison Avenue
Cincinnati, OH 45214
P: 513.557.2500

Oriana Comprehensive Sanction Center
1829 East 55th Street
Cleveland, OH 44103
P: 216.881.7882

Alvis House For Men
1755 Alum Creek Drive
Columbus, OH 43207
P: 614.443.4989

Alvis House For Women
868 Bryden Road
Columbus, OH 43205
P: 614.252.1788

Alvis House Cope Center
42 Arnold Place
Dayton, OH 45407
P: 937.278.8219

Ohio Link Community Correctional Treatment Center
2012 Madison Avenue
Toledo, OH 44304
P: 419.241.4308

Community Correctional Association
1764 Market Street
Youngstown, OH 44507
P: 330.742.8664

OKLAHOMA
The Oklahoma Halfway House
517 SW Second Street
Oklahoma City, OK 73109
P: 405.232.0231

Avalon Correctional Center
302 West Archer
Tulsa, OK 74103
P: 918.583.9445

OREGON
Deschutes County Work Release
63333 West Highway 20
Bend, OR 97701
P: 541.617.3331

Lane County Work Release
75 West 5th Avenue
Eugene, OR 97401
P: 541.682.2297

Clackamas County Work Release
9000 SE McBrod
Milwaukie, OR 97222
P: 503.655.8262

Oregon Halfway House
1413 SE 15th Avenue
Portland, OR 97214
P: 503.231.7785

Portland Progress House
5709 North Vancouver Avenue
Portland, OR 97217
P: 503.283.1650

Portland YWCA
17 SW 2nd Avenue
Portland, OR 97204
P: 503.294.7424

PENNSYLVANIA
Cumberland County Prison
1101 Claremont Road
Carlisle, PA 17013
P: 717.245.8787

Clearfield County Jail
410 21st Street
Clearfield, PA 16830
P: 814.765.0276

Bucks County Work Release
1730 South Easton Road
Doylestown, PA 18901
P: 215.345.3700

Westmoreland County Jail
3000 South Grande Boulevard
Greensburg, PA 15601
P: 724.830.6000

Capitol Pavilion Community Correctional Center
2012 North Fourth Street
Harrisburg, PA 17102
P: 717.236.0132

Blair County Prison, Hollidays, Pa
419 Market Square
Hollidaysburg, PA 16648
P: 814.693.3155

The Kintock Group CCC
325 North Broad Street
Philadelphia, PA 19107
P: 215.521.4308

The Kintock Group
331 North Broad Street
Philadelphia, PA 19107
P: 215.440.9730

Renewal, Inc.
339 Boulevard of The Allies
Pittsburgh, PA 15222
P: 412.697.1616

Catholic Social Services
409-411 Olive Street
Scranton, PA 18509
P: 570.342.1295

Conewago – Wernersville
Building 18-19 Sportsman Road
Wernersville, PA 19565
P: 610.685.3733

SOUTH CAROLINA
CSC – Alston Wilkes Society
1218 Bull Street
Columbia, SC 29201
P: 803.765.1394

CCC – Bannum, Incorporated
1219 West Evans Street
Florence, SC 29501
P: 843.676.0051

CCC – Alston Wilkes Society
614 Pendleton Street
Greenville, SC 29601
P: 864.242.0808

CCC – Harbor Place, Incorporated
1929 Iris Street
North Charleston, SC 29405
P: 843.566.9629

SOUTH DAKOTA
Community Alcohol/Drug Center
901 South Miller
Mitchell, SD 57301
P: 605.995.8180

Community Alternatives
5025 Highway 79 South, Box 2273
Rapid City, SD 57709
P: 605.341.4240

Pennington County Sheriff's Department
725 North Lacrosse
Rapid City, SD 57701
P: 605.394.6128

Glory House of Sioux Falls
4000 SW Avenue, P.O. 88145
Sioux Falls, SD 57105
P: 605.332.3273

TENNESSEE
Salvation Army Center, Chattanooga
800 McCallie Avenue
Chattanooga, TN 37404
P: 423.756.1023

Midway Rehab Center, Knoxville
1715 East Magnolia Avenue
Knoxville, TN 37927
P: 865.522.0301

Memphis Community Service Center
15 South Cleveland Street
Memphis, TN 38104
P: 901.274.2942

Dismas Charities
808 Lea Street
Nashville, TN 37203
P: 615.254.0006

TEXAS
Salvation Army
1726 Butternut
Abilene, TX 79604
P: 915.677.1408

McCabe Center CSC
1915 East Martin Luther King
Austin, TX 78702
P: 512.322.0925

Bannum Inc., Beaumont, Texas
1310 Pennsylvania
Beaumont, TX 77701
P: 409.835.7575

Reality House
405 East Washington
Brownsville, TX 78520
P: 956.541.2771

Bannum, Inc.
2801 South Port
Corpus Christi, TX 78405
P: 361.879.0047

Correctional Systems, Inc.
402 West Chapin Street
Edinburg, TX 78539
P: 956.383.0663

Dismas Charities, CSC
7011 Alameda Avenue
El Paso, TX 79915
P: 915.781.1122

Volunteers of America
2710 Avenue "J"
Fort Worth, TX 76105
P: 817.429.1087

Liedel Sanction Center
1819 Commerce Street
Houston, TX 77002
P: 713.224.0984

Volunteers of America
800 West Wintergreen Road
Hutchins, TX 75141
P: 972.225.5472

Bannum Place
2920 East Saunders
Laredo, TX 78041
P: 956.712.8783

Bannum, Inc.
2920 East Saunders
Laredo, TX 78041
P: 956.712.8783

CCC Dismas Charities
709 EAST 49th Street
Lubbock, TX 79404
P: 806.747.5055
Dismas Charities CSC
24 Industrial Loop
Midland, TX 79701
P: 915.686.9188

Crosspoint CSC
420 Baltimore Street
San Antonio, TX 78215
P: 210.225.0864

County Rehabilitation Center
313 Ferrell Place
Tyler, TX 75702
P: 903.593.3131

Salvation Army CSC
500 Fourth Street
Waco, TX 76703
P: 254.756.7271

UTAH
Cornell Corrections, Inc.
1585 West 2100 South
Salt Lake City, UT 84119
P: 801.973.3800

VIRGINIA
Lebanon Community Correctional Center
168 Rogers Street, P.O. Box 879
Lebanon, VA 24266
P: 276.889.1530

Rehabilitation Services #2
7718 Warwick Boulevard
Newport News, VA 23607
P: 757.244.0027

Rehabilitation Services #1
300 West 20th Street
Norfolk, VA 23517
P: 757.625.3507

Clarke/Frederick/Winchester Pre-Release Center
141 Fort Collier Road
Winchester, VA 22603
P: 540.665.6380

VERMONT
Marble Valley Regional Correctional Facility
167 State Street
Rutland, VT 05701
P: 802.786.5830

North East Regional Correctional Facility
#3 Route 5 South
St. Johnsbury, VT 05819
P: 802.748.8151

WASHINGTON
Franklin County Work Release
1015 North 5th
Pasco, WA 99301
P: 509.545.3549

Pioneer Fellowship House
220 11th Avenue
Seattle, WA 98122
P: 206.667.9674

Geiger Work Release Center
P.O. Box 19202
Spokane, WA 99219
P: 509.477.1542

Turner House
West 925 Broadway
Spokane, WA 99201
P: 509.326.6606

Tacoma CSC
922 South "J" Street
Tacoma, WA 98405
P: 253.274.0248

Tacoma Progress House
1119 South Altheimer Street
Tacoma, WA 98405
P: 253.627.0246

WISCONSIN
Fahrman Center
3136 Craig Road
Eau Claire, WI 54701
P: 715.835.9110

Alternative Program
203 West Sunny Lane Road
Janesville, WI 53546
P: 608.741.4510

Arc House/Dayton Facility
2009 East Dayton Street
Madison, WI 53704
P: 608.241.7616

Schwert House
3501 Kipling Drive
Madison, WI 53704
P: 608.249.6226

Horizon House
2511 West Vine Street
Milwaukee, WI 53205
P: 414.342.3237

Parsons House
2930 North, 25 Street
Milwaukee, WI 53206
P: 414.445.3301

WEST VIRGINIA
Bannum Place of Clarksburg
260 Monticello Road
Clarksburg, WV 26301
P: 304.624.7634

Mothers & Infants Together
HC 64 Box 126
Hillsboro, WV 24946
P: 304.653.4882

Bannum Place of Charleston
5904 Maccorkle Avenue, SW
St. Albans, WV 25177
P: 304.768.4002

WYOMING
Community Alternatives of Casper
10081 Landmark Lane
Mills, WY 82644
P: 307.266.2592

APPENDIX 2-A: STATE DRIVER LICENSE & IDENTIFICATION CARD OFFICES

The Department of Motor Vehicles provides information and assistance with the issuance, renewal, and suspension of state-issued driver licensees and identification cards. The Department of Motor Vehicles may also oversee vehicle title, registration and insurance matters.

ALABAMA
Alabama Department of Public Safety
Driver License Division
P.O. Box 1471
Montgomery, AL 36102
P: 334.242.4400
I: http://dps.alabama.gov

ALASKA
Alaska Department of Administration
Division of Motor Vehicles
1300 West Benson Boulevard, Suite 200
Anchorage, AK 99503
P: 907.269.5551
I: http://doa.alaska.gov/dmv

ARIZONA
Arizona Department of Transportation
Motor Vehicle Division
P.O. Box 2100, Mail Drop 504M
Phoenix, AZ 85001
P: 602.712.8152
I: http://www.azdot.gov/mvd/index.asp

ARKANSAS
Arkansas Office of Driver Services
P.O. Box 1272, Room 1130
Little Rock, AR 72203
P: 501.682.7207
I: http://www.dfa.arkansas.gov

CALIFORNIA
California Department of Motor Vehicles
Information Services Branch
P.O. Box 944247, MS G199
Sacramento, CA 94244
P: 916.657.8098
I: http://www.dmv.ca.gov

COLORADO
Colorado Division of Motor Vehicles
Driver Control Section
181 Pierce Street, Room 150
Lakewood, CO 80214
P: 303.205.5613
I: http://www.colorado.gov/revenue/dmv

CONNECTICUT
Connecticut Department of Motor Vehicles
Driver Services Division
60 State Street
Wethersfield, CT 03161
P: 860.263.5720
I: http://www.ct.gov/dmv

DELAWARE
Delaware Division of Motor Vehicles
Driver's License Unit
P. O. Box 698
Dover, DE 19903
P: 302.744.2506
I: http://www.dmv.de.gov

DISTRICT OF COLUMBIA
District of Columbia Department of Motor Vehicles
95 M Street, SW
Washington, DC 20024
P: 202.737.4404
I: http://dmv.dc.gov

FLORIDA
Department of Highway Safety and Motor Vehicles
Division of Motorist Services
P.O. Box 5775
Tallahassee, FL 32314
P: 850.617.2000
I: http://www.flhsmv.gov

GEORGIA
Georgia Department of Driver Services
Licensing and Records Division
P.O. Box 80447
Conyers, GA 30013
P: 678.413.8400
I: http://www.dds.ga.gov

HAWAII
Hawaii Department of Transportation
Motor Vehicle Safety Office
601 Kamokila Boulevard, 511
Kapolei, HI 96707
P: 808.692.7650
I: http://www.hawaii.gov/dot/highways/

IDAHO
Idaho Transportation Department
Driver Services
P.O. Box 34
Boise, ID 83731
P: 208.334.4443
I: http://www.itd.idaho.gov/dmv

ILLINOIS
Illinois Driver Services Department
2701 South Dirksen Parkway
Springfield, IL 62723
P: 217.782.6212
I: http://www.cyberdriveillinois.com

INDIANA
Indiana Bureau of Motor Vehicles
Indiana Government Center North
100 North Senate Avenue, Room N412
Indianapolis, IN 46204
P: 888.692.6841
I: http://www.mybmv.com

IOWA
Iowa Department of Transportation
Office of Driver Services
P.O. Box 9204
Des Moines, IA 50306
P: 515.237.3253
I: http://www.iowadot.gov/mvd/index.htm

KANSAS
Kansas Department of Revenue
Division of Vehicles, Driver Control Bureau
P.O. Box 12021
Topeka, KS 66612
P: 785.296.3601
I: http://ksrevenue.org/vehicle.html

KENTUCKY
Kentucky Division of Driver Licensing
Transportation Office Building
200 Mero Street
Frankfort, KY 40622
P: 502.564.6800
I: http://transportation.ky.gov

LOUISIANA
Louisiana Department of Public Safety
Office of Motor Vehicles
P.O. Box 64886
Baton Rouge, LA 70896
P: 225.925.6388
I: http://www.expresslane.org

MAINE
Maine Bureau of Motor Vehicles
Driver License Services
29 State House Station
Augusta, ME 04333
P: 207.624.9000
I: http://www.maine.gov/sos/bmv

MARYLAND
Maryland Motor Vehicle Administration
6601 Ritchie Highway
Glen Burnie, MD 21062
P: 410.768.7274
I: http://www.mva.maryland.gov

MASSACHUSETTS
Massachusetts Registry of Motor Vehicles
P.O. Box 55889
Boston, MA 02205
P: 857.368.9460
I: http://www.massrmv.com

MICHIGAN
Michigan Department of State
Driver and Vehicle Records Division
7064 Crowner Drive
Lansing, MI 48918
P: 888.767.6424
I: http://www.michigan.gov/sos

MINNESOTA
Minnesota Department of Public Safety
Driver and Vehicle Services
445 Minnesota Street
St. Paul, MN 55101
P: 651.296.6911
I: https://dps.mn.gov

MISSISSIPPI
State Department of Public Safety
Driver Services Bureau
P.O. Box 958
Jackson, MS 39205
P: 601.987.1287
I: http://www.dps.state.ms.us

MISSOURI
Missouri Department of Revenue
Motor Vehicle and Driver Licensing Division
P.O. Box 629
Jefferson City, MO 65105
P: 573.526.1827
I: http://dor.mo.gov

MONTANA
Department of Justice
Motor Vehicle Division
P.O. Box 201430
Helena, MT 59620
P: 406.444.3292
I: https://doj.mt.gov/driving

NEBRASKA
Nebraska Department of Motor Vehicles
301 Centennial Mall South
Lincoln, NE 68509
P: 402.471.3861
I: http://www.dmv.ne.gov

NEVADA
Nevada Department of Motor vehicles
555 Wright Way
Carson City, NV 89711
P: 775.684.4549
I: http://www.dmvnv.com

NEW HAMPSHIRE
New Hampshire Department of Safety
Division of Motor Vehicles
23 Hazen Drive
Concord, NH 03305
P: 603.227.4050
I: http://www.nh.gov/safety/divisions/dmv

NEW JERSEY
New Jersey Motor Vehicle Commission
225 East State Street
P.O. Box 174
Trenton, NJ 08666
P: 609.292.6500
I: http://www.state.nj.us/mvc

NEW MEXICO
New Mexico Motor Vehicle Division
P.O. Box 1028
Santa Fe, NM 87504
P: 505.827.2296
I: http://www.mvd.newmexico.gov

NEW YORK
New York Department of Motor Vehicles
6 Empire State Plaza
Albany, NY 12228
P: 518.486.9786
I: http://www.dmv.ny.gov

NORTH CAROLINA
North Carolina Department of Transportation
Division of Motor Vehicles
3101 Mail Service Center
Raleigh, NC 27699
P: 919.715.7000
I: http://www.ncdot.gov/dmv

NORTH DAKOTA
North Dakota Department of Transportation
Driver's Licensing Division
608 East Boulevard Avenue
Bismarck, ND 58505
P: 701.328.4353
I: http://www.dot.nd.gov/public/licensing.htm

OHIO
Ohio Bureau of Motor Vehicles
P.O. Box 16520
Columbus, OH 43216
P: 614.752.7600
I: http://www.bmv.ohio.gov

OKLAHOMA
State Department of Public Safety
3600 North Martin Luther King Boulevard
Oklahoma City, OK 73111
P: 405.425.2001
I: http://www.dps.state.ok.us

OREGON
Oregon Department of Motor Vehicles
1905 Lana Avenue, NE
Salem, OR 97314
P: 503.945.5000
I: http://www.oregon.gov/odot/dmv

PENNSYLVANIA
Pennsylvania Department of Transportation
Bureau of Driver Licensing
Riverfront Office Center, 4th Floor
1101 South Front Street
Harrisburg, PA 17104
P: 717.391.6190
I: http://www.dmv.state.pa.us

PUERTO RICO
Puerto Rico Department of Transportation
Driver Services Division
P.O. Box 41243
San Juan, PR 00940
P: 787.722.2929
I: http://www.dtop.gov/pr/servicios/index.asp

RHODE ISLAND
Rhode Island Division of Motor Vehicles
Operator Control
600 New London Avenue
Cranston, RI 02920
P: 401.462.4368
I: http://www.dmv.ri.gov

SOUTH CAROLINA
South Carolina Department of Motor Vehicles
P.O. Box 1498
Blythewood, SC 29016
P: 803.896.5599
I: http://www.scdmvonline.com

SOUTH DAKOTA
State Department of Public Safety
Driver Licensing Program
118 West Capitol
Pierre, SD 57501
P: 605.773.6883
I: http://dps.sd.gov/licensing/default.aspx

TENNESSEE
Tennessee Department of Safety
Driver Services Division
P.O. Box 945
Nashville, TN 37202
P: 615.253.5221
I: http://www.tn.gov/safety/dlmain.shtml

TEXAS
Texas Department of Public Safety
Driver License Division
P.O. Box 4087
Austin, TX 78773
P: 512.424.2600
I: http://www.dps.texas.gov

UTAH
Utah Department of Public Safety
Driver License Division
P.O. Box 144501
Salt Lake City, UT 84114
P: 801.965.4437
I: http://publicsafety.utah.gov/dld/

VERMONT
Vermont Department of Motor Vehicles
120 State Street
Montpelier, VT 05603
P: 802.828.2011
I: http://dmv.vermont.gov

VIRGINIA
Virginia Department of Motor Vehicles
P.O. Box 27412
Richmond, VA 23269
P: 804.367.6602
I: http://www.dmvnow.com

WASHINGTON
Washington Department of Licensing
P.O. Box 9030
Olympia, WA 98507
P: 360.902.3850
I: http://www.dol.wa.gov

WEST VIRGINIA
West Virginia Department of Transportation
Division of Motor Vehicles
5707 MacCorkle Avenue, SE
P.O. Box 17300
Charleston, WV 25317
P: 304.926.3871
I: http://www.transportation.wv.gov/dmv

WISCONSIN
Wisconsin Division of Motor Vehicles
Bureau of Driver Services
P.O. Box 7983
Madison, WI 53707
P: 608.266.9890
I: http://www.dot.wisconsin.gov/drivers/

WYOMING
Wyoming Department of Transportation
Motor Vehicle Services
5300 Bishop Boulevard
Cheyenne, WY 82009
P: 307.777.4800
I: http://www.dot.state.wy.us/wydot

APPENDIX 2-B: STATE VITAL RECORD OFFICES

The Office of Vital Records maintains and issues certified copies of birth, death, marriage and divorce records within a particular jurisdiction and makes them available to authorized individuals pursuant to statutory guidelines.

ALABAMA
Alabama Center for Health Statistics
Alabama Department of Public Health
P.O. Box 5625
Montgomery, AL 36103
P: 334.206.5418
I: http://www.cdc.gov/nchs/w2w/alabama.htm

ALASKA
Alaska Bureau of Vital Statistics
Department of Health and Social Services
5441 Commercial Boulevard
Juneau, AK 99801
P: 907.465.3391
I: http://www.cdc.gov/nchs/w2w/alaska.htm

ARIZONA
Arizona Department of Health Services
Office of Vital Records
P.O. Box 3887
Phoenix, AZ 85030
P: 602.364.1300
I: http://www.cdc.gov/nchs/w2w/arizona.htm

ARKANSAS
Arkansas Department of Health
Vital Records Section
4815 West Markham Street, Slot 44
Little Rock, AR 72205
P: 501.661.2336
I: http://www.cdc.gov/nchs/w2w/arkansas.htm

CALIFORNIA
California Department of Public Health
Office of Vital Records
P.O. Box 997410, Mail Stop: 5103
Sacramento, CA 95855
P: 916.445.2684
I: http://www.cdc.gov/nchs/w2w/california.htm

COLORADO
Colorado Department of Public Health
Vital Records Section
4300 Cherry Creek Drive, South, HSVRD-VS-A1
Denver, CO 80246
P: 303.692.2200
I: http://www.cdc.gov/nchs/w2w/colorado.htm

CONNECTICUT
Connecticut Department of Public Health
Vital Records Section
410 Capitol Avenue, Mail Stop: 11
Hartford, CT 06134
P: 860.509.7897
I: http://www.cdc.gov/nchs/w2w/connecticut.htm

DELAWARE
Delaware Division of Public Health
Office of Vital Statistics
417 Federal Street
Dover, DE 19901
P: 302.744.4549
I: http://www.cdc.gov/nchs/w2w/delaware.htm

DISTRICT OF COLUMBIA
District of Columbia Department of Health
Vital Records Division
899 North Capitol Street, NE, 1st Floor
Washington, DC 20002
P: 202.671.5000
I: http://www.cdc.gov/nchs/w2w/dc.htm

FLORIDA
Florida Department of Health
Bureau of Vital Statistics
1217 P.O. Box 210
Jacksonville, FL 32231
P: 904.359.6900
I: http://www.cdc.gov/nchs/w2w/florida.htm

GEORGIA
Georgia Department of Public Health
Vital Records
2600 Skyland Drive, NE
Atlanta, GA 30319
P: 404.679.4702
I: http://www.cdc.gov/nchs/w2w/georgia.htm

HAWAII
Hawaii Department of Health
Office of Health Status Monitoring
P.O. Box 3378
Honolulu, HI 96801
P: 808.586.4533
I: http://www.cdc.gov/nchs/w2w/hawaii.htm

IDAHO
Idaho Bureau of Vital Records and Health Statistics
Vital Records Unit
P.O. Box 83720
Boise, ID 83720
P: 208.334.5988
I: http://www.cdc.gov/nchs/w2w/idaho.htm

ILLINOIS
Illinois Department of Public Health
Division of Vital Records
925 East Ridgely Avenue
Springfield, IL 62702
P: 217.782.6553
I: http://www.cdc.gov/nchs/w2w/illinois.htm

INDIANA
Indiana State Department of Health
Vital Records
P.O. Box 7125
Indianapolis, IN 46206
P: 317.233.2700
I: http://www.cdc.gov/nchs/w2w/indiana.htm

IOWA
Iowa Department of Public Health
Bureau of Vital Records
321 East 12th Street, 1st Floor
Des Moines, IA 50319
P: 515.281.4944
I: http://www.cdc.gov/nchs/w2w/iowa.htm

KANSAS
Kansas Office of Vital Statistics
Curtis State Office Building
1000 SW Jackson Street, Suite 120
Topeka, KS 66612
P: 785.296.1400
I: http://www.cdc.gov/nchs/w2w/kansas.htm

KENTUCKY
Kentucky Department of Public Safety
Office of Vital Statistics
275 East Main Street, IE-A
Frankfort, KY 40621
P: 502.564.4212
I: http://www.cdc.gov/nchs/w2w/kentucky.htm

LOUISIANA
Louisiana Office of Public Health
Vital Records Registry
P.O. Box 60630
New Orleans, LA 70160
P: 504.219.4500
I: http://www.cdc.gov/nchs/w2w/LOUISIANA.htm

MAINE
Maine Department of Health & Human Services
Vital Records Office
244 Water Street, 11 State House Station
Augusta, ME 04333
P: 207.287.3181
I: http://www.cdc.gov/nchs/w2w/maine.htm

MARYLAND
Maryland Department of Health and Mental Hygiene
Division of Vital Records
6550 Reisterstown Road, P.O. Box 68760
Baltimore, MD 21215
P: 410.764.3038
I: http://www.cdc.gov/nchs/w2w/maryland.htm

MASSACHUSETTS
Massachusetts Registry of Vital records and Statistics
150 Mount Vernon Street, 1st Floor
Dorchester, MA 02125
P: 617.740.2600
I: http://www.cdc.gov/nchs/w2w/massachusetts.htm

MICHIGAN
State of Michigan
Vital Records Request
P.O. Box 30721
Lansing, MI 48909
P: 517.335.8656
I: http://www.cdc.gov/nchs/w2w/michigan.htm

MINNESOTA
Minnesota Department of Health
Central Cashiering – Vital Records
P.O. Box 64499
St. Paul, MN 55164
P: 651.201.5970
I: http://www.cdc.gov/nchs/w2w/minnesota.htm

MISSISSIPPI
State Department of Health
Mississippi Vital records
P.O. Box 1700
Jackson, MS 39215
P: 601.576.7981
I: http://www.cdc.gov/nchs/w2w/mississippi.htm

MISSOURI
Missouri Department of Health and Senior Services
Bureau of Vital Records
930 Wildwood, P.O. Box 570
Jefferson City, MO 65102
P: 573.751.6387
I: http://www.cdc.gov/nchs/w2w/missouri.htm

MONTANA

Department of Public Health and Human Services
111 North Sanders, Room 209
P.O. Box 4210
Helena, MT 59604
P: 406.444.2685
I: http://www.cdc.gov/nchs/w2w/montana.htm

NEBRASKA

Nebraska Vital Records Office
1033 O Street, Suite 130
Lincoln, NE 68509
P: 402.471.2871
I: http://www.cdc.gov/nchs/w2w/nebrasks.htm

NEVADA

Nevada Office of Vital Records
4150 Technology Way, Suite 104
Carson City, NV 89706
P: 775.684.4242
I: http://www.cdc.gov/nchs/w2w/nevada.htm

NEW HAMPSHIRE

Division of Vital Records Administration
Archives Building
71 South Fruit Street
Concord, NH 03301
P: 603.271.4654
I: http://www.cdc.gov/nchs/w2w/new_hampshire.htm

NEW JERSEY

New Jersey Department of Health and Senior Services
Bureau of Vital Statistics
P.O. Box 370
Trenton, NJ 08625
P: 866.469.8726
I: http://www.cdc.gov/nchs/w2w/new_jersey.htm

NEW MEXICO

New Mexico Vital records
P.O. Box 25767
Santa Fe, NM 87125
P: 866.543.0051
I: http://www.cdc.gov/nchs/w2w/new_mexico.htm

NEW YORK (EXCEPT NEW YORK CITY)

New York State Vital Records Section
Certification Unit
800 North Pearl Street, 2nd Floor
Menands, NY 12204
P: 518.474.3075
I: http://www.cdc.gov/nchs/w2w/new_york.htm

NEW YORK CITY (ALL BOROUGHS)

New York City Health Department
Office of Vital Records
125 Worth Street, CN4, Room 133
New York, NY 10013
P: 212.639.9675
I: http://www.cdc.gov/nchs/w2w/new_york_city.htm

NORTH CAROLINA

North Carolina Vital Records
1903 Mail Service Center
Raleigh, NC 27699
P: 919.733.3000
I: http://www.cdc.gov/nchs/w2w/north_carolina.htm

NORTH DAKOTA

North Dakota Department of Health
Division of Vital Records
600 East Boulevard Avenue, Department 301
Bismarck, ND 58505
P: 701.328.2360
I: http://www.cdc.gov/nchs/w2w/north_dakota.htm

OHIO

Ohio Department of Health
Vital Statistics
P.O. Box 15089
Columbus, OH 43215
P: 614.466.2531
I: http://www.cdc.gov/nchs/w2w/ohio.htm

OKLAHOMA

State Department of Health
Vital records Service
1000 Northeast 10th Street
Oklahoma City, OK 73117
P: 405.271.4040
I: http://www.cdc.gov/nchs/w2w/oklahoma.htm

OREGON

Oregon Health Administration - Vital Records
P.O. Box 14050
Portland, OR 97293
P: 971.673.1190
I: http://www.cdc.gov/nchs/w2w/oregon.htm

PENNSYLVANIA

Pennsylvania Division of Vital Records
101 South Mercer Street, Room 401
P.O. Box 1528
New Castle, PA 16103
P: 724.656.3100
I: http://www.cdc.gov/nchs/w2w/pennsylvania.htm

PUERTO RICO
Puerto Rico Department of Health
Demographic Registry
P.O. Box 11584
Fernandez Juncos Station
San Juan, PR 00910
P: 787.767.9120
I: http://www.cdc.gov/nchs/w2w/puerto_rico.htm

RHODE ISLAND
Rhode Island Department of Health
Office of Vital Records
3 Capitol Hill, Room 101
Providence, RI 02908
P: 401.222.2811
I: http://www.cdc.gov/nchs/w2w/rhode_island.htm

SOUTH CAROLINA
South Carolina Office of Vital Records
2600 Bull Street
Columbia, SC 29201
P: 803.898.3630
I: http://www.cdc.gov/nchs/w2w/south_carolina.htm

SOUTH DAKOTA
State Department of Health
Vital Records
207 East Missouri Avenue, Suite 1-A
Pierre, SD 57501
P: 605.773.4961
I: http://www.cdc.gov/nchs/w2w/south_dakota.htm

TENNESSEE
Tennessee Vital Records
Central Services Building
4215th Avenue, North
Nashville, TN 37243
P: 615.741.1763
I: http://www.cdc.gov/nchs/w2w/tennessee.htm

TEXAS
Department of State Health Services
Texas Vital Records
P.O. Box 12040
Austin, TX 78711
P: 512.776.7111
I: http://www.cdc.gov/nchs/w2w/texas.htm

UTAH
Utah Department of Health
Office of Vital Records and Statistics
288 North 1460 West
P.O. Box 141012
Salt Lake City, UT 84114
P: 801.538.6105
I: http://www.cdc.gov/nchs/w2w/utah.htm

VERMONT
Vermont Department of Health
Vital Records Section
108 Cherry Street, P.O. Box 70
Burlington, VT 05402
P: 802.863.7275
I: http://www.cdc.gov/nchs/w2w/vermont.htm

VIRGINIA
State Health Department
Division of Vital Records
P.O. Box 1000
Richmond, VA 23218
P: 804.662.6200
I: http://www.cdc.gov/nchs/w2w/virginia.htm

WASHINGTON
Washington Department of Health
Center for Health Statistics
P.O. Box 47814
Olympia, WA 98504
P: 360.236.4300
I: http://www.cdc.gov/nchs/w2w/washington.htm

WEST VIRGINIA
Vital Records Office
350 Capitol Street, Room 165
Charleston, WV 25301
P: 304.558.2931
I: http://www.cdc.gov/nchs/w2w/west_virginia.htm

WISCONSIN
State of Wisconsin
Vital Records Office
One West Wilson Street, P.O. Box 309
Madison, WI 53701
P: 608.266.1373
I: http://www.cdc.gov/nchs/w2w/wisconsin.htm

WYOMING
Wyoming Vital Statistics Services
Hathaway Building
Cheyenne, WY 82002
P: 307.777.7591
I: http://www.cdc.gov/nchs/w2w/wyoming.htm

APPENDIX 3-A: STATE DEPARTMENT OF LABOR OFFICES

The State Department of Labor provides direct oversight of employment, training and career exploration delivery systems for individuals entering and reentering the workforce within a specific jurisdiction.

ALABAMA
Alabama Department of Labor
649 Monroe Street
Montgomery, AL 36131
P: 334.242.8055
I: http://www.labor.alabama.gov

ALASKA
Alaska Department of Labor and Workforce Development
P.O. Box 11149
Juneau, AK 99811
P: 907.465.2700
I: http://www.labor.state.ak.us

ARIZONA
Industrial Commission of Arizona
800 West Washington Street
Phoenix, AZ 85001
P: 602.542.4411
I: http://www.ica.state.az.us

ARKANSAS
Arkansas Department of Labor
10421 West Markham
Little Rock, AR 72205
P: 501.682.4500
I: http://www.labor.ar.gov

CALIFORNIA
California Department of Industrial Relations
1515 Clay Street, 17th Floor
Oakland, CA 94612
P: 510.286.3800
I: http://www.labor.ca.gov

COLORADO
Colorado Department of Labor and Employment
633 17th Street, Suite 201
Denver, CO 80202
P: 303.318.8000
I: http://www.coworkforce.com

CONNECTICUT
Connecticut Department of Labor
200 Folly Brook Boulevard
Wethersfield, CT 06109
P: 860.263.6000
I: http://www.ct.gov/dol

DELAWARE
Delaware Department of Labor
4425 North Market Street, 4th Floor
Wilmington, DE 19802
P: 302.761.8200
I: http://www.delawareworks.com

DISTRICT OF COLUMBIA
District of Columbia Department of Employment Services
4058 Minnesota Avenue, NE
Washington, DC 20019
P: 202.671.1900
I: http://www.does.dc.gov

FLORIDA
Florida Department of Business and Professional Relations
The Caldwell Building
107 East Madison Street, Suite 100
Tallahassee, FL 32399
P: 800.342.3450
I: http://www.floridajobs.org

GEORGIA
Georgia Department of Labor
Sussex Place, Room 600
148 Andrew Young International Boulevard, NE
Atlanta, GA 30303
P: 404.232.7300
I: http://www.dol.state.ga.us

HAWAII
Hawaii Department of Labor and Industrial Relations
830 Punchbowl Street, Room 321
Honolulu, HI 96813
P: 808.586.8844
I: http://www.hawaii.gov/labor

IDAHO
Idaho Department of Labor
317 West Main Street
Boise, ID 83735
P: 208.332.3579
I: http://www.labor.idaho.gov

ILLINOIS
Illinois Department of Labor
160 North LaSalle Street, 13th Floor, Suite C-1300
Chicago, IL 60601
P: 312.793.2800
I: http://www.state.il.us/agency/idol

INDIANA
Indiana Department of Labor
Indiana Government Center South
402 West Washington Street, Room W-195
Indianapolis, IN 46204
P: 317.232.2655
I: http://www.in.gov/labor

IOWA
Iowa Labor Services Division
1000 East Grand Avenue
Des Moines, IA 50319
P: 515.281.5387
I: http://www.iowaworkforce.org/labor

KANSAS
Kansas Department of Labor
401 Southwest Topeka Boulevard
Topeka, KS 66603
P: 785.296.5000
I: http://www.dol.ks.gov

KENTUCKY
Kentucky Labor Cabinet
1047 US Highway 127 South, Suite 4
Frankfort, KY 40601
P: 502.564.3070
I: http://www.labor.ky.gov

LOUISIANA
Louisiana Workforce Commission
P.O. Box 94094
Baton Rouge, LA 70804
P: 225.342.3111
I: http://www.ldol.state.la.us

MAINE
Maine Department of Labor
54 State House Station Drive
P.O. Box 259
Augusta, ME 04332
P: 207.623.7900
I: http://www.state.me.us/labor

MARYLAND
Maryland Department of Labor, Licensing and Regulation
500 North Calvert Street, Suite 401
Baltimore, MD 21202
P: 410.230.6020
I: http://www.dllr.state.md.us

MASSACHUSETTS
Massachusetts Office of Labor and Workforce
Development
One Ashburton Place, Room 2112
Boston, MA 02108
P: 617.626.7122
I: http://www.mass.gov/eolwd

MICHIGAN
Department of Licensing and Regulatory Affairs
611 West Ottawa
Lansing, MI 48909
P: 517.373.1820
I: http://www.michigan.gov/lara

MINNESOTA
Minnesota Department of Labor and Industry
443 Lafayette Road, North
St. Paul, MN 55155
P: 651.284.5010
I: http://www.doli.state.mn.us

MISSISSIPPI
Mississippi Department of Employment Security
1235 Echelon Parkway
P.O. Box 1699
Jackson, MS 39215
P: 601.321.6000
I: http://www.mdes.ms.gov

MISSOURI
Missouri Labor and Industrial Relations Commission
3315 West Truman Boulevard
P.O. Box 504
Jefferson City, MO 65102
P: 573.751.3215
I: http://www.labor.mo.gov

MONTANA
Montana Department of Labor and Industry
P.O. Box 1728
Helena, MT 59624
P: 406.444.2071
I: http://www.dli.mt.gov

NEBRASKA
Nebraska Department of Labor
550 South 16th Street
P.O. Box 94600
Lincoln, NE 68508
P: 402.471.9000
I: http://www.dol.nebraska.gov

NEVADA
Nevada Department of Business and Industry
555 East Washington Avenue, Suite 4100
Las Vegas, NV 89101
P: 702.486.2650
I: http://www.laborcommissioner.com

NEW HAMPSHIRE
New Hampshire Department of Labor
State Office Park South
95 Pleasant Street
Concord, NH 03301
P: 603.271.3176
I: http://www.labor.state.nh.us

NEW JERSEY
Department of Labor and Workforce Development
1 John Fitch Plaza, 13th Floor, Suite D
P.O. Box 110
Trenton, NJ 08625
P: 609.659.9045
I: http://www.lwd.dol.state.nj.us/labor

NEW MEXICO
New Mexico Department of Workforce Solutions
401 Broadway, NE
P.O. Box 1928
Albuquerque, NM 87102
P: 505.841.8405
I: http://www.dws.state.nm.us

NEW YORK
New York Department of Labor
State Office Building, #2
W.A. Harriman Campus
Albany, NY 12240
P: 518.457.2741
I: http://www.labor.ny.gov

NORTH CAROLINA
North Carolina Department of Labor
4 West Edenton Street
Raleigh, NC 27699
P: 919.807.2796
I: http://www.nclabor.com

NORTH DAKOTA
North Dakota Department of Labor
State Capitol Building
600 East Boulevard Avenue, Department 406
Bismarck, ND 58505
P: 701.328.2660
I: http://www.nd.gov/labor

OHIO
Ohio Department of Commerce
77 South High Street, 22nd Floor
Columbus, OH 43215
P: 614.64.2239
I: http://www.com.state.oh.us

OKLAHOMA
Oklahoma Department of Labor
3017 North Stiles Avenue, Suite 100
Oklahoma City, OK 73105
P: 405.521.6100
I: http://www.ok.gov/odol

OREGON
Oregon Bureau of Labor and Industries
800 Northeast Oregon Street, #1045
Portland, OR 97232
P: 971.673.0761
I: http://www.oregon.gov/boli

PENNSYLVANIA
Pennsylvania Department of Labor and Industry
1700 Labor and Industry Building
7th and Forester Streets
Harrisburg, PA 17120
P: 717.787.5279
I: http://www.dli.state.pa.us

PUERTO RICO
Puerto Rico Department of Labor and Human Resources
Edificio Prudencio Rivera Martinez
505 Muniz Rivera Avenue
G.P.O. Box 308
Hato Rey, PR 00918
P: 787.754.2120
I: http://www.dtrh.gobierno.pr

RHODE ISLAND
Rhode Island Department of Labor and Training
1511 Pontiac Avenue
Cranston, RI 02920
P: 401.462.8000
I: http://www.dlt.state.ri.us

SOUTH CAROLINA
South Carolina Department of Labor, Licensing and
Regulations
P.O. Box 11329
Columbia, SC 29211
P: 803.896.4300
I: http://www.llr.state.sc.us

SOUTH DAKOTA
South Dakota Department of Labor and Regulation
700 Governors Drive
Pierre, SD 57501
P: 605.773.3101
I: http://www.dlr.sd.gov

TENNESSEE
Tennessee Department of Labor and Workforce
Development
220 French Landing Drive
Nashville, TN 37243
P: 615.741.6642
I: http://www.state.tn.us/labor-wfd

TEXAS
Texas Workforce Commission
101 East 15th Street
Austin, TX 78778
P: 512.463.2829
I: http://www.twc.state.tx.us

UTAH
Utah Labor Commission
160 East 300 South, Suite 300
Salt Lake City, UT 84111
P: 801.530.6800
I: http://www.laborcommission.utah.gov

VERMONT
Vermont Department of Labor
5 Green Mountain Drive
P.O. Box 488
Montpelier, VT 05601
P: 802.828.4022
I: http://www.labor.vermont.gov

VIRGINIA
Virginia Department of Labor and Industry
Main Street Centre
600 East Main Street, Suite 207
Richmond, VA 23219
P: 804.371.2327
I: http://www.doli.virginia.gov

WASHINGTON
Washington Department of Labor and Industries
P.O. Box 44000
Olympia, WA 98504
P: 360.902.5800
I: http://www.lni.wa.gov

WEST VIRGINIA
West Virginia Division of Labor
State Capitol Complex, 749-B, Building 6
1900 Kanawha Boulevard
Charleston, WV 25305
P: 304.558.7890
I: http://www.wvlabor.com

WISCONSIN
Wisconsin Department of Workforce Development
201 East Washington Avenue, A-400
P.O. Box 7946
Madison, WI 53707
P: 608.266.3131
I: http://www.dwd.wisconsin.gov

WYOMING
Wyoming Department of Workforce Services
1510 East Pershing Boulevard
Cheyenne, WY 82002
P: 307.777.8728
I: http://www.wyomingworkforce.org

APPENDIX 3-B: STATE & REGIONAL OFFICES OF APPRENTICESHIP

The U.S. Department of Labors' Department of Apprenticeship & Training provides oversight of state apprenticeship and training programs. Apprenticeship programs are a combination of on-the-job training and related instruction in which workers learn the practical and theoretical aspects of a highly skilled occupation.

ALABAMA
U.S. Department of Labor
Employment and Training Administration
Office of Apprenticeship
Medical Forum Building
950 22nd Street North, Room 648
Birmingham, AL 35203
P: 205.731.1308

ALASKA
U.S. Department of Labor
Employment and Training Administration
Office of Apprenticeship
605 West 4th Avenue, Room G-30
Anchorage, AK 99501
P: 907.271.5035

ARIZONA
U.S. Department of Labor
Employment and Training Administration
Office of Apprenticeship
600 South Las Vegas Boulevard, Suite 520
Las Vegas, NV 89101
P: 702.388.6771

ARKANSAS
U.S. Department of Labor
Employment and Training Administration
Office of Apprenticeship
700 West Capitol Street, Rom 3507
Little Rock, AR 72201
P: 501.324.5415

CALIFORNIA
U.S. Department of Labor
Employment and Training Administration
Office of Apprenticeship
801 I Street, Room 202
Sacramento, CA 95814
P: 916.414.2389

COLORADO
U.S. Department of Labor
Employment and Training Administration
Office of Apprenticeship
U.S. Custom House
721 19th Street, Room 465
Denver, CO 80202
P: 303.844.6362

CONNECTICUT
The U.S. Department of Labor, Employment and Training Administration, Office of Apprenticeship does not maintain a state office within this jurisdiction. Please refer to regional listing at end of section.

DELAWARE
The U.S. Department of Labor, Employment and Training Administration, Office of Apprenticeship does not maintain a state office within this jurisdiction. Please refer to regional listing at end of section.

DISTRICT OF COLUMBIA
The U.S. Department of Labor, Employment and Training Administration, Office of Apprenticeship does not maintain a state office within this jurisdiction. Please refer to regional listing at end of section.

FLORIDA
U.S. Department of Labor
Employment and Training Administration
Office of Apprenticeship
400 West Bay Street, Suite 934
Jacksonville, FL 32202
P: 904.359.9252

GEORGIA
U.S. Department of Labor
Employment and Training Administration
Office of Apprenticeship
61 Forsyth Street, SW, Room 6T80
Atlanta, GA 30303
P: 404.302.5897

HAWAII
U.S. Department of Labor
Employment and Training Administration
Office of Apprenticeship
300 Ala Moana Boulevard, Room 5-117
Honolulu, HI 96850
P: 808.541.2519

IDAHO
U.S. Department of Labor
Employment and Training Administration
Office of Apprenticeship
1387 South Vinnell Way, 110
Boise, ID 83706
P: 208.321.2972

ILLINOIS

U.S. Department of Labor
Employment and Training Administration
Office of Apprenticeship
230 South Dearborn Street, Room 656
Chicago, IL 60604
P: 312.596.5508

INDIANA

U.S. Department of Labor
Employment and Training Administration
Office of Apprenticeship
Federal Building & U.S. Courthouse
46 East Ohio Street, Room 511
Indianapolis, IN 46204
P: 317.226.7001

IOWA

U.S. Department of Labor
Employment and Training Administration
Office of Apprenticeship
210 Walnut Street, Room 715
Des Moines, IA 50309
P: 515.284.4690

KANSAS

U.S. Department of Labor
Employment and Training Administration
Office of Apprenticeship
444 Southeast Quincy Street, Room 247
Topeka, KS 66683
P: 785.295.2624

KENTUCKY

U.S. Department of Labor
Employment and Training Administration
Office of Apprenticeship
Federal Building, Room 168
600 Martin Luther King Place
Louisville, KY 40202
P: 502.582.5223

LOUISIANA

The U.S. Department of Labor, Employment and Training
Administration, Office of Apprenticeship does not maintain
a state office within this jurisdiction. Please refer to
regional listing at end of section.

MAINE

The U.S. Department of Labor, Employment and Training
Administration, Office of Apprenticeship does not maintain
a state office within this jurisdiction. Please refer to
regional listing at end of section.

MARYLAND

U.S. Department of Labor
Employment and Training Administration
Office of Apprenticeship
Federal Building
31 Hopkins Plaza, Room 430-B
Baltimore, MD 21201
P: 410.962.2676

MASSACHUSETTS

The U.S. Department of Labor, Employment and Training
Administration, Office of Apprenticeship does not maintain
a state office within this jurisdiction. Please refer to
regional listing at end of section.

MICHIGAN

U.S. Department of Labor
Employment and Training Administration
Office of Apprenticeship
315 West Allegan, Room 209
Lansing, MI 48933
P: 517.377.1747

MINNESOTA

U.S. Department of Labor
Employment and Training Administration
Office of Apprenticeship
316 North Robert Street, Room 144
St. Paul, MN 55101
P: 312.596.5508

MISSISSIPPI

U.S. Department of Labor
Employment and Training Administration
Office of Apprenticeship
100 West Capitol Street
Jackson, MS 39269
P: 601.965.4346

MISSOURI

U.S. Department of Labor
Employment and Training Administration
Office of Apprenticeship
Robert A. Young Federal Building
1222 Spruce Street, Room 9.102E
St. Louis, MO 63103
P: 314.539.2522

MONTANA

The U.S. Department of Labor, Employment and Training
Administration, Office of Apprenticeship does not maintain
a state office within this jurisdiction. Please refer to
regional listing at end of section.

NEBRASKA
U.S. Department of Labor
Employment and Training Administration
Office of Apprenticeship
111 South 18th Plaza, Suite C-49
Omaha, NE 68102
P: 402.221.3281

NEVADA
U.S. Department of Labor
Employment and Training Administration
Office of Apprenticeship
600 South Las Vegas Boulevard, Suite 520
Las Vegas, NV 89101
P: 702.38.6771

NEW HAMPSHIRE
U.S. Department of Labor
Employment and Training Administration
Office of Apprenticeship
55 Pleasant Road
Concord, NH 03301
P: 603.225.1444

NEW JERSEY
U.S. Department of Labor
Employment and Training Administration
Office of Apprenticeship
190 Middlesex Essex Turnpike
Iselin, NJ 08830
P: 732.750.0766

NEW MEXICO
U.S. Department of Labor
Employment and Training Administration
Office of Apprenticeship
500 4th Street, NW, Suite 401
Albuquerque, NM 87102
P: 505.248.6530

NEW YORK
U.S. Department of Labor
Employment and Training Administration
Office of Apprenticeship
190 Middlesex Essex Turnpike
Iselin, NJ 08830
P: 732.750.0766

NORTH CAROLINA
The U.S. Department of Labor, Employment and Training
Administration, Office of Apprenticeship does not maintain
a state office within this jurisdiction. Please refer to
regional listing at end of section.

NORTH DAKOTA
U.S. Department of Labor
Employment and Training Administration
Office of Apprenticeship
304 Broadway, Room 332
Bismarck, ND 58501
P: 701.250.4700

OHIO
U.S. Department of Labor
Employment and Training Administration
Office of Apprenticeship
200 North High Street, Room 605
Columbus, OH 43215
P: 614.469.7375

OKLAHOMA
U.S. Department of Labor
Employment and Training Administration
Office of Apprenticeship
215 Dean A. McGee Avenue, Suite 346
Oklahoma City, OK 73102
P: 405.231.4338

OREGON
U.S. Department of Labor
Employment and Training Administration
Office of Apprenticeship
300 Fifth Avenue, Suite 1260
Seattle, WA 98104
P: 206.757.6772

PENNSYLVANIA
U.S. Department of Labor
Employment and Training Administration
Office of Apprenticeship
Federal Building
228 Walnut Street, Room 356
Harrisburg, PA 17108
P: 717.221.3496

PUERTO RICO
The U.S. Department of Labor, Employment and Training
Administration, Office of Apprenticeship does not maintain
a state office within this jurisdiction. Please refer to
regional listing at end of section.

RHODE ISLAND
U.S. Department of Labor
Employment and Training Administration
Office of Apprenticeship
JFK Federal Building
15 New Sudbury Street, Room 370
Boston, MA 02203
P: 617.788.0177

SOUTH CAROLINA
U.S. Department of Labor
Employment and Training Administration
Office of Apprenticeship
61 Forsyth Street, SW, Room 6T80
Atlanta, GA 30303
P: 404.302.5483

SOUTH DAKOTA
U.S. Department of Labor
Employment and Training Administration
Office of Apprenticeship
221 South Central Avenue
Pierre, SD 57501
P: 605.224.7983

TENNESSEE
U.S. Department of Labor
Employment and Training Administration
Office of Apprenticeship
Airport Executive Plaza
1321 Murfreesboro Road, Suite 541
Nashville, TN 37217
P: 615.781.5318

TEXAS
U.S. Department of Labor
Employment and Training Administration
Office of Apprenticeship
300 East 8th Street, Suite 914
Austin, TX 79701
P: 512.916.5435

UTAH
U.S. Department of Labor
Employment and Training Administration
Office of Apprenticeship
125 State Street, Room 914
Salt Lake City, UT 84138
P: 801.524.5451

VERMONT
The U.S. Department of Labor, Employment and Training
Administration, Office of Apprenticeship does not maintain
a state office within this jurisdiction. Please refer to
regional listing at end of section.

VIRGINIA
U.S. Department of Labor
Employment and Training Administration
Office of Apprenticeship
Federal Building
400 North 8th Street, Suite 404
Richmond, VA 23219
P: 804.771.2488

WASHINGTON
U.S. Department of Labor
Employment and Training Administration
Office of Apprenticeship
300 Fifth Avenue, Suite 1260
Seattle, WA 98104
P: 206.757.6772

WEST VIRGINIA
U.S. Department of Labor
Employment and Training Administration
Office of Apprenticeship
405 Capitol Street, Suite 409
Charleston, WV 25301
P: 304.347.5794

WISCONSIN
U.S. Department of Labor
Employment and Training Administration
Office of Apprenticeship
740 Regent Street, Suite 104
Madison, WI 53715
P: 608.441.5377

WYOMING
U.S. Department of Labor
Employment and Training Administration
Office of Apprenticeship
American National Bank Building
1912 Capitol Avenue, Room 508
Cheyenne, WY 82001
P: 307.772.2448

REGION 1
U.S. Department of Labor
Employment and Training Administration
Office of Apprenticeship
JFK Federal Building, Room E-370
Boston, MA 02203
P: 617.788.0177

Note: This office serves the following states: Connecticut,
Maine, Massachusetts, New Hampshire, New Jersey, New
York, Puerto Rico, Rhode Island, Vermont, and the Virgin
Islands.

REGION 2
U.S. Department of Labor
Employment and Training Administration
Office of Apprenticeship
170 South Independence Mall, West, Suite 820-East
Philadelphia, PA 19106
P: 215.861.4830

Note: This office serves the following states: Delaware, Maryland, Pennsylvania, Virginia, West Virginia, and District of Columbia.

REGION 3

U.S. Department of Labor
Employment and Training Administration
Office of Apprenticeship
61 Forsyth Street, SW, Room 6T71
Atlanta, GA 30303
P: 404.302.5478

Note: This office serves the following states: Alabama, Florida, Georgia, Kentucky, Mississippi, North Carolina, South Carolina, and Tennessee.

REGION 4

U.S. Department of Labor
Employment and Training Administration
Office of Apprenticeship
Federal Building
525 South Griffin Street, Room 303
Dallas, TX 75202
P: 972.850.4681

Note. This office serves the following states: Arkansas, Colorado, Louisiana, Montana, New Mexico, North Dakota, Oklahoma, South Dakota, Texas, Utah, and Wyoming.

REGION 5

U.S. Department of Labor
Employment and Training Administration
Office of Apprenticeship
230 South Dearborn Street, Room 656
Chicago, IL 60604
P: 312.596.5500

Note: This office serves the following states: Illinois, Indiana, Iowa, Kansas, Michigan, Minnesota, Missouri, Nebraska, Ohio, and Wisconsin.

REGION 6

U.S. Department of Labor
Employment and Training Administration
Office of Apprenticeship
90 7th Street, Suite 17-100
San Francisco, CA 94103
P: 415.625.2230

Note: This office serves the following states: Alaska, Arizona, California, Hawaii, Idaho, Nevada, Oregon, and Washington.

APPENDIX 3-C: AMERICAN JOB CENTER WEBSITES

American Job Centers provide a full range of assistance to job seekers in one convenient location. The following websites are coordinated and administered by states with guidance and funding provided by the U.S. Department of Labor under the Workforce Innovation and Opportunity Act.

ALABAMA
https://joblink.alabama.gov/ada/?wfoffice=1

ALASKA
http://www.jobs.state.ak.us/

ARIZONA
https://egov/azdes.gov/cmsinternet/main.aspx?menu=260&id=2214

ARKANSAS
http://www.state.ar.us/esd/

CALIFORNIA
http://www.edd.ca.gov/one-stop/default.htm

COLORADO
http://www.coworkforce.com/EMP/WFCs.asp

CONNECTICUT
http://www.ctdol.state.ct.us/ContactInfo/CTWorks/Directory.htm

DELAWARE
http://www.vcnet.net

DISTRICT OF COLUMBIA
http://does.ci.washington.dc.us

FLORIDA
http://www.floridajobs.org/onestop/onestopdir/

GEORGIA
http://www.dol.state.ga.us

HAWAII
http://dlir.state.hi.us/wdd/esaddr.htm

IDAHO
http://www.idahoworks.state.id.us/IW_career.shtml

ILLINOIS
http://www.ides.state.il.us/ietc/map.htm

INDIANA
http://www.in.gov/dwd/job_seekers/workone_centers.html

IOWA
http://www.iowaworkforce.org/

KANSAS
http://www.kansascommerce.com/IndexPages/Div06a.aspx

KENTUCKY
http://www.dtr.ky.gov/one-stop.htm

LOUISIANA
http://www.ldol.state.la.us/

MAINE
http://www.mainecareercenter.com

MARYLAND
http://www.careernet.state.md.us

MASSACHUSETTS
http://www.detma.org/offices/careercenters.htm

MICHIGAN
http://www.michiganworks.org/

MINNESOTA
http://www.mnworkforcecenter.org/

MISSISSIPPI
http://www.wininmississippi.org/

MISSOURI
http://www.ded.mo.gov/Home/WFD/Missouri%20Career%20Centers.aspx

MONTANA
http://dli.mt.gov/

NEBRASKA
http://www.dol.state.ne.us/

NEVADA
http://www.nevadajobconnect.com

NEW HAMPSHIRE
http://www.nhworks.org/

NEW JERSEY
http://www.wnjpin.state.nj.us/

NEW MEXICO
http://www.dws.state.nm.us/

NEW YORK
http://labor.ny.gov/workforcenypartners/osview.asp

NORTH CAROLINA
http://www.joblink.state.nc.us

NORTH DAKOTA
http://www.state.nd.us/jsnd/

OHIO
http://jfs.ohio.gov/owd/wia/wiamap.stm

OKLAHOMA
http://www.oesc.state.ok.us

OREGON
http://findit.emp.state.or.us/offices/

PENNSYLVANIA
http://www.pacareerlink.state.pa.us/

PUERTO RICO
Information pertaining to Puerto Rico was not available during the creation of this document. Please see future editions for updates and/or revisions or visit http://www.gobierno.pr for more information.

RHODE ISLAND
http://www.dlt.state.ri.us

SOUTH CAROLINA
http://www.sccommerce.com/WorkForceDev.html

SOUTH DAKOTA
http://www.state.sd.us/dol/

TENNESSEE
http://www.state.tn.us/labor-wfd/

TEXAS
http://www.twc.state.tx.us/twc.html

UTAH
http://dwsa.state.ut.us

VERMONT
http://www.det.state.vt.us

VIRGINIA
http://www.careerconnect.state.va.us/

WASHINGTON
http://www.wa.gov/esd/1stop/

WEST VIRGINIA
https://www.workforcewv.org/

WISCONSIN
http://www.wisconsinjobcenter.org/directory/map/mapdefault.htm

WYOMING
http://onestop.state.wy.us/appview/wjn_home.asp

APPENDIX 3-D: STATE LABOR MARKET INFORMATION OFFICES

The State Department of Labors' Labor Market Information Office provides a wide range of labor market information from regional wages for specific occupations to statistics on employment within a specific geographic area.

ALABAMA
Alabama Department of Industrial Relations
Labor Market Information Division
649 Monroe Street, Room 422
Montgomery, AL 36131
P: 334.242.8859
I: http://dir.alabama.gov

ALASKA
Alaska Department of Workforce Development
Research and Analysis Section
P.O. Box 25501
Juneau, AK 99802
P: 907.465.4518
I: http://almis.labor.state.ak.us

ARIZONA
Arizona Department of Economic Security
Research and Analysis Section
P.O. Box 6123, SC 733A
Phoenix, AZ 85005
P: 602.542.5984
I: http://www.workforce.az.gov

ARKANSAS
Arkansas Department of Workforce Services
Research and Analysis Section
P.O. Box 2981
Little Rock, AR 72203
P: 501.682.3198
I: http://www.arkansas.gov/esd

CALIFORNIA
California Employment Development Department
Labor Market Information Division
P.O. Box 826880
Sacramento, CA 94280
P: 916.262.2160
I: http://www.calmis.cahwnet.gov

COLORADO
Colorado Department of Labor and Employment Work
Labor Market Information
633 17th Street, Suite 600
Denver, CO 80202
P: 303.318.8850
I: http://www.coworkforce.com/lmi

CONNECTICUT
Connecticut Department of Labor
Office of Research
200 Folly Brook Boulevard
Wethersfield, CT 06109
P: 860.263.6275
I: http://www.ctdol.state.ct.us/lmi

DELAWARE
Delaware Department of Labor
Office of Occupational and Labor Market Information
4425 North Market Street
Wilmington, DE 19809
P: 302.761.8069
I: http://www.delawareworks.com

DISTRICT OF COLUMBIA
Government of the District of Columbia
Department of Employment Services
Office of Labor Market Research and Information
64 New York Avenue, NE, Suite 3035
Washington, DC 20002
P: 202.671.1633
I: http://www.does.dc.gov/does

FLORIDA
Florida Agency for Workforce Innovation
Labor Market Statistics
107 East Madison Street, MSC G-020
Tallahassee, FL 32399
P: 850.245.7205
I: http://www.labormarketinfo.com

GEORGIA
Georgia Department of Labor
Workforce Information and Analysis
223 Courtland Street
Atlanta, GA 30303
P: 404.232.3875
I: http://www.dol.state.ga.us

HAWAII
Hawaii Department of Labor and Industrial Relations
Research and Statistics Office
830 Punchbowl Street, Room 304
Honolulu, HI 96813
P: 808.586.8999
I: http://www.hiwi.org

IDAHO
Idaho Department of Commerce and Labor
Research and Analysis Bureau
317 West Main Street
Boise, ID 83704
P: 208.332.3570
I: http://lmi.idaho.gov

ILLINOIS
Illinois Department of Employment Security
Workforce and Career Information
33 South State Street, 9th Floor
Chicago, IL 60603
P: 312.793.2316
I: http://lmi.ides.state.il.us

INDIANA
Indiana Workforce Development
Research and Analysis
10 North Senate Avenue, SE, Suite 211
Indianapolis, IN 46204
P: 317.232.7460
I: http://www.in.gov/dwd

IOWA
Iowa Workforce Development
Policy and Information Division
1000 East Grand Avenue
Des Moines, IA 50319
P: 515.281.6642
I: http://www.iowaworkforce.org/lmi

KANSAS
Kansas Department of Labor
Labor Market Information Services
401 Southwest Topeka Boulevard
Topeka, KS 66603
P: 785.296.5058
I: http://laborstats.dol.ks.gov

KENTUCKY
Kentucky Office of Employment and Training
Research and Statistics Branch
275 East Main Street, 2W-G
Frankfort, KY 40621
P: 502.564.7976
I: http://www.workforcekentucky.ky.gov

LOUISIANA
Louisiana Department of Labor
Research and Statistics Division
1001 North 23rd Street
Baton Rouge, LA 70804
P: 225.342.3141
I: http://www.laworks.net

MAINE
Maine Department of Labor
Labor Market Information Services
19 Union Street
Augusta, ME 04332
P: 207.287.2271
I: http://www.state.me.us/labor/lmis/index.html

MARYLAND
Maryland Department of Labor, Licensing and Regulation
Office of Labor Market Analysis and Information
1100 North Eutaw Street, Room 316
Baltimore, MD 21201
P: 410.767.2250
I: http://www.dllr.state.md.us/lmi/index.htm

MASSACHUSETTS
Massachusetts Division of Unemployment Assistance
Department of Economic Research
19 Staniford Street
Boston, MA 02421
P: 617.626.6556
I: http://www.detma.org/lmidataprog.htm

MICHIGAN
Michigan Department of Labor and Economic Growth
Bureau of Labor Market Information
3024 West Grand Boulevard, Suite 9-100
Detroit, MI 48202
P: 313.456.3100
I: http://www.michlmi.org

MINNESOTA
Department of Employment and Economic Development
Labor Market Information Office
332 Minnesota Street, Suite E-200
St. Paul, MN 55101
P: 651.296.6545
I: http://www.deed.state.mn.us/lmi

MISSISSIPPI
Mississippi Department of Employment Security
Labor Market Information Division
1235 Echelon Parkway
Jackson, MS 39213
P: 601.321.6262
I: http://mdes.ms.gov

MISSOURI
Missouri Economic Research and Information Center
Labor Market Information Division
P.O. Box 3150
Jefferson City, MO 65101
P: 573.751.3637
I: http://www.missourieconomy.org

MONTANA
Montana Department of Labor and Industry
Research and Analysis Bureau
P.O. Box 1728
Helena, MT 59624
P: 406.444.2430
I: http://www.ourfactsyourfuture.org

NEBRASKA
Nebraska Department of Workforce Development
Labor Market Information Division
P.O. Box 4600
Lincoln, NE 68509
P: 402.471.2600
I: http://www.dol.state.ne.us/lmi/index.htm

NEVADA
Nevada Department of Employment and Training
Research and Analysis
500 East Third Street
Carson City, NV 89713
P: 775.684.0387
I: http://www.detr.state.nv.us/lmi/index.htm

NEW HAMPSHIRE
New Hampshire Department of Employment Security
Economic and Labor Market Information Bureau
32 South Main Street
Concord, NH 03301
P: 603.228.4123
I: http://www.nhes.state.nh.us/elmi

NEW JERSEY
New Jersey Department of Labor
Labor Market and Demographic Research Division
P.O. Box 388
Trenton, NJ 08625
P: 609.984.2593
I: http://www.state.nj.us/labor/lra

NEW MEXICO
New Mexico Department of Labor
Economic Research and Analysis
501 Mountain Road, NE
Albuquerque, NM 87102
P: 505.222.4684
I: http://www.dol.state.nm.us/dol_lmif.html

NEW YORK
New York State Department of Labor
Research and Statistics
State Office Campus
Building 12, Room 400
Albany, NY 12240
P: 518.457.3805
I: http://www.labor.state.ny.us

NORTH CAROLINA
North Carolina Employment Security Commission
Labor Market Information Division
700 Wade Avenue
Raleigh, NC 27605
P: 919.733.2936
I: http://www.ncesc.com

NORTH DAKOTA
North Dakota Department of Labor
Labor Market Information
P.O. Box 5507
Bismarck, ND 58506
P: 701.328.3136
I: http://www.jobsnd.com/data/index.html

OHIO
Ohio Office of Workforce Development
Bureau of Labor Market Information
4300 Kimberly Parkway
Columbus, OH 43232
P: 614.752.9494
I: http://www.ohioworkforceinformer.org

OKLAHOMA
Oklahoma Employment Security Commission
Labor Market Information
2401 North Lincoln Boulevard
P.O. Box 52003
Oklahoma City, OK 73152
P: 405.557.7221
I: http://www.oesc.state.ok.us/lmi/default.htm

OREGON
Oregon Employment Department Partnership
Research Division
875 Union Street, NE, Room 207
Salem, OR 97311
P: 503.947.1200
I: http://www.qualityinfo.org/olmisj/OlmisZine

PENNSYLVANIA
Pennsylvania Department of Labor and Industry
Center for Workforce Information and Analysis
220 Labor and Industry Building
Seventh and Forester Streets
Harrisburg, PA 17121
P: 877.493.3282
I: http://www.paworkstats.state.pa.us

PUERTO RICO
Department of Labor and Human Resources
Labor Market Information Office
P.O. Box 195540
San Juan, PR 00919
P: 787.754.5347
I: http://www.net-empleopr.org/almis23/index.jsp

RHODE ISLAND
Rhode Island Department of Labor and Training
Labor Market information
1511 Pontiac Avenue
Cranston, RI 02920
P: 401.462.8767
I: http://www.dlt.ri.gov/lmi

SOUTH CAROLINA
South Carolina Employment Security Commission
Labor Market Information Department
631 Hampton Street
Columbia, SC 29202
P: 803.737.2660
I: http://www.sces.org/lmi/index.asp

SOUTH DAKOTA
South Dakota Department of Labor
Labor Market Information Center
420 South Roosevelt Street
Aberdeen, SD 57402
P: 605.626.2314
I: http://www.state.sd.us/dol/lmic/index.htm

TENNESSEE
Department of Labor and Workforce Development
Research and Statistics Division
500 James Robertson Parkway, 11th Floor
Nashville, TN 37245
P: 615.741.2284
I: http://www.state.tn.us/labor-wfd/lmi.htm

TEXAS
Texas Workforce Commission
Labor Market Information
9001 North IH-35, Suite 103A
Austin, TX 75753
P: 512.491.4800
I: http://www.tracer2.com

UTAH
Utah Department of Workforce Services
Workforce Information
140 East 300 South
Salt Lake City, UT 84111
P: 801.526.9401
I: http://jobs.utah.gov/opencms/wi

VERMONT
Vermont Department of Labor
Research and Analysis
P.O. Box 488
Montpelier, VT 05601
P: 802.828.4202
I: http://www.labor.vermont.gov

VIRGINIA
Virginia Employment Commission
Economic Information Services
703 East Main Street, Room 327
Richmond, VA 23218
P: 804.786.5496
I: http://www.velma.virtuallmi.com

WASHINGTON
Washington Employment Security Department
Labor Market and Economic Analysis
P.O. Box 9046
Olympia, WA 98507
P: 360.438.4804
I: http://www.workforceexplorer.com

WEST VIRGINIA
West Virginia Division of Labor
Research, Information and Analysis Division
112 California Avenue
Charleston, WV 25303
P: 304.558.2660
I: http://www.wvbep.org/bep/lmi

WISCONSIN
Wisconsin Department of Workforce Development
Bureau of Workforce Information
201 East Washington Avenue
Madison, WI 53702
P: 608.266.8212
I: http://worknet.wisconsin.gov/worknet

WYOMING
Wyoming Department of Employment
Research and Planning
P.O. Box 2760
Casper, WY 82602
P: 307.473.3807
I: http://www.doe.state.wy.us/lmi

APPENDIX 3-E: STATE JOB BANK WEBSITES

Job Banks provide Internet access to a wide range of job-opportunities within a specific geographic area or occupational cluster.

ALABAMA
https://joblink.alabama.gov/ada/

ALASKA
http://www.jobs.state.ak.us/jobseeker.htm

ARIZONA
https://www.azjobconnection.gov/ada/

ARKANSAS
https://www.arjoblink.arkansas.gov/ada/default.cfm

CALIFORNIA
https://www.caljobs.ca.gov/vosnet/default.aspx

COLORADO
http://www.connectingcolorado.com/

CONNECTICUT
http://connecticut.us.jobs/index.asp

DELAWARE
https://joblink.delaware.gov/ada/r/

DISTRICT OF COLUMBIA
https://www.dcnetworks.org/vosnet/default.aspx

FLORIDA
https://www.employflorida.com/vosnet/default.aspx

GEORGIA
http://www.dol.state.ga.us/js/job_info_system.htm

HAWAII
https://www.hirenethawaii.com/vosnet/default.aspx

IDAHO
http://labor.idah.gov/dnn/default.aspx

ILLINOIS
https://illiniosjoblink.illinois.gov

INDIANA
https://www.indianacareerconnect.com/vosnet/default.aspx

IOWA
https://www1.iowajobs.org/jobs/login.seek

KANSAS
https://www.kansasworks.com/ada/r/

KENTUCKY
https://focuscareer.ky.gov/career/

LOUISIANA
https://www.louisianaworks.net/hire/vosnet/default.aspx

MAINE
https://gateway.maine.gov/dol/mjb/jobseeker/jobseekerwelcome.aspx

MARYLAND
https://mwejobs.maryland.gov/vosnet/default.aspx

MASSACHUSETTS
https://web.detma.org/jobquest/default.aspx

MICHIGAN
http://www.mitalent.org

MINNESOTA
https://www.minnesotaworks.net/

MISSISSIPPI
https://wings.mdes.ms.gov/wings/welcome.jsp

MISSOURI
http://jobs.mo.gov/

MONTANA
https://jobs.mt.gov/jobs/login.seek

NEBRASKA
http://dol.nebraska.gov/

NEVADA
http://www.nevada.us.jobs/

NEW HAMPSHIRE
https://nhworksjobmatch.nhes.nh.gov/vosnet/default.aspx

NEW JERSEY
http://jobs4jersey.com/

NEW MEXICO
https://www.jobs.state.nm.us/vosnet/default.aspx

NEW YORK
http://newyork.us.jobs/index.asp

NORTH CAROLINA
https://www.ncworks.gov/vosnet/default.aspx

NORTH DAKOTA
http://jobsnd.com/

OHIO
https://jobseeker.ohiomeansjobs.monster.com

OKLAHOMA
https://okjobmatch.com/ada/

OREGON
http://www.emp.state.or.us/jobs/

PENNSYLVANIA
https://www.jobgateway.pa.gov

PUERTO RICO
http://puertorico.us.jobs/

RHODE ISLAND
https://www.employri.org/vosnet/default.aspx

SOUTH CAROLINA
https://jobs.scworks.org/vosnet/default.aspx

SOUTH DAKOTA
http://dlr.sd.gov/

TENNESSEE
https://www.jobs4tn.gov/vosnet.default.aspx

TEXAS
https://wit.twc.state.tx.us/workintexas/wtx?

UTAH
https://jobs.utah.gov/jsp/utahjobs/seeker/search/search.do

VERMONT
https://www.vermontjoblink.com/ada/

VIRGINIA
https://www.vawc.virginia.gov/vosnet/default.aspx

WASHINGTON
https://fortress.wa.gov/esd/worksource/employment.aspx

WEST VIRGINIA
http://www.wvcommerce.org/business/workforcewv/job_seekers/default.aspx

WISCONSIN
https://jobcenterofwisconsin.com/

WYOMING
https://www.wyomingatwork.com/vosnet/default.aspx

APPENDIX 3-F: STATE FEDERAL BONDING
PROGRAM COORDINATORS

The Federal Bonding Program provides fidelity bonding insurance coverage to individuals with criminal histories and other high-risk job applicants to protect employers from loss of theft due to employee dishonesty.

ALABAMA

Alabama State Employment Services
Bonding Services Coordinator
Industrial Relations Building, Room 2805
649 Monroe Street
Montgomery, AL 36131
P: 334.242.8039

ALASKA

Alaska Department of Labor and Workforce Development
Bonding Services Coordinator
P.O. Box 115509
Juneau, AK 99811
P: 907.465.5955

ARIZONA

Arizona Department of Economic Security
Employment and Training Administration
Bonding Services Coordinator
Site Code 734-T
P.O. Box 6123
Phoenix, AZ 85005
P: 602.771.0906

ARKANSAS

Arkansas Department of Workforce Services
Bonding Services Coordinator
2200 Ft. Root Drive, Building 89, Room 106
North Little Rock, AR 72214
P: 501.554.1343

CALIFORNIA

California Employment Development Department
Bonding Services Coordinator
800 Capitol Mall, MIC-50
Sacramento, CA 95814
P: 916.654.7799

COLORADO

Colorado Department of Labor and Employment
Workforce Programs
Bonding Services Coordinator
633 17th Street, Suite 700
Denver, CO 80202
P: 303.318.8961

CONNECTICUT

Connecticut Department of Labor
Bonding Services Coordinator
200 Folly Brook Boulevard, 3rd Floor
Wethersfield, CT 06109
P: 860.263.6017

DELAWARE

Delaware Department of Labor
Division of Employment Services
Bonding Services Coordinator
4425 North Market Street, 3rd Floor
Wilmington, DE 19802
P: 302.761.8039

DISTRICT OF COLUMBIA

District of Columbia Department of Employment Services
Bonding Services Coordinator
4058 Minnesota Avenue, NE, 2nd Floor
Washington, DC 20002
P: 202.698.3753

FLORIDA

Florida Department of Economic Opportunity
Bonding Services Coordinator
107 East Madison Street
Tallahassee, FL 32399
P: 850.245.7451

GEORGIA

Georgia Department of Labor
Bonding Services Coordinator
148 Andrew Young International Boulevard, NE,
Suite 400
Atlanta, GA 30303
P: 404.232.3509

HAWAII

Hawaii Department of Employment Services
Workforce Development Division
Bonding Services Coordinator
830 Punchbowl Street, Room 329
Honolulu, HI 96813
P: 808.586.8819

IDAHO
Idaho Department of Commerce and Labor
Bonding Services Coordinator
317 West Main Street
Boise, ID 83735
P: 208.332.3570

ILLINOIS
Illinois Department of Employment Security
Bonding Services Coordinator
33 South State Street, Suite 800
Chicago, IL 60603
P: 312.793.2913

INDIANA
Indiana Workforce Development
Bonding Services Coordinator
10 North Senate Avenue, Room SE-304
Indianapolis, IN 46204
P: 317.232.3623

IOWA
Iowa Workforce Development
Bonding Services Coordinator
1000 East Grand Avenue
Des Moines, IA 50319
P: 515.725.2007

KANSAS
Kansas Department of Commerce
Bonding Services Coordinator
1000 Southwest Jackson Street, Suite 100
Topeka, KS 66612
P: 785.296.7435

KENTUCKY
Kentucky Department of Corrections
Bonding Services Coordinator
275 East Main Street
Frankfort, KY 40601
P: 502.782.2256

LOUISIANA
Louisiana Department of Labor
Bonding Services Coordinator
1001 North 23rd Street
P.O. Box 94094
Baton Rouge, LA 70804
P: 225.342.2939

MAINE
Maine Bureau of Employment Services
Bonding Services Coordinator
54 State House Station Drive
P.O. Box 259
Augusta, ME 04332
P: 207.623.7977

MARYLAND
Maryland Department of Economic and Employment
Division
Bonding Services Coordinator
1100 North Eutaw Street, Suite 209
Baltimore, MD 21201
P: 410.767.2018

MASSACHUSETTS
Massachusetts Division of Employment and Training
Administration
Bonding Services Coordinator
19 Staniford Street, 1st Floor
Boston, MA 02114
P: 617.626.5733

MICHIGAN
Michigan Bureau of Workforce Transition
Bonding Services Coordinator
201 North Washington Square, 3rd Floor, Suite 3-West
Lansing, MI 48913
P: 517.335.4316

MINNESOTA
Department of Employment and Economic Development
Bonding Services Coordinator
332 Minnesota Street, Suite E-200
St. Paul, MN 55101
P: 651.259.7521

MISSISSIPPI
Mississippi Department of Employment Security
Bonding Services Coordinator
1235 Echelon Parkway
Jackson, MS 39215
P: 601.321.6054

MISSOURI
Missouri Department of Economic Development
Division of Workforce Development
Bonding Services Coordinator
421 East Dunklin, P.O. Box 1087
Jefferson City, MO 65102
P: 573.526.8217

MONTANA
Montana Department of Labor and Industry
Bonding Services Coordinator
P.O. Box 1728
Helena, MT 59624
P: 406.444.7895

NEBRASKA
Nebraska Department of Labor
Employment and Training Administration
Bonding Services Coordinator
550 South 16th Street
Lincoln, NE 68509
P: 402.471.9977

NEVADA
Nevada Department of Employment and Training
Bonding Services Coordinator
500 East Third Street
Carson City, NV 89713
P: 775.684.0320

NEW HAMPSHIRE
New Hampshire Department of Employment Security
Bonding Services Coordinator
32 South Main Street
Concord, NH 03301
P: 603.228.4079

NEW JERSEY
New Jersey Department of Labor
Division of Workforce Grant and Program Management
Bonding Services Coordinator
P.O. Box 055, 7th Floor
Trenton, NJ 08625
P: 609.292.5763

NEW MEXICO
New Mexico Employment Security Department
Employment and Training Support Section
Bonding Services Coordinator
P.O. Box 1928
Albuquerque, NM 87103
P: 505.841.8444

NEW YORK
New York Department of Labor
Bonding Services Coordinator
State Office Campus
Building 12, Room 425
Albany, NY 12240
P: 518.485.2151

NORTH CAROLINA
North Carolina Department of Commerce
Bonding Services Coordinator
313 Chapanoke Road
P.O. Box 27625
Raleigh, NC 27611
P: 919.814.0457

NORTH DAKOTA
North Dakota Department of Labor
Bonding Services Coordinator
P.O. Box 5507
Bismarck, ND 58506
P: 701.328.3034

OHIO
Ohio Central School System
Bonding Services Coordinator
P.O. Box 779
London, OH 43140
P: 740.845.3240

OKLAHOMA
Oklahoma Employment Security Division
Bonding Services Coordinator
2401 North Lincoln Boulevard, Suite 454
P.O. Box 52003
Oklahoma City, OK 73152
P: 405.557.5474

OREGON
Oregon Employment Department Partnership
Bonding Services Coordinator
875 Union Street, NE
Salem, OR 97311
P: 503.947.1680

PENNSYLVANIA
Pennsylvania Department of Labor and Industry
Bonding Services Coordinator
651 Boas Street
Harrisburg, PA 17121
P: 717.783.3676

PUERTO RICO
American Job Centers of Puerto Rico, Inc.
Bonding Services Coordinator
Condonminio Plaza Universadid 200
Calle Anasco 839 Local 5
Rio Piedras, PR 00928
P: 787.296.1785

RHODE ISLAND
Rhode Island Department of Labor and Training
Bonding Services Coordinator
1511 Pontiac Avenue, Building 73-3
Cranston, RI 02920
P: 401.462.8724

SOUTH CAROLINA
South Carolina Department of Employment and Workforce
Bonding Services Coordinator
1550 Gadsden Street
P.O. Box 1406
Columbia, SC 29202
P: 803.737.2636

SOUTH DAKOTA
South Dakota Department of Labor
Bonding Services Coordinator
420 South Roosevelt Street
P.O. Box 4730
Aberdeen, SD 57402
P: 605.626.7652

TENNESSEE
Tennessee Department of Labor and Workforce
Development
Bonding Services Coordinator
220 French Landing Drive
Nashville, TN 37243
P: 615.253.6389

TEXAS
Texas Workforce Commission
Bonding Services Coordinator
101 East 15th Street, Room 440-AT
Austin, TX 78778
P: 512.463.9647

UTAH
Utah Department of Workforce Services
Bonding Services Coordinator
140 East 300 South, 5th Floor
Salt Lake City, UT 84111
P: 801.526.9876

VERMONT
Vermont Department of Labor
Bonding Services Coordinator
5 Green Mountain Drive, P.O. Box 480
Montpelier, VT 05601
P: 802.828.4342

VIRGINIA
Virginia Department of Corrections
Bonding Services Coordinator
6900 Atmore Drive
Richmond, VA 23225
P: 804.887.8262

WASHINGTON
Washington Department of Employment Security
Offender Employment Services
Bonding Services Coordinator
P.O. Box 9046
Olympia, WA 98507
P: 360.902.9685

WEST VIRGINIA
West Virginia Division of Labor
Bonding Services Coordinator
112 California Avenue, Room 112
Charleston, WV 25305
P: 304.558.1138

WISCONSIN
Wisconsin Department of Workforce Development
Bonding Services Coordinator
201 East Washington Avenue
P.O. Box 7972
Madison, WI 53707
P: 608.267.7259

WYOMING
Wyoming Department of Workforce Services
Bonding Services Coordinator
851 Werner Court, Suite 120
Casper, WY 82601
P: 307.233.4623

APPENDIX 3-G: STATE WORK OPPORTUNITY
TAX CREDIT COORDINATORS

The Work Opportunity Tax Credit is a tax credit to reduce the federal tax liability of private sector employers. It is intended to be used as an incentive for employers to hire individuals with criminal histories and other target groups.

ALABAMA
Alabama Department of Industrial Relations
Work Opportunity Tax Credit Coordinator
649 Monroe Street, Room 2813
Montgomery, AL 36131
P: 334.242.8037

ALASKA
Alaska Department of Workforce Development
Employment Security Division, ESS1B
Work Opportunity Tax Credit Coordinator
P.O. Box 115509
Juneau, AK 99811
P: 907.465.5952

ARIZONA
Arizona Department of Economic Security
Employment and Training Administration
Work Opportunity Tax Credit Coordinator
P.O. Box 6123
Phoenix, AZ 85005
P: 602.542.6320

ARKANSAS
Arkansas Department of Workforce Services
Work Opportunity Tax Credit Coordinator
P.O. Box 2981
Little Rock, AR 72203
P: 501.682.1354

CALIFORNIA
California Employment Development Department
Work Opportunity Tax Credit Coordinator
2901 50th Street
Sacramento, CA 95817
P: 916.227.2301

COLORADO
Colorado Department of Labor and Employment Work
Opportunity Tax Credit Coordinator
633 17th Street, Suite 700
Denver, CO 80202
P: 303.318.8845

CONNECTICUT
Connecticut Department of Labor
Work Opportunity Tax Credit Coordinator
200 Folly Brook Boulevard
Wethersfield, CT 06109
P: 860.263.6066

DELAWARE
Delaware Department of Labor
Division of Employment and Training
Work Opportunity Tax Credit Coordinator
4425 North Market Street, 3rd Floor
Wilmington, DE 19802
P: 302.761.8145

DISTRICT OF COLUMBIA
Government of the District of Columbia
Department of Employment Services
Work Opportunity Tax Credit Coordinator
4058 Minnesota Avenue, NE, Suite 3001
Washington, DC 20019
P: 202.698.5136

FLORIDA
Florida Department of Economic Opportunity
Work Opportunity Tax Credit Coordinator
107 East Madison Street, MSC G-300
Tallahassee, FL 32399
P: 850.921.3299

GEORGIA
Georgia Department of Labor
Work Opportunity Tax Credit Coordinator
148 Andrew Young International Boulevard, Suite 400
Atlanta, GA 30303
P: 404.232.3567

HAWAII
Hawaii Department of Employment Services
Workforce Development Division
Work Opportunity Tax Credit Coordinator
830 Punchbowl Street, Room 329
Honolulu, HI 96813
P: 808.586.8820

IDAHO
Idaho Department of Commerce and Labor
Work Opportunity Tax Credit Coordinator
317 West Main Street
Boise, ID 83704
P: 208.332.3570

ILLINOIS
Illinois Department of Employment Security
Work Opportunity Tax Credit Coordinator
33 South State Street, 8th Floor South
Chicago, IL 60603
P: 312.793.2913

INDIANA
Indiana Workforce Development
Work Opportunity Tax Credit Coordinator
10 North Senate Avenue
Indianapolis, IN 46204
P: 317.232.7746

IOWA
Iowa Workforce Development
Work Opportunity Tax Credit Coordinator
1000 East Grand Avenue, 3rd Floor East
Des Moines, IA 50319
P: 515.725.2810

KANSAS
Kansas Department of Commerce
Work Opportunity Tax Credit Coordinator
1000 Southwest Jackson Street, Suite 100
Topeka, KS 66612
P: 785.296.7435

KENTUCKY
Kentucky Department of Workforce Investment
Work Opportunity Tax Credit Coordinator
275 East Main Street, 2W-A
Frankfort, KY 40621
P: 502.782.3069

LOUISIANA
Louisiana Department of Labor
Work Opportunity Tax Credit Coordinator
1001 North 23rd Street
P.O. Box 94094
Baton Rouge, LA 70804
P: 225.342.2939

MAINE
Maine Bureau of Employment Services
Work Opportunity Tax Credit Coordinator
54 State House Station Drive
Augusta, ME 04333
P: 207.623.7981

MARYLAND
Maryland Department of Labor, Licensing and Regulation
Work Opportunity Tax Credit Coordinator
1100 North Eutaw Street, Room 201-203
Baltimore, MD 21201
P: 410.767.2047

MASSACHUSETTS
Massachusetts Division of Employment and Training
Administration
Work Opportunity Tax Credit Coordinator
19 Staniford Street, 1st Floor
Boston, MA 02114
P: 617.626.5730

MICHIGAN
Michigan Unemployment Insurance Agency
Work Opportunity Tax Credit Coordinator
3024 West Grand Boulevard, Suite 11-500
Detroit, MI 48202
P: 313.456.3363

MINNESOTA
Department of Employment and Economic Development
Work Opportunity Tax Credit Coordinator
332 Minnesota Street, Suite E-200
St. Paul, MN 55101
P: 651.259.7521

MISSISSIPPI
Mississippi Department of Employment Security
Work Opportunity Tax Credit Coordinator
1235 Echelon Parkway
P.O. Box 1699
Jackson, MS 39213
P: 601.321.6084

MISSOURI
Missouri Department of Economic Development
Work Opportunity Tax Credit Coordinator
421 East Dunklin
Jefferson City, MO 65102
P: 573.522.9501

MONTANA
Montana Department of Labor and Industry
Work Opportunity Tax Credit Coordinator
P.O. Box 1728
Helena, MT 59624
P: 406.444.9046

NEBRASKA
Nebraska Department of Labor
Employment and Training Administration
Work Opportunity Tax Credit Coordinator
550 South 16th Street
Lincoln, NE 68509
P: 402.471.9977

NEVADA
Nevada Department of Employment and Training
Work Opportunity Tax Credit Coordinator
500 East Third Street
Carson City, NV 89713
P: 775.684.0321

NEW HAMPSHIRE
New Hampshire Department of Employment Security
Work Opportunity Tax Credit Coordinator
32 South Main Street
Concord, NH 03301
P: 603.228.4079

NEW JERSEY
New Jersey Department of Labor
Work Opportunity Tax Credit Coordinator
P.O. Box 058
Trenton, NJ 08625
P: 609.292.5525

NEW MEXICO
New Mexico Department of Workforce Solutions
Business Services Division
Work Opportunity Tax Credit Coordinator
P.O. Box 1928
Albuquerque, NM 87103
P: 505.841.8501

NEW YORK
New York Department of Labor
Work Opportunity Tax Credit Coordinator
State Office Campus
Building 12, Room 200
Albany, NY 12240
P: 518.457.6823

NORTH CAROLINA
North Carolina Department of Commerce
Work Opportunity Tax Credit Coordinator
4216 Mail Service Center
Raleigh, NC 27699
P: 919.814.0439

NORTH DAKOTA
North Dakota Department of Labor
Work Opportunity Tax Credit Coordinator
P.O. Box 5507
Bismarck, ND 58506
P: 701.328.2997

OHIO
Ohio Office of Workforce Development
Work Opportunity Tax Credit Coordinator
4020 East Fifth Avenue
Columbus, OH 43219
P: 888.296.7541

OKLAHOMA
Oklahoma Employment Security Division
Work Opportunity Tax Credit Coordinator
2401 North Lincoln Boulevard
P.O. Box 52003
Oklahoma City, OK 73152
P: 405.557.7128

OREGON
Oregon Employment Department Partnership
Work Opportunity Tax Credit Coordinator
875 Union Street, NE, Room 201
Salem, OR 97311
P: 503.947.1478

PENNSYLVANIA
Pennsylvania Department of Labor and Industry
Work Opportunity Tax Credit Coordinator
651 Boas Street, 12-W
Harrisburg, PA 17121
P: 717.783.3676

PUERTO RICO
Department of Labor and Human Resources
Bureau of Employment Security
Work Opportunity Tax Credit Coordinator
P.O. Box 195540
San Juan, PR 00919
P: 787.625.3137

RHODE ISLAND
Rhode Island Department of Labor and Training
Work Opportunity Tax Credit Coordinator
1511 Pontiac Avenue
Cranston, RI 02920
P: 401.462.8717

SOUTH CAROLINA
Department of Employment and Workforce
Work Opportunity Tax Credit Coordinator
1550 Gadsden Street, P.O. Box 1406, Room 1406
Columbia, SC 29202
P: 803.737.2592

SOUTH DAKOTA
South Dakota Department of Labor
Work Opportunity Tax Credit Coordinator
420 South Roosevelt Street
P.O. Box 4730
Aberdeen, SD 57402
P: 605.626.7652

TENNESSEE
Tennessee Department of Labor and Workforce
Development
Work Opportunity Tax Credit Coordinator
220 French Landing Drive
Nashville, TN 37243
P: 615.253.6664

TEXAS
Texas Workforce Commission
Work Opportunity Tax Credit Coordinator
101 East 15th Street, Room 202-T
Austin, TX 78778
P: 512.305.9602

UTAH
Utah Department of Workforce Services
Work Opportunity Tax Credit Coordinator
140 East 300 South
Salt Lake City, UT 84111
P: 801.390.4336

VERMONT
Vermont Department of Labor
Work Opportunity Tax Credit Coordinator
5 Green Mountain Drive, P.O. Box 488
Montpelier, VT 05601
P: 802.828.5250

VIRGINIA
Virginia Employment Commission
Work Opportunity Tax Credit Coordinator
703 East Main Street
Richmond, VA 23219
P: 804.786.2887

WASHINGTON
Washington Department of Employment Security
Work Opportunity Tax Credit Coordinator
P.O. Box 9046
Olympia, WA 98507
P: 360.407.1323

WEST VIRGINIA
West Virginia Division of Labor
Work Opportunity Tax Credit Coordinator
112 California Avenue, Room 200
Charleston, WV 25305
P: 304.558.5050

WISCONSIN
Wisconsin Department of Workforce Development
Work Opportunity Tax Credit Coordinator
201 East Washington Avenue, G-100
P.O. Box 7972
Madison, WI 53707
P: 608.266.1903

WYOMING
Wyoming Department of Workforce Services
Work Opportunity Tax Credit Coordinator
851 Werner Court, Suite 121
Casper, WY 82601
P: 307.233.4623

APPENDIX 3-H: COMPANIES WHO HIRE EX-OFFENDERS

The following list is comprised of the national headquarters of companies whose official hiring practices do not automatically restrict those individuals with criminal records.

AAMCO Transmissions, Inc.
201 Gibraltar Road
Horaham, PA 19044
P: 800.523.0401
I: http://www.aamco.com

Abbott Nutrition Products
625 Cleveland Avenue
Columbus, OH 43215
P: 800.227.5767
I: http://www.abbottnutrition.com

Abercrombie & Fitch
200 Abercrombie Way
New Albany, OH 43054
P: 866.681.3115
I: http://www.abercrombie.com

Adobe Systems, Inc.
345 Park Avenue
San Jose, CA 95110
P: 408.536.6000
I: http://www.adobe.com

AirTran Airways
1800 Phoenix Boulevard
Atlanta, GA 30349
P: 866.247.2428
I: http://www.airtran.com

Alamo Rent-a-Car
8420 St. John Industrial Drive
Saint Louis, MO 63114
P: 800.445.5664
I: http://www.alamo.com

Alaska Airlines
P.O. Box24948
Seattle, WA 98124
P: 800.654.5669
I: http://www.alaskaair.com

Albertsons, Inc.
175 South Howard Street
Spokane, WA 99201
P: 208.395.6200
I: http://www.albertsons.com

Allied Van Lines, Inc.
700 Oakmont Lane
Westmont, IL 60559
P: 800.470.2851
I: http://www.allied.com

Allstate Insurance Company
1819 Electric Road, SW
Roanoke, IL 24018
P: 847.402.5000
I: http://www.allstate.com

American Airlines, Inc.
P.O. Box 619612
Dallas/Fort Worth Airport, TX 75261
P: 817.967.2000
I: http://www.aa.com

American Eagle Outfitters
150 Thorn Hill Drive
Warrendale, PA 15086
P: 888.232.4535
I: http://www.ae.com

American Express Company
P.O. Box 981540
El Paso, TX 79998
P: 800.528.4800
I: http://www.americanexpress.com

American Greetings Corporation
One American Road
Cleveland, OH 44144
P: 800.777.4891
I: http://www.americangreeting.com

Anderson Windows, Inc.
100 4th Avenue, North
Bayport MN 55003
P: 888.888.2070
I: http://www.andersonwindows.com

Anheuser-Busch, Inc.
One Busch Place
St. Louis, MO 63118
P: 800.342.5283
I: http://www.anheuser-busch.com

Apple Computer, Inc.
One Infinite Loop
Cupertino, CA 95014
P: 408.996.1010
I: http://www.apple.com

Applebee's
8140 Ward Parkway
Kansas City, MO 64114
P: 888.592.7753
I: http://www.applebees.com

Arby's Restaurant Group, Inc.
1155 Perimeter Center, West
Atlanta, GA 30338
P: 678.514.4100
I: http://www.arbys.com

AT&T, Inc.
175 East Houston Street
San Antonio, TX 78205
P: Not Provided
I: http://www.att.com

Bally Total Fitness Corporation
P.O. Box 96241
Washington, DC 20090
P: 866.402.2559
I: http://www.ballyfitness.com

Banana Republic
5900 North Meadows Drive
Grove City, OH 42123
P: 888.277.8953
I: http://www.bananarepublic.com

Ben & Jerry's Homemade, Inc.
30 Community Drive
South Burlington, VT 05403
P: 802.846.1500
I: http://www.benjerry.com

Benihana, Inc.
8750 NW 36th Street, Suite 300
Miami, FL 33178
P: 800.327.3369
I: http://www.benihana.com

Best Buy Company, Inc.
P.O. Box 9312
Minneapolis, MN 55440
P: 888.237.8289
I: http://www.bestbuy.com

Best Western International, Inc.
P.O. Box 10203
Phoenix, AZ 85064
P: 800.528.1238
I: http://www.bestwestern.com

Big Lot Stores, Inc.
300 Phillipi Road
Columbus, OH 43228
P: 800.877.1253
I: http://www.biglots.com

BJ's Wholesale Club, Inc.
25 Research Drive
Westborough, MA 01581
P: 800.257.2582
I: http://www.bjs.com

Blockbuster Entertainment Corporation
3000 Redbud Boulevard
McKinney, TX 75270
P: 866.692.2789
I: http://www.blockbuster.com

Bloomingdales, Inc.
P.O. Box 8215
Mason, OH
P: 800.777.0000
I: http://www.bloomingdales.com

Bob Evans Farms, Inc.
3776 South High Street
Columbus, OH 43270
P: 800.939.2338
I: http://www.bobevans.com

Bojangles Restaurant, Inc.
4932 Southern Pine Boulevard
Charlotte, NC 28273
P: 888.300.4265
I: http://www.bojangles.com

BP Corporation
28301 Ferry Road
Warrenville, IL 60555
P: 800.333.3991
I: http://www.bp.com

Bridgestone Retail Operations
P.O. Box 6397
Bloomington, IL 60108
P: 800.367.3872
I: http://www.firestonecompleteautocare.com

Brio Tuscan Grill
777 Goodale Boulevard, Suite 100
Columbus, OH 43212
P: 888.452.7286
I: http://www.brioitalian.com

British Airways
P.O. Box 300686
Jamaica, NY 11430
P: 800.247.9297
I: http://www.britishairways.com

Budget Rent-A-Car, Inc.
Six Sylvan Way
Parsippany, NJ 07054
P: 800.214.6094
I: http://www.budget.com

Burger King Corporation
5505 Blue Lagoon Drive
Miami, FL 33126
P: 866.394.2493
I: http://www.bk.com

Canon USA, Inc.
One Canon Plaza
Lake Success, NY 11042
P: 800.652.2666
I: http://www.usa.canon.com

Carrier A/C Company
P.O. Box 4804
Syracuse, NY 13221
P: 800.227.7437
I: http://www.residential.carrier.com

Chase, J.P. Morgan
P.O. Box 36520
Louisville, KY 40233
P: 212.270.6000
I: http://www.chase.com

Cheesecake Factory
26901 Malibu Hills Road
Calabasas Hills, CA 91301
P: 818.871.3000
I: http://www.cheesecakefactory.com

Chevron Corporation
P.O. Box 4000
Bellaire, TX 77402
P: Not Provided
I: http://www.chevron.com

Chipotle Mexican Grill, Inc.
1401 Wynkoop Street, Suite 500
Denver, CO 80202
P: 303.595.4000
I: http://www.chipotle.com

Choice Hotels
6811 East Mayo Boulevard, Suite 100
Phoenix, AZ 85054
P: 800.300.8800
I: http://www.choicehotels.com

The Coca-Cola Company
P.O. Box 1734
Atlanta, GA 30301
P: Not Provided
I: http://www.thecocacolacompany.com

Costco Wholesale Corporation
PO Box 34331
Seattle, WA 98124
P: 800.774.2678
I: http://www.costco.com

Crate and Barrel
1860 West Jefferson Avenue
Naperville, IL 60540
P: 800.967.6696
I: http://www.crateandbarrel.com

Dairy Queen Corporation
7505 Metro Boulevard
Minneapolis, MN 55439
P: 952.830.0200
I: http://www.dairyqueen.com

Darden Restaurants
P.O Box 695011
Orlando, FL 32859
P: 407.245.4000
I: http://www.darden.com

Days Inn Worldwide, Inc.
P.O Box 4090
Aberdeen, SD 57401
P: 800.441.1618
I: http://www.daysinn.com

Delta Air Lines, Inc.
P.O Box 20980
Atlanta, GA 30320
P: 404.773.0305
I: http://www.delta.com

Denny's Corporation
203 East Main Street
Spartanburg, SC 29319
P: 800.733.6697
I: http://www.dennys.com

Dick's Sporting Goods
345 Court Street
Coraopolis, PA 15108
P: Not Provided
I: http://www.dickssportinggoods.com

Dillard's, Inc.
P.O Box 486
Little Rock, AR 72203
P: 501.376.5200
I: http://www.dillards.com

Dollar Rent-A-Car
P.O Box 33167
Tulsa, OK 74153
P: 918.669.3000
I: http://www.dollar.com

Domino's Pizza, Inc.
30 Frank Lloyd Wright Drive
Ann Arbor, MI 48106
P: 734.930.3030
I: http://www.dominos.com

Dunkin Donuts
130 Royal Street
Canton, MA 02021
P: 800.859.3539
I: http://www.donkindonuts.com

Eastman Kodak Company
343 State Street
Rochester, NY 14650
P: 800.235.6325
I: http://www.kodak.com

Eddie Bauer, Inc.
P.O Box 7001
Groveport, OH 43125
P: 800.426.8020
I: http://www.eddiebauer.com

Enterprise Rent-A-Car
600 Corporate Park Drive
St. Louis, MO 63015
P: 800.264.6350
I: http://www.enterprise.com

Exxon Mobil
P.O Box 1049
Buffalo, NY 14240
P: 800.234.9966
I: http://www.exxonmobile.com

FedEx Corporation
3875 Airways Boulevard
Memphis, TN 28116
P: 800.463.3339
I: http://www.fedex.com

Florsheim, Inc.
333 West Estabrook Boulevard
Glendale, WI 53212
P: 866.454.0449
I: http://www.florsheim.com

Food Lion, Inc.
P.O Box 1330
Salisbury, NC 28145
P: 800.210.9569
I: http://www.foodlion.com

Frito-Lay
P.O Box 660634
Dallas, TX 75266
P: 972.334.7000
I: http://www.fritolay.com

Fuji Photo Film USA, Inc.
1100 King George Post
Edison, NJ 08837
P: 800.800.3854
I: http://www.fujifilm.com

Gap, Inc.
100 Gap Drive
Grove City, OH 43123
P: 888.906.1104
I: http://www.gap.com

General Electric Company
3135 Easton Turnpike
Fairfield, CT 06828
P: 203.373.2211
I: http://www.ge.com

Giant Food, Inc.
8301 Professional Place
Landover, MD 20785
P: 301.341.4322
I: http://www.giantfood.com

Gold's Gym International
125 East John Carpenter Freeway
Irving, TX 75062
P: 214.574.4653
I: http://www.goldsgym.com

Goodrich Corporation
P.O. Box 19001
Greenville, SC 29602
P: 877.788.8899
I: http://www.bfgoodrichtires.com

Greyhound Lines, Inc.
P.O. Box 660362
Dallas, TX 75266
P: 214.849.8000
I: http://www.greyhound.com

Hallmark Cards, Inc.
P.O. Box 419034
Kansas City, MO 64141
P: 800.425.5627
I: http://www.hallmark.com

Hertz Corporation
P.O. Box 26120
Oklahoma City, OK 73126
P: 800.654.4173
I: http://www.hertz.com

Hilton Hospitality, Inc.
755 Crossover Lane
Memphis, TN 38117
P: 901.374.5000
I: http://www.hilton.com

Home Depot, Inc.
2455 Paces Ferry Road
Atlanta, GA 30339
P: 800.466.3337
I: http://www.homedepot.com

Howard Johnson, Inc.
P.O. Box 4090
Aberdeen, SD 57401
P: 800.544.9881
I: http://www.hojo.com

Hyatt Hotels & Resorts
9805 Q Street
Omaha, NE 68127
P: 800.323.7949
I: http://www.hyatt.com

IBM Corporation
One New Orchard Road
Armonk, NY 10504
P: 914.499.1900
I: http://www.ibm.com

IKEA
420 Alan Wood Road
Conshohocken, PA19428
P: 800.434.4532
I: http://www.ikea.com

InterContinental Hotels Group
P.O. Box 30321
Salt Lake City, UT 84130
P: Not Provided
I: http://www.ihgplc.com

Jack In The Box
9330 Balboa Avenue
San Diego, CA 92123
P: 800.955.5225
I: http://www.juckinthebox.com

J.C. Penney Company, Inc.
P.O. Box 10001
Dallas, TX 75301
P: 800.322.1189
I: http://www.jcpenney.com

Jiffy Lube International, Inc.
P.O. Box 4427
Houston, TX 77210
P: 800.344.6933
I: http://www.jiffylube.com

Kentucky Fried Chicken
P.O. Box 725489
Atlanta, GA31139
P: 800.225.5532
I: http://www.kfc.com

Kroger Company
1014 Vine Street
Cincinnati, OH 45202
P: 800.576.4377
I: http://www.kroger.com

L.A. Fitness International
P.O. Box 54170
Irvine, CA 92619
P: Not Provided
I: http://www.lafitness.com

Lowe's Home Improvement
P.O. Box 1111
North Wilkesboro, NC 28656
P: 800.445.6937
I: http://www.lowes.com

MAACO Enterprises, Inc.
610 Freedom Business Center
King Of Prussia, PA 19406
P: 800.523.1180
I: http://www.maaco.com

Macy's
P.O. Box 8113
Mason, OH 45040
P: 800.526.1202
I: http://www.macys.com

Marriott International, Inc.
1818 North 90th Street
Omaha, NE 68114
P: 800.535.4028
I: http://www.marriott.com

Mayflower Transit
One Mayflower Drive
St. Louis, MO 63026
P: Not Provided
I: http://www.mayflower.com

McDonald's Corporation
2111 McDonald's Drive
Oak Brook, IL 60523
P: 800.244.6227
I: http://www.mcdonalds.com

Meineke Car Care Centers, Inc.
128 South Tryon Street
Charlotte, NC 28202
P: 704.377.8855
I: http://www.meineke.com

Midas, Inc.
823 Donald Ross Road
Juno Beach, FL 33406
P: 800.621.8545
I: http://www.midas.com

Miller Coors
250 South Wacker Drive
Chicago, IL 60606
P: 800.645.5376
I: http://www.millercoors.com

Motel 6
P.O. Box 326
Worthington, OH 43085
P: 614.601.4089
I: http://www.motel6.com

National Car Rental Systems, Inc.
8420 University Avenue
St. Louis, MO 63114
P: 800.468.3334
I: http://www.nationalcar.com

Netflix
100 Winchester Circle
Los Gatos, CA 95032
P: 866.579.7172
I: http://www.netflix.com

North American Van Lines
P.O. Box 988
Ft. Wayne, IN 46801
P: 800.348.2111
I: http://www.navl.com

Office Depot, Inc.
6600 North Military Trail
Boca Raton, FL 33496
P: 800.463.3768
I: http://www.officedepot.com

Olive Garden
P.O. Box 695017
Orlando, FL 32869
P: 800.331.2729
I: http://www.olivegarden.com

Outback Steakhouse
2202 Northwest Shore Boulevard
Tampa, FL 33607
P: 813.282.1225
I: http://www.outback.com

Panera Bread
6710 Clayton Road
Richmond Heights, MO 63117
P: 800.301.5566
I: http://www.panerabread.com

Pep Boys Auto
3111 West Allegheny Avenue
Philadelphia, PA 19132
P: 800.737.2697
I: http://www.pepboys.com

Pepsi-Cola Company
One Pepsi Way
Somers, NY 10589
P: 800.433.2652
I: http://www.pepsico.com

P.F. Chang's China Bistro, Inc.
7676 East Pinnacle Peak Road
Scottsdale, AZ 85255
P: 866.732.4264
I: http://www.pfchangs.com

Pizza Hut
7100 Corporate Drive
Plano, TX 75024
P: 972.338.7700
I: http://www.pizzahut.com

Price Chopper Supermarkets
461 Nott Street
Schenectady, NY 12308
P: 518.355.5000
I: http://www.pricechopper.com

Public Supermarkets
P.O. Box 407
Lakeland, FL 33802
P: 800.242.1227
I: http://www.publix.com

Qdoba Mexican Grill
4865 Ward Road
Wheat Ridge, CO 80033
P: 720.898.2300
I: http://www.qdoba.com

Safeway, Inc.
P.O. Box 10501
Phoenix, AZ 85038
P: 877.723.3929
I: http://www.safeway.com

Staples, Inc.
500 Staples Drive
Framingham, MA 01702
P: 800.378.2753
I: http://www.staples.com

Starbucks
P.O. Box 3717
Seattle, WA 98124
P: 800.782.7282
I: http://www.starbucks.com

Stop & Shop Supermarkets, Inc.
1385 Hancock Street
Quincy, MA 02169
P: 800.767.7772
I: http://www.stopandshop.com

Target Stores
P.O. Box 9350
Minneapolis, MN 55440
P: 800.440.0680
I: http://www.target.com

TJX Companies, Inc.
770 Cockituate Road
Framingham, MA 01701
P: 508.390.1000
I: http://www.tjx.com

Trader Joe's
P.O. Box 5049
Monrovia, CA 91016
P: 626.599.3817
I: http://www.traderjoes.com

True Value Company
8600 West Bryn Mawr Avenue
Chicago, IL 60631
P: 877.502.4641
I: http://www.truevalue.com

U-Haul International
2727 North Central Avenue
Phoenix, AZ 85004
P: 800.789.3638
I: http://www.uhaul.com

United Parcel Service
55 Glenlake Parkway, NE
Atlanta, GA 30328
P: 800.742.5877
I: http://www.ups.com

United Van Lines, Inc.
One United Drive
St. Louis, MO 63026
P: 800.948.4885
I: http://www.unitedvanlines.com

Wal-Mart Stores, Inc.
702 SW 8th Street
Bentonville, AZ 72716
P: 800.925.6278
I: http://www.wal-mart.com

Wendy's International, Inc.
One Dave Thomas Boulevard
Dublin, OH 43017
P: 614.764.3100
I: http://www.wendys.com

APPENDIX 3-I: INTERNET SITES FOR CAREER PLANNING

These links include many resources, services, and tools which assist users in exploring careers, planning for the future, searching for employment, and finding the additional training necessary to pursue a dream. Most of these resources are free, and several were developed in countries other than the United States. This is a mere sample of what is available online, but it can serve as a starting point for career counselors or for career-seekers.

The following links are from the book, The Internet: A Tool for Career Planning, (Third Edition, 2011) by Debra S. Osborn, Margaret Riley Dikel, & James P. Sampson, Jr. [Note: These links were updated in August 2015].

DIRECTORY OF ONLINE EMPLOYMENT INFORMATION

Job-Hunt.org
http://www.job-hunt.org/

One of the earliest websites to provide Internet job search guidance, Job-Hunt.org offers numerous articles and other web resources related to executing a job search. Users can search for jobs by key word, industry (limited), and location using the "Find Jobs" tab. Special sections of the site are dedicated to Career Changers and those experiencing job-loss.

JobHuntersBible.com
http://www.jobhuntersbible.com/

This website was created and is maintained by Richard Bolles, author of What Color is My Parachute. It was developed to supplement his print publications and includes job search resources for both job-seekers, HR professionals, and Career Development Facilitators (under the tab "Career Coaches.")

The Riley Guide
http://www.rileyguide.com/

This site describes itself as "The Web's premier gateway for job search, career exploration, and school information, since 1994." The Riley Guide links to hundreds of sources of information for job leads, career exploration, and potential employers. It contains information to help job seekers find the best ways to use the Internet in their job search, explore new careers, research new places to live, and consider new education and training options. Founded by a university librarian, Margaret Riley Dikel and now operated by Schools Eye Media, LLC, the directory continues to be a free resource for all users.

SELF-ASSESSMENT

Casey Life Skills
http://caseylifeskills.force.com/

Casey Life Skills (CLS) is a free tool that assesses the behaviors and competencies youth (particularly those in foster care) need to achieve their long term goals. It aims to set youth on their way toward developing healthy, productive lives. CLS is designed to be used in a collaborative conversation between an educator, mentor, case worker, or other service provider and any youth between the ages of 14 and 21. It is appropriate for all youth regardless of whether they are in foster care, live with their biological parents, or reside in a group home." Providers need to register for a free account, and they will then establish accounts for their clients. You can preview a sample of the tool prior to registering and review their privacy policy at the same time. To view a copy of the assessment
http://www.casey.org/media/CLS_assessments_LifeSkills.pdf
(and scroll to page 3).

The iSeek Skills Assessment
http://www.iseek.org/careers/skillsAssessment

This skills assessment is based on data from O*NET and is a fairly simple tool that allows the user to rate him or herself on 35 different skills and then see what occupations match those skills identified as the being most important to the user. The entire tool takes 5–10 minutes to complete, and the results are presented immediately upon completion, offering the user information on each career, how his or her skills match this profile, and the level of education or training usually required to perform this particular job. The user interface is relatively simple and should not pose a problem for persons with limited computer skills. Individuals can print the results page, e-mail it to a career practitioner or other person, or save the results to a free iSeek account.

Queendom.com
http://www.queendom.com/

Queendom offers a variety of personality, intelligence, career, and health quizzes. Many are available for fun and conversation. Because of limited technical information on the assessments, when taking the quiz users are cautioned "I agree to use this test for personal purposes only." All users can register for free and take a short form of most of these assessments and tests at no cost, but some tests as well as extended personalized result reports will cost.

Take the MAPP
http://www.assessment.com/

This is an interest survey designed by the International Assessment Network in Minneapolis, MN. A free sample MAPP Career Analysis is provided to help individuals identify their preferences for working with people or things, and other job characteristics; it also suggests some occupations that match these preferences. The assessment takes about 20 minutes to complete, but it is possible to stop the inventory and resume it at a later time. The resulting report is sent to the user via e-mail, outlining his or her "natural motivations and talent for work" and matching these to five occupational descriptions from O*NET. More extensive reporting is available for less than $100.

CDDQ.org
http://kivunim.huji.ac.il/cddq/

These assessments are based on research performed at the Hebrew University of Jerusalem and The Ohio State University by a team led by Professors Itamar Gati and Samuel H. Osipow. This site includes eight assessments designed to assist individuals in the process of making a career decision by helping them clarify what their specific difficulties are, by providing a framework for a systematic process for career decision making organized into a three-stage process, and by providing the career professional with information about and access to Making Better Career Decisions (MBCD), an Internet based career planning system. All of the assessments are free to use, and the supporting documentation is available for perusal.

CAREER DEVELOPMENT PROCESS

Career Development eManual
https://emanual.uwaterloo.ca/

This manual, available for a fee to non-Waterloo community, contains sections on self-assessment, research, career decision making, marketing yourself, work, and work life planning. Several exercises are contained in each section ultimately attempt to help you find a career that is right for you. A demo of the contents is available at https://emanual.uwaterloo.ca/register/demo.aspx.

iSeek, Minnesota's Career, Education, and Job Resource
http://www.iseek.org/

This simple guide helps users of all types answer the question of "What do you seek?" by covering career exploration, education planning, and job search in a single source. Sponsored by iSeek Solutions, a Minnesota partnership formed in 1999 to work with the state's workforce development and education authorities to develop and inform policy and to strategize services, this site allows users to decide where to start and how to progress. The ultimate goal is the help the user create a career development plan, including instructions on how to implement it. Users can register for free accounts in order to customize their personal interests and receive updates. Information is geared to residents of Minnesota or those interested in jobs or education there, but can be helpful to others as well. One nice feature appears at the bottom of the front page where information guides for specific users (e.g., recent immigrants, ex-offenders, veterans, and the disabled) are provided.

Kuder Journey
http://www.kuderjourney.com/

Developed by Kuder specifically for postsecondary schools and adult career changers, Kuder Journey is a career guidance product designed to guide these older and often more experienced users through the process of planning for a career, making a career change, or merely making sure a career is still on track. Access to the information is available via a licensed organization or an individual purchase. As users complete their initial registration, the system asks about needs, personal situation, and potential barriers to career and employment, and also asks for the user to identify his or her user type, including career changer, veteran or active-duty military, disabled adult, ex-offender, or retiree.

OCCUPATIONAL INFORMATION

Career Outlook
http://www.bls.gov/CareerOutlook/

Career Outlook is published quarterly by the Bureau of Labor Statistics. It is a web version of the former Occupational Outlook Quarterly (OOQ) and maintains some of the same features such as a major article, "You're a What?", quick tips, "An interview with...", and data on display. This site covers a wide variety of career and work-related topics, such as new and emerging occupations, training opportunities, salary trends, and results of new studies from the Bureau of Labor Statistics. Articles from the OOQ have been archived and are still accessible. Access to the website is free.

CareerOneStop
http://www.careeronestop.org/

CareerOneStop offers visitors a variety of tools and resources for career exploration, education information, and job search. Its purpose is to help users explore career opportunities and make informed employment and education choices. The site features user-friendly occupation and industry information, salary data, career videos, education resources, self-assessment tools, career exploration assistance, and other resources that support career exploration and development for today's workforce. Specific sections offer information and resources targeted to transitioning military personnel, workers with a criminal conviction, workers with disabilities, the older worker, laid-off workers, entry-level workers and career changers.

Myfuture
http://myfuture.edu.au/

This product of Australian federal, state, and territory governments is a career and occupational guide geared toward persons finishing school and finding a career, looking for a job, or wanting to locate education and training. Individual users can register for a free account which allows them to customize the site and save information while exploring occupations and planning careers, but users can also review the facts of this site, browsing information on careers, work and employment, and education and training. Under the heading of "Assist Your Child" are resources and activities to help parents help children and adolescents with career planning and employability. The occupation and industry data, as well as jobs and training, is specific to Australia and New Zealand.

O*NET Online
http://www.onetonline.org/

This site was created to provide broad access to the O*NET (Occupational Information Network) database of occupational information, which includes information on skills, abilities, work activities, and interests associated with around 950 occupations. This user-friendly resource allows visitors to browse occupations by career cluster, industry, job family, job zone (level of education, training and experience usually required), green economy or STEM (science / technology / engineering / math) discipline. Users can also search for possible careers by skills or tools and technology, interests, knowledge, skills, abilities, work style, work content, and work values needed. Some users will also appreciate the crosswalks, allowing them to match careers and jobs to Military Occupational Classifications (MOC), apprenticeship codes, or titles from the Registered Apprenticeship Partners Information Data System (RAPIDS) or other systems. Occupational information is from job incumbent surveys. National employment trends and wage data are available and can be narrowed down to a specific state. A listing of related occupations and supplementary resources are also provided for each occupation. O*Net is updated on a regular cycle making the information relevant to good occupational research and decision making.

The Occupational Outlook Handbook (OOH)
http://www.bls.gov/ooh/

The OOH is one of the most quoted and cited career information websites available. It is a career reference that describes the job duties, working conditions, education and training requirements, earnings levels, current employment levels, projected employment change, and employment prospects for hundreds of occupations. It presents the results of research and analysis conducted by the Bureau of Labor Statistics' Office of Occupational Statistics and Employment Projections to help students and job seekers identify and learn about careers. Users can search the handbook using median pay, projected number of new jobs, educational level, amount of training, and projected growth rate. The information is also organized by occupations groups using the links and menus on the left, or scan the A–Z index for ideas. Each profile also includes a list of related occupations and sources for additional information, usually professional or trade associations and other quality related organizations. Each profile can be easily printed in PDF format by clicking on the link at the top of each page. The guide is updated every two years, and a Spanish version is available. All of the various online versions of this product are free.

Virginia Career VIEW (Vital Information for Education and Work)
http://www.vaview.org/

This is a source for career and education information in the Commonwealth of Virginia with sections focused on students (divided by grade/age), parents, and professionals. Career explorers can quickly find information on various careers either by Career Cluster or by selecting a specific career that interests them. Students in younger grades will find numerous age-appropriate tools and resources for them. Parents will find helpful guides and tools to work with their children in examining career options. Professionals will find guides, links to associations and training, and even more resources to help them guide their clients and students in their efforts. While the occupational data and primary education information is linked to Virginia, many users may find this to be a source of information and guidance.

EMPLOYMENT TRENDS

Labor Market Information State by State
http://www.rileyguide.com/trends.html#gov

This section of The Riley Guide includes links to state-sponsored sites containing labor market information on employment, wages, industries, and other factors affecting the world of work. It also has a link to the Milken Institute's "Best Performing Cities" survey as well as other resources for tracking employment trends.

Occupational data from the U.S. Bureau of Labor Statistics

http://www.bls.gov/emp/ep_data_occupational_data.htm

This site presents a specific page containing tables, analyses, articles, and more, giving users an accessible and understandable view of occupational employment projections from 2008 to 2018. Users also have the ability to review current and projected earnings for the same period. The second section, titled "Data Tables," displays quick links to popular data charts which depict fastest growing occupations, occupations showing largest employment growth, job decline, etc. The BLS has a wealth of data which can be confusing to users who attempt to view it on their own.

SALARY INFORMATION

CareerOneStop.org: Salaries and Benefits Information

http://www.careeronestop.org/explorecareers/plan/salaries.aspx

Users may appreciate the easy-to-find and easy-to-understand wage and salary information found here. From this page, click on the "Salaries" link to search salaries by keyword or use the drop-down industry lists to select a specific occupation. Other links that users may find helpful are "Negotiating Salary," "Highest Paying Occupations," and "Wages by Occupation and Local Area." All wage data is provided by the Occupational Employment Statistics program of the U.S. Bureau of Labor Statistics.

Occupational Employment Statistics (OES)

http://www.bls.gov/oes/

This BLS program produces employment and wage estimates for more than 800 occupations. These are estimates of wages paid to the number of people employed in certain occupations. Self-employed persons are not included in these estimates. Estimates are available for the nation as a whole, for individual states, and for metropolitan areas; national occupational estimates for specific industries are also available. As with much of the data produced by BLS, the various reports and datasets can be overwhelming for many users. Practitioners can start with the OES Charts as these will present the most relevant data in the most readable fashion. Then, if more detail is preferred, users can go to the full database to create a customized report. The article "How Jobseekers and Employers Can Use Occupational Employment Statistics (OES) Data during Wage and Salary Discussions" (www.bls.gov/oes/highlight_wage_discussions.htm) offers an excellent discussion of how location, and even industry, affects earnings and relevant discussions with employers.

Salary.com

http://www.salary.com/

This site offers users free access to more than just salary data. Salary.com gives users information on total compensation, not only what is in the paycheck but also the possible benefits and perks received on the job. The US Salary Wizard (http://www.salary.com/category/salary/) allows users to search for base, median, and top-level earnings in hundreds of jobs in many occupational areas; many of these projections are local as well as national. Users have the option to create a free account and tailor salary projections to meet their experience level, education, evaluation results, and more for an estimate of salary range they can expect for a particular occupation in a specific area. Salary.com uses a team of compensation specialists to add value to salary surveys done by others, such as the Bureau of Labor Statistics. Users will find helpful articles and exercises on topics such as benefits, stock options, bonuses (and how to get them), and salary negotiations. Users can choose to purchase a Personal Salary Report, a detailed examination of their earning power based on their personal work history and geographic location (cost ranges from $29.95-$79.95). The Cost of Living calculator and resources found under the "Work & Life"" tab may also provide helpful information for those researching and/or evaluating compensation. These do not require registration to view.

EDUCATIONAL INFORMATION

CareerOneStop: Find Local Training

http://www.careeronestop.org/FindTraining/find-Training.aspx

This website allows a person to find various types of training that can help them prepare for success in the workforce. Sections include the opportunity to find training for high school equivalency, adult basic education, short term training, college, certification, apprenticeships, internships and professional development. Most of these sections allow for the individuals to use an occupational title and location to find related training. In some instances a person is directed to America's Job Centers for more localized information. Information on certifications is found on the link to the Certifications Finder. A section of this website also provides information on paying for education and training and finding your path.

CareerOneStop: Training and Education Center

http://www.careeronestop.org/EducationTraining/tduIraining.aspx?frd=true

This is a free resource for information on degree programs, specialty training opportunities, financial aid, certification and accreditation, and licensing for the various states. It also includes career information and links it to education and training plans. There are links to additional training and education information and articles on how to ensure the quality of the training before signing up for a program. The Training and Education Center is part of America's Career Infonet, a subsection of CareerOneStop. To find it from the front page, select America's Career Infonet from the More Resources tab in the upper-right part of the front page.

College Navigator
http://nces.ed.gov/collegenavigator/

This research tool allows access to information on more than 9,000 colleges, universities, and postsecondary vocational and technical schools in the U.S. Users may search the database by location, type of institution, program and majors offered, availability of housing, and many more options. Users have the option of selecting several school profiles for side-by-side comparisons, and all search results can be sent to a valid e-mail address, printed, or exported as an Excel spreadsheet. The site and all of its information is also available in Spanish. There is a link to the College Affordability and Transparency Center which has information on how much it costs to go to different colleges. This is a product of the National Center for Education Statistics (NCES), part of the U.S. Department of Education's Institute of Education Sciences.

Distance Education Accrediting Commission (DEAC)
http://www.deac.org/

DETC is a nonprofit educational association that sponsors a nationally recognized accrediting agency for distance education programs. The site includes distance education activities within an institution and it provides a single source of nationally recognized accreditation from the secondary school level through professional doctoral degree-granting institutions. Users visiting the website can find a search-able directory of accredited high school and college degree programs, including some offered by federal and military schools.

GoCollege
http://www.gocollege.com/

This free searchable guide includes information on how to finance and succeed in college. Visitors can review information on admissions (selecting schools, test preparation, application essays, and more), financial aid (loans, scholarships, and grants), education options (types of schools and varieties of programs), and college survival (money maintenance, study tips, and dealing with dorm life). GoCollege has searchable databases for financial aid as well as information on and links to loan providers. There is a lot of information here to guide potential students, including older students who are considering a return to school or the pursuit of additional degrees or certifications.

Peterson's
https://www.petersons.com/

This well-known publisher of guides to colleges provides this free searchable resource for information on a variety of training and education programs, including undergraduate and graduate programs, online schools, and help for international students. Among the many descriptions of institutions and degree possibilities are articles on applying for college (both undergraduate and graduate), selecting a school and a program, and much more. Within the Undergraduate section is a financial-aid search system which requires registration along with numerous practice programs for the many standardized tests an individual may encounter (fee). Persons interested in graduate school will find helpful articles.

SeminarInformation.com
https://www.seminarinformation.com/index.cfm

Originally founded in 1981 and turned into an online resource in 1999, SeminarInformation.com lists over 360,000 seminars and conferences hosted by more than 600 providers including associations, private organizations, and universities. Users of this free site can use the Quick Search to find upcoming programs by provider, state or topic using keywords from the title or description. You can browse the category lists to see what is offered in any given area, or target upcoming programs by location. Each listing includes a full description of the training program offered, the host, the location, and the cost. Users can register immediately through the page or print the training brochure for later referral.

USNews.com: Education
http://www.usnews.com/education

The publisher of U.S. News and World Report has consistently produced one of the most outstanding guides to education information on the web. Dedicated sections of this area of the website focus on high schools, colleges, community colleges, graduate schools, online programs, and global universities. Various articles are provided on topic such as financial aid, STEM, writing essays, college applications, etc. USNews.com also lists the annual rankings of colleges and graduate schools.

FINANCIAL AID INFORMATION

Federal Student Aid
https://studentaid.ed.gov/sa/

This is a one-stop center for all of the U.S. Department of Education's Federal Student Aid (FSA) programs. Available in English and Spanish, this site will guide the user through the process of preparing for college, selecting and applying to schools, securing funding from a variety of sources, attending college, and repaying loans. Information is available for high school, undergraduate, and graduate students as well as parents, international students, and other targeted student populations. The site links to FAFSA, the Free Application for Federal Student Aid (www.fafsa.gov) for easy access and application processing. A few portions of the site require the user to create a login and password, but this is to allow the users to save profile information, store applications, and customize areas for specific needs. Users can review their extensive privacy policy from the link at the bottom of each page for information on how this data is used and protected.

FinAid
http://www.finaid.org/

Established in 1994, FinAid is possibly the finest single source for information and resources for all types of educational financial aid including scholarships, loans savings, and military aid programs. Visitors will find comprehensive information on various programs, advice on how to approach each, important legislative information, warnings about potential problems and much more. There are numerous calculators to help students and parents figure out how much is needed, the true cost of a loan, and almost anything else a user could dare to ask. Information for educators is also included with guides to help them work with students and parents. This continues to be a premiere site for financial aid information online, and it continues to be free.

Sallie Mae: Plan for College
https://www.salliemae.com/plan-for-college/

This sites has a variety of financial information. Placing your cursor over the "Plan for College" section uncovers additional links on saving for college, scholarships, grants, financial aid, types of loans and a college planning toolbox. The tool box offers several calculators and articles of interest.

APPRENTICESHIPS AND OTHER ALTERNATIVE TRAINING OPPORTUNITIES

About Trades, ApprenticeSearch.com
http://www.apprenticesearch.com/AboutTrades

This Canadian site for employers and apprentices includes a list of trades that have apprenticeships and a detailed listing which is found in the "About Trades" section. For each of the trades there is more specific information such as personal qualities, skills, interests, associated wages, future trends, etc. Many have associated videos.

CareerOneStop: Apprenticeship
http://www.careeronestop.org/FindTraining/Types/apprenticeships.aspx?&frd=true

An apprenticeship is a system of training that is done on-the-job. An apprentice works for an employer who helps the apprentice learn their trade. This page at CareerOneStop will connect you to apprenticeship resources on the Department of Labor website through the Apprenticeship Finder, including links to apprenticeship programs in all states and registered programs within states you can explore.

CareerOneStop: Certification
http://www.careeronestop.org/FindTraining/Types/certifications.aspx?&frd=true

Certifications are examinations that test or enhance your knowledge, experience, or skills in an occupation or profession. Users can search for certifications by keyword, industry, or occupation by using the Certifications Finder. Certifications are generally voluntary but may be required by some employers in some occupations. In some cases, there are additional certifications that licensed individuals may want to pursue in order to advance into a new specialty, but in other cases these are more useful for demonstrating a specific skill or a continued improvement in skills which are applicable to your current employment situation.

The Corporation for National and Community Service
http://www.nationalservice.gov/

Established in 1993, the Corporation for National and Community Service oversees programs engaging more than a million Americans each year in service to their communities. The Corporation's three major service initiatives are AmeriCorps, Learn and Serve America, and the Senior Corps, but it also supports other initiatives such as the Martin Luther King, Jr. Day of Service. The AmeriCorps program provides credits and/or awards to assist with the payment of education costs or loans. There are two Americorps residential programs, the National Civilian Community Corps and FEMA (Federal Emergency Management Agency) Corps.

The Job Corps
http://www.jobcorps.gov/home.aspx

Job Corps is a free education and training program that helps young people learn a career, earn a high school diploma or GED, and find and keep a good job. For eligible young people at least 16 years of age that qualify as low income, Job Corps provides the all-around skills needed to succeed in a career and in life.

My Next Move. Careers with Registered Apprenticeships

http://www.mynextmove.org/find/apprenticeship

Created by the National Center for O*Net Development for the USDOL Employment and Training Administration, This section of My Next Move lists career fields with Registered Apprenticeship programs and links to information on those programs. This is probably the easiest way to find the data you need.

Peace Corps

http://www.peacecorps.gov/

Founded in 1961 by President John F. Kennedy, the Peace Corps was established to promote world peace and friendship. This site contains background information on the organization, recruiting, diversity, and reach of this volunteer service program

Regional Offices of Apprenticeship, US Employment and Training Administration

http://www.doleta.gov/oa/regdirlist.cfm

The Federal Office of Apprenticeship within the United States Employment and Training Administration has a presence in almost all 50 states plus many territories, and interested persons can contact the relevant state or responsible regional office for information on programs available in his or her state of residence.

State Apprenticeship Agencies

http://www.doleta.gov/OA/sainformation.cfm

These lists will connect you with the many states registered apprenticeship programs, with much more specific information and documents for interested individuals.
Job Search Instruction and Advice

Executive Gateway

http://www.wendyenelow.com/

Wendy Enelow is a Master Resume Writer (MRW), Credentialed Career Manager (CCM), Certified Professional Resume Writer (CPRW), and a Certified Job and Career Transition Coach (JCTC), who has combined all of that plus a career of more than 20 years into this source for both job seekers and career practitioners. Two different libraries of articles are shown under "Articles," and the collection for the Executive Job Seeker is actually useful for job seekers at all levels of experience. The articles for Career Practitioners offer advice in preparing resumes for clients as well as business advice for practitioners.

GoinGlobal

http://www.goinglobal.com/

GoinGlobal is a provider of both country-specific and USA city-specific career and employment information. Use of the resources on this site are open only to individuals associated with one of the participating customers, which are typically universities. Their e-books are researched by in-country career experts and updated annually to include information such as application and interviewing customs, employment trends, work permit and visa regulations, major employers, and much more. The individual guides are available to all for a moderate fee, and anyone working with international candidates, trailing spouses, or clients interested in exploring international possibilities will find these to be extremely useful.

Susan Ireland's Resume Site

http://susanireland.com/

This is much more than the title indicates. It includes extensive information on resume preparation, job search correspondence (it's more than just cover letters), and even interviewing. There are also terrific samples for users to review and use as templates for their own documents. Susan apprenticed under the late resume writer Yana Parker, and then trained others who are now members of her resume team.

Using Employment Kiosks and Online Job Applications

http://www.rileyguide.com/kiosk.html

This page of the Riley Guide links to several free resources and services practitioners that clients can use to develop a familiarity with application kiosks and online job applications and even develop a printed application to be carried along to assist in submitting applications through in-house electronic stations. This is part of The Riley Guide's collection of articles on How to Job Search (rileyguide.com/execute.html).

Wall Street Journal: Careers

http://www.wsj.com/public/page/news-career-jobs.html

This portion of the WSJ website continues to offer articles and information covering all aspects of the job search and career management. The content is updated daily and focuses on career, management, business, education and other workplace related issues.

JOB BANKS

Career Builder

http://www.careerbuilder.com/

One of the larger and more dynamic sites for job and career information. Registration is free of charge and allows a job seeker to store a resume online without posting it in the database. Registered users can create up to five personal search profiles to track new jobs added to the database, and an e-mail message can be generated to a user when a match is discovered.

College Grad Job Hunter
https://collegegrad.com/

This website is a cornucopia of resources and information to guide college students and others through a complete job search. It has job databases for those seeking internships, entry-level job seekers, and experienced job seekers as well as a searchable database of more than 8,000 employers. It also offers advice on careers, the job search, resume preparation, and more.

GrooveJob
http://www.groovejob.com/

GrooveJob specializes in seasonal, part-time, and hourly jobs along with jobs for teens and students. Users can easily target jobs in their location by city/state or zip code to find possibilities with specific employers within 15 miles. Users must complete the free registration which includes a resume in order to apply for any listings found here.

Monster.com
http://www.monster.com/

Monster.com is one of the most recognized names in the online job search community. It offers an impressive variety of job and career resources for everyone from college students to contractors to chief executives; most are served with their own communities that include job listings and career advice. It also offers several industry/job field communities, including healthcare, human resources, and finance.

NationJob
http://www.nationjob.com/

Perhaps not as well-known as some other sites, NationJob features an impressive collection of job openings, company information, and a variety of ways to search the database. It divides into many sources of occupation-and/or industry-related resources, creating an excellent source of information for all. Users can easily search for jobs by keyword and location or browse by Communities, Industries, or Employers.

US.jobs
http://us.jobs/

US.jobs is operated by the Direct Employers Association, a nonprofit consortium of leading U.S. corporations, in alliance with the National Association of State Workforce Agencies. This association was established in 2001 by a consortium of employers who wanted to increase recruiting efficiency while reducing costs. Users will find numerous

postings placed here by employers, with links leading back to employer websites for application purposes. Sections of this site are targeted to diverse audiences.

CAREER SEARCH ENGINES

CareerJet
http://www.careerjet.com/

Careerjet is a job search engine designed to make the process of finding a job on the internet easier for the user. It maps the huge selection of job offerings available on the internet in one extensive database by referencing job listings originating from job boards, recruitment agency websites and large specialist recruitment sites. Using a fast and straightforward interface, users can query this database and save themselves the trouble of visiting each site individually. The job offerings themselves are not hosted by Careerjet and users are always redirected to the original job listing. ly, Careerjet acts as traffic driver to those sites.

Careerjet's job search engine network encompasses over 90 countries, featuring separate interfaces that are translated into 28 languages.

Indeed
http://www.indeed.com/

As the world's #1 job site, with over 180 million unique visitors every month from over 50 different countries, Indeed has become the catalyst for putting the world to work. Indeed is intensely passionate about delivering the right fit for every hire. Indeed helps companies of all sizes hire the best talent and offers the best opportunity for job seekers to get hired.

RESOURCES FOR DIVERSE AUDIENCES

Black Collegian Online
http://blackcollegian.com/

This free career and job site for African-American college students offers African-American and other students of color information on careers, job opportunities, graduate and professional schools, internships, study abroad programs, and much more. This site and the magazine are published by IMDiversity, Inc., who also operates the Diversity Employers website, below. The Black Collegian print magazine has been integrated into Diverslty Employers magazine, from the same organization.

Diversity Employers
http://www.diversityemployers.com/

DIVERSITY EMPLOYERS/IMDiversity is dedicated to providing career and self-development information to all minorities, specifically African Americans, Asian Americans and Pacific Islanders, Latino/Hispanic Americans, Native Americans and women. The site includes a listing of employers that support diversity and a list of jobs from those employers. Individuals can search jobs by keyword and location. The site is free to job seekers although registration is requested. Employers can post jobs and track applicants for a fee.

Feminist Jobs
http://jobs.feminist.org/

Founded in 1987, the Feminist Majority Foundation (FMF) is dedicated to women's equality, reproductive health, and nonviolence. The jobs posted here include opportunities with academic institutions, nonprofit organizations, and other associations that also support the FMF mission. In addition, there are some opportunities in nontraditional career fields such as law enforcement and construction. This free site is open to all visitors.

ISNA Careers
http://www.isna.net/careers.html

This free listing includes jobs with the Islamic Society of North America (ISNA) as well as jobs posted by other organizations. Applicants are free to review the announcements and apply directly to the hiring organization according to the instructions given.

LatPro
http://www.latpro.com/

LatPro is dedicated to Hispanic and bilingual professionals (Spanish/English and Portuguese/English). LatPro.com offers a searchable resume database that employers can access and job postings for job seekers. The site is available in English, Spanish, and Portuguese.

The OU Job Board, The Orthodox Union
http://www.oujobs.org/

This is a free source of job listings for the U.S., Canada, and Israel, some of which are in Jewish faith-based organizations. Job seekers are also welcome to create a free account and upload a resume, but it is not necessary. This site is operated by The Union of Orthodox Jewish Congregations of America, more popularly known as the Orthodox Union (OU), one of the oldest Orthodox Jewish organizations in the United States. The main website connects with additional social services offered by this organization.

Out and Equal
http://www.outandequal.org/resources/lgbt-careerlink/

Out and Equal is a website dedicated to compiling resources for the LGBT community. LGBT CareerLink, one portion of the site, offers visitors and users the opportunity to view job opportunities from a broad variety of diversity-friendly employers, review career resources, and learn about upcoming events for the LGBT community. Most areas of the site are available to all, but individuals are encouraged to register for free and, if desired, create a full profile, upload a resume, and connect with other registered users and employers.

The Tribal Employment Newsletter
http://www.nativejobs.com/

Founded in 1996, The Tribal Employment Newsletter is a nationwide job bank for Native Americans seeking professional and technical opportunities. There are numerous job listings at any time, and the listings are constantly updated. There is no registration for the site; everything is free and easily accessible.

RESOURCES AND SERVICES FOR EX-OFFENDERS

Career Resource Centers: An Emerging Strategy for Improving Offender Employment Outcomes
http://nicic.gov/library/023066

This bulletin from the National Institute of Corrections, provides a step-by-step guide for setting up a Career Resource Center in a correctional facility, a parole or probation office, or a community-based organization. It includes a companion multimedia DVD that contains many of the resources needed to operate an effective center, including assessment software and documents related to career exploration, offender re-entry, collaboration building and more.

National HIRE Network
http://www.hirenetwork.org/

Established by the Legal Action Center, the National HIRE Network is a national clearinghouse for information as well as an advocate for policy change. The goal of this organization is to increase the number and quality of job opportunities available to people with criminal records by changing public policies, employment practices, and public opinion. The Network also provides training and technical assistance to agencies working to improve the employment prospects for people with criminal records. Practitioners can use the Resources list to find state agencies and local organizations to assist clients and practitioners.

The National Institute of Corrections
http://nicic.gov/

This agency of the U. S. Department of Justice and the Federal Bureau of Prisons provides training, technical assistance, information services, and policy/program development assistance to federal, state, and local corrections agencies. NIC also provides leadership to influence correctional policies, practices, and operations nationwide in areas of emerging interest and concern to correctional executives and practitioners as well as public policymakers. For counselors and other career practitioners working with this group, there are numerous free documents and products available to assist clients as well as practitioners.

National Resource Center on Children and Families of the Incarcerated at Rutgers University—Camden
http://nrccfi.camden.rutgers.edu/

The center, which began as the Federal Resource Center on Children of Prisoners in the 1990s, joined forces with the Family and Corrections Network in 2003 creating the oldest and largest organization to focus on the children and families of the incarcerated. The website includes links to numerous local groups offering services and support to the incarcerated and their families during and after their separation along with research, information, and resources for the families and those that support them.

Simulated Online/Kiosk Job Application
http://nicic.gov/library/022996

This free product produced by the National Institute of Corrections can be used by any individual to practice completing employment applications on a computer that does not have access to the Internet. This simulation training program provides basic information about computerized employment applications on kiosks, tips for completing online job applications, a printable worksheet that can be used to prepare offenders for using these systems, and a full-length interactive application with context sensitive help. You can download the installation package from the website or order a free CD-ROM to be sent to you.

RESOURCES AND SERVICES FOR YOUTH, TEEN AND YOUNG ADULTS

BLS K-12
http://www.bls.gov/k12/

Those who work with students will appreciate BLS K-12 and the introductory career information offered in this simplified version of the Occupational Outlook Handbook (OOH). The BLS K-12 site features games and quizzes, student resources such as career information, resources for teachers such as classroom activities, and an interactive timeline of the history of BLS. According to the Bureau of Labor and Statistics (BLS), "wording and labor market concepts have been simplified and some statistical detail has been eliminated. In addition, the occupations on the site are categorized according to interests and hobbies common among students." The Teacher's Desk (http://www.bls.gov/k12/teachers.htm) offers more information on this site, how it differs from the full OOH, and additional resources available from BLS.

California CareerZone
http://www.cacareerzone.org/

This is a career exploration and planning system designed especially for students in California, and it can be used by others. Users are encouraged to work through the assessment based on the Holland Codes for self-exploration. Comprehensive information on 900 occupations includes state specific wages, worker attributes, job characteristics, and much more. The Make Money Choices section is a great introduction to the concept of how much money is needed for life after high school. Users need to register, but it is free and will allow them to save their data to a profile.

Federal Internships, The Washington DC Job Source
http://www.dcjobsource.com/fedinterns.html

From this page users can link to internship opportunities available in each agency or department of the Federal Government. The page also includes links to all members of the U.S. House of Representatives and the U.S. Senate who offer internships in their DC or home offices.

One Day, One Job
http://www.onedayonejob.com/

This started as a blog about entry-level jobs. Every day, author Willy Franzen and his collaborators look at one employer and the jobs offered for young, talented individuals. Visitors to this free site will also find job search advice.

RESOURCES AND SERVICES THE OLDER CLIENT

AARP: Work & Retirement
http://www.aarp.org/work/

This is a collection of articles and resources covering various topics in work and employment for older people. Issues discussed include discrimination, career changes, retirement, and starting your own business. While looking at these resources, take some time to look at AARP's National Employer Team, a list of member organizations who recognize the value of the more experienced worker and actively recruit and hire older workers.

Encore Careers
http://encore.org/

This site encourages older persons to pursue second careers to provide personal fulfillment doing paid work and producing a windfall of human talent to solve society's problems. There are no jobs listed but there are examples, suggestions, fellowships, and an extensive network of like-minded individuals who are now interested in making a change in a way that serves society and others. This site is operated by Civic Ventures, a group working to engage the baby boomer generation as a vital workforce for change.

iLostMyJob.com
http://www.ilostmyjob.com/

This site is designed to support persons in transition, either voluntarily or involuntarily. The site is filled with good articles on surviving the transition and executing a job search, and also provides links to resources such as state job banks and unemployment claims offices. Registered members get early notifications of new videos and articles posted on the site as well as email newsletters.

Networking and Job Search Support by State, Job-Hunt.org
http://www.job-hunt.org/job-search-networking/job-search-networking.shtml

This collection of listings for all 50 states plus the District of Columbia will help users find and connect with local networking and support groups while searching for new or better opportunities. From this page, users can also access lists of company/corporate, military, and government "alumni" groups as well as a list of more than 1,500 professional associations and societies by industry.

What's Next
http://www.whatsnext.com/

This organization provides information, inspiration and resources for individuals interested in changing careers, finding more fulfilling work, or improving their work-life balance. While all are welcome, there is an emphasis on those who are in midcareer or approaching retirement. This site includes advice on second careers (Career 2.0), financial planning, and a searchable directory of advisors who can assist with your career change or life plans. Under "Tools" is a collection of free and fee-based assessment tools and financial planning calculators along with links to some very good jobs for experienced professionals. Not everything is free, but there is a lot of helpful advice and resources available here.

RESOURCES FOR PEOPLE WITH DISABILITIES

CareerConnect, American Foundation for the Blind
http://www.afb.org/info/living-with-vision-loss/for-job-seekers/12

This is a free resource where the blind or visually impaired can learn about the range and diversity of the jobs performed throughout the United States and Canada by other who are blind or visually impaired. CareerConnect takes users through the process of examining what they have to offer employers. Users explore careers; review tips on finding work, getting hired, and making that job work; and examine information on assistive technology for

use on the job. Users can even build a resume online in MyCareerConnect and search for a volunteer mentor to offer some guidance while proceeding through the exploration and search. Finally, users can link to resources for employment listings. All visitors can read the articles and search the databases, but to contact a mentor or set up My CareerConnect, an individual must fill out the free registration form.

Entry Point
http://ehrweb01.aaas.org/entrypoint/

This program of the American Association for the Advancement of Science (AAAS) offers students with disabilities outstanding internship opportunities in science, engineering, mathematics, computer science, and some fields of business. Application and program information is available on the site.

GettingHired
http://www.gettinghired.com/

This is a free website designed to create employment opportunities for people with disabilities. Several very good employers are associated with this resource and the database is well populated with opportunities. Users must register in order to view any piece of the real site, including the job listings, and in some cases the user must have "an active jobseeker profile" (a resume) in the system in order to use resources such as the career assessment.

Hire Disability Solutions
http://www.hireds.com/

This organization works to empower individuals with disabilities to reach their goals by providing them with the tools to succeed. The website presents information and resources for individuals to connect with employers such as nonprofit organizations and numerous corporations. This site works to assist individuals to find meaningful employment while also aiding employers in finding employees for their organizations. Individuals can easily search the database of employment opportunities and view contact information for the posting organization, but a user will need to create a Monster.com account in order to apply for these positions. Users can also post a resume on the HireDS.com site by completing their quick registration (name, e-mail address, and a password).

Workplace & Employment: American Association of People with Disabilities
http://www.aapd.com/what-we-do/employment/

According to their website, AAPD is the largest national nonprofit cross-disability member organization in the United States, dedicated to ensuring economic self-sufficiency and political empowerment for the more than 50 million Americans with disabilities. They not only partner with several employers to offer internship programs specifically for young persons with disabilities, they actively recruit Washington DC - based organizations to participate in the Greater Washington Internship Coalition, offering even more opportunities to talented students and young professionals.

RESOURCES TO AID SEPARATING MILITARY PERSONNEL AND VETERANS

CivilianJobs.com
http://www.civilianjobs.com/

Owned by Bradley-Morris Inc., CivilianJobs.com was created to offer an online recruiting solution to employers for candidates that are currently transitioning out of the military. There are numerous job listings and live career fairs across the country. Under Career Advice, there are listings of transition offices, veterans associations and resume writing services.

Military to Civilian
http://www.militarytocivilian.com/

This is a gateway to the many sites and services provided by Bradley-Morris, Inc., "the largest military-focused job placement firm in the U.S." Veterans and personnel preparing to separate from the service can review their many resources and select those that work best for the individual, from career and job search advice to resume assistance to job placement.

Re-entering the Civilian Job Market - National Job Search Resources for Veterans, Job-Hunt.org
http://www.job-hunt.org/

This site offers the reader several articles and resources for military members in transition. It is authored by Job-Hunt.org editor and publisher Susan Joyce, a veteran of the U.S. Marine Corps.

Resources for Veterans and Military Personnel and Their Families
http://www.rileyguide.com/vets.html

This page of The Riley Guide is dedicated to sites, services, and resources that support current and former military personnel and their families. Along with job search advice and resources it also lists information for employers who want to attract these qualified candidates, information on pay rates and employment verification, and employment and financial rights for reservists called to active duty.

RESEARCHING EMPLOYERS

Company Research Guide, Rutgers University Libraries
http://libguides.rutgers.edu/companies

The Rutgers librarians have created a company research guide resource to assist individuals seeking to learn about a company. Listings for the top business research sources (both print and online) are provided, and the site is organized by the logical steps of the research process. The research process cites both online and print resources. Users outside of Rutgers should check with their local public or college library for access.

Hoovers Online
http://www.hoovers.com/

Hoovers is a well-known and respected publisher of business almanacs. Users can access a tremendous amount of free information from the website, but paid subscribers will have access to even more detailed profiles. Hoover's covers U.S. and non-U.S. companies as well as Initial Public Offerings through IPO Central (www.hoovers.com/ip-central/100004160-1.html). Individuals should check with local public or college library to inquire about free access before purchasing this on their own.

Vault
http://www.vault.com/

Vault is a resource for career management and job search information, including insider intelligence on specific employers, salaries, hiring practices, and company cultures. The website offers both free and paid subscription content to users who want to research employers, professions, and industries. There is a public job bank; users will need to create a free basic account to apply for positions listed here. Vault still publishes numerous print guides to various careers, employers, and industries.

Wetfeet.com
https://www.wetfeet.com/

Wetfeet.com offers articles and guides on career related topics such as interviewing, resumes, career change and many others. The site provides information on the top 100 companies and good insights into the company's culture, diversity, social responsibility, training, and development, etc. The information is sent to the user by email and the data are from employees who post comments. Additionally you can access a lot of company information on this site that will help prepare a person for a job interview.

SOCIAL NETWORKING SITES

Blogger
https://accounts.google.com/ServiceLogin?service=blogger&hl=en&passive=1209600&continue=https://www.blogger.com/home#identifier

Blogger is a free weblog (blog) publishing system. Users can have their blog hosted free of charge on the site. An individual can use a blog to highlight skills, experiences, accomplishments, and reflections. Photos and videos can be uploaded, and individuals can choose to follow a person's blog. The blog can be linked to an individual's social networking site(s). Blogger is part of the Google network of sits and requires sign-in to a Google account.

Facebook
http://www.facebook.com/

Used for both social and professional networking, Facebook is the most frequently used social networking site. According to the site, there are currently about 1.5 billion active users. About 936 million use Facebook daily. "Friendships" are initiated and either confirmed or ignored. Individuals provide information on a profile page and can upload links, photos, videos, or text. Brief status updates are used to inform contacts of a person's activities for the moment or day. Notes can be sent and friends "tagged," both of which show up on their "wall" and in their email. Individuals can join groups and become fans of employers, organizations, movie stars, hobby sites, social causes, and the like. Instant chatting is also available through their Message feature, and privacy settings can be set to allow only certain information to be shared.

LinkedIn
http://www.linkedin.com/

LinkedIn is a professional social networking site boasting over 364 million users, with executives from all Fortune 500 companies, 170 industries, and a million companies represented. They provide a "gated access" to members, where contacts must know each other or be introduced to each other from a common contact. LinkedIn provides discussion groups for a variety of industries, topics, and interests. In addition, members can write "recommendations" of other contacts and endorse a persons skill via keywords. A personal profile can include links to publicly available sites or resources as well as supporting documents for projects or positions you have held, turning a resume into a portfolio. Members can use the search feature at the top of all pages to find people, jobs, companies (profit and non-profit organizations), groups, and others with similar interests.

Second Life
http://www.secondlife.com/

Second Life (SL) is a virtual world in which members choose avatars to represent themselves and interact with other avatars from around the world. Many members are paid for services provided "in world" such as through designing "skins" or "builds" or even for providing counseling services. Corporations, universities, and professional organizations are represented in SL. Because the avatars represent real people, SL provides a unique opportunity to expand a social network.

Twitter
http://www.twitter.com/

In addition to following individual or organizational tweets, guests and members can also search for tweets about career, job, and interviewing. NCDA has a Twitter account at http://twitter.com/NCDAwebeditor. Twellow is a Twitter tool that searches bios and URLs based on a variety of factors. One can search by company or industry, and the software provides a list of those people who are on Twitter. Other job search aids in Twitter include http://www.Twitjobsearch.com (a job search engine that provides listings that match keywords).

ZoomInfo
http://www.zoominfo.com/

ZoomInfo is a source boasting 95 million summaries of business professionals and 7 million company profiles that allows employers to locate "passive" job candidates, i.e., individuals who are currently employed and not looking for a job, but might be open to a new opportunity. ZoomInfo pulls public information on specific employees from various web sources, and also allows (for a fee) individuals to build a profile or add to its summaries.

APPENDIX 4-A: STATE CRIMINAL RECORD REPOSITORIES

Criminal record repositories maintain and provide access to criminal record information based on state privacy and accessibility laws.

ALABAMA
Alabama Bureau of Investigation
Identification Unit – Record Checks
P.O. Box 1511
Montgomery, AL 36102
P: 334.353.4340
I: http://dps.alabama.gov/ABI/cic.aspx

ALASKA
Alaska Department of Public Safety
Records and Identification
5700 East Tudor Road
Anchorage, AK 99507
P: 907.269.5767
I: http://www.dps.state.ak.us

ARIZONA
Arizona Department of Public Safety
Applicant Team One
P.O. Box 18430, Mail Code 2250
Phoenix, AZ 85005
P: 602.223.2223
I: http://www.azdps.gov

ARKANSAS
Arkansas State Police
Identification Bureau
1 State Police Plaza Drive
Little Rock, AR 72209
P: 501.618.8500
I: http://www.asp.arkansas.gov

CALIFORNIA
California Department of Justice
Records Security Section
P.O. Box 903417
Sacramento, CA 94203
P: 916.227.3849
I: http://www.caag.state.ca.us

COLORADO
Colorado Bureau of Investigation
State Repository, Identification Unit
690 Kipling Street, Suite 3000
Denver, CO 80215
P: 303.239.4208
I: http://www.cbi.state.co.us

CONNECTICUT
Connecticut Department of Public Safety
Bureau of Identification
1111 Country Club Road
Middletown, CT 06457
P: 860.685.8480
I: http://www.ct.gov/dps/site/default.asp

DELAWARE
Delaware State Police
State Bureau of Identification
P.O. Box 430
Dover, DE 19903
P: 302.739.2134
I: http://dps.delaware.gov/default.shtml

DISTRICT OF COLUMBIA
Metropolitan Police Department
Identification and Records Section
300 Indiana Avenue, NW, Room 3055
Washington, DC 20001
P: 202.727.4245
I: http://mpdc.dc.gov/mpdc/site/default.asp

FLORIDA
Florida Department of Law Enforcement
User Services Bureau/Public Records
P.O. Box 1489
Tallahassee, FL 32302
P: 850.410.8109
I: http://www.flde.state.fl.us

GEORGIA
Georgia Bureau of Investigation
P.O. Box 370748
Decatur, GA 30037
P: 404.244.2639
I: http://www.ganet.org/gbi

HAWAII
Hawaii Criminal Justice Data Center
Criminal Record Request
465 South King Street, Room 101
Honolulu, HI 96813
P: 808.587.3279
I: http://www.hawaii.gov/ag/hcjdc/

IDAHO
Idaho Bureau of Criminal Identification
State Repository
P.O. Box 700
Meridian, ID 83680
P: 208.884.7130
I: http://www.isp.state.id.us

ILLINOIS
Illinois State Police Bureau of Identification
Civil Processing Unit
260 North Chicago Street
Joliet, IL 60432
P: 815.740.5160
I: http://www.isp.state.il.us

INDIANA
Indiana State Police
Criminal History Records
P.O. Box 6188
Indianapolis, IN 46206
P: 317.232.5424
I: http://www.in.gov/isp

IOWA
Iowa Department of Public Safety
Division of Criminal Investigation, Records Unit
215 East 7th Street
Des Moines, IA 50319
P: 515.725.6066
I: http://www.dps.state.ia.us/dci/index.shtml

KANSAS
Kansas Bureau of Investigation
Criminal Records Division
1620 Southwest Tyler
Topeka, KS 66612
P: 785.296.8200
I: http://www.accesskansas.org/kbi

KENTUCKY
Kentucky State Police
Criminal Identification and Records Branch
1250 Louisville Road
Frankfort, KY 40601
P: 502.227.8713
I: http://www.kentuckystatepolice.org

LOUISIANA
Louisiana State Police
Bureau of Identification
7919 Independence Boulevard
Baton Rouge, LA 70806
P: 225.925.6095
I: http://www.lsp.org/index.html

MAINE
Maine State Police
State Bureau of Identification
State House Station, #42
Augusta, ME 04333
P: 207.624.7240
I: http://www.informe.org/pcr

MARYLAND
Maryland Criminal Justice Information System
Public Safety and Correctional Records
P.O. Box 32708
Pikeville, MD 21282
P: 410.764.4510
I: http://www.dpscs.state.md.us

MASSACHUSETTS
Massachusetts Criminal History Systems Board
200 Arlington Street, Suite 2200
Chelsea, MA 02150
P: 617.660.4640
I: http://www.mass.gov/chsb

MICHIGAN
Michigan State Police
Criminal Justice Information Center
7150 Harris Drive
Lansing, MI 48913
P: 517.322.1956
I: http://www.michigan.gov/msp

MINNESOTA
Minnesota Bureau of Criminal Apprehension
Criminal History Access Unit
1430 Maryland Avenue, East
St. Paul, MN 55106
P: 651.793.2400
I: http://www.bca.state.mn.us

MISSISSIPPI
Mississippi Department of Public Safety
Criminal Information Center
P.O. Box 958
Jackson, MS 39205
P: 601.933.2600
I: http://www.dps.state.ms.us

MISSOURI
Missouri State Highway Patrol
Criminal Record and Identification Division
1510 East Elm Street
Jefferson City, MO 65102
P: 573.526.6153
I: http://www.mshp.dps.missouri.gov

MONTANA
Montana Department of Justice
Criminal Records
P.O. Box 201403
Helena, MT 59620
P: 406.444.3625
I: http://www.doj.mt.gov

NEBRASKA
Nebraska State Patrol
P.O. Box 94907
Lincoln, NE 68509
P: 402.471.4545
I: http://www.nsp.state.ne.us

NEVADA
Nevada Department of Public Safety
Records and Technology Division
333 West Nye Lane, Suite 100
Carson City, NV 89706
P: 775.684.6262
I: http://www.nvrepository.state.nv.us

NEW HAMPSHIRE
New Hampshire State Police Headquarters
Criminal Records
33 Hazen Drive
Concord, NH 03305
P: 603.271.2538
I: http://www.nh.gov

NEW JERSEY
New Jersey Division of State Police
Records and Identification Section
P.O. Box 7068
West Trenton, NJ 08628
P 609.882.2000
I: http://www.njsp.org

NEW MEXICO
New Mexico Department of Public Safety
Criminal Records Bureau
P.O. Box 1628
Santa Fe, NM 87504
P: 505.827.9181
I: http://www.dps.nm.org

NEW YORK
New York State Division of Criminal Justice Services
Record Review Unit
4 Tower Place, Stuyvesant Plaza
Albany, NY 12203
P: 518.457.6043
I: http://www.criminaljustice.state.ny.us

NORTH CAROLINA
North Carolina Bureau of Investigation
P.O. Box 29500
Raleigh, NC 27626
P: 919.662.4500
I: http://www.ncsbi.gov

NORTH DAKOTA
North Dakota Bureau of Criminal Investigation
Criminal Records Section
P.O. Box 1054
Bismarck, ND 58502
P: 701.328.5500
I: http://www.ag.state.nd.us

OHIO
Ohio Bureau of Investigation
Civilian Background Section
P.O. Box 365
London, OH 43140
P: 740.845.2000
I: http://www.ag.state.oh.us

OKLAHOMA
Oklahoma State Bureau of Investigation
Criminal History Reporting
6600 North Harvey
Oklahoma City, OK 73116
P: 405.848.6724
I: http://www.ok.gov/osbi

OREGON
Oregon State Police
Identification Services Section, Unit 11
P.O. Box 4395
Portland, OR 97208
P: 503.378.3070
I: http://egov.oregon.gov/osp/id

PENNSYLVANIA
Pennsylvania State Police
Central Repository, Suite 164
1800 Elmerton Avenue
Harrisburg, PA 17110
P: 717.783.5494
I: http://www.psp.state.pa.us

PUERTO RICO
Information pertaining to Puerto Rico was not available during the creation of this document. Please see future editions for updates and/or revisions or visit http://www.gobierno.pr for more information.

RHODE ISLAND

Rhode Island Department of Attorney General
Bureau of Criminal Identification
150 South Main Street
Providence, RI 02903
P: 401.274.4400
I: http://www.riag.ri.gov

SOUTH CAROLINA

South Carolina Law Enforcement Division
Criminal Records Section
P.O. Box 21398
Columbia, SC 29221
P: 803.896.7043
I: http://www.sled.sc.gov

SOUTH DAKOTA

South Dakota Division of Criminal Investigation
Identification Section
1302 East Highway 14, Suite 5
Pierre, SD 57501
P: 605.773.3331
I: http://dci.sd.gov

TENNESSEE

Tennessee Bureau of Investigation
Open Records Information Service
901 R.S. Gass Boulevard
Nashville, TN 37216
P: 615.744.4057
I: http://www.tbi.state.tn.us

TEXAS

Texas Department of Public Safety
Access and Dissemination Bureau
Crime Records Service
P.O. Box 15999
Austin, TX 78761
P: 512.424.2474
I: https://records.txdps.state.tx.us

UTAH

Utah Bureau of Criminal Identification
P.O. Box 148280
Salt Lake City, UT 84114
P: 801.965.4555
I: http://publicsafety.utah.gov/bci

VERMONT

Vermont Criminal Information Center
Criminal Record Check Section
103 South Main Street
Waterbury, VT 05671
P: 802.244.8727
I: http://www.dps.state.vt.us

VIRGINIA

Virginia State Police
P.O. Box 85076
Richmond, VA 23261
P: 804.674.6750
I: http://www.vsp.state.va.us

WASHINGTON

Washington State Patrol
Identification and Criminal History Section
P.O. Box 42633
Olympia, WA 98504
P: 360.705.5100
I: http://www.wsp.wa.gov

WEST VIRGINIA

West Virginia State Police
Criminal Records Section
725 Jefferson Road
Charleston, WV 25309
P: 304.746.2179
I: http://www.wvstatepolice.com

WISCONSIN

Wisconsin Department of Justice
Crime Information Bureau, Record Check Unit
P.O. Box 2688
Madison, WI 53701
P: 608.266.5764
I: http://www.doj.state.wi.us

WYOMING

Wyoming Division of Criminal Investigation
Criminal Record Unit
316 West 22nd Street
Cheyenne, WY 82002
P: 307.777.7523
I: http://www.attorneygeneral.state.wy.us

APPENDIX 4-B: STATE BAR ASSOCIATIONS

Bar associations provides licensure and oversight of attorneys within a particular state or geographic area. They may also provide assistance with obtaining low-cost legal services for qualified individuals.

ALABAMA
Alabama State Bar
415 Dexter Avenue
Montgomery, AL 36104
P: 334.269.1515
I: http://www.alabar.org

ALASKA
Alaska Bar Association
P.O. Box 100279
550 West 7th Avenue, Suite 1990
Anchorage, AK 99510
P: 907.272.7469
I: http://www.alaskabar.org

ARIZONA
State Bar of Arizona
111 West Monroe, Suite 1800
Phoenix, AZ 85003
P: 602.252.4804
I: http://www.azbar.org

ARKANSAS
Arkansas Bar Association
400 West Markham
Little Rock, AR 72201
P: 501.375.4606
I: http://www.arkbar.com

CALIFORNIA
California State Bar Association
180 Howard Street
San Francisco, CA 94105
P: 415.538.2000
I: http://www.calbar.ca.gov

COLORADO
Colorado Bar Association
1900 Grant Street, Suite 950
Denver, CO 80203
P: 303.860.1115
I: http://www.cobar.org

CONNECTICUT
Connecticut Bar Association
30 bank Street
New Britain, CT 06050
P: 860.223.4400
I: http://www.ctbar.org

DELAWARE
Delaware State Bar Association
301 North Market Street
Wilmington, DE 19801
P: 302.658.5279
I: http://www.dsba.org

DISTRICT OF COLUMBIA
The District of Columbia Bar
1101 K Street, NW, Suite 200
Washington, DC 20005
P: 202.737.4700
I: http://www.dcbar.org

FLORIDA
The Florida Bar
651 East Jefferson Street
Tallahassee, FL 32399
P: 850.561.5600
I: http://www.flabar.org

GEORGIA
State Bar of Georgia
104 Marietta Street, NW, Suite 100
Atlanta, GA 30303
P: 404.527.8700
I: http://www.gabar.org

HAWAII
Hawaii State Bar Association
1132 Bishop Street, Suite 906
Honolulu, HI 96813
P: 808.537.1868
I: http://www.hsba.org

IDAHO
Idaho State Bar and Idaho Law Foundation
P.O. Box 895
Boise, ID 83701
P: 208.334.4500
I: http://www.state.id.us/isb

ILLINOIS
Information pertaining to Illinois was not available during the creation of this document. Please see future editions for updates and/or revisions or visit http://www.iardc.org for more information.

INDIANA
Indiana State Bar Association
230 East Ohio Street, 4th Floor
Indianapolis, IN 46204
P: 317.639.5465
I: http://www.inbar.org

IOWA
Iowa State Bar Association
521 East Locust, Suite 300
Des Moines, IA 50309
P: 515.243.3179
I: http://www.iowabar.org

KANSAS
Kansas Bar Association
1200 Southwest Harrison Street
Topeka, KS 66612
P: Not Available
I: http://www.ksbar.org

KENTUCKY
Kentucky Bar Association
514 West Main Street
Frankfort, KY 40601
P: 502.564.3795
I: http://www.kybar.org

LOUISIANA
Louisiana State Bar Association
601 St. Charles Avenue
New Orleans, LA 70130
P: 504.566.1600
I: http://www.lsba.org

MAINE
Maine State Bar Association
P.O. Box 788
Augusta, ME 04322
P: 207.622.7523
I: http://www.mainebar.org

MARYLAND
Maryland State Bar Association
520 West Fayette Street
Baltimore, MD 21201
P: 410.685.7878
I: http://www.msba.org

MASSACHUSETTS
Massachusetts Bar Association
20 West Street
Boston, MA 02111
P: 617.338.0694
I: http://www.massbar.org

MICHIGAN
State Bar of Michigan
306 Townsend Street
Lansing, MI 48933
P: 800.968.1442
I: http://www.michbar.org

MINNESOTTA
Minnesota State Bar Association
600 Nicollet Mall, Suite 380
Minneapolis, MN 55402
P: 612.333.1183
I: http://www.mnbar.org

MISSISSIPPI
Mississippi Bar Association
P.O. Box 2168
Jackson, MS 39225
P: 601.948.4471
I: http://www.msbar.org

MISSOURI
Missouri State Bar Association
326 Monroe
Jefferson City, MO 65102
P: 573.638.2235
I: http://www.mobar.org

MONTANA
The State Bar of Montana
P.O. Box 577
Helena, MT 59624
P: 406.442.7660
I: http://www.montanabar.org

NEBRASKA
Nebraska State Bar Association
635 South 14th Street
P.O. Box 81809
Lincoln, NE 68501
P: 402.475.7091
I: http://www.nebar.com

NEVADA
State Bar of Nevada
600 East Charleston Boulevard
Las Vegas, NV 89104
P: 702.382.2200
I: http://www.nvbar.org

NEW HAMPSHIRE
New Hampshire Bar Association
112 Pleasant Street
Concord, NH 03301
P: 603.224.6942
I: http://www.nhbar.org

NEW JERSEY
New Jersey State Bar Association
New Jersey Law Center
One Constitution Square
New Brunswick, NJ 08901
P: 732.249.5000
I: http://www.njsba.com

NEW MEXICO
State Bar of New Mexico
121 Tijeras Street, NE
P.O. Box 25883
Albuquerque, NM 87102
P: 505.842.6132
I: http://www.nmexam.org

NEW YORK
New York State Bar Association
1 Elk Street
Albany, NY 12207
P: 518.463.3200
I: http://www.nysba.org

NORTH CAROLINA
North Carolina Bar Association
P.O. Box 3688
Cary, NC 27519
P: 919.677.0561
I: http://www.ncbar.org

NORTH DAKOTA
State Bar Association of North Dakota
515 ½ East Broadway, Suite 101
Bismarck, ND 58501
P: 701.255.1404
I: http://www.sband.org

OHIO
Ohio State Bar Association
1700 Lake Shore Drive
Columbus, OH 43204
P: 614.487.2050
I: http://www.ohiobar.org

OKLAHOMA
Oklahoma Bar Association
1901 North Lincoln Boulevard
Oklahoma City, OK 73152
P: 405.416.7000
I: http://www.okbar.org

OREGON
Oregon State Bar Association
5200 Southwest Meadow Road
Lake Oswego, OR 97035
P: 503.620.0222
I: http://www.osbar.org

PENNSYLVANIA
Pennsylvania Bar Association
100 South Street
P.O. Box 186
Harrisburg, PA 17108
P: 717.238.6715
I: http://www.pabar.org

PUERTO RICO
Information pertaining to Puerto Rico was not available during the creation of this document. Please see future editions for updates and/or revisions or visit http://www.gobierno.pr for more information.

RHODE ISLAND
Rhode Island Bar Association
15 Cedar Street
Providence, RI 02903
P: 401.421.5740
I: http://www.ribar.com

SOUTH CAROLINA
South Carolina Bar Association
950 Taylor Street
Columbia, SC 29202
P: 803.799.6653
I: http://www.scbar.org

SOUTH DAKOTA
South Dakota State Bar Association
222 East Capitol
Pierre, SD 57501
P: 605.224.7554
I: Not Available

TENNESSEE
Tennessee Bar Association
221 Fourth Avenue, North
Nashville, TN 37219
P: 615.383.7421
I: http://www.tba.org

TEXAS
The State Bar of Texas
1414 Colorado
Austin, TX 78701
P: 512.463.1463
I: http://www.texasbar.com

UTAH
Utah State Bar Association
645 South 200 East
Salt Lake City, UT 84111
P: 801.531.9077
I: http://www.utahbar.org

VERMONT
Vermont State Bar Association
35-37 Court Street
P.O. Box 100
Montpelier, VT 05620
P: 802.223.2020
I: Not Available

VIRGINIA
Virginia Bar Association
701 East Franklin Street, Suite 1120
Richmond, VA 23219
P: 804.644.0041
I: http://www.vba.org

WASHINGTON
Washington State Bar Association
2101 Fourth Avenue, Suite 400
Seattle, WA 98121
P: 206.443.9722
I: http://www.wsba.org

WEST VIRGINIA
West Virginia Bar Association
2006 Kanawha Boulevard, East
Charleston, WV 25311
P: 304.558.2456
I: http://www.wvbar.org

WISCONSIN
State Bar of Wisconsin
5302 Eastpark Boulevard
Madison, WI 53718
P: 608.257.3838
I: http://www.wisbar.org

WYOMING
Wyoming State Bar
500 Randall Avenue
P.O. Box 109
Cheyenne, WY 82003
P: 307.632.9061
I: http://www.wyomingbar.org

APPENDIX 4-C: STATE VOTER REGISTRATION AUTHORITIES

Voter registration authorities provide oversight of state-specific voting rights and laws. Where applicable, they may also provide assistance with the restoration of voting rights on an individual basis for persons with criminal histories.

ALABAMA
Alabama Secretary of State
Elections Division
State Capitol E-208
P.O. Box 5616
Montgomery, AL 36103
P: 334.242.7210
I: http://www.sos.alabama.gov/elections/default.aspx

ALASKA
Alaska Division of Elections
P.O. Box 110017
Juneau, AK 99811
P: 907.465.4611
I: http://www.elections.alaska.gov

ARIZONA
Arizona Secretary of State
Election Division
1700 West Washington, 7th Floor
Phoenix, AZ 85007
P: 602.542.8683
I: http://www.azsos.gov/election

ARKANSAS
Arkansas Secretary of State
Voter Services
State Capitol, Room 026
Little Rock, AR 72201
P: 501.682.3204
I: http://www.sosweb.state.ar.us/elections.html

CALIFORNIA
California Secretary of State
Elections Division
1500 11th Street, 5th Floor
Sacramento, CA 95814
P: 916.657.2166
I: http://www.sos.ca.gov/elections/elections.htm

COLORADO
Colorado Department of State
Elections Department
1700 Broadway, Suite 270
Denver, CO 80290
P: 303.894.2200
I: http://www.elections.colorado.gov

CONNECTICUT
Connecticut Secretary of State
Election Services Division
30 Trinity Street, 2nd Floor
Hartford, CT 06106
P: 860.509.6100
I: http://www.sots.ct.gov/sots/site/default.asp

DELAWARE
Delaware Commissioner of Elections
Voter Registration Division
111 South West Street, Suite 10
Dover, DE 19904
P: 302.739.4277
I: http://elections.delaware.gov

DISTRICT OF COLUMBIA
District of Columbia Board of Elections and Ethics
Voter Registration Division
441 4th Street, NW, Suite 250 North
Washington, DC 20001
P: 202.727.2525
I: http://www.dcboee.org

FLORIDA
Florida Department of State
Division of Elections
500 South Bronough Street, Room 216
Tallahassee, FL 32399
P: 850.245.6200
I: http://elections.dos.state.fl.us

GEORGIA
Georgia Secretary of State
Elections Division
1104 West Tower, 2 Martin Luther King Drive, SE
Atlanta, GA 30334
P: 404.656.2871
I: http://sos.georgia.gov/elections

HAWAII
Hawaii Office of Elections
Voter registration
802 Lehua Avenue
Honolulu, HI 96782
P: 808.453.8683
I: http://hawaii.gov/elections

IDAHO
Idaho Secretary of State
State Elections Office
P.O. Box 83720
Boise, ID 83720
P: 208.334.2852
I: http://www.idahovotes.gov

ILLINOIS
Illinois State Board of Elections
Voter Registration Services
1020 South Spring
Springfield, IL 62704
P: 217.782.4141
I: http://www.elections.state.il.us

INDIANA
Indiana Secretary of State
Elections Division
302 Washington, Room E-204
Indianapolis, IN 46204
P: 317.232.3939
I: http://www.in.gov/sos/elections

IOWA
Iowa Secretary of State
Voter Registration
321 East 12th Street
Lucas Building, 1st Floor
Des Moines, IA 50319
P: 515.281.0145
I: http://www.sos.state.ia.us/elections/index.html

KANSAS
Kansas Secretary of State
Elections Division
Memorial Hall, 1st Floor
120 Southwest 10th Avenue
Topeka, KS 66612
P: 785.296.4561
I: http://www.kssos.org

KENTUCKY
Kentucky State Board of Elections
140 Walnut
Frankfort, KY 40601
P: 502.573.7100
I: http://elect.ky.gov/registrationinfo

LOUISIANA
Louisiana Secretary of State
Elections Division
P.O. Box 94125
Baton Rouge, LA 70804
P: 225.922.0900
I: http://www.sos.louisiana.gov

MAINE
Maine Secretary of State
Department of Elections
101 State House Station, 4th Floor
Augusta, ME 04333
P: 207.624.7650
I: http://www.maine.gov/sos/cec/elec

MARYLAND
Maryland Board of Elections
P.O. Box 6486
Annapolis, MD 21401
P: 410.269.2840
I: http://www.elections.state.md.us

MASSACHUSETTS
Massachusetts Secretary of the Commonwealth
Elections Division
One Ashburton Place, Room 1705
Boston, MA 02108
P: 617.727.2828
I: http://www.sec.state.ma.us/ele/eleidx.htm

MICHIGAN
Michigan Secretary of State
Bureau of Elections
P.O. Box 20126
Lansing, MI 48901
P: 517.3736.2540
I: http://www.michigan.gov/sos

MINNESOTA
Minnesota Secretary of State
Election Division
180 State Office Building
100 Rev. Martin Luther King Jr. Boulevard
St. Paul, MN 55155
P: 651.215.1440
I: http://www.sos.state.mn.us

MISSISSIPPI
Mississippi Secretary of State
Elections Division
P.O. Box 136
Jackson, MS 39205
P: 601.576.2550
I: http://www.sos.state.ms.us/elections/elections.asp

MISSOURI
Missouri Secretary of State
Division of Elections
P.O. Box 1767
Jefferson City, MO 65102
P: 573.751.2301
I: http://www.sos.mo.gov/elections

MONTANA

Montana Secretary of State
Elections Bureau
P.O. Box 202801
Helena, MT 59620
P: 406.444.5376
I: http://www.sos.mt.gov/elections/index.asp

NEBRASKA

Nebraska Secretary of State
Elections Division
P.O. Box 94608
Lincoln, NE 68509
P: 402.471.2555
I: http://www.sos.state.ne.us/elec

NEVADA

Nevada Secretary of State
Elections Division
101 North Carson Street, Suite 3
Carson City, NV 89701
P: 775.684.5705
I: http://nvsos.gov/elections

NEW HAMPSHIRE

New Hampshire Secretary of State
Elections Division
107 North Main Street, State House Room 204
Concord, NH 03301
P: 603.271.3242
I: http://www.sos.nh.gov/elections.htm

NEW JERSEY

New Jersey Department of Law and Public Safety
Division of Elections
P.O. Box 304
Trenton, NJ 08625
P: 609.292.3760
I: http://www.njelections.org

NEW MEXICO

New Mexico Secretary of State
Bureau of Elections
325 Don Gaspar, Suite 300
Santa Fe, NM 87503
P: 505.827.3621
I: http://www.sos.state.nm.us/sos-elections.html

NEW YORK

New York State Board of Elections
Public Information Officer
40 Steuben Street
Albany, NY 12207
P: 518.474.1953
I: http://www.elections.state.ny.us

NORTH CAROLINA

North Carolina Board of Elections
P.O. Box 27255
Raleigh, NC 27611
P: 919.733.7173
I: http://www.sboe.state.nc.us

NORTH DAKOTA

North Dakota Secretary of State
Elections Division
600 East Boulevard Avenue, Suite 108
Bismarck, ND 58505
P: 701.328.4146
I: http://www.nd.gov/sos/electvote

OHIO

Ohio Secretary of State
Elections Division
180 East Broad Street, 15th Floor
Columbus, OH 43215
P: 614.466.2585
I: http://www.sos.state.oh.us

OKLAHOMA

Oklahoma State Election Board
P.O. Box 53156
Oklahoma City, OK 73152
P: 405.521.2391
I: http://www.elections.state.ok.us

OREGON

Oregon Secretary of State
Elections Division
141 State Capitol
Salem, OR 97310
P: 503.986.1518
I: http://www.sos.state.or.us/elections

PENNSYLVANIA

Pennsylvania Board of Commissions and Elections
Voter Registration
210 North Office Building
Harrisburg, PA 17120
P: 717.787.5280
I: http://www.dos.state.pa.us/bcel/site/default.asp

PUERTO RICO

Information pertaining to Puerto Rico was not available during the creation of this document. Please see future editions for updates and/or revisions or visit http://www.gobierno.pr for more information.

RHODE ISLAND
Rhode Island Secretary of State
Elections Division
148 West River Street
Providence, RI 02904
P: 401.222.2340
I: http://www.sec.state.ri.us/elections

SOUTH CAROLINA
South Carolina Election Commission
P.O. Box 5987
Columbia, SC 29250
P: 803.734.9060
I: http://www.scvote.org

SOUTH DAKOTA
South Dakota Secretary of State
Elections Division
500 East Capitol, Suite 204
Pierre, SD 57501
P: 605.773.3537
I: http://www.sdsos.gov/elections

TENNESSEE
Tennessee Secretary of State
Division of Elections
312 Rosa L. Parks Avenue, 9th Floor
Snodgrass Tower
Nashville, TN 37243
P: 615.741.7956
I: http://www.state.tn.us/sos/election/index.htm

TEXAS
Texas Secretary of State
Elections Division
P.O. Box 12060
Austin, TX 78711
P: 800.252.8683
I: http://www.sos.state.tx.us

UTAH
Utah Office of the Lt. Governor
Elections Section
P.O. Box 142325
State Capitol Suite 220
Salt Lake City, UT 84114
P: 801.538.1041
I: http://elections.utah.gov

VERMONT
Vermont Secretary of State
Election Division
26 Terrace Street
Montpelier, VT 05609
P: 802.828.2464
I: http://vermont-elections.org

VIRGINIA
Virginia State Board of Elections
200 North 9th Street, Suite 101
Richmond, VA 23219
P: 804.786.6551
I: http://www.sbe.virginia.gov/cms

WASHINGTON
Washington Secretary of State
Office of Elections Division
P.O. Box 40229
Olympia, WA 98504
P: 360.902.4180
I: http://www.secstate.wa.gov/elections

WEST VIRGINIA
West Virginia Secretary of State
Election Division
Building 1, #157-K
190 Kanawha Boulevard East
Charleston, WV 25305
P: 304.558.6000
I: http://www.wvsos.com/elections/main.htm

WISCONSIN
Wisconsin State Elections Board
P.O. Box 2973
Madison, WI 53701
P: 608.266.8005
I: http://elections.wi.gov

WYOMING
Wyoming Secretary of State
Election Division
200 West 24th Street
Wyoming State Capitol
Cheyenne, WY 82002
P: 307.777.7186
I: http://soswy.state.wy.us/election/election.htm

APPENDIX 4-D: STATE SEXUAL OFFENDER REGISTRIES

Sexual offender registries maintain and coordinate the registration of individuals convicted of certain sexual offenses. They may also provide registered sexual offenders with information regarding their legal obligations under applicable state law and assistance with understanding or addressing any issues related to offense classification.

ALABAMA
Alabama Department of Public Safety
Sexual Offender Registry
P.O. Box 1511
Montgomery, AL 36102
P: 334.353.1172
I: http://community.dps.alabama.gov

ALASKA
Alaska Department of Public Safety
Statewide Services – DIV SOCKR Unit
5700 East Tudor Road
Anchorage, AK 99507
P: 907.269.0396
I: http://www.dps.state.ak.us/sorweb/sorweb.aspx

ARIZONA
Arizona Department of Public Safety
Sex Offender Compliance
P.O. Box 6638, Mail Code 9999
Phoenix, AZ 85005
P: 602.255.0611
I: http://az.gov/webapp/offender/main.do

ARKANSAS
Arkansas Crime Information Center
Sexual Offender Registry
One Capitol Mall, 4D200
Little Rock, AR 72201
P: 501.682.7441
I: http://www.acic.org/registration/index.htm

CALIFORNIA
California Department of Justice
Sexual Offender Program
P.O. Box 903387
Sacramento, CA 94203
P: 916.227.4974
I: http://www.meganslaw.ca.gov

COLORADO
Colorado Bureau of Investigation
Sexual Offender Registry
690 Kipling Street, Suite 3000
Denver, CO 80215
P: 303.239.4222
I: http://sor.state.co.us

CONNECTICUT
Connecticut Department of Public Safety
Sex Offender Registry Unit
1111 Country Club Road
Middletown, CT 06457
P: 860.685.8060
I: http://www.ct.gov/dps

DELAWARE
Delaware State Police
Sex Offender Central Registry
P.O. Box 430
Dover, DE 19903
P: 302.672.5306
I: http://sexoffender.dsp.delaware.gov

DISTRICT OF COLUMBIA
Metropolitan Police Department
Sex Offender Registry Unit
300 Indiana Avenue, NW, Room 3009
Washington, DC 20001
P: 202.727.4407
I: http://mpdc.dc.gov/mpdc/site/default.asp

FLORIDA
Florida Department of Law Enforcement
Offender Registration and Tracking Services
P.O. Box 1489
Tallahassee, FL 32302
P: 850.410.8572
I: http://offender.fdle.state.fl.us

GEORGIA
Georgia Bureau of Investigation
Sexual Offender Registry
P.O. Box 370808
Decatur, GA 30037
P: 404.244.2600
I: http://services.georgia.gov/gbi/gbisor/disclaim.html

HAWAII
Hawaii Criminal Justice Data Center
Sexual Offender Registry
465 South King Street, Room 101
Honolulu, HI 96813
P: 808.587.3100
I: http://sexoffenders.ehawaii.gov

IDAHO

Idaho State Repository
Central Sexual Offender Registry
P.O. Box 700
Meridian, ID 83680
P: 208.884.7305
I: http://isp.state.id.us

ILLINOIS

Illinois State Police
Sexual Offender Registry Unit
801 South 7th Street, #200 South
Springfield, IL 62794
P: 217.785.0653
I: http://www.isp.state.il.us/sor

INDIANA

Indiana Sex and Violent Offender Directory Manager
Indiana Government Center, South E334
302 West Washington Street
Indianapolis, IN 46204
P: 317.232.1232
I: http://www.insor.org/insasoweb

IOWA

Iowa Division of Criminal Investigation
Sexual Offender registry Unit
215 East 7th Street
Des Moines, IA 50319
P: 515.725.6050
I: http://www.iowasexoffender.com

KANSAS

Kansas Bureau of Investigation
Offender Registration
1620 Southwest Tyler
Topeka, KS 66612
P: 785.296.2841
I: http://www.kansas.gov/kbi/ro.shtml

KENTUCKY

Kentucky State Police
Criminal Identification and Records Branch
1250 Louisville Road
Frankfort, KY 40601
P: 502.227.8700
I: http://kspsor.state.ky.us

LOUISIANA

Louisiana State Police
Sex Offender and Child Predator Registry
P.O. Box 66614, Box A-6
Baton Rouge, LA 70896
P: 225.925.6100
I: http://lasocpr1.lsp/org

MAINE

Maine State Police
State Bureau of Identification
Sex Offender Registry
State House Station, #42
Augusta, ME 04333
P: 207.624.7270
I: http://sor.informe.org/sor

MARYLAND

Maryland Criminal Justice Information System
Sexual Offender Registry Unit
P.O. Box 32708
Pikeville, MD 21282
P: 410.585.3649
I: http://www.socem.info

MASSACHUSETTS

Massachusetts Sex Offender Registry Board
P.O. Box 4547
Salem, MA 01970
P: 978.740.6400
I: http://www.mass.gov/sorb

MICHIGAN

Michigan State Police
Sexual Offender Registry Section
7150 Harris Drive
Lansing, MI 48913
P: 517.322.4938
I: http://www.mipsor.state.mi.us

MINNESOTA

Minnesota Bureau of Criminal Apprehension
Minnesota Predatory Offender Program
1430 Maryland Avenue, East
St. Paul, MN 55106
P: 651.793.7070
I: http://por.state.mn.us

MISSISSIPPI

Mississippi Department of Public Safety
Sexual Offender Registry
P.O. Box 958
Jackson, MS 39205
P: 601.987.1540
I: http://www.sor.mdps.state.ms.us

MISSOURI

Missouri State Highway Patrol
Sexual Offender Registry
1510 East Elm Street
Jefferson City, MO 65102
P: 573.526.6153
I: http://www.mshp.mo.gov

MONTANA
Montana Department of Justice
Sexual and Violent Offender Registry
P.O. Box 201417
Helena, MT 59620
P: 406.444.2497
I: http://doj.mt.gov/svor

NEBRASKA
Nebraska State Patrol
Sexual Offender Registry
P.O. Box 94907
Lincoln, NE 68509
P: 402.471.8647
I: http://www.nsp.state.ne.us/sor

NEVADA
Nevada Records and Identification Bureau
Sex Offender Registry
333 West Nye Lane, Suite 100
Carson City, NV 89706
P: 775.684.6256
I: http://www.nvsexoffenders.gov

NEW HAMPSHIRE
New Hampshire State Police Headquarters
Special Investigations Unit - SOR
33 Hazen Drive
Concord, NH 03305
P: 603.271.6344
I: http://www.egov.nh.gov/nsor

NEW JERSEY
New Jersey Division of State Police
Sexual Offender registry
P.O. Box 7068
West Trenton, NJ 08628
P 609.882.2000
I: http://www.njsp.org

NEW MEXICO
New Mexico Department of Public Safety
Records Bureau
P.O. Box 1628
Santa Fe, NM 87504
P: 505.827.9297
I: http://www.nmsexoffender.dps.state.nm.us

NEW YORK
New York State Division of Criminal Justice Services
Sexual Offender Registry
4 Tower Place, Room 604
Albany, NY 12203
P: 518.457.3167
I: http://www.criminaljustice.state.ny.us/nsor/index.htm

NORTH CAROLINA
North Carolina Bureau of Investigation
Criminal Investigation and Identification Section
Sexual Offender Registry Section
P.O. Box 29500
Raleigh, NC 27626
P: 919.662.4500
I: http://ncfindoffender.com/disclaimer.aspx

NORTH DAKOTA
North Dakota Bureau of Criminal Investigation
Sexual Offender Registry Unit
P.O. Box 1054
Bismarck, ND 58502
P: 701.328.5500
I: http://www.sexoffender.nd.gov

OHIO
Ohio Bureau of Investigation
Sexual Offender Registry
P.O. Box 365
London, OH 43140
P: 866.406.4534
I: http://www.esorn.ag.oh.us/secured/p1.aspx

OKLAHOMA
Oklahoma Department of Corrections
Sex Offender Registry
3400 Martin Luther King Avenue
Oklahoma City, OK 73106
P: 405.425.2872
I: http://www.doc.state.ok.us

OREGON
Oregon State Police
Sexual Offender Registry Unit
255 Capitol Street, SE, 4th Floor
Salem, OR 97310
P: 503.378.3725
I: http://egov.oregon.gov/osp/sor/index.shtml

PENNSYLVANIA
Pennsylvania State Police
Bureau of Records and Identification
Megan's Law Unit
1800 Elmerton Avenue
Harrisburg, PA 17110
P: 717.783.4363
I: www.pameganslaw.state.pa.us

PUERTO RICO
Information pertaining to Puerto Rico was not available during the creation of this document. Please see future editions for updates and/or revisions or visit http://www.gobierno.pr for more information.

RHODE ISLAND

Rhode Island Sex Offender Community Notification Unit
40 Howard Avenue
Cranston, RI 02920
P: 401.462.0905
I: http://www.paroleboard.ri.gov

SOUTH CAROLINA

South Carolina Law Enforcement Division
Sex Offender Registry
P.O. Box 21398
Columbia, SC 29221
P: 803.896.7043
I: http://services.sled.sc.gov/sor/

SOUTH DAKOTA

South Dakota Division of Criminal Investigation
Identification Section — SOR Unit
1302 East Highway 14, Suite 5
Pierre, SD 57501
P: 605.773.3331
I: http://sor.sd.gov

TENNESSEE

Tennessee Bureau of Investigation
Sexual Offender Registry
901 R.S. Gass Boulevard
Nashville, TN 37216
P: 888.837.4170
I: http://www.ticic.state.tn.us

TEXAS

Texas Department of Public Safety
Sex Offender Registration
P.O. Box 4143
Austin, TX 78765
P: 512.424.2800
I: https://records.txdps.state.tx.us

UTAH

Utah Department of Corrections
Sex Offenders Registration Program
14717 South Minuteman Drive
Draper, UT 84020
P: 801.495.7700
I: http://corrections.utah.gov/asp-bin/sonar.asp

VERMONT

Vermont Criminal Information Center
State Repository
103 South Main Street
Waterbury, VT 05671
P: 802.244.8727
I: http://www.dps.state.vt.us/cjs/s_registry.htm

VIRGINIA

Virginia State Police
Criminal Records
Sex Offenders and Crimes Against Minors Registry
P.O. Box 85076
Richmond, VA 23261
P: 804.674.6750
I: http://sex-offender.vsp.state.va.us/sor

WASHINGTON

Washington State Patrol
Sexual Offender Registry
P.O. Box 42633
Olympia, WA 98504
P: 360.534.2000
I: http://www.wsp.wa.gov

WEST VIRGINIA

West Virginia State Police
Sexual Offender Registry
725 Jefferson Road
Charleston, WV 25309
P: 304.746.2133
I: http://www.wvstatepolice.com/sexoff

WISCONSIN

Wisconsin Department of Corrections
Sex Offender Registry Program
P.O. Box 7925
Madison, WI 53707
P: 608.240.5830
I: http://offender.doc.state.wi.us/public

WYOMING

Wyoming Division of Criminal Investigation
Sexual Offender Registry
316 West 22nd Street
Cheyenne, WY 82002
P: 307.777.7809
I: http://wysors.dci.wyo.gov/sor/home.htm

APPENDIX 6-A: STATE PUBLIC TRANSPORTATION WEBSITES

Public transportation agencies are available in most areas. The links below will direct you to available agencies within a particular geographic area.

ALABAMA
http://www.apta.com/resources/links/unitedstates/Pages/AlabamaTransitLinks.aspx

ALASKA
http://www.apta.com/resources/links/unitedstates/Pages/AlaskaTransitLinks.aspx

ARIZONA
http://www.apta.com/resources/links/unitedstates/Pages/ArizonaTransitLinks.aspx

ARKANSAS
http://www.apta.com/resources/links/unitedstates/Pages/ArkansasTransitLinks.aspx

CALIFORNIA
http://www.apta.com/resources/links/unitedstates/Pages/CaliforniaTransitLinks.aspx

COLORADO
http://www.apta.com/resources/links/unitedstates/Pages/ColoradoTransitLinks.aspx

CONNECTICUT
http://www.apta.com/resources/links/unitedstates/Pages/ConnecticutTransitLinks.aspx

DELAWARE
http://www.apta.com/resources/links/unitedstates/Pages/DelawareTransitLinks.aspx

DISTRICT OF COLUMBIA
http://www.apta.com/resources/links/unitedstates/Pages/DistrictofColumbiaTransitLinks.aspx

FLORIDA
http://www.apta.com/resources/links/unitedstates/Pages/FloridaTransitLinks.aspx

GEORGIA
http://www.apta.com/resources/links/unitedstates/Pages/GeorgiaTransitLinks.aspx

HAWAII
http://www.apta.com/resources/links/unitedstates/Pages/HawaiiTransitLinks.aspx

IDAHO
http://www.apta.com/resources/links/unitedstates/Pages/IdahoTransitLinks.aspx

ILLINOIS
http://www.apta.com/resources/links/unitedstates/Pages/IllinoisTransitLinks.aspx

INDIANA
http://www.apta.com/resources/links/unitedstates/Pages/IndianaTransitLinks.aspx

IOWA
http://www.apta.com/resources/links/unitedstates/Pages/IowaTransitLinks.aspx

KANSAS
http://www.apta.com/resources/links/unitedstates/Pages/KansasTransitLinks.aspx

KENTUCKY
http://www.apta.com/resources/links/unitedstates/Pages/KentuckyTransitLinks.aspx

LOUISIANA
http://www.apta.com/resources/links/unitedstates/Pages/LouisianaTransitLinks.aspx

MAINE
http://www.apta.com/resources/links/unitedstates/Pages/MaineTransitLinks.aspx

MARYLAND
http://www.apta.com/resources/links/unitedstates/Pages/MarylandTransitLinks.aspx

MASSACHUSETTS
http://www.apta.com/resources/links/unitedstates/Pages/MassachusettsTransitLinks.aspx

MICHIGAN
http://www.apta.com/resources/links/unitedstates/Pages/MichiganTransitLinks.aspx

MINNESOTA
http://www.apta.com/resources/links/unitedstates/Pages/MinnesotaTransitLinks.aspx

MISSISSIPPI
http://www.apta.com/resources/links/unitedstates
/Pages/MIssissippiTransitLinks.aspx

MISSOURI
http://www.apta.com/resources/links/unitedstates
/Pages/MissouriTransitLinks.aspx

MONTANA
http://www.apta.com/resources/links/unitedstates
/Pages/MontanaTransitLinks.aspx

NEBRASKA
http://www.apta.com/resources/links/unitedstates
/Pages/NebraskaTransitLinks.aspx

NEVADA
http://www.apta.com/resources/links/unitedstates
/Pages/NevadaTransitLinks.aspx

NEW HAMPSHIRE
http://www.apta.com/resources/links/unitedstates
/Pages/NewHampshireTransitLinks.aspx

NEW JERSEY
http://www.apta.com/resources/links/unitedstates
/Pages/NewJerseyTransitLinks.aspx

NEW MEXICO
http://www.apta.com/resources/links/unitedstates
/Pages/NewMexicoTransitLinks.aspx

NEW YORK
http://www.apta.com/resources/links/unitedstates
/Pages/NewYorkTransitLinks.aspx

NORTH CAROLINA
http://www.apta.com/resources/links/unitedstates
/Pages/NorthCarolinaTransitLinks.aspx

NORTH DAKOTA
http://www.apta.com/resources/links/unitedstates
/Pages/NorthDakotaTransitLinks.aspx

OHIO
http://www.apta.com/resources/links/unitedstates
/Pages/OhioTransitLinks.aspx

OKLAHOMA
http://www.apta.com/resources/links/unitedstates
/Pages/OklahomaTransitLinks.aspx

OREGON
http://www.apta.com/resources/links/unitedstates
/Pages/OregonTransitLinks.aspx

PENNSYLVANIA
http://www.apta.com/resources/links/unitedstates
/Pages/PennsylvaniaTransitLinks.aspx

PUERTO RICO
http://www.apta.com/resources/links/unitedstates
/Pages/PuertoRicoTransitLinks.aspx

RHODE ISLAND
http://www.apta.com/resources/links/unitedstates
/Pages/RhodeIslandTransitLinks.aspx

SOUTH CAROLINA
http://www.apta.com/resources/links/unitedstates
/Pages/SouthCarolinaTransitLinks.aspx

SOUTH DAKOTA
http://www.apta.com/resources/links/unitedstates
/Pages/SouthDakotaTransitLinks.aspx

TENNESSEE
http://www.apta.com/resources/links/unitedstates
/Pages/TennesseeTransitLinks.aspx

TEXAS
http://www.apta.com/resources/links/unitedstates
/Pages/TexasTransitLinks.aspx

UTAH
http://www.apta.com/resources/links/unitedstates
/Pages/UtahTransitLinks.aspx

VERMONT
http://www.apta.com/resources/links/unitedstates
/Pages/VermontTransitLinks.aspx

VIRGINIA
http://www.apta.com/resources/links/unitedstates
/Pages/VirginiaTransitLinks.aspx

WASHINGTON
http://www.apta.com/resources/links/unitedstates
/Pages/WashingtonTransitLinks.aspx

WEST VIRGINIA
http://www.apta.com/resources/links/unitedstates
/Pages/WestVirginiaTransitLinks.aspx

WISCONSIN

http://www.apta.com/resources/links/unitedstates
/Pages/WisconsinTransitLinks.aspx

WYOMING

http://www.apta.com/resources/links/unitedstates
/Pages/WyomingTransitLinks.aspx

APPENDIX 7-A: CHANGING A CHILD SUPPORT ORDER

The Office of Child Support Enforcement has created a series of documents highlighting how to change a child support order in a specific state or territory. Use the links below to determine if your state or territory has options for reducing child support orders while incarcerated.

ALABAMA
http://www.acf.hhs.gov/sites/default/files/programs/css/al_cs_order.pdf

ALASKA
http://www.acf.hhs.gov/sites/default/files/programs/css/ak_cs_order.pdf

ARIZONA
http://www.acf.hhs.gov/sites/default/files/programs/css/az_cs_order.pdf

ARKANSAS
http://www.acf.hhs.gov/sites/default/files/programs/css/ar_cs_order.pdf

CALIFORNIA
http://www.acf.hhs.gov/sites/default/files/programs/css/ca_cs_order.pdf

COLORADO
http://www.acf.hhs.gov/sites/default/files/programs/css/co_cs_order.pdf

CONNECTICUT
http://www.acf.hhs.gov/sites/default/files/programs/css/ct_cs_order.pdf

DELAWARE
http://www.acf.hhs.gov/sites/default/files/programs/css/de_cs_order.pdf

DISTRICT OF COLUMBIA
http://www.acf.hhs.gov/sites/default/files/programs/css/dc_cs_order.pdf

FLORIDA
http://www.acf.hhs.gov/sites/default/files/programs/css/fl_cs_order.pdf

GEORGIA
http://www.acf.hhs.gov/sites/default/files/programs/css/ga_cs_order.pdf

HAWAII
http://www.acf.hhs.gov/sites/default/files/programs/css/hi_cs_order.pdf

IDAHO
http://www.acf.hhs.gov/sites/default/files/programs/css/id_cs_order.pdf

ILLINOIS
http://www.acf.hhs.gov/sites/default/files/programs/css/il_cs_order.pdf

INDIANA
http://www.acf.hhs.gov/sites/default/files/programs/css/in_cs_order.pdf

IOWA
http://www.acf.hhs.gov/sites/default/files/programs/css/ia_cs_order.pdf

KANSAS
http://www.acf.hhs.gov/sites/default/flles/programs/css/ks_cs_order.pdf

KENTUCKY
http://www.acf.hhs.gov/sites/default/files/programs/css/ky_cs_order.pdf

LOUISIANA
http://www.acf.hhs.gov/sites/default/files/programs/css/la_cs_order.pdf

MAINE
http://www.acf.hhs.gov/sites/default/files/programs/css/me_cs_order.pdf

MARYLAND
http://www.acf.hhs.gov/sites/default/files/programs/css/md_cs_order.pdf

MASSACHUSETTS
http://www.acf.hhs.gov/sites/default/files/programs/css/ma_cs_order.pdf

MICHIGAN
http://www.acf.hhs.gov/sites/default/files/programs/css/mi_cs_order.pdf

MINNESOTA
http://www.acf.hhs.gov/sites/default/files/programs/css/mn_cs_order.pdf

MISSISSIPPI
http://www.acf.hhs.gov/sites/default/files/programs/css/ms_cs_order.pdf

MISSOURI
http://www.acf.hhs.gov/sites/default/files/programs/css/mo_cs_order.pdf

MONTANA
http://www.acf.hhs.gov/sites/default/files/programs/css/mt_cs_order.pdf

NEBRASKA
http://www.acf.hhs.gov/sites/default/files/programs/css/ne_cs_order.pdf

NEVADA
http://www.acf.hhs.gov/sites/default/files/programs/css/nv_cs_order.pdf

NEW HAMPSHIRE
http://www.acf.hhs.gov/sites/default/files/programs/css/nh_cs_order.pdf

NEW JERSEY
http://www.acf.hhs.gov/sites/default/files/programs/css/nj_cs_order.pdf

NEW MEXICO
http://www.acf.hhs.gov/sites/default/files/programs/css/nm_cs_order.pdf

NEW YORK
http://www.acf.hhs.gov/sites/default/files/programs/css/ny_cs_order.pdf

NORTH CAROLINA
http://www.acf.hhs.gov/sites/default/files/programs/css/nc_cs_order.pdf

NORTH DAKOTA
http://www.acf.hhs.gov/sites/default/files/programs/css/nd_cs_order.pdf

OHIO
http://www.acf.hhs.gov/sites/default/files/programs/css/oh_cs_order.pdf

OKLAHOMA
http://www.acf.hhs.gov/sites/default/files/programs/css/ok_cs_order.pdf

OREGON
http://www.acf.hhs.gov/sites/default/files/programs/css/or_cs_order.pdf

PENNSYLVANIA
http://www.acf.hhs.gov/sites/default/files/programs/css/pa_cs_order.pdf

PUERTO RICO
http://www.acf.hhs.gov/sites/default/files/programs/css/pr_cs_order.pdf

RHODE ISLAND
http://www.acf.hhs.gov/sites/default/files/programs/css/ri_cs_order.pdf

SOUTH CAROLINA
http://www.acf.hhs.gov/sites/default/files/programs/css/sc_cs_order.pdf

SOUTH DAKOTA
http://www.acf.hhs.gov/sites/default/files/programs/css/sd_cs_order.pdf

TENNESSEE
http://www.acf.hhs.gov/sites/default/files/programs/css/tn_cs_order.pdf

TEXAS
http://www.acf.hhs.gov/sites/default/files/programs/css/tx_cs_order.pdf

UTAH
http://www.acf.hhs.gov/sites/default/files/programs/css/ut_cs_order.pdf

VERMONT
http://www.acf.hhs.gov/sites/default/files/programs/css/vt_cs_order.pdf

VIRGINIA
http://www.acf.hhs.gov/sites/default/files/programs/css/va_cs_order.pdf

WASHINGTON
http://www.acf.hhs.gov/sites/default/files/programs/css/wa_cs_order.pdf

WEST VIRGINIA
http://www.acf.hhs.gov/sites/default/files/programs/css/wv_cs_order.pdf

WISCONSIN

http://www.acf.hhs.gov/sites/default/files/programs/css/wi_cs_order.pdf

WYOMING

http://www.acf.hhs.gov/sites/default/files/programs/css/wy_cs_order.pdf

APPENDIX 7-B: STATE CHILD SUPPORT ENFORCEMENT OFFICES

State child support programs locate noncustodial parents, establish paternity, establish and enforce child support orders, modify orders when appropriate, collect and distribute child support payments, and refer parents to other services when appropriate.

ALABAMA
Alabama Department of Human Resources
Child Support Enforcement Division
50 Ripley Street
P.O. Box 304000
Montgomery, AL 36130
P: 334.242.9300

ALASKA
Alaska Department of Revenue
Child Support Services Division
550 West 7th Avenue, Suite 280
Anchorage, AK 99501
P: 907.269.6900

ARIZONA
Arizona Department of Economic Security
Division of Child Support Enforcement
3443 North Central Avenue, 16th Floor
Phoenix, AZ 85012
P: 602.771.8190

ARKANSAS
Arkansas Department of Finance and Administration
Office of Child Support Enforcement
P.O. Box 8133
Little Rock, AR 72203
P: 501.682.6169

CALIFORNIA
California Department of Child Support Services
P.O. Box 419064, Mail Station 100
Rancho Cordova, CA 95741
P: 916.464.5300

COLORADO
Colorado Department of Human Services
Division of Child Support Enforcement
1575 Sherman Street, 5th Floor
Denver, CO 80203
P: 303.866.4300

CONNECTICUT
Connecticut Department of Social Services
Bureau of Child Support Enforcement
25 Sigourney Street
Hartford, CT 06106
P: 860.424.4989

DELAWARE
Delaware Health and Social Services
Division of Child Support Enforcement
P.O. Box 11223
Wilmington, DE 19850
P: 302.395.6500

DISTRICT OF COLUMBIA
District of Columbia Office of the Attorney General
Child Support Services Division
441 Fourth Street, NW, 550 N
Washington, DC 20001
P: 202.724.2131

FLORIDA
Florida Department of Revenue
Child Support Enforcement
P.O. Box 8030
Tallahassee, FL 32399
P: 850.717.7000

GEORGIA
Georgia Department of Human Resources
Child Support Services
2 Peachtree Street
Atlanta, GA 30303
P: 404.657.3851

HAWAII
Hawaii Department of the Attorney General
Child Support Enforcement Agency
601 Kamokila Boulevard, Suite 207
Kapolei, HI 96707
P: 808.692.7000

IDAHO
Idaho Department of Health and Welfare
Bureau of Child Support Services
P.O. Box 83720
Boise, ID 83720
P: 800.356.9868

ILLINOIS
Illinois Department of Healthcare and Family Services
Division of Child Support Services
509 South 6th Street
Springfield, IL 62701
P: 800.447.4278

INDIANA
Indiana Department of Child Services
Child Support Bureau
402 West Washington Street, Room W360
Indianapolis, IN 46204
P: 317.233.5437

IOWA
Iowa Department of Human Services
Child Support Program
400 Southwest 8th Street, Suite H
Des Moines, IA 50309
P: 888.229.9223

KANSAS
Kansas Department for Children and families
Child Support Services
P.O. Box 497
Topeka, KS 66601
P: 888.757.2445

KENTUCKY
Kentucky Department of Income and Support, Cabinet for
Families and Children
Child Support Enforcement Program
730 Schenkel Lane, P.O. Box 2150
Frankfort, KY 40602
P: 502.564.2285

LOUISIANA
Louisiana Office of Family Support
Support Enforcement Services Division
627 North Fourth Street, P.O. Box 94065
Baton Rouge, LA 70802
P: 225.342.4780

MAINE
Maine Division of Child Support Enforcement and Recovery
11 State House Station, 19 Union Street
Augusta, ME 04333
P: 207.624.4100

MARYLAND
Maryland Department of Human Resources
Child Support Enforcement Administration
311 West Saratoga Street, Room 301
Baltimore, MD 21201
P: 410.767.7065

MASSACHUSETTS
Massachusetts Department of Revenue
Child Support Enforcement Division
P.O. Box 9561
Boston, MA 02114
P: 800.332.2733

MICHIGAN
Michigan Department of Human Services
Office of Child Support
235 South Grand Avenue, P.O. Box 30478
Lansing, MI 48909
P: 517.241.7460

MINNESOTA
Minnesota Department of Human Services
Office of Child Support Enforcement
444 Lafayette Road, P.O. Box 64946
St. Paul, MN 55164
P: 651.431.4400

MISSISSIPPI
Mississippi Department of Human Services
Division of Child Support Enforcement
750 North State Street
Jackson, MS 39202
P: 601.359.4861

MISSOURI
Missouri Department of Social Services
Family Support Division
P.O. Box 6790
Jefferson City, MO 65102
P: 866.313.9960

MONTANA
Montana Department of Public Health and Human Services
Child Support Division
3075 North Montana Avenue, Suite 112
Helena, MT 59620
P: 406.444.9855

NEBRASKA
Nebraska Department of Health and Human Services
Division of Child Support Enforcement
220 South 17th Street, P.O. Box 94728
Lincoln, NE 68509
P: 402.471.1400

NEVADA
Nevada Division of Welfare and Supportive Services
Child Support Enforcement Program
1470 College Parkway
Carson City, NV 89706
P: 775.684.0705

NEW HAMPSHIRE
New Hampshire Department of Health and Human Services
Division of Child Support Services
129 Pleasant Street
Concord, NH 03301
P: 603.271.4427

NEW JERSEY
New Jersey Department of Human Services
Office of Child Support Services
P.O. Box 716
Trenton, NJ 08625
P: 877.655.4371

NEW MEXICO
New Mexico Human Services Department
Child Support Enforcement Division
P.O. Box 25110
Santa Fe, NM 87502
P: 505.476.7207

NEW YORK
New York State
Division of Child Support Enforcement
40 North Pearl Street, 13th Floor
Albany, NY 12243
P: 888.208.4485

NORTH CAROLINA
North Carolina Department of Health and Human Services
Office of Child Support Enforcement
P.O. Box 20800
Raleigh, NC 27619
P: 919.855.4755

NORTH DAKOTA
North Dakota Department of Human Services
Child Support Enforcement Program
P.O. Box 7190
Bismarck, ND 58507
P: 701.328.3582

OHIO
Ohio Department of Human Services and Job and Family Services
Office of Child Support Enforcement
30 east Broad Street, 31st Floor
Columbus, OH 43215
P: 614.752.6561

OKLAHOMA
Oklahoma Department of Human Services
Child Support Services
P.O. Box 53552
Oklahoma City, OK 73152
P: 405.522.2874

OREGON
Oregon Department of Justice
Division of Child Support
1162 Court Street, NE
Salem, OR 97301
P: 503.947.4388

PENNSYLVANIA
Pennsylvania Department of Public Welfare
Bureau of Child Support Enforcement
P.O. Box 8018
Harrisburg, PA 17105
P: 800.932.0211

PUERTO RICO
Administration for Child Support Enforcement
P.O. Box 70376
San Juan, PR 00936
P: 787.767.1500

RHODE ISLAND
Rhode Island Department of Human Services
Office of Child Support Services
77 Dorrance Street
Providence, RI 02904
P: 401.458.4400

SOUTH CAROLINA
South Carolina Department of Social Services
Child Support Enforcement Division
P.O. Box 1469
Columbia, SC 29202
P: 803.898.9210

SOUTH DAKOTA
South Dakota Department of Social Services
Division of Child Support
700 Governor's Drive
Pierre, SD 57501
P: 605.773.3641

TENNESSEE
Tennessee Department of Human Services
Child Support Division
400 Deaderick Street, 15th Floor
Nashville, TN 37243
P: 615.313.4880

TEXAS
Texas Office of the Attorney General
Child Support Division
P.O. Box 12017
Austin, TX 78711
P: 800.252.8014

UTAH
Utah Department of Human Services
Child Support Services
P.O. Box 45033
Salt Lake, Utah 84145
P: 807.536.8500

VERMONT
Vermont Department of Children and Families
Office of Child Support
103 South Main Street
Waterbury, VT 05671
P: 800.786.3214

VIRGINIA
Virginia Department of Social Services
Division of Child Support Enforcement
801 East Main Street, 12th Floor
Richmond, VA 23219
P: 800.257.9986

WASHINGTON
Washington Department of Social and Health Services
Division of Child Support
P.O. Box 9162
Olympia, WA 98507
P: 360.664.5000

WEST VIRGINIA
West Virginia Department of Health and Human Services
Bureau of Child Support Enforcement
350 Capitol Street, Room 147
Charleston, WV 25301
P: 800.249.3778

WISCONSIN
Wisconsin Division of Economic Support
Bureau of Child Support
201 East Washington Avenue, E-200
Madison, WI 53707
P: 608.266.9909

WYOMING
Wyoming Department of Family Services
Child Support Enforcement
122 West 25th Herschler Building, 1301 1st Floor East
Cheyenne, WY 82002
P: 307.777.6948

APPENDIX 8-A: STATE GED ADMINISTRATIVE OFFICES

State GED Administrative Offices serves as the primary point-of-contact for identifying local G.E.D. Testing Centers and maintain and disseminate Official G.E.D. Score Reports.

ALABAMA
Alabama Department of Postsecondary Education
GED Testing Program
P.O. Box 302130
Montgomery, AL 36130
P: 800.392.8086

ALASKA
Alaska Department of Labor and Workforce Development
GED Testing Program
1111 West 8th Street
P.O. Box 115509
Juneau, AK 99811
P: 907.465.8714

ARIZONA
GED Testing Program
1535 West Jefferson
Phoenix, AZ 85007
P: 602.364.2777

ARKANSAS
Arkansas Department of Career Education
GED Testing Program
Three Capitol Mall
Little Rock, AR 72201
P: 501.682.1980

CALIFORNIA
California Department of Education
GED Testing Program
1430 North Street, Suite 4202
Sacramento, CA 95814
P: 916.445.9438

COLORADO
Colorado Department of Education
GED Testing Program
201 East Colfax Avenue, Room 100
Denver, CO 80203
P: 303.866.6613

CONNECTICUT
Connecticut State Department of Education
GED Testing Program
25 Industrial Park Road
Middletown, CT 06457
P: 860.807.2102

DELAWARE
Delaware Department of Education
GED Testing Program
35 Commerce Way, Suite 1
Dover, DE 11904
P: 302.857.3342

DISTRICT OF COLUMBIA
University of the District of Columbia
Adult Education Agency
GED Testing Program
441 4th Street, NW, Suite 350-N
Washington, DC 20001
P: 202.274.7173

FLORIDA
Florida Department of Education
Bureau of Program Planning and Development
GED Testing Program
325 West Gaines Street, Room 634
Tallahassee, FL 32399
P: 850.245.0449

GEORGIA
Technical College System of Georgia
GED Testing Program
1800 Century Place, NE, Suite 300B
Atlanta, GA 30345
P: 404.679.4959

HAWAII
Hawaii Department of Education
Community Education Section
GED Testing Program
475 22nd Avenue, Room 202
Honolulu, HI 96816
P: 808.203.5511

IDAHO
Idaho Division of Professional-Technical Education
GED Testing Program
650 West State Street, Suite 324
Boise, ID 83720
P: 208.334.3216

ILLINOIS
Illinois Community College Board
GED Testing Program
401 East Capitol Avenue
Springfield, IL 62701
P: 217.558.5668

INDIANA
Indiana Department of Workforce Development
Education and Training Programs
GED Testing Program
10 North Senate Avenue
Indianapolis, IN 46204
P: 317.234.7746

IOWA
Iowa Department of Education
GED Testing Program
400 East 14th Street
Des Moines, IA 50319
P: 515.281.7308

KANSAS
Kansas Board of Regents
GED Testing Program
1000 Southwest Jackson, Suite 520
Topeka, KS 66612
P: 785.296.3191

KENTUCKY
Kentucky Council on Postsecondary Education
GED Testing Program
1024 Capital Center Drive, Suite 250
Frankfort, KY 40601
P: 502.573.5114

LOUISIANA
Louisiana Community and Technical College System
GED Testing Program
265 South Foster Drive
Baton Rouge, LA 70806
P: 225.922.2800

MAINE
Maine Department of Education
GED Testing Program
23 State House Station
Augusta, ME 04333
P: 207.624.6752

MARYLAND
Maryland Department of Labor, License and Regulation
GED Testing Program
1100 North Eutaw Street
Baltimore, MD 21201
P: 410.767.0069

MASSACHUSETTS
Massachusetts Department of Elementary and Secondary Education
GED Testing Program
75 Pleasant Street
Malden, MA 02148
P: 781.338.6625

MICHIGAN
Michigan Department of Energy, Labor and Economic Growth
GED Testing Program
201 North Washington Square, 2nd Floor
Lansing, MI 48913
P: 517.373.1692

MINNESOTA
Minnesota Department of Education
GED Testing Program
1500 Highway 36 West
Roseville, MN 55113
P: 651.582.8437

MISSISSIPPI
State Board for Community and Junior Colleges
GED Testing Program
3825 Ridgewood Road
Jackson, MS 39211
P: 601.432.6338

MISSOURI
State Department of Elementary and Secondary Education
GED Testing Program
P.O. Box 480
Jefferson City, MO 65102
P: 573.751.3504

MONTANA
Montana Office of Public Instruction
GED Testing Program
1300 11th Avenue, Box 202501
Helena, MT 59620
P: 406.444.4443

NEBRASKA
Nebraska Department of Education
Division of Adult Education
GED Testing Program
301 Centennial Mall South, P.O. Box 94987
Lincoln, NE 68509
P: 402.471.4807

NEVADA
Nevada Department of Education
Adult Education Office
GED Testing Program
755 North Roop Street, Suite 201
Carson City, NV 89701
P: 775.687.7289

NEW HAMPSHIRE
New Hampshire Department of Education
Bureau of Adult Education
GED Testing Program
21 South Fruit Street, Suite 20
Concord, NH 03301
P: 603.271.6699

NEW JERSEY
New Jersey Department of Education
GED Testing Program
P.O. Box 500
Trenton, NJ 08625
P: 609.341.3071

NEW MEXICO
New Mexico Department of Education
GED Testing Program
300 Don Gaspar, Room 122
Santa Fe, NM 87501
P: 505.827.6507

NEW YORK
New York State Education Department
GED Testing Program
89 Washington Avenue, Room 374
Albany, NY 12234
P: 518.473.9897

NORTH CAROLINA
North Carolina Community College System
GED Testing Program
5016 Mail Service Center
Raleigh, NC 27699
P: 919.807.7214

NORTH DAKOTA
North Dakota Department of Public Instruction
Adult Education and Literacy
GED Testing Program
State Capitol Building
600 East Boulevard Avenue
Bismarck, ND 58505
P: 701.328.4138

OHIO
Ohio Department of Education
GED Testing Program
25 South Front Street, 1st Floor, Mailstop 106
Columbus, OH 43215
P: 614.466.1577

OKLAHOMA
Oklahoma Department of Education
Lifelong Learning Section
GED Testing Program
2500 North Lincoln Boulevard
Oklahoma City, OK 73105
P: 405.521.3321

OREGON
Oregon Department of Community Colleges/Workforce
Development
GED Testing Program
255 Capitol Street, NE
Salem, OR 97310
P: 503.947.2446

PENNSYLVANIA
Pennsylvania Department of Education
GED Testing Program
333 Market Street, 12th Floor
Harrisburg, PA 17126
P: 717.787.5532

PUERTO RICO
Puerto Rico Department of Education
Examinations, Diplomas and Certificates Unit
GED Testing Program
P.O. Box 190759
San Juan, PR 00919
P: 787.773.4881

RHODE ISLAND
Department of Elementary and Secondary Education
GED Testing Program
255 Westminster Street
Providence, RI 02903
P: 401.222.8949

SOUTH CAROLINA
South Carolina Department of Education
GED Testing Program
1429 Senate Street, Suite 402
Columbia, SC 29201
P: 803.734.8347

SOUTH DAKOTA
South Dakota Department of Labor
Adult Education and Literacy
GED Testing Program
700 Governors Drive
Pierre, SD 57501
P: 605.773.5017

TENNESSEE
Tennessee Department of Labor and Workforce
Development
GED Testing Program
220 French Landing Drive
Nashville, TN 37243
P: 615.741.7055

TEXAS
Texas Department of Education
GED Testing Program
1701 North Congress Avenue, CC350
Austin, TX 78701
P: Not Provided

UTAH
Utah State Office of Education
GED Testing Program
250 East 500 South
P.O. Box 144200
Salt Lake City, UT 84114
P: 801.538.7824

VERMONT
Vermont Department of Education
GED Testing Program
120 State Street
Montpelier, VT 05620
P: 802.828.3133

VIRGINIA
Virginia Office of Adult Education and Literacy
GED Testing Program
101 North 14th Street, P.O. Box 2120
Richmond, VA 23218
P: 804.371.2333

WASHINGTON
State Board for Community and Technical Colleges
GED Testing Program
1300 Quince Street, SE, P.O. Box 42495
Olympia, WA 98504
P: 360.704.4321

WEST VIRGINIA
West Virginia Department of Education
GED Testing Program
Capitol Complex, Building 6, Room 250
1900 Kanawha Boulevard East
Charleston, WV 25305
P: 304.558.6315

WISCONSIN
Wisconsin Department of Public Instruction
GED Testing Program
125 South Webster Street
P.O. Box 7841
Madison, WI 53707
P: 608.267.1062

WYOMING
Wyoming Department of Workforce Services
GED Testing Program
2020 Carey Avenue, 8th Floor
Cheyenne, WY 82002
P: 307.777.5897

APPENDIX 8-B: STATE VOCATIONAL REHABILITATION AGENCIES

Vocational Rehabilitation Agencies coordinate and provide counseling, evaluation and job placement services for individuals with disabilities within a specific jurisdiction.

ALABAMA
Alabama Department of Rehabilitation Services
Vocational Rehabilitation Services
602 South Lawrence Street
Montgomery, AL 36104
P: 334.281.8780
I: http://www.rehab.state.al.us

ALASKA
Alaska Division of Vocational Rehabilitation
Division of Vocational Rehabilitation
801 West 10th Street, Suite A
Juneau, AK 99801
P: 907.465.2814
I: http://www.labor.state.ak.us/dvr/home.htm

ARIZONA
Arizona Rehabilitation Services Division
103 West Highland Avenue, Suite 202
Phoenix, AZ 85013
P: 800.562.1221
I: http://www.azdes.gov/rsa

ARKANSAS
Arkansas Vocational Rehabilitation Services Administration
1616 Brookwood Drive
Little Rock, AR 72202
P: 501.296.1600
I: http://www.arsinfo.org

Arkansas Department of Human Services
Division of Services for the Blind
700 Main Street
P.O. Box 3237
Little Rock, AR 72203
P: 501.682.5463
I: http://www.state.ar.us/dhs/dsb

CALIFORNIA
California Department of Rehabilitation
721 Capitol Mall
P.O. Box 94422
Sacramento, CA 95814
P: 916.324.1313
I: http://www.rehab.cahwnet.gov

COLORADO
Colorado Division of Vocational Rehabilitation
1574 Sherman Avenue, 4th Floor
Denver, CO 80203
P: 303.866.4150
I: http://www.dvrcolorado.com

CONNECTICUT
Connecticut Department of Social Services
Bureau of Rehabilitation Services
25 Sigourney Street
Hartford, CT 06106
P: 860.424.4840
I: http://www.brs.state.ct.us

State of Connecticut Board of Education and Services for the Blind
184 Windsor Avenue
Windsor, CT 06095
P: 860.602.4000
I: http://www.besb.state.ct.us

DELAWARE
Delaware Division of Vocational Rehabilitation
4425 North Market Street
Wilmington, DE 19089
P: 302.761.8300
I: http://delawareworks.com/dvr/welcome.shtml

Delaware Health and Social Services
Division for the Visually Impaired
1901 North Du Pont Highway
New Castle, DE 19720
P: 302.255.9040
I: http://www.state.de.us/dhss/dvi/index.html

DISTRICT OF COLUMBIA
District of Columbia Department on Disability Services
1125 15th Street, NW
Washington, DC 20005
P: 202.730.1700
I: http://dds.dc.gov/dc/dds

FLORIDA

Florida Division of Vocational Rehabilitation
2002 Old Saint Augustine Road, Building A
Tallahassee, FL 32301
P: 850.245.3399
I: http://www.rehabworks.org

Florida Division of Blind Services
1320 Executive Center Drive, Room 201
Tallahassee, FL 32399
P: 850.245.0370
I: http://dbs.myflorida.com

GEORGIA

Georgia Department of Labor
Vocational Rehabilitation Program
1700 Century Circle, Suite 300
Atlanta, GA 30345
P: 404.486.6331
I: http://www.vocrehabga.org

HAWAII

State Vocational Rehabilitation and Services for the Blind
Division
1901 Bachelor Street
Honolulu, HI 96813
P: 808.586.9744
I: http://www.hawaiivr.org

IDAHO

Idaho Division of Vocational rehabilitation
650 West State Street, Room 150
Boise, ID 83720
P: 208.334.3390
I: http://www.vr.idaho.gov

Idaho Commission for the Blind and Visually Impaired
341 West Washington Street
Boise, ID 83702
P: 208.334.3220
I: http://www.icbvi.state.id.us

ILLINOIS

Illinois Department of Human Services
Office of Rehabilitation Services
100 South Grand Avenue, E
Springfield, IL 62762
P: 800.843.6154
I: http://www.dhs.state.il.us/ors

INDIANA

Indiana Vocational Rehabilitation Services
138 East Lincoln Highway
Schererville, IN 46375
P: 219.864.8163
I: http://www.in.gov/fssa/2328.htm

IOWA

Indiana Vocational Rehabilitation Services
510 East 12th Street
Des Moines, IA 50319
P: 515.281.4211
I: http://www.ivrs.iowa.gov

Iowa Department for the Blind
524 Fourth Street
Des Moines, IA 50309
P: 515.281.1333
I: http://www.blind.state.ia.us

KANSAS

Kansas Rehabilitation Services Commission
915 Southwest Harrison, 9th Floor, N
Topeka, KS 66612
P: 785.368.7471
I: http://www.srs.ks.gov

KENTUCKY

Kentucky Department of Vocational Rehabilitation
275 East Main Street, 2E-K
Frankfort, KY 40621
P: 502.564.4440
I: http://ovr.ky.gov

Kentucky Office for the Blind
209 St. Clair Street
P.O. Box 757
Frankfort, KY 40602
P: 502.564.4754
I: http://www.blind.ky.gov

LOUISIANA

Louisiana Workforce Commission
Division of Rehabilitation Services
627 North Fourth Street
Baton Rouge, LA 70821
P: 225.219.2225
I: http://www.laworks.net

MAINE

Maine Bureau of Rehabilitation Services
150 State House Station
Augusta, ME 04333
P: 207.624.5950
I: http://www.maine.gov/rehab

MARYLAND

Maryland Department of Education
Division of Rehabilitation Services
2301 Argonne Drive
Baltimore, MD 21218
P: 410.554.9442
I: http://www.dors.state.md.us

MASSACHUSETTS

Massachusetts Rehabilitation Commission
27 Wormwood Street, Suite 600
Boston, MA 02210
P: 617.204.3600
I: http://www.state.ma.us/mrc

Massachusetts State Commission for the Blind
48 Boylston Street
Boston, MA 02116
P: 617.727.5550
I: http://www.state.ma.us.mcb

MICHIGAN

Michigan Rehabilitative Services
201 North Washington Square, 4th Floor
P.O. Box 30010
Lansing, MI 48909
P: 517.373.2062
I: http://www.michigan.gov/mdcd

Michigan Commission for the Blind
201 North Washington Square, 2nd Floor
P.O. Box 30652
Lansing, MI 48909
P: 517.373.2062
I: http://www.michigan.gov/dleg

MINNESOTA

Minnesota Department of Employment and Economic Development
332 Minnesota Street, Suite E200
St. Paul, MN 55101
P: 651.259.7366
I: http://www.deed.state.mn.us/rehab

Minnesota State Services for the Blind
2200 University Avenue, Suite 240
St. Paul, MN 55114
P: 651.642.0500
I: http://www.mnssb.org

MISSISSIPPI

Mississippi Department of Rehabilitation Services
1281 Highway 51
P.O. Box 1698
Madison, MS 39110
P: 800.443.1000
I: http://www.mdrs.state.ms.us

MISSOURI

Missouri Division of Vocational Rehabilitation
3024 DuPont Circle
Jefferson City, MO 65109
P: 573.751.3251
I: http://dese.mo.gov/vr

Missouri Department of Social Services
Rehabilitation Services for the Blind
615 Howerton Court
P.O. Box 2320
Jefferson City, MO 65102
P: 573.751.4249
I: http://dss.mo.gov/fsd/rsb/index.htm

MONTANA

Montana Vocational Rehabilitation
111 Sanders, Suite 307
P.O. Box 4210
Helena, MT 59604
P: 406.444.2590
I: http://www.dphhs.mt.gov

NEBRASKA

Nebraska Department of Education
Vocational rehabilitation
P.O. Box 94987
Lincoln, NE 68509
P: 402.471.3644
I: http://www.vocrehab.state.ne.us

Nebraska Commission for the Blind and Visually Impaired
4600 Valley Road, Suite 100
Lincoln, NE 69510
P: 402.471.2891
I: http://www.ncbvi.ne.gov

NEVADA

Nevada Bureau of Vocational Rehabilitation
1370 South Curry Street
Carson City, NV 89703
P: 775.684.4040
I: http://detr.state.nv.us/rehab

NEW HAMPSHIRE
New Hampshire Vocational Rehabilitation
21 South Fruit Street, Suite 20
Concord, NH 03301
P: 603.271.3471
I: http://education.nh.gov/career/vocational

NEW JERSEY
New Jersey Division of Vocational Rehabilitation Services
135 East State Street, 3rd Floor
P.O. Box 398
Trenton, NJ 08625
P: 609.292.5987
I: http://lwd.dol.state.nj.us/labor/dvrs

NEW MEXICO
New Mexico Division of Vocational Rehabilitation
435 Saint Michaels Drive, Building D
Santa Fe, NM 87505
P: 505.954.8500
I: http://www.dvrgetjobs.com

NEW YORK
New York State Office of Children and Family Services
Commission for the Blind and Visually Handicapped
52 Washington Street
South Building, Room 201
Renssalaer, NY 12144
P: 518.474.6812

New York Department of Education
Adult Career and Continuing Education Services
Vocational Rehabilitation (ACCESS-VR)
One Commerce Plaza, Room 1603
Albany, NY 12234
P: 518.474.1711
I: http://www.access.nysed.gov/vr

NORTH CAROLINA
North Carolina Division of Vocational Rehabilitation
Services
2801 Mail Service Center
Raleigh, NC 27699
P: 919.855.3500
I: http://www.ncdhhs.gov/dvrs

NORTH DAKOTA
North Dakota Vocational Rehabilitation
117 1st Street, E
Dickinson, ND 58601
P: 701.227.7600
I: http://www.nd.gov/dhs

OHIO
Ohio Rehabilitation Services Commission
400 East Campus View Boulevard, SW3C
Columbus, OH 43235
P: 614.438.1200
I: http://www.state.oh.us/rsc/index.asp

OKLAHOMA
Oklahoma Department of Rehabilitative Services
3535 Northwest 58th Street, Suite 500
Oklahoma City, OK 73112
P: 405.951.3400
I: http://www.okrehab.org

OREGON
State of Oregon Vocational Rehabilitation Division
500 Summer Street, NE, E87
Salem, OR 97301
P: 503.945.5880
I: http://www.oregon.gov/dhs/vr

PENNSYLVANIA
Pennsylvania Office of Vocational Rehabilitation
1521 North 6th Street
Harrisburg, PA 17102
P: 717.787.5244
I: Not Provided

PUERTO RICO
Puerto Rico Vocational Rehabilitation Administration
Address Not Provided
P: 787.728.6620
I: http://www.gobierno.pr/gprportal/inicio

RHODE ISLAND
Rhode Island Office of Rehabilitative Services
40 Fountain Street
Providence, RI 02903
P: 401.421.7005
I: http://www.ors.state.ri.us

SOUTH CAROLINA
South Carolina Vocational Rehabilitation Department
1410 Boston Avenue
P.O. Box 15
West Columbia, SC 29171
P: 803.896.6500
I: http://www.scvrd.net

SOUTH DAKOTA
South Dakota Division of Rehabilitation Services
3800 East Highway 34
500 East Capitol
Pierre, SD 57501
P: 605.773.3195
I: http://dhs.sd.gov/drs/vocrehab/vr.aspx

TENNESSEE
Tennessee Division of Vocational Rehabilitation Services
400 Deaderick Street, 2nd Floor
Nashville, TN 37243
P: 615.313.4891
I: http://www.tennessee.gov/humanserv/rehab

TEXAS
Texas Department of Assistive and Rehabilitative Services
4900 North Lamar Boulevard
Austin, TX 78751
P: 800.628.5115
I: http://www.dars.state.tx.us

UTAH
Utah State Office of Rehabilitation
P.O. Box 144200
Salt Lake City, UT 84114
P: 801.538.7530
I: http://www.usor.utah.gov

VERMONT
Vermont Division of Vocational Rehabilitation
103 South Main Street, Weeks 1A
Waterbury, VT 05671
P: 866.879.6757
I: http://vocrehab.vermont.gov

VIRGINIA
Virginia Department for Aging and Rehabilitative Services
8004 Franklin Farms Drive
Henrico, VA 23299
P: 804.662.7000
I: http://www.vadrs.org

Virginia Department for the Blind and Vision Impaired
397 Azalea Avenue
Richmond, VA 23227
P: 804.371.3145
I: http://www.vdbvi.org

WASHINGTON
Washington State Division of Vocational Rehabilitation
P.O. Box 45340
Olympia, WA 98504
P: 360.725.3636
I: http://www.dshs.wa.gov/dvr

WEST VIRGINIA
West Virginia Division of Rehabilitative Services
P.O. Box 1004
Institute, WV 25112
P: 304.766.4600
I: http://www.wvdrs.org

WISCONSIN
Wisconsin Division of Vocational Rehabilitation
201 East Washington Avenue
P.O. Box 7852
Madison, WI 53707
P: 608.261.0050
I: http://dwd.wisconsin.gov/dvr

WYOMING
Wyoming Department of Vocational Rehabilitation
122 West 25th Street
Cheyenne, WY 82002
P: 307.777.7389
I: http://wyomingworkforce.org/vr

APPENDIX 8-C: STATE HIGHER EDUCATION AGENCIES

Higher Education Agencies provide information on state educational programs, colleges and universities, financial aid assistance programs, grants, scholarships, continuing education programs, and career opportunities.

ALABAMA
Alabama Commission on Higher Education
P.O. Box 302000
Montgomery, AL 36130
P: 334.242.1998
I: http://www.ache.alabama.gov

ALASKA
Alaska Commission on Postsecondary Education
P.O. Box 110505
Juneau, AK 99811
P: 907.465.2962
I: http://alaskaadvantage.state.ak.us

ARIZONA
Arizona Commission for Postsecondary Education
2020 North Central Avenue, Suite 650
Phoenix, AZ 85004
P: 602.258.2435
I: http://www.azhighered.gov/home.aspx

ARKANSAS
Arkansas Department of Higher Education
423 Main Street, Suite 400
Little Rock, AR 72201
P: 501.371.2000
I: http://www.adhe.edu

CALIFORNIA
California Student Aid Commission
P.O. Box 419027
Rancho Cordova, CA 95741
P: 916.526.7590
I: http://www.csac.ca.gov

COLORADO
Colorado Department of Higher Education
1560 Broadway, Suite 1600
Denver, CO 80202
P: 303.866.2723
I: http://highered.colorado.gov

CONNECTICUT
Connecticut Department of Higher Education
61 Woodland Street
Hartford, CT 06105
P: 860.947.1800
I: http://www.ctdhe.org

DELAWARE
Delaware Higher Education Commission
820 North French Street, 5th Floor
Wilmington, DE 19801
P: 302.577.5240
I: http://www.doe.k12.de.us/dhec

DISTRICT OF COLUMBIA
Office of the State Superintendent of Education
State Board of Education
441 Fourth Street, NW, Suite 350 N
Washington, DC 20001
P: 202.727.6436
I: http://osse.dc.gov

FLORIDA
Florida Office of Student Financial Assistance
1940 North Monroe Street, Suite 70
Tallahassee, FL 32303
P: 850.410.5180
I: http://www.floridastudentfinancialaid.org

GEORGIA
Georgia Student Finance Commission
2082 East Exchange Place
Tucker, GA 30084
P: 770.724.9000
I: http://www.gsfc.org

HAWAII
Hawaii Postsecondary Education Commission
Office of the Board of Regents
2444 Dole Street, Room 209
Honolulu, HI 96822
P: 808.956.8213
I: http://www.hawaii.edu/offices/bor

IDAHO
Idaho State Board of Education
650 West State Street
P.O. Box 83720
Boise, ID 83720
P: 208.334.2270
I: http://www.boardofed.idaho.gov

ILLINOIS
Illinois Student Assistance Commission
1755 Lake Cook Road
Deerfield, IL 60015
P: 847.948.8500
I: http://www.collegezone.com

INDIANA
Indiana Commission for Higher Education
101 West Ohio Street, Suite 550
Indianapolis, IN 46204
P: 317.464.4400
I: http://www.che.in.gov

State Student Assistance Commission of Indiana
150 West Market Street, Suite 500
Indianapolis, IN 46204
P: 317.232.2350
I: http://www.ssaci.in.gov

IOWA
Iowa College Student Aid Commission
603 East 12th Street, 5th Floor
Des Moines, IA 50319
P: 515.725.3400
I: http://www.iowacollegeaid.gov

KANSAS
Kansas Board of Regents
1000 Southwest Jackson Street, Suite 520
Topeka, KS 66612
P: 785.296.3421
I: http://www.kansasregents.org

KENTUCKY
Kentucky Higher Education Assistance Authority
P.O. Box 798
Frankfort, KY 40602
P: 502.696.7200
I: http://www.kheaa.com

LOUISIANA
Louisiana Office of Student Financial Assistance
P.O. Box 91202
Baton Rouge, LA 70821
P: 225.933.1012
I: http://www.osfa.la.gov

MAINE
Finance Authority of Maine
P.O. Box 949
Augusta, ME 04332
P: 207.623.0095
I: http://www.famemaine.com

MARYLAND
Maryland Higher Education Commission
839 Bestgate Road, Suite 400
Annapolis, MD 21401
P: 410.260.4500
I: http://www.mhec.state.md.us

MASSACHUSETTS
Massachusetts Department of Higher Education
One Ashburton Place, Room 1401
Boston, MA 02108
P: 617.994.6950
I: http://www.mass.edu

TERI College Planning Center
Boston Public Library
700 Boylston Street, Concourse Level
Boston, MA 02116
P: 617.536.0200
I: http://www.tericollegeplanning.org

MICHIGAN
Michigan Student Financial Services Bureau
430 West Allegan, 3rd Floor
P.O. Box 30047
Lansing, MI 48909
P: 800.642.5626
I: http://www.michigan.gov/studentaid

MINNESOTA
Minnesota Office of Higher Education
1450 Energy Park Drive, Suite 350
St. Paul, MN 55108
P: 651.642.0567
I: http://www.ohe.state.mn.us

MISSISSIPPI
Mississippi Institutions of Higher Learning
3825 Ridgewood Road
Jackson, MS 39211
P: 601.432.6623
I: http://www.ihl.state.ms.us

MISSOURI
Missouri Department of Higher Education
205 Jefferson Street
P.O. Box 1469
Jefferson City, MO 65109
P: 573.751.2361
I: http://www.dhe.mo.gov

MONTANA

Montana University System
2500 Broadway
P.O. Box 203201
Helena, MT 59620
P: 406.444.6570
I: http://www.mus.edu

NEBRASKA

Coordinating Commission for Postsecondary Education
140 North Eighth Street, Suite 300
P.O. Box 95005
Lincoln, NE 68509
P: 402.471.2847
I: http://www.ccpe.state.ne.us

NEVADA

Nevada does not currently have a designated office of higher education.

NEW HAMPSHIRE

New Hampshire Postsecondary Education Commission
3 Barrell Court, Suite 300
Concord, NH 03301
P: 603.271.2555
I: http://www.state.nh.us/postsecondary

NEW JERSEY

Higher Education Student Assistance Authority
P.O. Box 540
Trenton, NJ 08625
P: 609.588.3226
I: http://www.hesaa.org

New Jersey Commission on Higher Education
20 West State Street
P.O. Box 542
Trenton, NJ 08625
P: 609.292.4310
I: http://www.state.nj.us/highereducation/index.htm

NEW MEXICO

New Mexico Higher Education Department
1068 Cerrillos Road
Santa Fe, NM 87505
P: 505.476.8400
I: http://www.hed.state.nm.us

NEW YORK

New York State Higher Education Services Corporation
99 Washington Avenue
Albany, NY 12255
P: 518.473.1574
I: http://www.hesc.org

NORTH CAROLINA

North Carolina State Education Assistance Authority
P.O. Box 13663
Research Triangle Park, NC 27709
P: 919.549.8614
I: http://www.cfnc.org

NORTH DAKOTA

North Dakota Student Financial Assistance Program
600 East Boulevard Avenue, Suite 215
Bismarck, ND 58505
P: 701.328.4114
I: http://www.ndus.edu

OHIO

Ohio Board of Regents
25 South Front Street
Columbus, OH 43215
P: 614.466.6000
I: http://www.ohiohighered.org

OKLAHOMA

Oklahoma State Regents for Higher Education
655 Research Parkway, Suite 200
Oklahoma City, OK 73104
P: 405.225.9100
I: http://www.okhighered.org

OREGON

Oregon Student Assistance Commission
1500 Valley River Drive, Suite 100
Eugene, OR 97401
P: 541.687.7400
I: http://www.osac.state.or.us

Oregon University System
P.O. Box 3175
Eugene, OR 97403
P: 541.346.5700
I: http://www.ous.edu

PENNSYLVANIA

Office of Postsecondary and Higher Education
State Department of Education
333 Market Street, 12th Floor
Harrisburg, PA 17126
P: 717.787.5041

Pennsylvania Higher Education Assistance Agency
1200 North Seventh Street
Harrisburg, PA 17102
P: 717.720.2800
I: http://www.pheaa.org

PUERTO RICO
Council on Education of Puerto Rico
P.O. Box 19900
Ave. Ponce de Leon 268
Edificio Hato Rey Center Piso 15
Hato Rey, PR 00918
P: 787.641.7100
I: http://www.ce.pr.gov

RHODE ISLAND
Rhode Island Higher Education Assistance Authority
560 Jefferson Boulevard, Suite 100
Warwick, RI 02886
P: 401.736.1100
I: http://www.riheaa.org

Rhode Island Office of Higher Education
74 West Road
Cranston, RI 02920
P: 401.462.9300
I: http://www.ribghe.org

SOUTH CAROLINA
South Carolina Commission on Higher Education
1333 Main Street, Suite 200
Columbia, SC 29201
P: 803.737.2260
I: http://www.che.sc.gov

SOUTH DAKOTA
South Dakota Board of Regents
306 East Capitol Avenue, Suite 200
Pierre, SD 57501
P: 605.773.3455
I: http://www.sdbor.edu

TENNESSEE
Tennessee Higher Education Commission
404 James Robertson Parkway, Suite 1900
Nashville, TN 37243
P: 615.741.3605
I: http://www.state.tn.us/thec

TEXAS
Texas Higher Education Coordinating Board
1200 East Anderson Lane
Austin, TX 78711
P: 512.427.6101
I: http://www.thecb.state.tx.us

UTAH
Utah System of Higher Education
State Board of Regents
60 South 400 West
Salt Lake City, UT 84101
P: 801.321.7103
I: http://www.utahsbr.edu

VERMONT
Vermont Student Assistance Corporation
10 East Allen Street
P.O. Box 2000
Winooski, VT 05404
P: 802.655.9602
I: http://www.vsac.org

VIRGINIA
State Council of Higher Education for Virginia
101 North 14th Street, 9th Floor
Richmond, VA 23219
P: 804.225.2600
I: http://www.schev.edu

WASHINGTON
Washington Higher Education Coordinating Board
917 Lakeridge Way
P.O. Box 43430
Olympia, WA 98504
P: 360.753.7800
I: http://www.hecb.wa.gov

WEST VIRGINIA
West Virginia Higher Education Policy Commission
1018 Kanawha Boulevard East, Suite 700
Charleston, WV 25301
P: 304.558.0699
I: http://www.hepc.wvnet.edu

WISCONSIN
Wisconsin Higher Education Aid Board
131 West Wilson Street, Suite 902
Madison, WI 53707
P: 608.267.2206
I: http://www.heab.state.wi.us

WYOMING
Wyoming Community College Commission
2020 Carey Avenue, 8th Floor
Cheyenne, WY 82002
P: 307.777.7763
I: http://www.commission.wcc.edu

APPENDIX 10-A: HUD FIELD & REGIONAL OFFICES

The U.S. Department of Housing & Urban Development oversees the Federal Housing Administration, regulates the housing industry and coordinates single family and multifamily housing to ensure access to public housing by all eligible individuals.

ALABAMA
U.S. Department of Housing and Urban Development
Alabama Field Office
950 22nd Street, North, Suite 900
Birmingham, AL 35203
P: 205.731.2619

ALASKA
U.S. Department of Housing and Urban Development
Alaska Field Office
3000 C Street, Suite 401
Anchorage, AK 99503
P: 907.677.9800

ARIZONA
U.S. Department of Housing and Urban Development
Phoenix Field Office
One North Central Avenue, Suite 600
Phoenix, AZ 85004
P: 602.379.7100

U.S. Department of Housing and Urban Development
Tucson Field Office
6245 East Broadway Boulevard, Suite 350
Tucson, AZ 85711
P: 520.308.3007

ARKANSAS
U.S. Department of Housing and Urban Development
Arkansas Field Office
425 West Capitol Avenue, Suite 1000
Little Rock, AR 72201
P: 501.918.5700

CALIFORNIA
U.S. Department of Housing and Urban Development
Fresno Field Office
855 M Street, Suite 970
Fresno, CA 93721
P: 559.487.5033

U.S. Department of Housing and Urban Development
Los Angeles Field Office
611 West Sixth Street, Suite 801
Los Angeles, CA 90017
P: 213.894.8000

U.S. Department of Housing and Urban Development
Sacramento Field Office
650 Capitol Mall, Room 4-200
Sacramento, CA 95814
P: 916.498.5220

U.S. Department of Housing and Urban Development
San Diego Field Office
750 B Street, Suite 1600
San Diego, CA 92101
P: 619.557.5305

U.S. Department of Housing and Urban Development
Santa Ana Field Office
34 Civic Center Plaza, Room 7015
Santa Ana, CA 92701
P: 714.796.5577

COLORADO
This area is served by a regional office; please refer to the regional office listings at the end of this section.

CONNECTICUT
U.S. Department of Housing and Urban Development
Hartford Field Office
20 Church Street, 10th Floor
Hartford, CT 06103
P: 860.240.4800

DELAWARE
U.S. Department of Housing and Urban Development
Wilmington Field Office
920 North King Street, Suite 404
Wilmington, DE 79801
P: 302.573.6300

DISTRICT OF COLUMBIA
U.S. Department of Housing and Urban Development
District of Columbia Field Office
820 First Street, NE, Suite 300
Washington, DC 20002
P: 202.275.9200

FLORIDA

U.S. Department of Housing and Urban Development
Miami Field Office
909 Southeast First Avenue, Room 500
Miami, FL 33131
P: 305.536.5678

U.S. Department of Housing and Urban Development
Jacksonville Field Office
400 West Bay Street, Suite 1015
Jacksonville, FL 32202
P: 904.232.2627

U.S. Department of Housing and Urban Development
Orlando Field Office
3751 Maguire Boulevard, Room 270
Orlando, FL 32803
P: 407.648.6441

GEORGIA

This area is served by a regional office; please refer to the regional office listings at the end of this section.

HAWAII

U.S. Department of Housing and Urban Development
Honolulu Field Office
1132 Bishop Street, Suite 1400
Honolulu, HI 96813
P: 808.457.4662

IDAHO

U.S. Department of Housing and Urban Development
Boise Field Office
800 Park Boulevard, Suite 220
Boise, ID 83712
P: 208.334.1990

ILLINOIS

U.S. Department of Housing and Urban Development
Springfield Field Office
77 West Jackson Boulevard
Chicago, IL 60604
P: 312.353.5680

INDIANA

U.S. Department of Housing and Urban Development
Indianapolis Field Office
151 North Delaware Street, Suite 1200
Indianapolis, IN 46204
P: 317.226.6303

IOWA

U.S. Department of Housing and Urban Development
Des Moines Field Office
210 Walnut Street, Suite 239
Des Moines, IA 50309
P: 515.284.4512

KANSAS

This area is served by a regional office; please refer to the regional office listings at the end of this section.

KENTUCKY

U.S. Department of Housing and Urban Development
Louisville Field Office
601 West Broadway, Room 110
Louisville, KY 40203
P: 502.582.5251

LOUISIANA

U.S. Department of Housing and Urban Development
New Orleans Field Office
500 Poydras Street, 9th Floor
New Orleans, LA 70130
P: 504.671.3000

U.S. Department of Housing and Urban Development
Shreveport Field Office
401 Edwards Street, Room 1510
Shreveport, LA 71101
P: 318.226.7030

MAINE

U.S. Department of Housing and Urban Development
Bangor Field Office
One Merchants Plaza, Suite 601
Bangor, ME 04401
P: 207.945.0467

MARYLAND

U.S. Department of Housing and Urban Development
Baltimore Field Office
10 South Howard Street, 5th Floor
Baltimore, MD 21201
P: 410.962.2520

MASSACHUSETTS

U.S. Department of Housing and Urban Development
Boston Field Office
10 Causeway Street, Room 301
Boston, MA 02222
P: 617.994.8223

MICHIGAN

U.S. Department of Housing and Urban Development
Detroit Field Office
477 Michigan Avenue
Detroit, MI 48226
P: 313.226.7900

U.S. Department of Housing and Urban Development
Flint Field Office
801 South Saginaw, 4th Floor
Flint, MI 48502
P: 810.766.5112

U.S. Department of Housing and Urban Development
Grand Rapids Field Office
99 Monroe Avenue, NW, Suite 402
Grand Rapids, MI 49503
P: 616.456.2100

MINNESOTA

U.S. Department of Housing and Urban Development
Minneapolis Field Office
920 Second Avenue South, Suite 1300
Minneapolis, MN 55402
P: 612.370.3000

MISSISSIPPI

U.S. Department of Housing and Urban Development
Jackson Field Office
100 West Capitol Street, Room 910
Jackson, MS 39269
P: 601.965.4757

MISSOURI

U.S. Department of Housing and Urban Development
St. Louis Field Office
1222 Spruce Street, Suite 3.203
St. Louis, MO 63103
P: 314.418.5400

MONTANA

U.S. Department of Housing and Urban Development
Helena Field Office
901 Front Street, Suite 1300
Helena, MT 59626
P: 406.449.5050

NEBRASKA

U.S. Department of Housing and Urban Development
Omaha Field Office
1616 Capitol Avenue, Suite 329
Omaha, NE 68102
P: 402.492.3100

NEVADA

U.S. Department of Housing and Urban Development
Las Vegas Field Office
302 East Carson Street, 4th Floor
Las Vegas, NV 89101
P: 702.366.2100

U.S. Department of Housing and Urban Development
Reno Field Office
745 West Moana Lane, Suite 360
Reno, NV 89509
P: 775.824.3700

NEW HAMPSHIRE

U.S. Department of Housing and Urban Development
Manchester Field Office
275 Chestnut Street, 4th Floor
Manchester, NH 03101
P: 603.666.7510

NEW JERSEY

U.S. Department of Housing and Urban Development
Newark Field Office
1085 Raymond Boulevard, 13th Floor
Newark, NJ 07102
P: 973.622.7900

NEW MEXICO

U.S. Department of Housing and Urban Development
Albuquerque Field Office
500 Gold Avenue, SW, 7th Floor, Suite 7301
P.O. Box 906
Albuquerque, NM 87103
P: 505.346.6463

NEW YORK

U.S. Department of Housing and Urban Development
Albany Field Office
52 Corporate Circle
Albany, NY 12203
P: 518.464.4200

U.S. Department of Housing and Urban Development
Buffalo Field Office
465 Main Street, 2nd Floor
Buffalo, NY 14203
P: 716.551.5755

U.S. Department of Housing and Urban Development
Syracuse Field Office
100 South Clinton Street
Syracuse, NY 13261
P: 315.477.0616

NORTH CAROLINA
U.S. Department of Housing and Urban Development
Greensboro Field Office
1500 Pinecroft Road, Suite 401
Greenville, NC 27407
P: 336.547.4000

NORTH DAKOTA
U.S. Department of Housing and Urban Development
Fargo Field Office
657 Second Avenue North, Room 366
Fargo, ND 58108
P: 701.239.5136

OHIO
U.S. Department of Housing and Urban Development
Cincinnati Field Office
632 Vine Street, 5th Floor
Cincinnati, OH 45202
P: 513.684.3451

U.S. Department of Housing and Urban Development
Cleveland Field Office
1350 Euclid Avenue, Suite 500
Cleveland, OH 44115
P: 216.357.7900

U.S. Department of Housing and Urban Development
Columbus Field Office
200 North High Street, 7th Floor
Columbus, OH 43215
P: 614.469.250

OKLAHOMA
U.S. Department of Housing and Urban Development
Oklahoma City Field Office
301 Northwest 6th Street, Suite 200
Oklahoma City, OK 73102
P: 405.609.8509

U.S. Department of Housing and Urban Development
Tulsa Field Office
Tower II Two West
Second Street, Suite 400
Tulsa, OK 74103
P: 918.292.8900

OREGON
U.S. Department of Housing and Urban Development
Portland Field Office
400 Southwest 6th Avenue, Suite 700
Portland, OR 97204
P: 971.222.2600

PENNSYLVANIA
U.S. Department of Housing and Urban Development
Pittsburgh Field Office
1000 Liberty Avenue, Suite 1000
Pittsburgh, PA 15222
P: 412.644.6428

PUERTO RICO
U.S. Department of Housing and Urban Development
San Juan Field Office
235 Federico Costa Street, Suite 200
San Juan, PR 00918
P: 787.766.5400

RHODE ISLAND
U.S. Department of Housing and Urban Development
Providence Field Office
121 South Main Street, Suite 300
Providence, RI 02903
P: 401.277.8300

SOUTH CAROLINA
U.S. Department of Housing and Urban Development
Columbia Field Office
1835 Assembly Street, 13th Floor
Columbia, SC 29201
P: 803.765.5592

SOUTH DAKOTA
U.S. Department of Housing and Urban Development
Sioux Falls Field Office
4301 West 57th Street, Suite 101
Sioux Falls, SD 57108
P: 605.330.4223

TENNESSEE
U.S. Department of Housing and Urban Development
Nashville Field Office
235 Cumberland Bend, Suite 200
Nashville, TN 37228
P: 615.736.5600

U.S. Department of Housing and Urban Development
Knoxville Field Office
710 Locust Street, SW, 3rd Floor
Knoxville, TN 37902
P: 865.545.4370

U.S. Department of Housing and Urban Development
Memphis Field Office
200 Jefferson Avenue, Suite 300
Memphis, TN 38103
P: 901.544.3367

TEXAS

U.S. Department of Housing and Urban Development
Dallas Field Office
525 Griffin Street, Suite 860
Dallas, TX 75202
P: 214.767.8300

U.S. Department of Housing and Urban Development
Houston Field Office
1301 Fannin, Suite 2200
Houston, TX 77002
P: 713.718.3199

U.S. Department of Housing and Urban Development
Lubbock Field Office
1205 Texas Avenue, Suite 511
Lubbock, TX 79401
P: 806.472.7265

U.S. Department of Housing and Urban Development
San Antonio Field Office
615 East Houston Street, Suite 347
San Antonio, TX 78205
P: 210.475.6806

UTAH

U.S. Department of Housing and Urban Development
Salt Lake City Field Office
125 South State Street, Suite 3001
Salt Lake City, UT 84138
P: 801.524.6070

VERMONT

U.S. Department of Housing and Urban Development
Burlington Field Office
95 Saint Paul Street, Suite 440
Burlington, VT 05401
P: 802.951.6290

VIRGINIA

U.S. Department of Housing and Urban Development
Richmond Field Office
600 East Broad Street, 3rd Floor
Richmond, VA 23219
P: 804.822.4805

WASHINGTON

U.S. Department of Housing and Urban Development
Spokane Field Office
920 West Riverside, Suite 588
Spokane, WA 99201
P: 509.368.3200

WEST VIRGINIA

U.S. Department of Housing and Urban Development
Charleston Field Office
405 Capitol Street, Suite 708
Charleston, WV 25301
P: 304.347.7000

WISCONSIN

U.S. Department of Housing and Urban Development
Milwaukee Field Office
310 West Wisconsin Avenue, Suite 1380
Milwaukee, WI 53203
P: 414.297.3214

WYOMING

U.S. Department of Housing and Urban Development
Casper Field Office
150 East B Street, Room 1010
Casper, WY 82601
P: 307.261.6250

REGION I

U.S. Department of Housing and Urban Development
Boston Regional Office
10 Causeway Street, 3rd Floor
Boston, MA 02222
P: 617.994.8200

Note: This office serves the following states: Connecticut, Maine, Massachusetts, New Hampshire, Rhode Island, and Vermont.

REGION II

U.S. Department of Housing and Urban Development
New York Regional Office
26 Federal Plaza, Suite 3541
New York, NY 10278
P: 212.264.8000

Note: This office serves the following states: New Jersey, New York and the Caribbean.

REGION III

U.S. Department of Housing and Urban Development
Philadelphia Regional Office
100 Penn Square East
Philadelphia, PA 19107
P: 215.656.0500

Note: This office serves the following states: Delaware, District of Columbia, Maryland, Pennsylvania, Virginia, and West Virginia.

REGION IV

U.S. Department of Housing and Urban Development
Atlanta Regional Office
40 Marietta Street
Atlanta, GA 30303
P: 404.331.5136

Note: This office serves the following states: Alabama, Florida, Georgia, Kentucky, Mississippi, North Carolina, South Carolina, and Tennessee.

REGION V

U.S. Department of Housing and Urban Development
Chicago Regional Office
77 West Jackson Boulevard
Chicago, IL 60604
P: 312.353.5680

Note: This office serves the following states: Illinois, Indiana, Michigan, Minnesota, Ohio, and Wisconsin

REGION VI

U.S. Department of Housing and Urban Development
Fort Worth Regional Office
801 Cherry Street, Unit 45, Suite 2500
Fort Worth, TX 76102
P: 817.978.5965

Note: This office serves the following states: Arkansas, Louisiana, New Mexico, Oklahoma, and Texas.

REGION VII

U.S. Department of Housing and Urban Development
Kansas City Regional Office
400 State Avenue, Room 200
Kansas City, KS 66101
P: 913.551.5462

Note: This office serves the following states: Iowa, Kansas, Missouri, and Nebraska.

REGION VIII

U.S. Department of Housing and Urban Development
Denver Regional Office
1670 Broadway, 25th Floor
Denver, CO 80202
P: 303.672.5440

Note: This office serves the following states: Colorado, Montana, North Dakota, South Dakota, Utah, and Wyoming.

REGION IX

U.S. Department of Housing and Urban Development
San Francisco Regional Office
600 Harrison Street, 3rd Floor
San Francisco, CA 94107
P: 415.489.6400

Note: This office serves the following states: American Samoa, Arizona, California, Guam, Hawaii, and Nevada.

REGION X

U.S. Department of Housing and Urban Development
Seattle Regional Office
909 First Avenue, Suite 200
Seattle, WA 98104
P: 206.220.5101

Note: This office serves the following states: Alaska, Idaho, Oregon, and Washington.

APPENDIX 10-B: USDA RURAL HOUSING SERVICE OFFICES

The U.S. Department of Agriculture, Rural Housing Service administers loan guarantee programs for low-income individuals and families in rural communities.

ALABAMA
U.S. Department of Agriculture
Rural Housing Service
4121 Carmichael Road, Suite 601
Montgomery, AL 36106
P: 334.279.3400
I: http://www.rurdev.usda.gov/al

ALASKA
U.S. Department of Agriculture
Rural Housing Service
800 West Evergreen, Suite 201
Palmer, AK 99645
P: 907.761.7707
I: http://www.rurdev.usda.gov/ak

ARIZONA
U.S. Department of Agriculture
Rural Housing Service
230 North First Avenue, Suite 206
Phoenix, AZ 85003
P: 602.280.8701
I: http://www.rurdev.usda.gov/az

ARKANSAS
U.S. Department of Agriculture
Rural Housing Service
700 West Capitol Avenue, Room 3416
Little Rock, AR 72201
P: 501.301.3200
I: http://www.rurdev.usda.gov/ar

CALIFORNIA
U.S. Department of Agriculture
Rural Housing Service
430 G Street, Suite 4169
Davis, CA 95616
P: 530.792.5800
I: http://www.rurdev.usda.gov/ca

COLORADO
U.S. Department of Agriculture
Rural Housing Service
Denver Federal Center
Building 56, Room 2300
P.O. Box 25426
Denver, CO 80225
P: 720.544.2903
I: http://www.rurdev.usda.gov/co

CONNECTICUT
U.S. Department of Agriculture
Rural Housing Service
451 West Street
Amherst, MA 01002
P: 413.253.4300
I: http://www.rurdev.usda.gov/ma

DELAWARE
U.S. Department of Agriculture
Rural Housing Service
1221 College Park Drive, Suite 200
Dover, DE 19904
P: 302.857.3580
I: http://www.rurdev.usda.gov/de

DISTRICT OF COLUMBIA
U.S. Department of Agriculture
National Headquarters
Rural Housing Service
1400 Independence Avenue, SW
Washington, DC 20250
P: 202.692.0090
I: http://www.rurdev.usda.gov

FLORIDA
U.S. Department of Agriculture
Rural Housing Service
4440 Northwest 25th Place
P.O. Box 147010
Gainesville, FL 32614
P: 352.338.3402
I: http://www.rurdev.usda.gov/fl

GEORGIA
U.S. Department of Agriculture
Rural Housing Service
355 East Hancock Avenue, Suite 300
Athens, GA 30601
P: 706.546.2162
I: http://www.rurdev.usda.gov/ga

HAWAII
U.S. Department of Agriculture
Rural Housing Service
154 Waianuenue Avenue, Room 311
Hilo, HI 96720
P: 808.933.8380
I: http://www.rurdev.usda.gov/hi

IDAHO

U.S. Department of Agriculture
Rural Housing Service
9713 West Barnes Drive, Suite A-1
Boise, ID 83709
P: 208.378.5600
I: http://www.rurdev.usda.gov/id

ILLINOIS

U.S. Department of Agriculture
Rural Housing Service
2118 West Park Court, Suite A
Champaign, IL 61821
P: 217.403.6200
I: http://www.rurdev.usda.gov/il

INDIANA

U.S. Department of Agriculture
Rural Housing Service
5975 Lakeside Boulevard
Indianapolis, IN 46278
P: 317.290.3100
I: http://www.rurdev.usda.gov/in

IOWA

U.S. Department of Agriculture
Rural Housing Service
210 Walnut Street, Room 873
Des Moines, IA 50309
P: 515.284.4663
I: http://www.rurdev.usda.gov/ia

KANSAS

U.S. Department of Agriculture
Rural Housing Service
1303 Southwest First American Place, Suite 100
Topeka, KS 66604
P: 785.271.2700
I: http://www.rurdev.usda.gov/ks

KENTUCKY

U.S. Department of Agriculture
Rural Housing Service
771 Corporate Drive, Suite 200
Lexington, KY 40503
P: 859.224.7300
I: http://www.rurdev.usda.gov/ky

LOUISIANA

U.S. Department of Agriculture
Rural Housing Service
3727 Government Street
Alexandria, LA 71302
P: 318.473.7920
I: http://www.rurdev.usda.gov/la

MAINE

U.S. Department of Agriculture
Rural Housing Service
967 Illinois Avenue, Suite 4
Bangor, ME 04401
P: 207.990.9160
I: http://www.rurdev.usda.gov/me

MARYLAND

U.S. Department of Agriculture
Rural Housing Service
1221 College Park Drive, Suite 200
Dover, DE 19904
P: 302.857.3580
I: http://www.rurdev.usda.gov/md

MASSACHUSETTS

U.S. Department of Agriculture
Rural Housing Service
451 West Street
Amherst, MA 01002
P: 413.253.4300
I: http://www.rurdev.usda.gov/ma

MICHIGAN

U.S. Department of Agriculture
Rural Housing Service
3001 Coolidge Road, Suite 200
East Lansing, MI 48823
P: 517.324.5190
I: http://www.rurdev.usda.gov/mi

MINNESOTA

U.S. Department of Agriculture
Rural Housing Service
375 Jackson Street, Suite 410
St. Paul, MN 55101
P: 651.602.7800
I: http://www.rurdev.usda.gov/mn

MISSISSIPPI

U.S. Department of Agriculture
Rural Housing Service
100 West Capitol Street, Suite 831
Jackson, MS 39269
P: 601.965.4316
I: http://www.rurdv.usda.gov/ms

MISSOURI

U.S. Department of Agriculture
Rural Housing Service
601 Business Loop 70 West, Suite 235
Columbia, MO 65203
P: 573.876.0976
I: http://www.rurdev.usda.gov/mo

MONTANA
U.S. Department of Agriculture
Rural Housing Service
2229 Boot Hill Court
Bozeman, MT 59715
P: 406.585.2530
I: http://www.rurdev.usda.gov/mt

NEBRASKA
U.S. Department of Agriculture
Rural Housing Service
100 Centennial Mall North, Suite 208
Lincoln, NE 68508
P: 402.437.5551
I: http://www.rurdev.usda.gov/ne

NEVADA
U.S. Department of Agriculture
Rural Housing Service
1390 South Curry Street
Carson City, NV 89703
P: 775.887.1222
I: http://www.rurdev.usda.gov/nv

NEW HAMPSHIRE
U.S. Department of Agriculture
Rural Housing Service
89 Main Street, 3rd Floor
Montpelier, VT 05602
P: 802.828.6080
I: http://www.rurdev.usda.gov/vt

NEW JERSEY
U.S. Department of Agriculture
Rural Housing Service
8000 Midlantic Drive, 5th Floor North, Suite 500
Mt. laurel, NJ 08054
P: 856.787.7700
I: http://www.rurdev.usda.gov/nj

NEW MEXICO
U.S. Department of Agriculture
Rural Housing Service
6200 Jefferson Street, Room 255
Albuquerque, NM 78109
P: 505.761.4950
I: http://www.rurdev.usda.gov/nm

NEW YORK
U.S. Department of Agriculture
Rural Housing Service
441 South Salina Street, Suite 357
Syracuse, NY 13202
P: 315.477.6400
I: http://www.rurdev.usda.gov/ny

NORTH CAROLINA
U.S. Department of Agriculture
Rural Housing Service
4405 Bland Road, Suite 260
Raleigh, NC 27609
P: 919.873.2000
I: http://www.rurdev.usda.gov/nc

NORTH DAKOTA
U.S. Department of Agriculture
Rural Housing Service
220 East Rosser, Room 208
P.O. Box 1737
Bismarck, ND 58502
P: 701.530.2037
I: http://www.rurdev.usda.gov/nd

OHIO
U.S. Department of Agriculture
Rural Housing Service
200 North High Street, Room 507
Columbus, OH 43215
P: 614.255.2400
I: http://www.rurdev.usda.gov/oh

OKLAHOMA
U.S. Department of Agriculture
Rural Housing Service
100 USDA, Suite 108
Stillwater, OK 74074
P: 405.742.1000
I: http://www.rurdev.usda.gov/ok

OREGON
U.S. Department of Agriculture
Rural Housing Service
1201 Northeast Lloyd Boulevard, Suite 801
Portland, OR 97232
P: 503.414.3300
I: http://www.rurdev.usda.gov/or

PENNSYLVANIA
U.S. Department of Agriculture
Rural Housing Service
1 Credit Union Place, Suite 330
Harrisburg, PA 17110
P: 717.237.2299
I: http://www.rurdev.usda.gov/pa

PUERTO RICO
U.S. Department of Agriculture
Rural Housing Service
654 Munoz Rivera Avenue, Suite 601
San Juan, PR 00936
P: 787.766.5095
I: http://www.rurdev.usda.gov/pr

RHODE ISLAND

U.S. Department of Agriculture
Rural Housing Service
451 West Street
Amherst, MA 01002
P: 413.253.4300
I: http://www.rurdev.usda.gov/ma

SOUTH CAROLINA

U.S. Department of Agriculture
Rural Housing Service
1835 Assembly Street, Room 1007
Columbia, SC 29201
P: 803.765.5163
I: http://www.rurdev.usda.gov/sc

SOUTH DAKOTA

U.S. Department of Agriculture
Rural Housing Service
200 Fourth Street, SW, Room 210
Huron, SD 57350
P: 605.352.1100
I: http://www.rurdev.usda.gov/sd

TENNESSEE

U.S. Department of Agriculture
Rural Housing Service
3322 West End Avenue, Suite 300
Nashville, TN 37203
P: 615.783.1300
I: http://www.rurdev.usda.gov/tn

TEXAS

U.S. Department of Agriculture
Rural Housing Service
101 South Main, Suite 102
Temple, TX 76501
P: 254.742.9700
I: http://www.rurdev.usda.gov/tx

UTAH

U.S. Department of Agriculture
Rural Housing Service
125 South State Street, Room 4311
Salt Lake City, UT 84138
P: 801.524.4321
I: http://www.rurdev.usda.gov/ut

VERMONT

U.S. Department of Agriculture
Rural Housing Service
89 Main Street, 3rd Floor
Montpelier, VT 05602
P: 802.828.6080
I: http://www.rurdev.usda.gov/vt

VIRGINIA

U.S. Department of Agriculture
Rural Housing Service
1606 Santa Rosa Road, Suite 238
Richmond, VA 23229
P: 804.287.1550
I: http://www.rurdev.usda.gov/va

WASHINGTON

U.S. Department of Agriculture
Rural Housing Service
1835 Blacklake Boulevard, SW, Suite B
Olympia, WA 98512
P: 360.704.7740
I: http://www.rurdev.usda.gov/wa

WEST VIRGINIA

U.S. Department of Agriculture
Rural Housing Service
1550 Earl Core Road, Suite 101
Morgantown, WV 26505
P: 304.284.4860
I: http://www.rurdev.usda.gov/wv

WISCONSIN

U.S. Department of Agriculture
Rural Housing Service
5417 Clem's Way
Stevens Point, WI 54482
P: 715.345.7600
I: http://www.rurdev.usda.gov/wi

WYOMING

U.S. Department of Agriculture
Rural Housing Service
100 East B Street, Room 1005
P.O. Box 11005
Casper, WY 82601
P: 307.233.6700
I: http://www.rurdev.usda.gov/wy

APPENDIX 10-C: HUD REGIONAL OFFICES OF FAIR HOUSING & EQUAL HOUSING OPPORTUNITY

The U.S. Department of Housing & Urban Development, Office of Fair Housing and Equal Opportunity enforces federal laws and establishes policies that ensure all Americans have equal access to the housing of their choice.

REGION I

U.S. Department of Housing and Urban Development
Boston Regional Office of Fair Housing and Equal Opportunity
10 Causeway Street, Room 321
Boston, MA 02222
P: 617.994.8300

Note: This office serves the following states: Connecticut, Maine, Massachusetts, New Hampshire, Rhode Island, and Vermont.

REGION II

U.S. Department of Housing and Urban Development
New York Regional Office of Fair Housing and Equal Opportunity
26 Federal Plaza, Suite 3532
New York, NY 10278
P: 212.542.7519

Note: This office serves the following states: New Jersey, New York and the Caribbean.

REGION III

U.S. Department of Housing and Urban Development
Philadelphia Regional Office of Fair Housing and Equal Opportunity
100 Penn Square East, 12th Floor
Philadelphia, PA 19107
P: 215.861.7646

Note: This office serves the following states: Delaware, District of Columbia, Maryland, Pennsylvania, Virginia, and West Virginia.

REGION IV

U.S. Department of Housing and Urban Development
Atlanta Regional Office of Fair Housing and Equal Opportunity
40 Marietta Street, 16th Floor
Atlanta, GA 30303
P: 404.331.5140

Note: This office serves the following states: Alabama, Florida, Georgia, Kentucky, Mississippi, North Carolina, South Carolina, and Tennessee.

REGION V

U.S. Department of Housing and Urban Development
Chicago Regional Office of Fair Housing and Equal Opportunity
77 West Jackson Boulevard, Room 2101
Chicago, IL 60604
P: 312.353.7776

Note: This office serves the following states: Illinois, Indiana, Michigan, Minnesota, Ohio, and Wisconsin

REGION VI

U.S. Department of Housing and Urban Development
Fort Worth Regional Office of Fair Housing and Equal Opportunity
801 Cherry Street, Unit 45, Suite 2500
Fort Worth, TX 76102
P: 817.978.5900

Note: This office serves the following states: Arkansas, Louisiana, New Mexico, Oklahoma, and Texas.

REGION VII

U.S. Department of Housing and Urban Development
Kansas City Regional Office of Fair Housing and Equal Opportunity
400 State Avenue, Room 200
Kansas City, KS 66101
P: 913.551.6958

Note: This office serves the following states: Iowa, Kansas, Missouri, and Nebraska.

REGION VIII

U.S. Department of Housing and Urban Development
Denver Regional Office of Fair Housing and Equal Opportunity
1670 Broadway
Denver, CO 80202
P: 303.672.5437

Note: This office serves the following states: Colorado, Montana, North Dakota, South Dakota, Utah, and Wyoming.

REGION IX

U.S. Department of Housing and Urban Development
San Francisco Regional Office of Fair Housing and Equal
Opportunity
600 Harrison Street, 3rd Floor
San Francisco, CA 94107
P: 415.489.6524

Note: This office serves the following states: American
Samoa, Arizona, California, Guam, Hawaii, and Nevada.

REGION X

U.S. Department of Housing and Urban Development
Seattle Regional Office of Fair Housing and Equal
Opportunity
909 First Avenue, Suite 205
Seattle, WA 98104
P: 206.220.5170

Note: This office serves the following states: Alaska, Idaho,
Oregon, and Washington.

APPENDIX 12-A: STATE CONSUMER PROTECTION OFFICES

State Consumer Protection Offices offer a variety of important services. They mediate complaints, conduct investigations, prosecute offenders of consumer laws and regulate professionals, provide educational materials, and advocate in the consumer interest.

ALABAMA
Alabama Office of the Attorney General
Consumer Affairs Section
501 Washington Avenue
Montgomery, AL 36104
P: 334.242.7335
I: http://www.ago.state.al.us

ALASKA
Alaska Office of the Attorney General
Consumer Protection Unit
1031 West 4th Avenue, Suite 200
Anchorage, AK 99501
P: 907.269.5200
I: http://www.law.state.ak.us

ARIZONA
Arizona Office of the Attorney General
Consumer Information and Complaints
1275 West Washington Street
Phoenix, AZ 85007
P: 602.542.5763
I: http://www.azag.gov

Arizona Office of the Attorney General
Consumer Information and Complaints
400 West Congress Street, South Building, Suite 315
Tucson, AZ 85701
P: 520.628.6504
I: http://www.azag.gov

ARKANSAS
Arkansas Office of the Attorney General
Consumer Protection Division
323 Center Street, Suite 200
Little Rock, AR 72201
P: 501.682.2007
I: http://www.arkansasag.gov

CALIFORNIA
California Department of Consumer Affairs
Consumer Information Division
1625 North Market Boulevard, Suite N112
Sacramento, CA 95834
P: 916.445.1254
I: http://www.dca.ca.gov

California Office of the Attorney General
Public Inquiry Unit
P.O. Box 944255
Sacramento, CA 94244
P: 916.322.3360
I: http://caag.state.ca.us

COLORADO
Colorado Office of the Attorney General
Consumer Protection Section
1525 Sherman Street, 7th Floor
Denver, CO 80203
P: 303.866.5189
I: http://www.coloradoattorneygeneral.gov

CONNECTICUT
Connecticut Office of the Attorney General
55 Elm Street
Hartford, CT 06106
P: 860.808.5318
I: http://www.ct.gov/ag

Connecticut Department of Consumer Protection
165 Capitol Avenue
Hartford, CT 06106
P: 800.842.2649
I: http://www.ct.gov/dcp

DELAWARE
Delaware Department of Justice
Consumer Protection Division
820 North French Street, 5th Floor
Wilmington, DE 19801
P: 302.577.8600
I: http://www.attorneygeneral.delaware.gov

DISTRICT OF COLUMBIA
District of Columbia Department of Consumer and Regulatory Affairs
1100 4th Street, SW
Washington, DC 20024
P: 202.442.4400
I: http://www.consumer.dc.gov

District of Columbia Office of the Attorney General
Consumer Protection and Antitrust
441 4th Street, NW
Washington, DC 20001
P: 202.442.9828
I: http://www.oag.dc.gov

FLORIDA
Florida Department of Financial Services
Division of Consumer Services
200 East Gaines Street
Tallahassee, FL 32399
P: 850.413.3089
I: http://www.myfloridacfo.com

Florida Office of the Attorney General
The Capitol, PL-01
Tallahassee, FL 32399
P: 850.414.3990
I: http://www.myfloridalegal.com

GEORGIA
Georgia Governors Office of Consumer Affairs
Two Martin Luther King, Jr. Drive, SE, Suite 356
Atlanta, GA 30334
P: 404.651.8600
I: http://www.consumer.georgia.gov

HAWAII
Hawaii Department of Commerce and Consumer Affairs
Office of Consumer Protection
235 South Beretania Street, Suite 801
Honolulu, HI 96813
P: 808.586.2630
I: http://www.hawaii.gov/dcca/ocp

IDAHO
Idaho Office of the Attorney General
Consumer Protection Division
954 West Jefferson, 2nd Floor
P.O. Box 83720
Boise, ID 83720
P: 208.334.2424
I: http://www.ag.idaho.gov

ILLINOIS
Illinois Office of the Attorney General
Consumer Fraud Bureau
601 South University Avenue
Carbondale, IL 62901
P: 618.529.6400
I: http://www.illinoisattorneygeneral.gov

Illinois Office of the Attorney General
Consumer Fraud Bureau
100 West Randolph Street
Chicago, IL 60601
P: 312.814.3000
I: http://www.illinoisattorneygeneral.gov

Illinois Office of the Attorney General
Consumer Fraud Bureau
500 South 2nd Street
Springfield, IL 62706
P: 217.782.1090
I: http://www.illinoisattorneygeneral.gov

INDIANA
Indiana Office of the Attorney General
Consumer Protection Division
Government Center South, 5th Floor
302 West Washington Street
Indianapolis, IN 46204
P: 317.232.6330
I: http://www.indianaconsumer.com

IOWA
Iowa Office of the Attorney General
Consumer Protection Division
1305 East Walnut Street
Des Moines, IA 50319
P: 515.281.5926
I: http://www.iowaattorneygeneral.org

KANSAS
Kansas Office of the Attorney General
Consumer Protection and Antitrust Division
120 Southwest 10th Street, Suite 430
Topeka, KS 66612
P: 785.296.3751
I: http://www.ag.ks.gov

KENTUCKY
Kentucky Office of the Attorney General
Consumer Protection Division
1024 Capital Center Drive
Frankfort, KY 40601
P: 502.696.5389
I: http://www.ag.ky.gov/cp

Kentucky Office of the Attorney General
Consumer Protection Division
310 Whittington Parkway, Suite 101
Louisville, KY 40222
P: 502.429.7134
I: http://www.ag.ky.gov/cp

Kentucky Office of the Attorney General
Consumer Protection Division
361 North Lake Drive
Prestonsburg, KY 41653
P: 606.889.1821
I: http://www.ag.ky.gov/cp

LOUISIANA
Louisiana Office of the Attorney General
Consumer Protection Section
1885 North 3rd Street
Baton Rouge, LA 70802
P: 225.326.6465
I: http://www.ag.state.la.us

MAINE
Maine Bureau of Consumer Credit Protection
35 State House Station
Augusta, ME 04333
P: 207.624.8527
I: http://www.credit.maine.gov

Maine Office of the Attorney General
6 State House Station
Augusta, ME 04333
P: 207.626.8849
I: http://www.maine.gov/ag

MARYLAND
Maryland Office of the Attorney General
Consumer Protection Division
200 Saint Paul Place
Baltimore, MD 21202
P: 410.576.6550
I: http://www.oag.state.md.us/consumer

MASSACHUSETTS
Massachusetts Office of the Attorney General
Consumer Protection Division
One Ashburton Place
Boston, MA 02108
P: 617.727.8400
I: http://www.mass.gov/ago

Massachusetts Office of Consumer Affairs and Business Regulation
10 Park Plaza, Suite 5170
Boston, MA 02116
P: 617.973.8700
I: http://www.mass.gov/consumer

MICHIGAN
Michigan Office of the Attorney General
Consumer Protection Division
P.O. Box 30213
Lansing, MI 48909
P: 517.373.1140
I: http://www.michigan.gov/ag

MINNESOTA
Minnesota Office of the Attorney General
Consumer Services Division
1400 Bremer Tower
445 Minnesota Street
St. Paul, MN 55101
P: 651.296.3353
I: http://www.ag.state.mn.us

MISSISSIPPI
Mississippi Office of the Attorney General
Consumer Protection Division
P.O. Box 22947
Jackson, MS 39225
P: 601.359.4230
I: http://www.ago.state.ms.us

MISSOURI
Missouri Office of the Attorney General
Consumer Protection Unit
P.O. Box 899
Jefferson City, MO 65102
P: 573.751.3321
I: http://www.ago.mo.gov

MONTANA
Montana Office of Consumer Protection
Office of Consumer Protection
P.O. Box 200151
2225 11th Avenue
Helena, MT 59620
P: 406.444.4500
I: http://www.doj.mt.gov/consumer

NEBRASKA
Nebraska Office of the Attorney General
Consumer Protection Division
2115 State Capitol
Lincoln, NE 68509
P: 402.471.2682
I: http://www.ago.ne.gov

NEVADA
Nevada Department of Business and Industry
Fight Fraud Task Force
I: http://www.fightfraud.nv.gov

NEW HAMPSHIRE
New Hampshire Office of the Attorney General
Consumer Protection and Antitrust Bureau
33 Capitol Street
Concord, NH 03301
P: 603.271.3641
I: http://www.doj.nh.gov/consumer

NEW JERSEY
New Jersey Department of Law and Public Safety
Division of Consumer Affairs
124 Halsey Street
Newark, NJ 07102
P: 973.504.6200
I: http://www.njconsumeraffairs.gov

NEW MEXICO
New Mexico Office of the Attorney General
Consumer Protection Division
P.O. Drawer 1508
Santa Fe, NM 87504
P: 505.827.6060
I: http://www.nmag.gov

NEW YORK
New York State Department of State
Division of Consumer Protection
Consumer Assistance Unit
99 Washington Avenue
Albany, NY 12231
P: 518.474.8583
I: http://www.nysconsumer.gov

New York State Office of the Attorney General
Bureau of Consumer Frauds and Protection
State Capitol
Albany, NY 12224
P: 518.474.5481
I: http://www.ag..ny.gov

New York State Office of the Attorney General
Bureau of Consumer Frauds and Protection
120 Broadway, 3rd Floor
New York, NY 10271
P: 212.416.8000
I: http://www.ag..ny.gov

NORTH CAROLINA
North Carolina Office of the Attorney General
Consumer Protection Division
Mall Service Center 9001
Raleigh, NC 27699
P: 919.716.6000
I: http://www.ncdoj.gov

NORTH DAKOTA
North Dakota Office of the Attorney General
Consumer Protection and Antitrust Division
1050 East Interstate Avenue, Suite 200
Bismarck, ND 58503
P: 701.328.3404
I: http://www.ag.nd.gov

OHIO
Ohio Office of the Attorney General
Consumer Protection Section
30 east Broad Street, 14th Floor
Columbus, OH 43215
P: 614.466.4320
I: http://www.ohioattorneygeneral.gov

OKLAHOMA
Oklahoma Department of Consumer Credit
3616 Northwest 56th Street, Suite 240
Oklahoma City, OK 73112
P: 405.521.3653
I: http://www.ok.gov/okdocc

Oklahoma Office of the Attorney General
Consumer Protection Unit
313 Northeast 21st Street
Oklahoma City, OK 73105
P: Not Provided
I: http://www.oag.ok.gov

OREGON
Oregon Department of Justice
Financial Fraud/Consumer Protection Section
1162 Court Street, NE
Salem, OR 97301
P: 503.378.4320
I: http://www.doj.state.or.us

PENNSYLVANIA
Pennsylvania Office of the Attorney General
Bureau of Consumer Protection
Strawberry Square, 14th Floor
Harrisburg, PA 17120
P: 717.787.9707
I: http://www.attorneygeneral.gov

PUERTO RICO
Puerto Rico Department de Asuntos Del Consumidor
Apartado 41059
Minillas Station
Santurce, PR 00940
P: 787.722.7555
I: http://www.daco.gobierno.pr

RHODE ISLAND

Rhode Island Office of the Attorney General
Consumer Protection Unit
150 South Main Street
Providence, RI 02903
P: 401.247.4400
I: http://www.riag.state.ri.us

SOUTH CAROLINA

South Carolina Department of Consumer Affairs
P.O. Box 5757
Columbia, SC 29250
P: 803.734.4200
I: http://www.scconsumer.gov

SOUTH DAKOTA

South Dakota Office of the Attorney General
Consumer Protection
1302 East Highway 14, Suite 3
Pierre, SD 57501
P: 605.773.4400
I: http://www.state.sd.us.atg

TENNESSEE

Tennessee Office of the Attorney General
P.O. Box 20207
Nashville, TN 37202
P: 615.741.1671
I: http://www.tn.gov/attorneygeneral

TEXAS

Texas Office of the Attorney General
Consumer Protection Division
P.O. Box 12548
Austin, TX 78711
P: 800.621.0508
I: http://www.oag.state.tx.us

UTAH

Utah Department of Commerce
Division of Consumer Protection
P.O. Box 146704
160 East 300 South, 2nd Floor
Salt Lake City, UT 84114
P: 801.530.6601
I: http://www.consumerprotection.utah.gov

VERMONT

Vermont Office of the Attorney General
Consumer Assistance Program
146 University Place
Burlington, VT 05405
P: 802.656.3183
I: http://www.atg.state.vt.us

VIRGINIA

Virginia Office of the Attorney General
Consumer Protection Section
900 East Main Street
Richmond, VA 23219
P: 804.786.2042
I: http://www.ag.virginia.gov

WASHINGTON

Washington Office of the Attorney General
Consumer Protection Division
P.O. Box 40100
1125 Washington Street, SE
Olympia, WA 98504
P: 206.464.7744
I: http://www.atg.wa.gov

WEST VIRGINIA

West Virginia Office of the Attorney General
Consumer Protection Division
P.O. Box 1789
Charleston, WV 25326
P: 304.558.8986
I: http://www.wvago.gov

WISCONSIN

Wisconsin Department of Agriculture, Trade and Consumer Protection
Bureau of Consumer Protection
P.O. Box 8911
2811 Agriculture Drive
Madison, WI 53708
P: 608.224.4953
I: http://www.datcp.state.wi.us

WYOMING

Wyoming Office of the Attorney General
Consumer Protection Unit
123 State Capitol
200 West 24th Street
Cheyenne, WY 82002
P: 307.777.5833
I: http://www.attorneygeneral.state.wy.us

APPENDIX 12-B: LOCAL BETTER BUSINESS BUREAUS

Better Business Bureaus are non-profit organizations that encourage honest advertising and selling practices, and are supported primarily by local businesses. They offer a variety of consumer services, including consumer education materials; business reports; mediation and arbitration services; and information about local charities.

ALABAMA
Birmingham Better Business Bureau
1210 South 20th Street
Birmingham, AL 35205
P: 205.558.2222

Cullman Better Business Bureau
202 1st Avenue, SE, Suite I
Cullman, AL 35055
P: 256.775.2917

Dothan Better Business Bureau
1971 South Brannon Stand Road, Suite 1
Dothan, AL 36305
P: 334.794.0492

Huntsville Better Business Bureau
210 A Exchange Place
Huntsville, AL 35806
P: 256.533.1640

Mobile Better Business Bureau
960 South Schillinger Road, Suite I
Mobile, AL 36695
P: 251.433.5494

Montgomery Better Business Bureau
4750 Woodmere Boulevard, Suite D
Montgomery, AL 36107
P: 334.273.5530

ALASKA
Anchorage Better Business Bureau
341 West Tudor Road, Suite 209
Anchorage, AK 99503
P: 907.562.0704

ARIZONA
Phoenix Better Business Bureau
4428 North 12th Street
Phoenix, AZ 85014
P: 602.264.1721

Prescott Better Business Bureau
1569 West Gurley Street
Prescott, AZ 86305
P: 928.772.3410

Tucson Better Business Bureau
5151 East Broadway Boulevard, Suite 100
Tucson, AZ 85711
P: 520.888.5353

ARKANSAS
Little Rock Better Business Bureau
12521 Kanis Road
Little Rock, AR 72211
P: 501.664.7274

CALIFORNIA
Bakersfield Better Business Bureau
1601 H Street, Suite 101
Bakersfield, CA 933301
P: 661.322.2074

Culver City Better Business Bureau
6125 Washington Boulevard, 3rd Floor
Culver City, CA 90232
P: 310.945.3166

Fresno Better Business Bureau
4201 West Shaw Avenue, Suite 107
Fresno, CA 93722
P: 559.222.8111

Long Beach Better Business Bureau
3363 Linden Avenue, Suite A
Long Beach, CA 90807
P: 562.216.9242

Los Angeles Better Business Bureau
315 North La Cadena Drive
Colton, CA 92324
P: 909.825.7280

Oakland Better Business Bureau
1000 Broadway, Suite 625
Oakland, CA 94607
P: 510.844.2000

Placentia Better Business Bureau
550 West Orangethorpe Avenue
Placentia, CA 92870
P: 714.985.8922

Sacramento Better Business Bureau
3075 Beacon Boulevard
West Sacramento, CA 95691
P: 714.985.8922

San Diego Better Business Bureau
5050 Murphy Canyon Road, Suite 110
San Diego, CA 92123
P: 858.496.2131

San Jose Better Business Bureau
1112 South Bascom Avenue
San Jose, CA 95128
P: 408.278.7400

Santa Barbara Better Business Bureau
P.O. Box 129
Santa Barbara, CA 93101
P: 805.963.8657

Stockton Better Business Bureau
11 South San Joaquin Street, 8th Floor
Stockton, CA 95202
P: 209.948.4880

COLORADO
Colorado Springs Better Business Bureau
25 North Wahsatch Avenue
Colorado Springs, CO 80903
P: 719.636.1155

Denver Better Business Bureau
1020 Cherokee Street
Denver, CO 80204
P: 303.758.2100

Fort Collins Better Business Bureau
8020 South County Road 5, Suite 100
Fort Collins, CO 80528
P: 970.484.1348

CONNECTICUT
Wallingford Better Business Bureau
94 South Turnpike Road
Wallingford, CT 06492
P: 203.269.2700

DELAWARE
Wilmington Better Business Bureau
60 Reads Way
New Castle, DE 19720
P: 302.221.5255

DISTRICT OF COLUMBIA
Washington Better Business Bureau
1411 K Street, NW, Suite 1000
Washington, DC 20005
P: 202.393.8000

FLORIDA
Clearwater Better Business Bureau
2655 McCormick Drive
Clearwater, FL 33759
P: 727.535.5522

Jacksonville Better Business Bureau
4417Beach Boulevard, Suite 202
Jacksonville, FL 32207
P: 904.721.2288

Miami Better Business Bureau
14750 Northwest 77 Court, Suite 317
Miami Lakes, FL 33016
P: 305.827.5363

Orlando Better Business Bureau
1600 South Grant Street
Longwood, FL 32750
P: 407.621.3300

Pensacola Better Business Bureau
912 East Gadsden Street
Pensacola, FL 32501
P: 850.429.0002

Stuart Better Business Bureau
101 East Ocean Boulevard, Suite 202
Stuart, FL 34994
P: 772.223.1492

West Palm Beach Better Business Bureau
4411 Beacon Circle, Suite 4
West Palm Beach, FL 33407
P: 561.842.1918

GEORGIA
Atlanta Better Business Bureau
503 Oak Place, Suite 590
Atlanta, GA 30349
P: 404.766.0875

Augusta Better Business Bureau
1227 Augusta West Parkway, Suite 15
Augusta, GA 30909
P: 706.210.7676

Columbus Better Business Bureau
500 12th Street
Columbus, GA 31901
P: 706.324.0712

Macon Better Business Bureau
277 Martin Luther King, Jr. Boulevard, Suite 102
Macon, GA 31201
P: 478.742.7999

Savannah Better Business Bureau
6555 Abercorn Street, Suite 120
Savannah, GA 31405
P: 912.354.7521

HAWAII
Honolulu Better Business Bureau
1132 Bishop Street, Suite 615
Honolulu, HI 96813
P: 808.536.6956

IDAHO
Boise Better Business Bureau
1200 North Curtis Road
Boise, ID 83706
P: 208.342.4649

Idaho Falls Better Business Bureau
453 River Parkway
Idaho Falls, ID 83402
P: 208.523.9754

ILLINOIS
Chicago Better Business Bureau
330 North Wabash Avenue, Suite 3120
Chicago, IL 60611
P: 312.832.0500

Peoria Better Business Bureau
112 Harrison Street
Peoria, IL 61602
P: 309.688.3741

Rockford Better Business Bureau
401 West State Street, Suite 500
Rockford, IL 61101
P: 815.963.2222

INDIANA
Evansville Better Business Bureau
3101 North Green River Road, Suite 410
Evansville, IN 47715
P: 812.473.0202

Fort Wayne Better Business Bureau
4011 Parnell Avenue
Fort Wayne, IN 46805
P: 260.423.4433

Indianapolis Better Business Bureau
151 North Delaware Street, Suite 2020
Indianapolis, IN 46204
P: 317.488.2222

Merriville Better Business Bureau
7863 Broadway, Suite 124
Merriville, IN 46410
P: 219.227.8400

Osceola Better Business Bureau
10775 McKinley Highway, Suite B
Osceola, IN 46561
P: 574.675.9315

IOWA
Bettendorf Better Business Bureau
2435 Kimberly Road, Suite 260 N
Bettendorf, IA 52722
P: 563.355.6344

Des Moines Better Business Bureau
505 5th Avenue, Suite 720
Des Moines, IA 50309
P: 515.243.8137

KANSAS
Wichita Better Business Bureau
345 North Riverview Street, Suite 720
Wichita, KS 67203
P: 316.263.3146

KENTUCKY
Lexington Better Business Bureau
1390 Olivia Lane, Suite 100
Lexington, KY 40511
P: 859.259.1008

Louisville Better Business Bureau
844 South 5th Street
Louisville, KY 40203
P: 502.583.6546

LOUISIANA
Alexandria Better Business Bureau
5220-C Rue Verdun
Alexandria, LA 71303
P: 318.473.4494

Baton Rouge Better Business Bureau
748 Main Street
Baton Rouge, LA 70802
P: 225.346.5222

Houma Better Business Bureau
801 Barrow Street, Suite 400
Houma, LA 70360
P: 985.868.3456

Lafayette Better Business Bureau
4007 West Congress Street, Suite B
Lafayette, LA 70506
P: 337.981.3497

Lake Charles Better Business Bureau
2309 East Prien Lake Road
Lake Charles, LA 70601
P: 337.478.6253

Monroe Better Business Bureau
1900 North 18th Street, Suite 411
Monroe, LA 71201
P: 318.387.4600

New Orleans Better Business Bureau
710 Baronne Street, Suite C
New Orleans, LA 70113
P: 504.581.6222

Shreveport Better Business Bureau
2006 East 70th Street
Shreveport, LA 71105
P: 318.797.1337

MAINE
Maine does not currently have any Better Business Bureaus.

MARYLAND
Baltimore Better Business Bureau
502 South Sharp Street, Suite 1200
Baltimore, MD 21201
P: 410.347.3990

MASSACHUSETTS
Marlborough Better Business Bureau
290 Donald Lynch Boulevard, Suite 102
Marlborough, MA 01752
P: 508.652.4800

Worcester Better Business Bureau
340 Main Street, Suite 802
Worcester, MA 01608
P: 508.755.2548

MICHIGAN
Detroit Better Business Bureau
26777 Central Park Boulevard, Suite 100
Southfield, MI 48076
P: 248.223.9400

Grand Rapids Better Business Bureau
40 Pearl Street, NW, Suite 354
Grand Rapids, MI 49503
P: 616.774.8236

MINNESOTA
Minneapolis/St. Paul Better Business Bureau
220 South River Ridge Circle
Burnsville, MN 55337
P: 651.699.1111

MISSISSIPPI
Jackson Better Business Bureau
505 Avalon Way, Suite B
Jackson, MS 39047
P: 601.398.1700

MISSOURI
Kansas City Better Business Bureau
8080 Ward Parkway, Suite 401
Kansas City, MO 64114
P: 816.421.7800

Springfield Better Business Bureau
430 South Glenstone Avenue, Suite A
Springfield, MO 65802
P: 417.862.4222

St. Louis Better Business Bureau
211 North Broadway, Suite 2060
St. Louis, MO 63102
P: 314.645.3300

MONTANA
Montana does not currently have any Better Business Bureaus.

NEBRASKA
Lincoln Better Business Bureau
3633 O Street, Suite 1
Lincoln, NE 68510
P: 402.436.2345

Omaha Better Business Bureau
11811 P Street
Omaha, NE 68137
P: 402.391.7612

NEVADA
Las Vegas Better Business Bureau
6040 South Jones Boulevard
Las Vegas, NV 89118
P: 702.320.4500

Reno Better Business Bureau
4834 Sparks Boulevard, Suite 102
Sparks, NV 89436
P: 775.322.0657

NEW HAMPSHIRE
Concord Better Business Bureau
48 Pleasant Street
Concord, NH 03301
P: 603.224.1991

NEW JERSEY
Trenton Better Business Bureau
1700 Whitehorse-Hamilton Square Road, Suite D-5
Trenton, NJ 08690
P: 609.588.0808

NEW MEXICO
Albuquerque Better Business Bureau
2625 Pennsylvania Street, NE, Suite 2050
Albuquerque, NM 87110
P: 505.346.0110

Farmington Better Business Bureau
308 North Locke Avenue
Farmington, NM 87401
P: 505.326.6501

NEW YORK
Buffalo Better Business Bureau
100 Bryant Woods South
Amherst, NY 14228
P: 716.881.5222

Farmingdale Better Business Bureau
399 Conklin Street, Suite 300
Farmingdale, NY 11735
P: 212.533.6200

New York Better Business Bureau
30 East 33rd Street, 12th Floor
New York, NY 10016
P: 212.533.6200

Tarrytown Better Business Bureau
150 White Plains Road, Suite 107
Tarrytown, NY 10591
P: 212.533.6200

NORTH CAROLINA
Asheville Better Business Bureau
112 Executive Park
Asheville, NC 28801
P: 828.253.2392

Charlotte Better Business Bureau
13860 Ballantyne Corporate Place, Suite 225
Charlotte, NC 28277
P: 704.927.8611

Greensboro Better Business Bureau
3608 West Friendly Avenue, Suite 212
Greensboro, NC 27410
P: 336.852.4240

Raleigh Better Business Bureau
5540 Munford Road, Suite 130
Raleigh, NC 27612
P: 919.277.4222

Winston-Salem Better Business Bureau
500 West 5th Street, Suite 202
Winston-Salem, NC 27101
P: 336.725.8348

NORTH DAKOTA
North Dakota does not currently have any Better Business Bureaus.

OHIO
Akron Better Business Bureau
222 West Market Street
Akron, OH 44303
P: 330.253.4590

Canton Better Business Bureau
1434 Cleveland Avenue, NW
Canton, OH 44703
P: 330.454.9401

Cincinnati Better Business Bureau
Seven West 7th Street, Suite 1600
Cincinnati, OH 45202
P: 513.421.3015

Cleveland Better Business Bureau
2800 Euclid Avenue, 4th Floor
Cleveland, OH 44115
P: 216.241.7678

Columbus Better Business Bureau
1169 Dublin Road
Columbus, OH 43215
P: 614.486.6336

Dayton Better Business Bureau
15 West 4th Street, Suite 300
Dayton, OH 45402
P: 937.222.5825

Lima Better Business Bureau
219 North McDonel Street
Lima, OH 45801
P: 419.223.7010

Toledo Better Business Bureau
7668 King's Pointe Road
Toledo, OH 43617
P: 419.531.3116

Youngstown Better Business Bureau
25 Market Street
Youngstown, OH 44503
P: 330.744.3111

OKLAHOMA
Oklahoma City Better Business Bureau
17 South Dewey Street
Oklahoma City, OK 73102
P: 405.239.6081

Tulsa Better Business Bureau
1722 South Carson Avenue, Suite 3200
Tulsa, OK 74119
P: 918.492.1266

OREGON
Lake Oswego Better Business Bureau
4004 Southwest Kruse Way Place, Suite 375
Lake Oswego, OR 97035
P: 503.212.3022

PENNSYLVANIA
Bethlehem Better Business Bureau
50 West North Street
Bethlehem, PA 18018
P: 610.866.8780

Harrisburg Better Business Bureau
1337 North Front Street
Harrisburg, PA 17102
P: 717.364.3250

Philadelphia Better Business Bureau
1880 John F. Kennedy Boulevard, Suite 1330
Philadelphia, PA 19103
P: 215.985.9313

Pittsburgh Better Business Bureau
400 Holiday Drive, Suite 220
Pittsburgh, PA 15220
P: 412.456.2700

Scranton/Wilkes-Barre Better Business Bureau
2099 Birney Avenue
Moosic, PA 18507
P: 570.342.5100

PUERTO RICO
San Juan Better Business Bureau
530 Avenida De La Constitucion, #206
San Juan, PR 00901
P: 787.289.8710

RHODE ISLAND
Rhode Island does not currently have any Better Business Bureaus.

SOUTH CAROLINA
Columbia Better Business Bureau
2442 Devine Street
Columbia, SC 29205
P: 803.254.2525

Conway Better Business Bureau
1121 3rd Avenue
Conway, SC 29526
P: 843.488.2227

Greenville Better Business Bureau
408 North Church Street, Suite C
Greenville, SC 29601
P: 864.242.5052

SOUTH DAKOTA
Sioux Falls Better Business Bureau
300 North Phillips Avenue, #100
Sioux Falls, SD 57104
P: 605.271.2066

TENNESSEE
Chattanooga Better Business Bureau
1010 Market Street, Suite 200
Chattanooga, TN 37402
P: 423.266.6144

Clarksville Better Business Bureau
214 Main Street
Clarksville, TN 37040
P: 931.503.2222

Columbia Better Business Bureau
502 North Garden Street, Suite 201
Columbia, TN 38401
P: 931.388.9222

Cookeville Better Business Bureau
18 North Jefferson Street
Cookeville, TN 38501
P: 931.520.0008

Franklin Better Business Bureau
367 Riverside Drive, Suite 110
Franklin, TN 37064
P: 615.242.4222

Knoxville Better Business Bureau
255 North Peters Road, Suite A
Knoxville, TN 37923
P: 865.692.1600

Memphis Better Business Bureau
3693 Tyndale Drive
Memphis, TN 38125
P: 901.759.1300

Murfreesboro Better Business Bureau
530 Uptown Square
Murfreesboro, TN 37129
P: 615.242.4222

Nashville Better Business Bureau
201 4th Avenue, N, Suite 100
Nashville, TN 37219
P: 615.242.4222

TEXAS
Abilene Better Business Bureau
3300 South 14th Street, Suite 307
Abilene, TX 79605
P: 325.691.1533

Amarillo Better Business Bureau
720 South Tyler Street, Suite B112
Amarillo, TX 79101
P: 806.379.6222

Austin Better Business Bureau
1005 La Posada Drive
Austin, TX 78752
P: 512.445.2911

Beaumont Better Business Bureau
550 Fannin Street, Suite 100
Beaumont, TX 77701
P: 409.835.5348

College Station Better Business Bureau
418 Tarrow Street
College Station, TX 77840
P: 979.260.2222

Corpus Christi Better Business Bureau
719 South Shoreline, Suite 304
Corpus Christi, TX 78401
P: 361.852.4949

Dallas Better Business Bureau
1601 Elm Street, Suite 3838
Dallas, TX 75201
P: 214.220.2000

El Paso Better Business Bureau
720 Arizona Avenue
El Paso, TX 79902
P: 915.577.0191

Fort Worth Better Business Bureau
101 Summit Avenue, Suite 707
Fort Worth, TX 76102
P: 817.332.7585

Harker Heights Better Business Bureau
445 East Central Texas Expressway, Suite 1
Harker Heights, TX 76584
P: 254.699.0694

Houston Better Business Bureau
1333 West Loop South, Suite 1200
Houston, TX 77027
P: 713.868.9500

Longview Better Business Bureau
2401 Judson Road, #102
Longview, TX 75605
P: 903.758.3222

Lubbock Better Business Bureau
3333 66th Street
Lubbock, TX 79412
P: 806.763.0459

Midland Better Business Bureau
10100 Liberator Lane
Midland, TX 79711
P: 432.563.1880

San Angelo Better Business Bureau
3134 Executive Drive, Suite A
San Angelo, TX 76904
P: 325.949.2989

San Antonio Better Business Bureau
425 Soledad Street, Suite 500
San Antonio, TX 78205
P: 210.828.9441

Tyler Better Business Bureau
3600 Old Bullard Road, Building 1, Suite 1
Tyler, TX 75701
P: 903.581.5704

Weslaco Better Business Bureau
502 East Expressway 83, Suite C
Weslaco, TX 78596
P: 956.968.3678

Wichita Falls Better Business Bureau
4245 Kemp Boulevard, Suite 1012
Wichita Falls, TX 76308
P: 940.691.1172

UTAH
Salt Lake City Better Business Bureau
5673 South Redwood Road, Suite 22
Salt lake City, UT 84123
P: 801.892.6009

VERMONT
Vermont does not currently have any Better Business
Bureaus.

VIRGINIA
Norfolk Better Business Bureau
586 Virginian Drive
Norfolk, VA 23505
P: 757.531.1300

Richmond Better Business Bureau
720 Moorefield Park Drive, Suite 300
Richmond, VA 23236
P: 804.648.0016

Roanoke Better Business Bureau
5115 Bernard Drive, Suite 202
Roanoke, VA 24018
P: 540.342.3455

WASHINGTON
DuPont Better Business Bureau
1000 Station Drive, Suite 222
DuPont, WA 98327
P: 206.431.2222

Spokane Better Business Bureau
152 South Jefferson Street, Suite 200
Spokane, WA 99201
P: 509.455.4200

WEST VIRGINIA
Charleston Better Business Bureau
1018 Kanawha Boulevard East, Suite 301
Charleston, WV 25301
P: 304.345.7502

WISCONSIN
Milwaukee Better Business Bureau
10101 West Greenfield Avenue, Suite 125
West Allis, WI 53214
P: 414.847.6000

WYOMING
Wyoming does not currently have any Better Business
Bureaus.

APPENDIX 12-C: STATE TAXPAYER ADVOCATE SERVICE OFFICES

The Taxpayer Advocate Service provides advocacy services to ensure that every taxpayer is treated fairly by the Internal Revenue Service while ensuring they know and understand their rights.

ALABAMA
Taxpayer Advocate Service
801 Tom Martin Drive, Room 151
Birmingham, AL 35211
P: 205.912.5631

ALASKA
Taxpayer Advocate Service
949 East 36th Avenue, Stop A-405
Anchorage, AK 99508
P: 907.271.6877

ARIZONA
Taxpayer Advocate Service
4041 North Central Avenue, MS-1005 PHX
Phoenix, AZ 85012
P: 602.636.9500

ARKANSAS
Taxpayer Advocate Service
700 West Capitol Avenue, Stop 1005 LIT
Little Rock, AR 72201
P: 501.396.5978

CALIFORNIA
Taxpayer Advocate Service
24000 Avila Road, Stop 3361
Laguna Niguel, CA 92677
P: 949.389.4804

Taxpayer Advocate Service
300 North Los Angeles Street
Room 5109, Stop 6710
Los Angeles, CA 90012
P: 213.576.3140

Taxpayer Advocate Service
1301 Clay Street, Suite 1540-S
Oakland, CA 94612
P: 510.637.2703

Taxpayer Advocate Service
4330 Watt Avenue, SA-5043
Sacramento, CA 95821
P: 916.974.5007

Taxpayer Advocate Service
55 South Market Street, Stop 0004
San Jan, CA 95113
P: 408.817.6850

COLORADO
Taxpayer Advocate Service
1999 Broadway, Stop 1005 DEN
Denver, CO 80202
P: 303.603.4600

CONNECTICUT
Taxpayer Advocate Service
135 High Street, Stop 219
Hartford, CT 06103
P: 860.756.4555

DELAWARE
Taxpayer Advocate Service
1352 Marrows Road, Suite 203
Newark, DE 19711
P: 302.286.1654

DISTRICT OF COLUMBIA
Taxpayer Advocate Service
77 K Street, NE, Suite 1500
Washington, DC 20002
P: 202.874.7203

FLORIDA
Taxpayer Advocate Service
7850 Southwest 6th Court, Room 265
Plantation, FL 33324
P: 954.423.7677

Taxpayer Advocate Service
400 West Bay Street
Room 535A, MSTAS
Jacksonville, FL 32202
P: 904.665.1000

GEORGIA
Taxpayer Advocate Service
401 West Peachtree Street, NW
Room 510, Stop 202-D
Atlanta, GA 30308
P: 404.338.8099

HAWAII
Taxpayer Advocate Service
1099 Alakea Street
MS H2200, Floor 22
Honolulu, HI 96813
P: 808.566.2950

IDAHO
Taxpayer Advocate Service
550 West Fort Street, MS 1005
Boise, ID 83724
P: 208.363.8900

ILLINOIS
Taxpayer Advocate Service
230 South Dearborn Street
Room 2820, Stop 1005 CHI
Chicago, IL 60604
P: 312.292.3800

Taxpayer Advocate Service
3101 Constitution Drive
Stop 1005 SPD
Springfield, IL 62704
P: 217.862.6382

INDIANA
Taxpayer Advocate Service
575 North Pennsylvania Street
Room 581, Stop TA 771
Indianapolis, IN 46204
P: 317.685.7840

IOWA
Taxpayer Advocate Service
210 Walnut Street
Stop 1005 DSM, Room 483
Des Moines, IA 50309
P: 515.564.6888

KANSAS
Taxpayer Advocate Service
271 West 3rd Street North
Stop 1005 WIC, Suite 2000
Wichita, KS 67202
P: 316.352.7506

KENTUCKY
Taxpayer Advocate Service
600 Dr. Martin Luther King, Jr. Place, Room 325
Louisville, KY 40202
P: 502.582.6030

LOUISIANA
Taxpayer Advocate Service
1555 Poydras Street
Suite 220, Stop 2
New Orleans, LA 70112
P: 504.558.3001

MAINE
Taxpayer Advocate Service
68 Sewall Street, Room 313
Augusta, ME 04330
P: 207.622.8528

MARYLAND
Taxpayer Advocate Service
31 Hopkins Plaza, Room 900A
Baltimore, MD 21201
P: 410.962.2082

MASSACHUSETTS
Taxpayer Advocate Service
15 New Sudbury Street, Room 725
Boston, MA 02203
P: 617.316.2690

MICHIGAN
Taxpayer Advocate Service
500 Woodward, Stop 07, Suite 1000
Detroit, MI 48226
P: 313.628.3670

MINNESOTA
Taxpayer Advocate Service
30 East 7th Street, Suite 817
Stop 1005 STP
St. Paul, MN 55101
P: 651.312.7999

MISSISSIPPI
Taxpayer Advocate Service
100 West Capitol Street, Stop 31
Jackson, MS 39269
P: 601.292.4800

MISSOURI
Taxpayer Advocate Service
1222 Spruce Street
Stop 1005 STL, Room 10.314
St. Louis, MO 63103
P: 314.612.4610

MONTANA
Taxpayer Advocate Service
10 West 15th Street, Suite 2319
Helena, MT 59626
P: 406.441.1022

NEBRASKA
Taxpayer Advocate Service
1616 Capitol Avenue, Suite 182
Mail Stop 1005
Omaha, NE 68102
P: 402.233.7272

NEVADA
Taxpayer Advocate Service
110 City Parkway, Stop 1005 LVG
Las Vegas, NV 89106
P: 702.868.5179

NEW HAMPSHIRE
Taxpayer Advocate Service
80 Daniel Street, Room 403
Portsmouth, NH 03801
P: 603.433.0571

NEW JERSEY
Taxpayer Advocate Service
955 South Springfield Avenue, 3rd Floor
Springfield, NJ 07081
P: 973.921.4043

NEW MEXICO
Taxpayer Advocate Service
5338 Montgomery Boulevard, NE
Stop 1005 ALB
Albuquerque, NM 87109
P: 505.837.5505

NEW YORK
Taxpayer Advocate Service
11- Clinton Avenue, Suite 354
Albany, NY 12207
P: 518.427.5413

Taxpayer Advocate Service
100 Myrtle Avenue, 7th Floor
Brooklyn, NY 11201
P: 718.488.2080

Taxpayer Advocate Service
130 South Elmwood Avenue, Room 265
Buffalo, NY 14202
P: 716.961.5300

Taxpayer Advocate Service
290 Broadway, 5th Floor
Manhattan, NY 10007
P: 212.436.1011

NORTH CAROLINA
Taxpayer Advocate Service
4905 Koger Boulevard, Suite 102, MS1
Greensboro, NC 27407
P: 336.574.6119

NORTH DAKOTA
Taxpayer Advocate Service
657 Second Avenue North
Stop 1005 FAR, Room 244
Fargo, ND 58102
P: 701.237.8342

OHIO
Taxpayer Advocate Service
550 Main Street, Room 3530
Cincinnati, OH 45202
P: 513.263.3260

Taxpayer Advocate Service
1240 East 9th Street, Room 423
Cleveland, OH 44199
P: 216.522.7134

OKLAHOMA
Taxpayer Advocate Service
55 North Robinson, Stop 1005 OKC
Oklahoma City, OK 73102
P: 405.297.4055

OREGON
Taxpayer Advocate Service
100 Southwest Main Street, Stop O-405
Portland, OR 97204
P: 503.415.7003

PENNSYLVANIA
Taxpayer Advocate Service
600 Arch Street, Room 7426
Philadelphia, PA 19106
P: 215.861.1304

Taxpayer Advocate Service
1000 Liberty Avenue, Room 1400
Pittsburgh, PA 15222
P: 412.395.5987

PUERTO RICO
Taxpayer Advocate Service
48 Carr 165, Suite 2000
Guaynabo, PR 00968
P: 787.522.8600

RHODE ISLAND
Taxpayer Advocate Service
380 Westminster Street, 4th Floor
Providence, RI 02903
P: 401.528.1921

SOUTH CAROLINA
Taxpayer Advocate Service
1835 Assembly Street
Room 466, MDP 03
Columbia, SC 29201
P: 803.253.3029

SOUTH DAKOTA
Taxpayer Advocate Service
115 4th Avenue, SE
Stop 1005 ABE, Suite 413
Aberdeen, SD 57401
P: 605.377.1600

TENNESSEE
Taxpayer Advocate Service
801 Broadway, Stop 22
Nashville, TN 37203
P: 615.250.5000

TEXAS
Taxpayer Advocate Service
300 East 8th Street
Stop 1005 AUS, Room 136
Austin, TX 78701
P: 512.499.5875

Taxpayer Advocate Service
1114 Commerce Street
MC 1005 DAL, Room 1001
Dallas, TX 75243
P: 214.413.6500

Taxpayer Advocate Service
1919 Smith Street
MC 1005 HOU
Houston, TX 77002
P: 713.209.3660

UTAH
Taxpayer Advocate Service
50 South 200 East
Stop 1005 SLC
Salt Lake City, UT 84111
P: 801.799.6958

VERMONT
Taxpayer Advocate Service
199 Main Street, Room 300
Burlington, VT 05401
P: 802.859.1052

VIRGINIA
Taxpayer Advocate Service
400 North 8th Street
Room 916, Box 25
Richmond, VA 23219
P: 804.916.3501

WASHINGTON
Taxpayer Advocate Service
915 2nd Avenue, Stop W-405
Seattle, WA 98174
P: 206.220.6037

WEST VIRGINIA
Taxpayer Advocate Service
425 Juliana Street, Room 2019
Parkersburg, WV 26101
P: 304.420.8695

WISCONSIN
Taxpayer Advocate Service
211 West Wisconsin Avenue
Room 507, Stop 1005 MIL
Milwaukee, WI 53203
P: 414.231.2390

WYOMING
Taxpayer Advocate Service
5353 Yellowstone Road
Cheyenne, WY 82009
P: 307.633.0800

APPENDIX 13-A: HHS OFFICE OF THE SECRETARY REGIONAL OFFICES

The U.S. Department of Health and Human Services, Office of the Secretary provides regional oversight of all agency administered health and human service programs.

REGION I
U.S. Department of Health and Human Services
Office of the Secretary
John F. Kennedy Federal Building
Government Center, Room 2100
Boston, MA 02203
P: 617.656.1500

Note: This office serves the following states: Connecticut, Maine, Massachusetts, New Hampshire, Rhode Island, and Vermont.

REGION II
U.S. Department of Health and Human Services
Office of the Secretary
26 Federal Plaza, Room 3835
New York, NY 10278
P: 212.264.4600

Note: This office serves the following states: New York, New Jersey, Puerto Rico, and the U.S. Virgin Islands.

REGION III
U.S. Department of Health and Human Services
Office of the Secretary
3535 Market Street, Room 11480
Philadelphia, PA 19104
P; 215.596.6492

Note: This office serves the following states: Delaware, District of Columbia, Maryland, Pennsylvania, Virginia, and West Virginia.

REGION IV
U.S. Department of Health and Human Services
Office of the Secretary
101 Marietta Tower, Suite 1515
Atlanta, GA 30323
P: 404.331.2442

Note: This office serves the following states: Alabama, Florida, Georgia, Kentucky, Mississippi, North Carolina, South Carolina, and Tennessee.

REGION V
U.S. Department of Health and Human Services
Office of the Secretary
105 West Adams, 23rd Floor
Chicago, IL 60603
P: 312.353.5160

Note: This office serves the following states: Illinois, Indiana, Michigan, Minnesota, Ohio, and Wisconsin.

REGION VI
U.S. Department of Health and Human Services
1301 Young Street, Suite 1124
Dallas, TX 75202
P: 214.767.3301

Note: This office serves the following states: Arkansas, Louisiana, New Mexico, Oklahoma and Texas.

REGION VII
U.S. Department of Health and Human Services
Office of the Secretary
601 East 12th Street, Room 210
Kansas City, MO 64106
P: 816.426.2821

Note: This office serves the following states: Iowa, Kansas, Missouri, and Nebraska.

REGION VIII
U.S. Department of Health and Human Services
Office of the Secretary
1961 Stout Street, Room 325
Denver, CO 80294
P: 303.844.3372

Note: This office serves the following states: Colorado, Montana, North Dakota, South Dakota, Utah, and Wyoming.

REGION IX
U.S. Department of Health and Human Services
50 united Nations Plaza, Room 431
San Francisco, CA 94102
P: 415.437.8500

Note: This office serves the following states: Arizona, California, Guam, Hawaii, and Nevada.

REGION X

U.S. Department of Health and Human Services
Office of the Secretary
2201 Sixth Avenue, Room 1208
Seattle, WA 98121
P: 206.615.2010

Note: This office serves the following states: Alaska, Idaho,
Oregon, and Washington

APPENDIX 13-B: SNAP APPLICATION AND LOCAL OFFICE LOCATOR LINKS

To apply for the Supplemental Nutrition Assistance Program (SNAP), you must fill out an application and return it to your local SNAP office. Each state has a different application. The links below will help you find the State SNAP application and location of the local SNAP office.

ALABAMA
http://www.fns.usda.gov/sites/default/files/snap/alabama-office.pdf

ALASKA
http://www.fns.usda.gov/sites/default/files/snap/alaska-office.pdf

ARIZONA
http://www.fns.usda.gov/sites/default/files/snap/arizona-office.pdf

ARKANSAS
http://www.fns.usda.gov/sites/default/files/snap/arkansas-office.pdf

CALIFORNIA
http://www.fns.usda.gov/sites/default/files/snap/california-office.pdf

COLORADO
http://www.fns.usda.gov/sites/default/files/snap/colorado-office.pdf

CONNECTICUT
http://www.fns.usda.gov/sites/default/files/snap/connecticut-office.pdf

DELAWARE
http://www.fns.usda.gov/sites/default/files/snap/delaware-office.pdf

DISTRICT OF COLUMBIA
http://www.fns.usda.gov/sites/default/files/snap/dc-office.pdf

FLORIDA
http://www.fns.usda.gov/sites/default/files/snap/florida-office.pdf

GEORGIA
http://www.fns.usda.gov/sites/default/files/snap/georgia-office.pdf

HAWAII
http://www.fns.usda.gov/sites/default/files/snap/hawaii-office.pdf

IDAHO
http://www.fns.usda.gov/sites/default/files/snap/idaho-office.pdf

ILLINOIS
http://www.fns.usda.gov/sites/default/files/snap/illinois-office.pdf

INDIANA
http://www.fns.usda.gov/sites/default/files/snap/indiana-office.pdf

IOWA
http://www.fns.usda.gov/sites/default/files/snap/iowa-office.pdt

KANSAS
http://www.fns.usda.gov/sites/default/files/snap/kansas-office.pdf

KENTUCKY
http://www.fns.usda.gov/sites/default/files/snap/kentucky-office.pdf

LOUISIANA
http://www.fns.usda.gov/sites/default/files/snap/louisiana-office.pdf

MAINE
http://www.fns.usda.gov/sites/default/files/snap/maine-office.pdf

MARYLAND
http://www.fns.usda.gov/sites/default/files/snap/maryland-office.pdf

MASSACHUSETTS
http://www.fns.usda.gov/sites/default/files/snap/massachusetts-office.pdf

MICHIGAN
http://www.fns.usda.gov/sites/default/files/snap/michigan-office.pdf

MINNESOTA
http://www.fns.usda.gov/sites/default/files/snap/minnesota-office.pdf

MISSISSIPPI
http://www.fns.usda.gov/sites/default/files/snap/mississippi-office.pdf

MISSOURI
http://www.fns.usda.gov/sites/default/files/snap/missouri-office.pdf

MONTANA
http://www.fns.usda.gov/sites/default/files/snap/montana-office.pdf

NEBRASKA
http://www.fns.usda.gov/sites/default/files/snap/nebraska-office.pdf

NEVADA
http://www.fns.usda.gov/sites/default/files/snap/nevada-office.pdf

NEW HAMPSHIRE
http://www.fns.usda.gov/sites/default/files/snap/new-hampshire-office.pdf

NEW JERSEY
http://www.fns.usda.gov/sites/default/files/snap/new-jersey-office.pdf

NEW MEXICO
http://www.fns.usda.gov/sites/default/files/snap/new-mexico-office.pdf

NEW YORK
http://www.fns.usda.gov/sites/default/files/snap/new-york-office.pdf

NORTH CAROLINA
http://www.fns.usda.gov/sites/default/files/snap/north-carolina-office.pdf

NORTH DAKOTA
http://www.fns.usda.gov/sites/default/files/snap/north-dakota-office.pdf

OHIO
http://www.fns.usda.gov/sites/default/files/snap/ohio-office.pdf

OKLAHOMA
http://www.fns.usda.gov/sites/default/files/snap/oklahoma-office.pdf

OREGON
http://www.fns.usda.gov/sites/default/files/snap/oregon-office.pdf

PENNSYLVANIA
http://www.fns.usda.gov/sites/default/files/snap/pennsylvania-office.pdf

RHODE ISLAND
http://www.fns.usda.gov/sites/default/files/snap/rhode-island-office.pdf

SOUTH CAROLINA
http://www.fns.usda.gov/sites/default/files/snap/south-carolina-office.pdf

SOUTH DAKOTA
http://www.fns.usda.gov/sites/default/files/snap/south-dakota-office.pdf

TENNESSEE
http://www.fns.usda.gov/sites/default/files/snap/tennessee-office.pdf

TEXAS
http://www.fns.usda.gov/sites/default/files/snap/texas-office.pdf

UTAH
http://www.fns.usda.gov/sites/default/files/snap/utah-office.pdf

VERMONT
http://www.fns.usda.gov/sites/default/files/snap/vermont-office.pdf

VIRGINIA
http://www.fns.usda.gov/sites/default/files/snap/virginia-office.pdf

WASHINGTON
http://www.fns.usda.gov/sites/default/files/snap/washington-office.pdf

WEST VIRGINIA

http://www.fns.usda.gov/sites/default/files/snap/west-virginia-office.pdf

WISCONSIN

http://www.fns.usda.gov/sites/default/files/snap/wisconsin-office.pdf

WYOMING

http://www.fns.usda.gov/sites/default/files/snap/wyoming-office.pdf

APPENDIX 13-C: STATE SUBSTANCE ABUSE TREATMENT AGENCIES

The following agencies provide oversight of state-specific substance abuse treatment programs and resources while coordinating multi-level treatment efforts of the U.S. Department of Health and Human Services.

ALABAMA

Alabama Department of Mental Health
Division of Mental Health and Substance Abuse Services
100 North Union Street
P.O. Box 301410
Montgomery, AL 36130
P: 334.242.3961
I: http://www.mh.alabama.gov

ALASKA

Alaska Department of Health and Social Services
Division of Behavioral Health
3601 C Street, Suite 934
Anchorage, AK 99503
P: 907.269.3410
I: http://dhss.alaska.gov

ARIZONA

Arizona Department of Health Services
Division of Behavioral Health Services
150 North 18th Avenue, Suite 500
Phoenix, AZ 85007
P: 602.364.4566
I: http://www.azdhs.gov/bhs

ARKANSAS

Arkansas Department of Health Services
Division of Behavioral Health Services
305 South Palm Street
Little Rock, AR 72205
P: 501.686.9164
I: Not Provided

CALIFORNIA

California Department of Health Care Services
1501 Capitol Avenue
P.O. Box 997412
Sacramento, CA 95389
P: 916.440.7400
I: http://www.dhcs.ca.gov

COLORADO

Colorado Department of Human Services
Office of Behavioral Health
3824 West Princeton Circle
Denver, CO 80236
P: 303.866.7400
I: Not Provided

CONNECTICUT

Connecticut Department of Mental Health and Addiction Services
P.O. Box 341431
Hartford, CT 06134
P: 860.418.6700
I: http://www.dmhas.state.ct.us

DELAWARE

Delaware Health and Social Services
Division of Substance Abuse and Mental Health
1901 North DuPont Highway, Main Building, 1st Floor
New Castle, DE 19720
P: 302.255.9404
I: http://www.dhss.delaware.gov

DISTRICT OF COLUMBIA

District of Columbia Department of Health
Addiction Prevention Recovery Administration
1300 First Street, NE, 3rd Floor
Washington, DC 20002
P: 202.727.8946
I: http://www.doh.dc.gov

FLORIDA

Florida Department of Children and Families
Substance Abuse and Mental Health Program Office
1317 Winewood Boulevard, Building 6, Room 275
Tallahassee, FL 32399
P; 850.921.8461
I: http://www.myflfamilies.com

GEORGIA

Georgia Department of Behavioral Health and Developmental Disabilities
Office of Addictive Diseases
2 Peachtree Street, NW, Suite 22-273
Atlanta, GA 30303
P: 404.657.2331
I: http://dbhdd.georgia.gov

HAWAII

Hawaii Department of Health
Alcohol and Drug Abuse Division
Kakuhhewa Building
601 Kamokila Boulevard, Room 360
Kapolei, HI 96707
P: 808.692.7507
I: http://hawaii.gov/health

IDAHO

Idaho Department of Health and Welfare
Division of Behavioral Health
Substance Use Disorder Services
450 West State Street, 3rd Floor
P.O. Box 83720
Boise, ID 83720
P: 208.334.6676
I: http://www.healthandwelfare.idaho.gov

ILLINOIS

Illinois Department of Human Services
Division of Alcohol and Substance Abuse
100 West Randolph Street, Suite 5-600
Chicago, IL 60601
P: 312.814.2300
I: http://www.dhs.state.il.us

INDIANA

Indiana Family and Social Services Administration
Division of Mental Health and Addiction
402 West Washington Street, Room W353
Indianapolis, IN 46204
P: 317.232.7845
I: http://www.in.gov/fssa/dmha/index.htm

IOWA

Iowa Department of Public Health
Division of Behavioral Health
321 East 12th Street, 4th Floor
Des Moines, IA 50319
P: 515.281.4417
I: http://www.idph.state.ia.us

KANSAS

Kansas Department for Aging and Disability Services
Division of Behavioral Health Services
Community Services and Programs
915 South West Harrison Street, 9th Floor South
Topeka, KS 66612
P: 785.368.6245
I: http://www.kdads.ks.gov

KENTUCKY

Kentucky Cabinet for Health and Family Services
Division of Behavioral Health
100 Fair Oaks Lane, 4E-D
Frankfort, KY 40621
P: 502.564.4456
I: http://www.odcp.ky.gov

LOUISIANA

Louisiana Department of Health and Hospitals
Office of Behavioral Health
628 North 4th Street
P.O. Box 4049
Baton Rouge, LA 70821
P: 225.342.6717
I: http://new.dhh.louisiana.gov

MAINE

Maine Department of Health and Human Services
Office of Substance Abuse and Mental Health Services
41 Anthony Avenue
11 State House Station
Augusta, ME 04333
P: 207.287.2595
I: http://www.maine.gov/dhhs/samhs

MARYLAND

Maryland Department of Health and Mental Hygiene
Alcohol and Drug Abuse Administration
55 Wade Avenue
Catonsville, MD 21228
P: 410.402.8615
I: http://www.adaa.dhmh.maryland.gov

MASSACHUSETTS

Massachusetts Department of Public Health
Bureau of Substance Abuse Services
250 Washington Street, 3rd Floor
Boston, MA 02108
P: 617.624.5124
I: http://www.mass.gov/dph/bsas

MICHIGAN

Michigan Department of Community Health
Behavioral Health and Developmental Disabilities
Administration
Bureau of Hospitals and Administrative Operations
320 South Walnut Street
Lansing, MI 48913
P: 517.335.0196
I: http://www.michigan.gov/mdch-bsaas

MINNESOTA

Minnesota Department of Human Services
Chemical and Mental Health Services Administration
Alcohol and Drug Abuse Division
P.O. Box 64977
St. Paul, MN 55164
P: 651.431.2467
I: http://www.mn.gov/dhs

MISSISSIPPI
Mississippi Department of Mental health
Bureau of Alcohol and Drug Abuse
239 North Lamar Street
1101 Robert E. Lee Building
Jackson, MS 39201
P: 601.359.6176
I: http://www.dmh.state.ms.us

MISSOURI
Missouri Department of Mental Health
Division of Alcohol and Drug Abuse
1706 East Elm Street
P.O. Box 687
Jefferson City, MO 65102
P: 573.751.9499
I: http://dmh.mo.gov/ada

MONTANA
Montana Department of Public Health and Human Services
Addictive and Mental Disorders Division
Chemical Dependency Bureau
P.O. Box 202905
Helena, MI 59620
P: 406.444.6981
I: http://www.dphhs.mt.gov/amdd

NEBRASKA
Nebraska Department of Health and Human Services
Division of Behavioral Health
301 Centennial Mall
P.O. Box 95026
Lincoln, NE 68509
P: 402.471.8553
I: http://dhhs.ne.gov

NEVADA
Nevada Department of Health and Human Services
Division of Mental Health and Developmental Services
Substance Abuse Prevention and Treatment Agency
4126 Technology Way, 2nd Floor
Carson City, NV 89706
P: 775.684.4190
I: http://mhds.state.nv.us

NEW HAMPSHIRE
New Hampshire Department of Health and Human Services
Division of Community Based Care Services
Bureau of Drug and Alcohol Services
105 Pleasant Street, 3rd Floor, N
Concord, NH 03301
P: 603.271.6110
I: http://www.dhhs.state.nh.us

NEW JERSEY
New Jersey Department of Human Services
Division of Mental Health and Addiction Services
50 East State Street
P.O. Box 727
Trenton, NJ 06862
P: 609.777.0711
I: http://www.state.nj.us/humanservices

NEW MEXICO
New Mexico Human Services Department
Behavioral Health Services Division
37 Plaza La Prensa
P.O. Box 2348
Santa Fe, NM 87504
P: 505.476.9295
I: http://www.hsd.state.nm.us/bhsd

NEW YORK
New York State Office of Alcohol and Substance Abuse Services
1450 Western Avenue
New York, NY 12203
P: 518.457.2061
I: http://www.oasas.ny.gov

NORTH CAROLINA
North Carolina Department of Health and Human Services
Division of Mental Health Developmental Disabilities and Substance Abuse
3007 Mail Service Center
Raleigh, NC 27699
P: 919.733.4670
I: http://www.ncdhhs.gov/mhddsas

NORTH DAKOTA
North Dakota Department of Human Services
Division of Mental Health and Substance Abuse Services
1237 West Divide Avenue, Suite 1C
Bismarck, ND 58501
P: 701.328.8924
I: http://www.nd.gov/dhs/services/mentalhealth

OHIO
Ohio Department of Mental Health and Addiction Services
30 East Broad Street, 36th Floor
Columbus, OH 43215
P: 614.466.2596
I: http://mha.ohio.gov

OKLAHOMA

Oklahoma Department of Mental Health and Substance
Abuse Services
1200 Northeast 13th Street
P.O. Box 53277
Oklahoma City, OK 73152
P: 405.522.3877
I: http://ok.gov/odmhsas

OREGON

Oregon Department of Human Services
Addiction and Mental Health Division
500 Summer Street, NE, E-86
Salem, OR 97301
P: 503.945.5879
I: http://www.oregon.gov/oha/amh/index.shtml

PENNSYLVANIA

Pennsylvania Department of Drug and Alcohol Programs
Health and Welfare Building
625 Forster Street, Room 903
Harrisburg, PA 17120
P: 717.214.1937
I: Not Provided

PUERTO RICO

Administracion de Servicios de Salud Mental y Contra la
Adiccion
P.O. Box 6070867
Bayamon, PR 00960
P: 787.763.7575
I: Not Provided

RHODE ISLAND

Rhode Island Department of Behavioral Healthcare
Services, Developmental Disabilities and Hospitals
14 Harrington Road, Barry Hall
Cranston, RI 02920
P: 401.462.2339
I: http://www.bhddh.ri.gov/sa

SOUTH CAROLINA

South Carolina Department of Alcohol and Drug Abuse
Services
2414 Bull Street, Suite 301
Columbia, SC 29201
P: 803.896.5555
I: http://www.doadas.state.sc.us

SOUTH DAKOTA

South Dakota Department of Social Services
700 Governor's Drive
Pierre, SD 57501
P: 605.773.3165
I: http://dss.sd.gov/behavioralhealthservices

TENNESSEE

Tennessee Department of Mental Health and Substance
Abuse Services
601 Mainstream Drive
Nashville, TN 37243
P: 615.532.6500
I: http://tn.gov/mental/a&d/index.htm

TEXAS

Texas Department of State Health Services
Mental Health and Substance Abuse Division
P.O. Box 149397, Mail Code 2053
Austin, TX 78714
P: 512.206.5968
I: http://www.dshs.state.tx.us

UTAH

Utah Department of Human Services
Division of Substance Abuse and Mental Health
195 North 1950 West
Salt Lake City, UT 84116
P: 801.538.4025
I: http://www.dsamh.utah.gov

VERMONT

Vermont Agency of Human Services
Alcohol and Drug Abuse Program Division
108 Cherry Street, P.O. Box 70
Burlington, VT 05402
P: 802.951.1258
I: http://healthvermont.gov

VIRGINIA

Virginia Department of Behavioral Health and
Developmental Services
1220 Bank Street, 13th Floor
P.O. Box 1797
Richmond, VA 23218
P: 804.786.3921
I: http://www.dmhmrsas.virginia.gov

WASHINGTON

Washington Department of Social and Health Services
Aging and Disability Services Administration
Division of Behavioral Health and Recovery
P.O. Box 45330
Olympia, WA 98504
P: 360.725.3700
I: http://www.dshs.wa.gov/dasa

WEST VIRGINIA

West Virginia Department of Health and Human Services
Bureau of Behavioral Health and Health Facilities
Division on Alcohol and Drug Abuse
350 Capitol Street, Room 350
Charleston, WV 25301
P: 304.356.4796
I: http://www.dhhr.wv.gov

WISCONSIN

Wisconsin Department of Health Services
Division of Mental Health and Substance Abuse Services
Bureau of Prevention Treatment and Recovery
1 West Wilson Street, Room 850
Madison, WI 53703
P: 608.266.1351
I: http://dhs.wisconsin.gov/substabuse

WYOMING

Wyoming Department of Health
Behavioral Health Division
6101 Yellowstone Road, Suite 186E
Cheyenne, WY 82002
P: 307.777.8763
I: http://health.wyo.gov/mhsa/index.html

APPENDIX 14-A: U.S. SMALL BUSINESS ADMINISTRATION DISTRICT & BRANCH OFFICES

The U.S. Small Business Administration helps Americans start, build and grow their businesses through an extensive network of district and branch offices.

ALABAMA
U.S. Small Business Administration
Alabama District Office
801 Tom Martin Drive, Suite 201
Birmingham, AL 35211
P: 205.290.7101

ALASKA
U.S. Small Business Administration
Alaska District Office
420 L Street, Suite 300
Anchorage, AK 99501
P: 907.271.4022

ARIZONA
U.S. Small Business Administration
Arizona District Office
2828 North Central Avenue, Suite 800
Phoenix, AZ 85004
P: 602.745.7200

ARKANSAS
U.S. Small Business Administration
Arkansas District Office
2120 Riverfront Drive, Suite 250
Little Rock, AR 72202
P: 501.324.7379

CALIFORNIA
U.S. Small Business Administration
Fresno District Office
801 R Street, Suite 201
Fresno, CA 93721
P: 559.487.5791

U.S. Small Business Administration
Los Angeles District Office
330 North Brand, Suite 1200
Glendale, CA 91203
P: 818.552.3215

U.S. Small Business Administration
Sacramento District Office
6501 Sylvan Road, Suite 100
Citrus Heights, CA 95601
P: 916.735.1700

U.S. Small Business Administration
San Diego District Office
550 West C Street, Suite 550
San Diego, CA 92101
P: 619.557.7250

U.S. Small Business Administration
San Francisco District Office
455 Market Street, 6th Floor
San Francisco, CA 94105
P: 415.744.6820

U.S. Small Business Administration
Santa Ana District Office
200 West Santa Ana Boulevard, Suite 700
Santa Ana, CA 92701
P: 714.550.7420

COLORADO
U.S. Small Business Administration
Colorado District Office
721 19th Street, Suite 426
Denver, CO 80202
P: 303.844.2607

CONNECTICUT
U.S. Small Business Administration
Connecticut District Office
330 Main Street, 2nd Floor
Hartford, CT 06106
P: 860.240.4700

DELAWARE
U.S. Small Business Administration
Delaware District Office
1007 North Orange Street, Suite 1120
Wilmington, DE 19801
P: 302.573.6294

DISTRICT OF COLUMBIA
U.S. Small Business Administration
Washington Metropolitan Area District Office
740 15th Street, NW, Suite 300
Washington, DC 20005
P: 202.272.0345

FLORIDA
U.S. Small Business Administration
North Florida District Office
7825 Baymeadows Way, Suite 1008
Jacksonville, FL 32256
P: 904.443.1900

U.S. Small Business Administration
South Florida District Office
100 South Biscayne Boulevard, 7th Floor
Miami, FL 33131
P: 305.536.5521

GEORGIA
U.S. Small Business Administration
Georgia District Office
233 Peachtree Street, NE, Suite 1900
Atlanta, GA 30303
P: 404.331.0100

HAWAII
U.S. Small Business Administration
Hawaii District Office
500 Ala Moana Boulevard, Suite 1-306
Honolulu, HI 96813
P: 808.541.2990

IDAHO
U.S. Small Business Administration
Boise District Office
380 East Parkcenter Boulevard, Suite 330
Boise, ID 83706
P: 208.334.9004

ILLINOIS
U.S. Small Business Administration
Illinois District Office
500 West Madison Street, Suite 1150
Chicago, IL 60661
P: 312.353.4528

U.S. Small Business Administration
Illinois Branch Office
3330 Ginger Creek Road, Suite B
Springfield, IL 62711
P: 217.793.5020

INDIANA
U.S. Small Business Administration
Indiana District Office
8500 Keystone Crossing, Suite 400
Indianapolis, IN 46240
P: 317.226.7272

IOWA
U.S. Small Business Administration
Des Moines District Office
210 Walnut Street, Room 749
Des Moines, IA 50309
P: 515.284.4422

U.S. Small Business Administration
Cedar Rapids Branch Office
2750 1st Avenue, NE, Suite 350
Cedar rapids, IA 52402
P: 319.362.6405

KANSAS
U.S. Small Business Administration
Wichita District Office
271 West 3rd Street, N, Suite 188
Wichita, KS 67202
P: 316.269.6616

KENTUCKY
U.S. Small Business Administration
Kentucky District Office
600 Dr. Martin Luther King, Jr. Place, Room 188
Louisville, KY 40202
P: 502.582.5971

LOUISIANA
U.S. Small Business Administration
New Orleans District Office
365 Canal Street, Suite 2820
New Orleans, LA 70130
P: 504.589.6685

MAINE
U.S. Small Business Administration
Maine District Office
68 Sewall Street, Room 512
Augusta, ME 04330
P: 207.622.8551

MARYLAND
U.S. Small Business Administration
Baltimore District Office
10 South Howard Street, Suite 6220
Baltimore, MD 21201
P: 410.962.6195

MASSACHUSETTS
U.S. Small Business Administration
Massachusetts District Office
10 Causeway Street, Room 265
Boston, MA 02222
P: 617.565.5590

U.S. Small Business Administration
Springfield Branch Office
One Federal Street, Building 101-R
Springfield, MA 01105
P: 413.785.0484

MICHIGAN
U.S. Small Business Administration
Michigan District Office
477 Michigan Avenue, Suite 515
Detroit, MI 48226
P: 313.226.6075

MINNESOTA
U.S. Small Business Administration
Minneapolis District Office
100 North Sixth Street, Suite 210-C
Minneapolis, MN 55403
P: 612.370.2324

MISSISSIPPI
U.S. Small Business Administration
Mississippi District Office
210 East Capitol Street, Suite 900
Jackson, MS 39201
P: 601.965.4378

U.S. Small Business Administration
Gulfport Branch Office
2510 14th Street, Suite 103
Gulfport, MS 39501
P: 228.863.4449

MISSOURI
U.S. Small Business Administration
Kansas City District Office
1000 Walnut, Suite 500
Kansas City, MO 64106
P: 816.426.4900

U.S. Small Business Administration
Springfield Branch Office
830 East Primrose, Suite 101
Springfield, MO 65807
P: 417.890.8501

U.S. Small Business Administration
St. Louis District Office
1222 Spruce Street, Suite 10.103
St. Louis, MO 63103
P: 314.539.6660

MONTANA
U.S. Small Business Administration
Montana District Office
10 West 15th Street, Suite 1100
Helena, MT 59626
P: 406.441.1081

NEBRASKA
U.S. Small Business Administration
Nebraska District Office
10675 Bedford Avenue, Suite 100
Omaha, NE 68134
P: 402.221.3620

NEVADA
U.S. Small Business Administration
Nevada District Office
400 South 4th Street, Suite 250
Las Vegas, NV 89101
P: 702.388.6611

U.S. Small Business Administration
Nevada District Office (Alternate Work Site)
745 West Moana Lane, Suite 375
Reno, NV 89509
P: 775.827.4923

NEW HAMPSHIRE
U.S. Small Business Administration
New Hampshire District Office
55 Pleasant Street, Suite 3101
Concord, NH 03301
P: 603.225.1400

NEW JERSEY
U.S. Small Business Administration
New Jersey District Office
Two Gateway Center, Suite 320
Newark, NJ 07102
P: 973.645.2434

NEW MEXICO
U.S. Small Business Administration
New Mexico District Office
625 Silver, SW, Suite 320
Albuquerque, NM 78102
P: 505.248.8225

NEW YORK
U.S. Small Business Administration
Buffalo District Office
130 South Elmwood Avenue, Suite 540
Buffalo, NY 14202
P: 716.551.4301

U.S. Small Business Administration
Elmira Branch Office
333 East Water Street, 4th Floor
Elmira, NY 14901
P: 607.734.8130

U.S. Small Business Administration
Long Island Branch Office
350 Motor Parkway, Suite 109
Hauppauge, NY 11788
P: 631.454.0750

U.S. Small Business Administration
New York District Office
26 Federal Plaza, Suite 3100
New York, NY 10278
P: 212.264.4354

U.S. Small Business Administration
Rochester Branch Office
100 State Street, Room 410
Rochester, NY 14614
P: 585.263.6700

U.S. Small Business Administration
Syracuse District Office
224 Harrison Street, Suite 506
Syracuse, NY 13202
P: 315.471.9393

NORTH CAROLINA
U.S. Small Business Administration
North Carolina District Office
6302 Fairview Road, Suite 300
Charlotte, NC 28210
P: 704.344.6563

NORTH DAKOTA
U.S. Small Business Administration
North Dakota District Office
675 2nd Avenue, N, Room 218
Fargo, ND 58108
P: 701.239.5131

OHIO
U.S. Small Business Administration
Cleveland District Office
1350 Euclid Avenue, Suite 211
Cleveland, OH 44115
P: 216.522.4180

U.S. Small Business Administration
Cincinnati Branch Office
525 Vine Street, Suite 1030
Cincinnati, OH 45202
P: 513.684.2814

U.S. Small Business Administration
Columbus District Office
401 North Front Street, Suite 200
Columbus, OH 43215
P: 614.469.6860

OKLAHOMA
U.S. Small Business Administration
Oklahoma City District Office
301 Northwest 6th Street, Suite 116
Oklahoma City, OK 73102
P: 405.609.8000

OREGON
U.S. Small Business Administration
Portland District Office
601 Southwest Second Avenue, Suite 950
Portland, OR 97204
P: 503.326.2682

PENNSYLVANIA
U.S. Small Business Administration
Harrisburg Branch Office
2601 North 3rd Street
Harrisburg, PA 17110
P: 717.782.3840

U.S. Small Business Administration
Philadelphia District Office
1150 First Avenue, Suite 1001
King of Prussia, PA 19406
P: 610.382.3062

U.S. Small Business Administration
Pittsburgh District Office
411 Seventh Avenue, Suite 1450
Pittsburgh, PA 15219
P: 412.395.6560

U.S. Small Business Administration
Wilkes-Barre Branch Office
7 North Wilkes-Bare Boulevard
Wilkes-Barre, PA 18702
P: Not Provided

PUERTO RICO
U.S. Small Business Administration
Puerto Rico District Office
273 Ponce de Leon Avenue
Plaza Scotiabank, Suite 510
San Juan, PR 00917
P: 787.766.5572

RHODE ISLAND
U.S. Small Business Administration
Rhode Island District Office
380 Westminster Street, Room 511
Providence, RI 02903
P: 401.528.4561

SOUTH CAROLINA
U.S. Small Business Administration
South Carolina District Office
1835 Assembly Street, Room 1425
Columbia, SC 29201
P. 803.765.5377

SOUTH DAKOTA
U.S. Small Business Administration
South Dakota District Office
2329 North Career Avenue, Suite 105
Sioux Falls, SD 57107
P: 605.330.4243

TENNESSEE
U.S. Small Business Administration
Tennessee District Office
50 Vantage Way, Suite 201
Nashville, TN 37228
P: 615.736.5881

U.S. Small Business Administration
Tennessee District Office (Alternate Work Site)
555 Beale Street
Memphis, TN 38103
P: 901.526.9300

TEXAS
U.S. Small Business Administration
Corpus Christi Branch Office
3649 Leopard Street, Suite 411
Corpus Christi, TX 78408
P: 361.879.0017

U.S. Small Business Administration
Dallas District Office
4300 Amon Carter Boulevard, Suite 114
Fort Worth, TX 76115
P: 817.684.5500

U.S. Small Business Administration
El Paso District Office
211 North Florence, Suite 201
El Paso, TX 79901
P: 915.834.4600

U.S. Small Business Administration
Houston District Office
8701 South Gessner Drive, Suite 1200
Houston, TX 77074
P: 713.773.6500

U.S. Small Business Administration
Lower Rio Grande Valley District Office
222 East Van Buren Avenue, Suite 500
Harlingen, TX 78550
P: 956.427.8533

U.S. Small Business Administration
Lubbock District Office
1205 Texas Avenue, Room 408
Lubbock, TX 79401
P: 806.472.7462

U.S. Small Business Administration
San Antonio District Office
17319 San Pedro, Building 2, Suite 200
San Antonio, TX 78232
P: 210.403.5900

UTAH
U.S. Small Business Administration
Utah District Office
125 South State Street, Room 2227
Salt Lake City, UT 84138
P: 801.524.3209

VERMONT
U.S. Small Business Administration
Vermont District Office
87 State Street, Room 205
Montpelier, VT 05601
P: 802.828.4422

VIRGINIA
U.S. Small Business Administration
Richmond District Office
400 North 8th Street, Suite 1150
Richmond, VA 23219
P: 804.771.2400

WASHINGTON

U.S. Small Business Administration
Seattle District Office
2401 Fourth Avenue, Suite 450
Seattle, WA 98121
P: 206.553.7310

U.S. Small Business Administration
Spokane Branch Office
801 West Riverside Avenue, Suite 444
Spokane, WA 99201
P: 509.353.2800

WEST VIRGINIA

U.S. Small Business Administration
West Virginia District Office
320 West Pike Street, Suite 330
Clarksburg, WV 26301
P: 304.623.5631

U.S. Small Business Administration
Charleston Branch Office
405 Capitol Street, Suite 412
Charleston, WV 25301
P: 304.347.5220

WISCONSIN

U.S. Small Business Administration
Wisconsin District Office
740 Regent Street, Suite 100
Madison, WI 53715
P: 608.441.5263

U.S. Small Business Administration
Milwaukee Branch Office
310 West Wisconsin Avenue, Room 400
Milwaukee, WI 53203
P: 414.297.3941

WYOMING

U.S. Small Business Administration
Wyoming District Office
100 East B Street
P.O. Box 44001
Casper, WY 82602
P: 307.261.6500

APPENDIX 15-A: ADDITIONAL RESOURCE MATERIALS

A compilation of Publications.USA.gov, the publications and brochures listed below were selected for inclusion because of their ability to provide information and assistance on a broad range of topics.

CONSUMER PROTECTION

2017 Consumer Action Handbook
http://publications.usa.gov/USAPubs.php?PubID=5131

Billed for Merchandise You Never Received? Here's What to Do
http://publications.usa.gov/USAPubs.php?PubID=140

Consumer Information Catalog
http://publications.usa.gov/USAPubs.php?PubID=9801

For Young Adults and Teens: Quick Tips for Managing Your Money
http://publications.usa.gov/USAPubs.php?PubID=6121

Guide to Assisting Identity Theft Victims
http://publications.usa.gov/USAPubs.php?PubID=2299

Identity Theft: Safeguard Your Personal Information
http://publications.usa.gov/USAPubs.php?PubID=856

Identity Theft: What to Know, What to Do
http://publications.usa.gov/USAPubs.php?PubID=645

Online Banking, Bill Paying and Shopping: 10 Ways to Protect Your Money
http://publications.usa.gov/USAPubs.php?PubID=6081

Practical Solutions for Protecting Your Money
http://publications.usa.gov/USAPubs.php?PubID=6127

Prepaid Phone Cards: What Consumers Should Know
http://publications.usa.gov/USAPubs.php?PubID=2235

Taking Charge: What to Do If Your Identity Is Stolen
http://publications.usa.gov/USAPubs.php?PubID=3326

Tax-Related Identity Theft
http://publications.usa.gov/USAPubs.php?PubID=2295

Tips for Avoiding Bill Shock on Your Mobile Phone
http://publications.usa.gov/USAPubs.php?PubID=2236

Understanding Your Telephone Bill
http://publications.usa.gov/USAPubs.php?PubID=830

Unwrapping Gift Cards: Know the Terms and Avoid Surprises
http://publications.usa.gov/USAPubs.php?PubID=6144

What You Need To Know: New Rules for Gift Cards
http://publications.usa.gov/USAPubs.php?PubID=307

EDUCATION

Application for Federal Student Aid 2016-17
http://publications.usa.gov/USAPubs.php?PubID=833

Banking Basics
http://publications.usa.gov/USAPubs.php?PubID=849

Building Wealth: A Beginner's Guide to Securing Your Financial Future
http://publications.usa.gov/USAPubs.php?PubID=289

Certificates: A Fast Track to Careers
http://publications.usa.gov/USAPubs.php?PubID=892

College Preparation Checklist
http://publications.usa.gov/USAPubs.php?PubID=220

Federal Student Aid Grant Programs Fact Sheet
http://publications.usa.gov/USAPubs.php?PubID=224

Federal Student Aid Loan Programs Fact Sheet
http://publications.usa.gov/USAPubs.php?PubID=225

Federal Student Aid for Adult Students
http://publications.usa.gov/USAPubs.php?PubID=930

Funding Your Education: The Guide to Federal Student Aid
http://publications.usa.gov/USAPubs.php?PubID=2274

Take Charge of Your Future: Get the Education and Training You Need
http://publications.usa.gov/USAPubs.php?PubID=2275

Your Federal Student Loans: Learn the Basics and Manage Your Debt
http://publications.usa.gov/USAPubs.php?PubID=509

EMPLOYMENT

Apprenticeship: Earn While You Learn
http://publications.usa.gov/USAPubs.php?PubID=2293

Career Myths and How to Debunk Them
http://publications.usa.gov/USAPubs.php?PubID=237

Careers in Wind Energy
http://publications.usa.gov/USAPubs.php?PubID=238

Catch the Spirit: A Student's Guide to Community Service
http://publications.usa.gov/USAPubs.php?PubID=5483

College to Career: Projected Job Openings in Occupations that Typically Require an Bachelor's Degree
http://publications.usa.gov/USAPubs.php?PubID=2294

Consulting Careers: Profiles of Three Occupations
http://publications.usa.gov/USAPubs.php?PubID=239

Employee Workplace Rights
http://publications.usa.gov/USAPubs.php?PubID=5531

Employment Background Checks
http://publications.usa.gov/USAPubs.php?PubID=240

Employment Matchmakers: Pairing People with Work
http://publications.usa.gov/USAPubs.php?PubID=241

Employment Options: Tips for Older Job Seekers
http://publications.usa.gov/USAPubs.php?PubID=811

Employment, Trends, and Training in Information Technology
http://publications.usa.gov/USAPubs.php?PubID=242

Environmental Jobs for Scientists and Engineers
http://publications.usa.gov/USAPubs.php?PubID=243

Skills to Getting a Job: What Young People with Disabilities Need to Know
http://publications.usa.gov/USAPubs.php?PubID=244

Flexible Work: Adjusting the When and Where of Your Job
http://publications.usa.gov/USAPubs.php?PubID=247

Focused Jobseeking: A Measured Approach to Looking for Work
http://publications.usa.gov/USAPubs.php?PubID=248

Getting Back to Work: Returning to the Labor Force After an Absence
http://publications.usa.gov/USAPubs.php?PubID=1339

Getting Uncle Sam to Enforce Your Civil Rights
http://publications.usa.gov/USAPubs.php?PubID=502

Handy Reference Guide to the Fair Labor Standards Act
http://publications.usa.gov/USAPubs.php?PubID=3097

High Wages After High School – Without a Bachelor's Degree
http://publications.usa.gov/USAPubs.php?PubID=850

House Work: Jobs in Residential Upkeep
http://publications.usa.gov/USAPubs.php?PubID=249

How to Get a Job in the Federal Government
http://publications.usa.gov/USAPubs.php?PubID=1338

Informational Interviewing: Get the Inside Scoop on Careers
http://publications.usa.gov/USAPubs.php?PubID=250

Interviewing: Seizing the Opportunity and the Job
http://publications.usa.gov/USAPubs.php?PubID=1321

Making the Move to Managing Your Own Personal Assistance Services
http://publications.usa.gov/USAPubs.php?PubID=6092

Resumes, Applications, and Cover Letters
http://publications.usa.gov/USAPubs.php?PubID=1207

The 2010-20 Job Outlook in Brief
http://publications.usa.gov/USAPubs.php?PubID=569

Working Abroad: Finding International Internships and Entry-Level Jobs
http://publications.usa.gov/USAPubs.php?PubID=255

Working Vacations: Jobs in Tourism and Leisure
http://publications.usa.gov/USAPubs.php?PubID=256

FAMILY

Adventures in Parenting
http://publications.usa.gov/USAPubs.php?PubID=2189

Domestic Violence: Older Women Can be Victims Too
http://publications.usa.gov/USAPubs.php?PubID=635

Helping Your Child through Early Adolescence
http://publications.usa.gov/USAPubs.php?PubID=766

How the Child Welfare System Works
http://publications.usa.gov/USAPubs.php?PubID=1139

Helping Your Child Become a Reader
http://publications.usa.gov/USAPubs.php?PubID=5605

Helping Your Child Become a Responsible Citizen
http://publications.usa.gov/USAPubs.php?PubID=800

Helping Your Child Learn History
http://publications.usa.gov/USAPubs.php?PubID=799

Helping Your Child Learn Mathematics
http://publications.usa.gov/USAPubs.php?PubID=3222

Helping Your Child Learn Science
http://publications.usa.gov/USAPubs.php?PubID=5321

Helping Your Child Succeed in School
http://publications.usa.gov/USAPubs.php?PubID=3206

Helping Your Child with Homework
http://publications.usa.gov/USAPubs.php?PubID=3262

Helping Your Preschool Child
http://publications.usa.gov/USAPubs.php?PubID=227

FEDERAL PROGRAMS

ADA: Know Your Rights – Returning Service Members with Disabilities
http://publications.usa.gov/USAPubs.php?PubID=607

Americans with Disabilities Act (ADA): Questions and Answers
http://publications.usa.gov/USAPubs.php?PubID=5333

An Employee's Guide to Health Benefits Under COBRA
http://publications.usa.gov/USAPubs.php?PubID=5936

Citizenship Foundation Skills and Knowledge Clusters
http://publications.usa.gov/USAPubs.php?PubID=521

Ending Hunger, Improving Nutrition, Combating Obesity
http://publications.usa.gov/USAPubs.php?PubID=547

Federal Benefits for Veterans, Dependents and Survivors
http://publications.usa.gov/USAPubs.php?PubID=1050

For Public Sale: Used Federal Government Personal Property
http://publications.usa.gov/USAPubs.php?PubID=3238

Guide to Disability Rights Laws
http://publications.usa.gov/USAPubs.php?PubID=5533

Handbook on Child Support Enforcement
http://publications.usa.gov/USAPubs.php?PubID=5001

How to Get Food Help
http://publications.usa.gov/USAPubs.php?PubID=549

Learn About the United States: Quick Civics Lessons for the Naturalization Test
http://publications.usa.gov/USAPubs.php?PubID=523

Medicare & You 2014
http://publications.usa.gov/USAPubs.php?PubID=2257

Medicare Coverage of Kidney Dialysis and Kidney Transplant Services
http://publications.usa.gov/USAPubs.php?PubID=5707

Medicare Hospice Benefits
http://publications.usa.gov/USAPubs.php?PubID=5652

Medicare and Your Mental Health Benefits
http://publications.usa.gov/USAPubs.php?PubID=5689

National Sellers List
http://publications.usa.gov/USAPubs.php?PubID=3298

Pathways to U.S. Citizenship
http://publications.usa.gov/USAPubs.php?PubID=527

Supplemental Nutrition Assistance Program
http://publications.usa.gov/USAPubs.php?PubID=551

The Citizen's Almanac
http://publications.usa.gov/USAPubs.php?PubID=529

Veterans Health Benefits Guide
http://publications.usa.gov/USAPubs.php?PubID=861

Welcome to the United States: A Guide for New Immigrants
http://publications.usa.gov/USAPubs.php?PubID=1340

You or Someone You Know May be Eligible for Help with Home Heating and Cooling Bills
http://publications.usa.gov/USAPubs.php?PubID=828

Your Guide to Medicare Medical Savings Account Plans
http://publications.usa.gov/USAPubs.php?PubID=864

Your Guide to Medicare Prescription Drug Coverage
http://publications.usa.gov/USAPubs.php?PubID=862

Your Rights to Federal Records
http://publications.usa.gov/USAPubs.php?PubID=6080

FOOD

Choose Smart Choose Health
http://publications.usa.gov/USAPubs.php?PubID=210

Cooking for Groups: A Volunteer's Guide to Food Safety
http://publications.usa.gov/USAPubs.php?PubID=5700

Delicious Heart Healthy Latino Recipes
http://publications.usa.gov/USAPubs.php?PubID=211

Dietary Supplements
http://publications.usa.gov/USAPubs.php?PubID=5801

Focus on Fruits
http://publications.usa.gov/USAPubs.php?PubID=649

Food Safety at Home
http://publications.usa.gov/USAPubs.php?PubID=5954

Got Your Dairy Today?
http://publications.usa.gov/USAPubs.php?PubID=653

Heart Healthy Home Cooking African American Style – With Every Heartbeat is Life
http://publications.usa.gov/USAPubs.php?PubID=214

Is It Done Yet?
http://publications.usa.gov/USAPubs.php?PubID=5908

Keep the Beat Recipes: Delicious Healthy Family Means
http://publications.usa.gov/USAPubs.php?PubID=215

Let's Eat for the Health of It
http://publications.usa.gov/USAPubs.php?PubID=1350

Make Half Your Grains Whole
http://publications.usa.gov/USAPubs.php?PubID=651

Recipes and Tips for Healthy, Thrifty Meals
http://publications.usa.gov/USAPubs.php?PubID=1317

Sample Menus for a 2000 Calorie Food Pattern
http://publications.usa.gov/USAPubs.php?PubID=648

HEALTH

4 Programs that Can Help You Pay Your Medical Expenses
http://publications.usa.gov/USAPubs.php?PubID=575

A Lifetime of Good Health: Your Guide to Staying Healthy
http://publications.usa.gov/USAPubs.php?PubID=260

A Quick Look at Medicare
http://publications.usa.gov/USAPubs.php?PubID=577

About the Health Insurance Marketplace
http://publications.usa.gov/USAPubs.php?PubID=971

Adult Stress: Frequently Asked Questions
http://publications.usa.gov/USAPubs.php?PubID=2191

Age Healthier Breathe Easier
http://publications.usa.gov/USAPubs.php?PubID=422

Alcohol: A Women's Health Issue
http://publications.usa.gov/USAPubs.php?PubID=512

Anxiety Disorders
http://publications.usa.gov/USAPubs.php?PubID=5450

Application for Health Coverage & Help Paying Costs
http://publications.usa.gov/USAPubs.php?PubID=972

Be Active Your Way – Consumer Booklet for Adults
http://publications.usa.gov/USAPubs.php?PubID=1347

Better Health and You – Tips for Adults
http://publications.usa.gov/USAPubs.php?PubID=2194

Depression
http://publications.usa.gov/USAPubs.php?PubID=442

Depression Fact Sheet
http://publications.usa.gov/USAPubs.php?PubID=5798

Do You Know the Health Risks of Being Overweight?
http://publications.usa.gov/USAPubs.php?PubID=3308

DrugFacts: Cigarettes and Other Tobacco Products
http://publications.usa.gov/USAPubs.php?PubID=966

Enrolling in Medicare Part A & Part B
http://publications.usa.gov/USAPubs.php?PubID=2120

FDA Approves First Medication to Reduce HIV Risk
http://publications.usa.gov/USAPubs.php?PubID=662

Genital Herpes Fact Sheet
http://publications.usa.gov/USAPubs.php?PubID=820

Get Ready to Enroll in the Marketplace
http://publications.usa.gov/USAPubs.php?PubID=973

Getting on Track: Physical Activity and Healthy Eating for Men
http://publications.usa.gov/USAPubs.php?PubID=629

Healthy Heart Handbook for Women
http://publications.usa.gov/USAPubs.php?PubID=1217

High Blood Pressure
http://publications.usa.gov/USAPubs.php?PubID=5965

Inked and Regretful: Removing Tattoos
http://publications.usa.gov/USAPubs.php?PubID=2148

Just Enough for You: About Food Portions
http://publications.usa.gov/USAPubs.php?PubID=2199

Marketplace Application Checklist
http://publications.usa.gov/USAPubs.php?PubID=990

Medicare Basics: A Guide for Families and Friends of People with Medicare
http://publications.usa.gov/USAPubs.php?PubID=6039

The Affordable Care Act and Women
http://publications.usa.gov/USAPubs.php?PubID=661

Things to Think About When Choosing a Health Plan
http://publications.usa.gov/USAPubs.php?PubID=974

Welcome to Medicare
http://publications.usa.gov/USAPubs.php?PubID=573

Who Cares: Sources of Information about Health Care Products and Services
http://publications.usa.gov/USAPubs.php?PubID=271

Women and HIV
http://publications.usa.gov/USAPubs.php?PubID=6003

Your Medicare Benefits
http://publications.usa.gov/USAPubs.php?PubID=5627

HOUSING

5 Tips for Shopping for a Mortgage
http://publications.usa.gov/USAPubs.php?PubID=275

A Consumer's Guide to Mortgage Refinancing
http://publications.usa.gov/USAPubs.php?PubID=3125

A Guide for Making Housing Decisions: Housing Options for Older Adults
http://publications.usa.gov/USAPubs.php?PubID=781

Act Fast to Avoid Foreclosure
http://publications.usa.gov/USAPubs.php?PubID=6116

Buying Your Home: Settlement Costs and Information
http://publications.usa.gov/USAPubs.php?PubID=1096

Consumer Handbook on Adjustable Rate Mortgages
http://publications.usa.gov/USAPubs.php?PubID=3081

HUD Home Buying Guide
http://publications.usa.gov/USAPubs.php?PubID=5459

Have a Mortgage? What You can Expect Under Federal Rules
http://publications.usa.gov/USAPubs.php?PubID=6162

How to Buy a Home with a Low Down Payment
http://publications.usa.gov/USAPubs.php?PubID=5399

How to Buy a Manufactured (Mobile) Home
http://publications.usa.gov/USAPubs.php?PubID=3066

Renters Insurance
http://publications.usa.gov/USAPubs.php?PubID=3390

Shopping for Your Home Loan: HUD's Settlement Cost Booklet
http://publications.usa.gov/USAPubs.php?PubID=286

Take Control to Avoid Foreclosure – A Checklist for Consumers
http://publications.usa.gov/USAPubs.php?PubID=6163

The 2014 "Make the Most of Your Mortgage" Checklist
http://publications.usa.gov/USAPubs.php?PubID=6166

Twelve Ways to Lower Your Homeowners Insurance Costs
http://publications.usa.gov/USAPubs.php?PubID=3257

MONEY

13 Things Everyone Should Know About Investing
http://publications.usa.gov/USAPubs.php?PubID=843

51 Ways to Save Hundreds on Loans and Credit Cards
http://publications.usa.gov/USAPubs.php?PubID=6030

Ask Questions: Questions You Should Ask About Your Investments
http://publications.usa.gov/USAPubs.php?PubID=5790

Bank Accounts Are Changing
http://publications.usa.gov/USAPubs.php?PubID=6089

Banking in a High-Tech World
http://publications.usa.gov/USAPubs.php?PubID=6147

Building a Better Credit Report
http://publications.usa.gov/USAPubs.php?PubID=3116

Check Your Credit Report
http://publications.usa.gov/USAPubs.php?PubID=6106

Consumer Financial Protection Bureau
http://publications.usa.gov/USAPubs.php?PubID=6105

Coping With Debt
http://publications.usa.gov/USAPubs.php?PubID=981

Credit Discrimination is Illegal
http://publications.usa.gov/USAPubs.php?PubID=6111

Credit Repair: How to Help Yourself
http://publications.usa.gov/USAPubs.php?PubID=292

Credit Reporting 101
http://publications.usa.gov/USAPubs.php?PubID=293

Credit and Your Consumer Rights
http://publications.usa.gov/USAPubs.php?PubID=2131

Debt Collection
http://publications.usa.gov/USAPubs.php?PubID=3024

Debt Collection Arbitration
http://publications.usa.gov/USAPubs.php?PubID=2176

Disputing Errors on Credit Reports
http://publications.usa.gov/USAPubs.php?PubID=3241

Electronic Banking
http://publications.usa.gov/USAPubs.php?PubID=3363

Fighting Fraud 101: Smart Tips for Investors
http://publications.usa.gov/USAPubs.php?PubID=6040

Filing a Claim for Your Retirement Benefits
http://publications.usa.gov/USAPubs.php?PubID=6012

Finding a Lost Pension
http://publications.usa.gov/USAPubs.php?PubID=1322

Focus on Finances: Preparing for Your Future
http://publications.usa.gov/USAPubs.php?PubID=976

Free Credit Reports
http://publications.usa.gov/USAPubs.php?PubID=978

How Credit Scores Affect the Price of Credit and Insurance
http://publications.usa.gov/USAPubs.php?PubID=2297

How to Find the Best Credit Card for You
http://publications.usa.gov/USAPubs.php?PubID=6138

Lost or Stolen Credit, ATM, and Debit Cards
http://publications.usa.gov/USAPubs.php?PubID=671

Mutual Finds: A Guide for Investors
http://publications.usa.gov/USAPubs.php?PubID=5783

New Credit Card Rules Effective August 22, 2010
http://publications.usa.gov/USAPubs.php?PubID=300

Pay Attention to Your Credit Report
http://publications.usa.gov/USAPubs.php?PubID=6118

Protecting Yourself from Overdraft and Bounced Check Fees
http://publications.usa.gov/USAPubs.php?PubID=3375

Saving and Investing for Students
http://publications.usa.gov/USAPubs.php?PubID=6091

Saving and Investing: A Roadmap to Your Financial Security through Saving and Investing
http://publications.usa.gov/USAPubs.php?PubID=5744

Savings Fitness: A Guide to Your Money and Your Financial Future
http://publications.usa.gov/USAPubs.php?PubID=5664

What You Should Know About Buying Life Insurance
http://publications.usa.gov/USAPubs.php?PubID=5460

Your Credit Score
http://publications.usa.gov/USAPubs.php?PubID=3379

Your Insured Deposits
http://publications.usa.gov/USAPubs.php?PubID=5833

BUSINESS

ADA Guide for Small Business
http://publications.usa.gov/USAPubs.php?PubID=5532

Advertising
http://publications.usa.gov/USAPubs.php?PubID=169

Buying a Franchise: A Consumer Guide
http://publications.usa.gov/USAPubs.php?PubID=3349

Choosing a Retirement Solution for Your Small Business
http://publications.usa.gov/USAPubs.php?PubID=5791

Contact the USPTO Before You Get Burned!
http://publications.usa.gov/USAPubs.php?PubID=924

Copyright Basics
http://publications.usa.gov/USAPubs.php?PubID=3284

Doing Business with GSA: Quick Guide 2013
http://publications.usa.gov/USAPubs.php?PubID=884

Doing Business with the CFPB: A Guide for Small Businesses
http://publications.usa.gov/USAPubs.php?PubID=6151

General Information Concerning Patents
http://publications.usa.gov/USAPubs.php?PubID=1041

How to Write a Business Plan
http://publications.usa.gov/USAPubs.php?PubID=173

Marketing for Small Business: An Overview
http://publications.usa.gov/USAPubs.php?PubID=175

Minding Your Own Business: Banking Tips for Small Companies
http://publications.usa.gov/USAPubs.php?PubID=6100

Planning and Goal Setting for Small Business
http://publications.usa.gov/USAPubs.php?PubID=176

Record Keeping in a Small Business
http://publications.usa.gov/USAPubs.php?PubID=178

Small Business Advantage
http://publications.usa.gov/USAPubs.php?PubID=179

OSHA Small Business Handbook
http://publications.usa.gov/USAPubs.php?PubID=180

Starting an Internet Business: Dream Job or Pipe Dream?
http://publications.usa.gov/USAPubs.php?PubID=403

APPENDIX 15-B: SUGGESTION FORM

Please complete this form, indicating if information within the Reentry Sourcebook has changed or needs updating. Additionally, we welcome new entries that would enhance the completeness of this project. Once completed, please e-mail or mail to the address below.

Public Information (Revision, Update, New)	
Date Submitted:	
Agency Name:	
Agency Type:	Please check all that apply: ☐ Administrative Issues ☐ Housing ☐ Clothing ☐ Legal ☐ Criminal Records ☐ Sex Offenders ☐ Education ☐ Shelters ☐ Emergency Assistance ☐ Substance Abuse ☐ Employment ☐ Support groups ☐ Faith-based Organizations ☐ Transportation ☐ Food and Nutrition Assistance ☐ Veterans ☐ Fuel Assistance ☐ Women and Families ☐ Hotlines ☐ Other: _____
Public Contact Name: (provided for consumers)	
Agency Street Address, City, Zip:	
Telephone #:	
Fax #:	
Website Address:	
Public Email Address:	
Description of Services Provided:	
Service Hours:	
Cost/Fees:	
Restrictions/Requirements: (e.g. residency, length of stay, verification of need, etc.)	
Wait Time:	
Public Transportation:	
Languages:	
Other Locations:	
Private Contact Information (For Internal Use Only)	
Private Contact Name, Title:	
Private Mailing Address, City, Zip:	
Private Contact Email:	
Private Contact Phone #:	

Please email this form to info@ReentryEssentials.org (TRULINCS friendly)

Or, mail to:

Reentry Essentials, Inc.
98 4th Street, Suite 414
Brooklyn, New York 11231

FREEDOM IS PRICELESS!

CONGRATULATIONS!

Your completion of this material demonstrates an ongoing commitment to personal growth and development.

CERTIFICATE
OF ACHIEVEMENT
THIS CERTIFICATE IS HEREBY AWARDED TO

Your Name Here

FOR SUCCESSFUL COMPLETION OF THE _____ HOUR
EVIDENCE-BASED RECIDIVISM REDUCTION PROGRAM ENTITLED,

Program Title Here

ISSUED AND VARIFIED BY REENTRY ESSENTIALS.
THIS CERTIFICATE ATTESTS TO YOUR KNOWLEDGE AND UNDERSTANDING OF THE CONCEPTS AND
THEORIES EXPLORED DURING THIS COURSE OF STUDY.

AWARDED ON THIS _____ DAY OF _____, 20 ___ .

Certificate verification available online at,
www.reentryessentials.org or via email at
certificate@reentryessentials.org

Ms. Michaiah
Director of

DEMONSTRATE REHABILITATION
Each of our unique Evidence-Based Recidivism Reduction (EBRR) Programs and Productive Activities (PA) include a transcript and certificate of achievement issued by Reentry Essentials. Ideal for demonstrating rehabilitation to a parole board, case manager, probation officer, judge, potential employer or even your family and friends.

REQUEST YOUR TRANSCRIPT AND CERTIFICATE TODAY!
Simply follow the below instructions based on how your materials were purchased and we will do the rest. We make receiving your certificate and transcript quick and easy!

- **Individual Purchase**
  Materials purchased by you directly or on your behalf by family or friends.
  Written requests should be submitted to the address below. All requests must include full committed name, inmate number and mailing address. Requests will be verified against our customer purchase history. Please allow 2 - 3 weeks for processing.

- **Organizational Purchase**
  Materials purchased by a government agency, nonprofit organization or community service provider. Please contact your program administrator for assistance. Program administrators may forward official requests for certification to, info@reentryessentials.org.

📍 Reentry Essentials, Inc., 2609 East 14 Street, Suite 1018, Brooklyn, NY 11235-3915
📞 347.973.0004   ✉ info@reentryessentials.org   🌐 www.reentryessentials.org

CAREER COMPASS
Success in all Directions

Made in the USA
Las Vegas, NV
07 September 2021